COSTELLO

COSTELLO

The True Story
of a Peninsular War Rifleman

(including *Adventures of a Soldier*)

Eileen Hathaway

SHINGLEPICKER
Swanage

© Eileen Hathaway 1997
ISBN 0-9522782-3-5

First published in the UK by
SHINGLEPICKER PUBLICATIONS
28 Bonfields Avenue
Swanage
Dorset BH19 1PL

British Library Cataloguing-in-Publication Data
A catalogue record for this book is available from the British Library

Printed and bound in Great Britain by:
Biddles Ltd
Guildford and King's Lynn

TABLE OF CONTENTS

ILLUSTRATIONS

MAPS

ACKNOWLEDGEMENTS

Research for this book was conducted with the help of the staff at Swanage Library, the British Library, the National Army Museum, the Public Record Offices in Kew and Chancery Lane, St. Catherine's House, the Greater London Record Library, Westminster Archives, the Hartley Library at the University of Southampton, the National Library of Ireland in Dublin, and the Catholic Library in Westminster. I would also like to thank Father Ian Dickie of the Westminster Diocesan Archives for allowing me to search the registers of the Westminster Chapel.

The pictures on pages 31, 55, 81, 94, 111, 127, 128, 158, 192, 222, 277 and 287 are reproduced with the courtesy of the Department of Prints and Drawings at the British Museum. The photographs on pages 50, 65, 112, 121, 144, 247 and 260 are part of Ian Fletcher's collection. Ian and photographer Andy Crane travelled to the Peninsular War battlefields to take photographs for their book *Fields of Fire*, and Ian now organises trips to those same locations for Midas Battlefield Tours.

The portraits of Jonathan Leach, Harry Smith, Thomas Smith and John Stewart, are all at the Royal Green Jackets Museum in Winchester. They are reproduced here thanks to the work of photographer Andrew Sollars, and with the kind permission of Major R. Cassidy, the Museum's curator, who also allowed me to consult the Museum's collection of the *Rifle Brigade Chronicle*.

I have received valuable support and encouragement from several of Costello's descendants, notably Celia and Richard de Lacy Costello of London, and Robert A. Costello of Winnipeg in Canada. I have Celia and Richard to thank for the portrait on page 317, and Robert for the photographs of Costello, and of his medals, on pages 316 and 318. Yeoman Warder Brian Harrison was enthusiastic in uncovering information about Costello's years at the Tower of London; I cannot thank him enough for his interest and his help.

George Caldwell, co-author with Robert Cooper of *Rifle Green at Waterloo*, has been a welcome correspondent. He supplied me with valuable information about the 95th Regiment's part in the Waterloo campaign. I can recommend their publication *Rifles at Waterloo*, which is still available from Bugle Horn Publications (£5). Also still available, but from Synjon Publications (£3), is *Where Duty Calls Me*, S and J Teague's edition of William Green's autobiography. The relevant addresses are listed in the bibliography. And thank you again, Dawn Waring, for your atmospheric painting of the storming of Ciudad Rodrigo, on the front cover of this book.

INTRODUCTION

Edward 'Ned' Costello joined the 95th Rifle Regiment in Londonderry in 1808, the year the Peninsular War began. Like Benjamin Harris, the subject of my previous book *A Dorset Rifleman*, he had been a shoemaker, although he does not appear to have practised this trade in the army as Harris did. Harris, who joined the 2nd battalion in 1806, fought in the first actions of the Peninsular War at Roliça and Vimeiro, but his active service life was brought to an end by 'Walcheren fever' in 1809. It was in that year that the active service life of Edward Costello began in the 1st battalion, therefore Costello's narrative acts as a continuation of the account, begun by Harris, of the campaigns of the 95th Regiment during the Peninsular War.

Born in Mountmellick, Ireland, in 1788, Costello joined the Dublin City Militia in 1805 before enlisting in the 1st battalion 95th in August 1808. His militia training meant that he was soon ready for active service, and in May 1809 he embarked at Dover for the Peninsula. His company was commanded by Peter O'Hare, the 1st battalion's senior captain, therefore Costello was soon in the forefront of the fighting. In March 1810, he was in the skirmish at Barba del Puerco where he and 42 of his comrades held off 600 French light-infantrymen for half an hour before being reinforced. He was wounded at the battle of the River Coa in July the same year, and in 1812 survived the storming of both Ciudad Rodrigo and Badajoz. He took an active part in the battle of Vitoria, and in the fighting in the Pyrenees in 1813, and in 1814 fought at Tarbes and Toulouse. He was also in the Waterloo campaign of 1815.

Like Harris, Costello remained a private throughout his active service life. Discharged from the army in 1819, he remained a civilian until 1836 when he again went to war, this time as a captain in the British Auxiliary Legion, fighting in the Carlist War in Spain on the side of the infant Queen Isabella. Within months of his arrival in Spain, he was wounded again, and was invalided to England. Two years later he obtained a post as a yeoman warder at the Tower of London.

Costello's autobiography, *Adventures of a Soldier* was published in 1841, but a large part of it, composed soon after his return from the Carlist War, first appeared in serialised form in Colbourn's *United Service Journal* of 1839-1840 as the *Memoirs of Edward Costello*. A second edition of the book was published in 1852. The only edition to appear since 1852 was that of Anthony Brett-James in 1967.

Costello was by no means the first rifleman to publish his recollections. In 1827, Volume 1 of William Napier's five-volume *History of the Peninsular War* was published, generating an interest in the War, which was promoted further by the new *United Service Journal* which, in 1829, started to publish serialised extracts of officers' memoirs. Among the first were *Twelve Years' Military Adventures*, by Major John Blakiston, formerly in the Portuguese Caçadores, and *Military Memoirs of Four Brothers* by R. Fernyhough, a lieutenant in the 95th Rifles. Both serialisations were later published as books. Although Fernyhough had been a rifle officer, it was Blakiston's *Military Adventures* which seems to have inspired another former rifle lieutenant to pen *his* recollections. This was John Kincaid, whose entertaining *Adventures in the Rifle Brigade* was published in 1830.

There was a particular interest in riflemen because they were, to some extent, Wellington's special forces. As skirmishers, they were usually the first into action, and the last out of it, and were sometimes in engagements which did not involve other regiments. For example, at Tarbes in 1814, the three battalions of the 95th, consisting of less than 1,500 men, successfully attacked a French Division of 5,000 men posted on the hill of Oleac. One eye-witness was Major Blakiston:

"I never saw such skirmishers at the 95th. They could do the work much better and with infinitely less loss than any other of our best light troops. They possessed an individual boldness, a mutual understanding, and a quickness of eye in taking advantage of the ground, which, taken altogether, I never saw equalled. They were as much superior to the French voltigeurs, as the latter were to our skirmishers in general. As our regiment was often employed in supporting them, I think I am fairly qualified to speak of their merits."

In the 1830s, this reputation for effectiveness in battle created for the riflemen a situation not dissimilar to that which we have witnessed in more recent times in relation to the SAS, with one volume of memoirs begetting another. Thus, in 1831, there appeared *Rough Sketches of the Life of an Old Soldier* by Jonathan Leach, a former captain in the Rifles. This was followed in 1833 by *Twenty-Five Years in the Rifle Brigade* by Quartermaster William Surtees. In 1835 it was Kincaid's turn again with *Random Shots from a Rifleman*. In 1841 the memoirs of the privates started to appear. First was Costello with *Adventures of a Soldier*, followed in 1848 by the *Recollections of Rifleman Harris*. Then in 1857, there was *A Brief Outline of the Travels and Adventures of William Green, Bugler, Rifle Brigade*. In more recent times, there have been *A British Rifle Man*, the Peninsular War journal and correspondence of Lt. George Simmons (1899), and *The Autobiography of Sir Harry Smith* (1901), who had joined the Rifles as a junior officer.

With the exception of Harris, all of these riflemen fought in the Peninsula after 1809. Six were in the 1st battalion; Surtees was with the 3rd. Furthermore, three of them - Costello, Green and Simmons - were in same company early on in the campaign, and in 1812, Jonathan Leach became Costello's captain. So relevant are these accounts to Costello's, that they have been studied and their contents used to validate and enhance his. I chose Costello to be the centrepiece of the book because his service with the battalion was unbroken from 1809 to 1815 and, apart from the battle of Waterloo, he was at the forefront in nearly all the major actions - and many minor ones - fought during that period. Also, he takes his readers into situations from which many officers shied away, eg the plunder and disorder in the streets of Ciudad Rodrigo and Badajoz after they had been stormed.

Another important factor in his story is his nationality. Costello was Irish, as were between a fifth and a quarter of the soldiers and officers in Wellington's army: the Duke of Wellington himself was born in Dublin. In the 95th, and in Costello's company in particular, the percentage appears to have been even higher. It is pleasing therefore, that one of these men should have penned his memoirs, and in such a way as to incorporate the personal experiences of many other veteran Irish riflemen, such as Tom Plunket, Tom Crawley, Tom Treacy, Daniel Kelly, Michael Dillon, and Robert Fairfoot, and of Irish officers like Peter O'Hare and John Uniacke.

Costello was able to recall accurately the names of many of his comrades, what happened to them and when, as official documents have confirmed. There are a few lapses and, on one occasion in particular, he strays badly by misrepresenting the exploits and death of his good friend and fellow rifle recruit, John Wilkie. However, to balance this, he helps to identify a volunteer rifle officer whom Kincaid disguised in his narrative with a false name. Where their accounts deal with the same events, we cannot know for sure whether Costello, who was literate, was influenced by Kincaid, Leach and Surtees, copies of whose books were published before his, but there is no doubt that most of the material is his own.

In preparing this book, I have used the texts of the 1841 and 1852 editions of *Adventures of a Soldier*, which I have edited. Some phrases and paragraphs have been relocated but, as with my previous books, the aim has been to reduce the word count and clarify the content, not to eliminate facts. However, I have chosen not to present in full the chapters detailing Costello's experiences in the Carlist War of 1835-1836 because, to do them justice, a separate volume would be required. For the chapters on the Peninsular War and the Waterloo campaign, much additional information is included, often in the form of quotations from the memoirs of other riflemen, but it is presented in a way which clearly distinguishes it from Costello's narrative. The punctuation of the quoted texts has sometimes been modified slightly to improve understanding, and placenames in Spain and Portugal have been generally modernised to those in use today.

This edition of Costello's memoirs has the advantage of maps, photographs, illustrations, and an index. Indeed, everything that can be done has been done to ensure that your progress with Ned Costello through the major events in his life, is a lot smoother for you as a reader than it was for him as a rifleman.

Eileen Hathaway
August 1997

FOR DAD
because this is a book
he would have loved to read.

CHAPTER 1

Militiaman and Recruit
October 1788 - February 1809

I was born in the town of Mountmellick, Queen's County, Ireland, on 26 October 1788[1]. When I was seven years old my father removed to Dublin, where he had been appointed to the situation of tidewaiter[2]. As soon as I became a good-sized youth, he bound me apprentice to a cabinet-maker in King William Street, Dublin[3], but I had a roving and restless spirit and soon grew tired of my occupation, which I left early one morning 'without beat of drum'.

Houses in the Square, Mountmellick, Co.Laois

I next went to live with an uncle, a shoemaker, who employed several men to work in his business[4]. Among these was an old soldier, who had lost a leg fighting in Egypt under Sir Ralph Abercromby[5]. It was from this old blade that I first acquired the martial ardour that so frequently infects young men in time of war. There was no resisting the old pensioner's description of glory, and I became red-hot for a soldier's life. Although rejected as too young for the regulars, I 'listed' as it is technically called, in the Dublin Militia on 17 June 1806[6].

At the latter end of the following year, our regiment was stationed at Londonderry in the north of Ireland, where I volunteered into the 95th - now the 'Rifle Brigade' - the only one from the regiment to join[7].

The sum allowed to those who volunteered from the militia was 18 guineas, £4 of which were deducted for my kit, which I was to have on joining. After receiving my bounty, I took the mail coach for Dublin, where I found a recruiting party of my new regiment. It consisted of a sergeant, a corporal, and six privates. I was highly delighted with the smart appearance of the men, and with their green uniform. The sergeant proposed that I remain in Dublin where, as I was almost a native of that city, he thought I might materially assist in raising recruits.

Recruiting on the pay of a private soldier is anything but pleasant, particularly if that soldier is confined to a shilling a day, doled out to him once a week, for he frequently spends it all the first night he receives it. I myself had woeful experience of this, and through my irregularities, and my unwillingness to let my friends know that I was so near them, I was for days without food.

One day, I was crawling about in this manner, heartily tired of my first sample of military life, and not having eaten for that or the whole of the previous day, when I was accosted by a smart young fellow. I was garbed in an old green jacket of the sergeant's, and after eyeing me rather shrewdly from head to foot for several seconds, this fellow said:

"I say, green boy, do you belong to the Croppies?[8] Damn me, but I like your dress. What bounty do you give?"

"Eighteen guineas," I replied.

"Come then, tip us a shilling. I'm your man."

Unfortunately, I had not a farthing, but knowing that we received £2 for every recruit, I hurried into a nearby public house and asked the landlord to lend me a shilling. When I told him why I wanted it, he very kindly did so, and I handed it over to the recruit who, chucking it instantly on the counter, called for its worth in whiskey. While we were drinking, the sergeant, whom I had sent for, arrived and supplied us with money.

The recruit passed the doctor and was sworn in for our corps. His name was Wilkie and he was an Englishman[9]. He was in Dublin because his father had been sent for from Manchester to superintend a glass manufactory in the city.

Wilkie was a fine young fellow about 5'8" in height. He possessed all the genuine qualities of a soldier, ie he was generous, quarrelsome, and brave, of which he gave us a specimen the evening he enlisted by quilting [beating] a pair of coal-heavers.

The £2 I received for enlisting Wilkie I handed over to my landlady in advance for future food, which my recent misfortunes had taught me to value. As is generally the case, this precaution was no longer necessary, for a short time after, we enlisted so many recruits that money became very plentiful and I was able to get coloured clothes[10].

After a few days, Wilkie introduced me to his parents and sister, and while we remained in Dublin I became a constant visitor at their house. Wilkie's sister was a remarkably pretty girl of about 17. I was but 19, and given my youth and early passions, Cupid tapped me very seriously on the shoulder. As his sister did not disapprove of my advances, a serious attachment followed, but war had claimed me as her proselyte and I went on recruiting. When the sergeant received orders for his party to join the regiment in Colchester, I was placed in a predicament: 'Mars and Cupid beat to arms', and I was like a donkey betwixt the haystacks, bewildered as to which to take[11], both being necessary to the calls of my nature. After a little private snivelling and simpering, and the usual vows of eternal fidelity, passion and remembrance - which last I have kept to this day - the time for parting arrived, and she and her mother accompanied Wilkie and myself towards the Pigeon House, Ringsend[12].

In something more than 24 hours, we found ourselves cheek by jowl with the quays of Liverpool. It was past midnight when we cast anchor. We were ordered to remain on board, but Wilkie and I were so anxious to see the place, we took advantage of a loop-hole in the waterman's pocket to get ashore in our coloured clothes. The hour was so late, we were obliged to take lodgings in a cellar. I had not been long asleep when I was woken by the bright glare of a bull's-eye lanthorn [lantern] staring me full in the face. Some five or six rough sailors, all armed to the teeth [ie a press gang], were standing before us. The first thing they did was to feel our hands. Finding them to be rather soft, one remarked to the others that we had never been sailors. Nevertheless, they took us as lawful prey. Wilkie wanted to fight with them, but was persuaded by these half a dozen bulldogs, and their cutlasses, to walk quietly to the tender. In this we should most probably have taken a voyage had we not been sea-sick. Next morning, on being examined by the officer on board, we gladly sent for our sergeant, who claimed us. We were accordingly liberated, and our party continued their march.

Wilkie, to whom I was growing exceedingly attached, became my companion, and as he was always in hot water, he got me into many a scrape. At Lichfield, we were caged for kicking up a disturbance amongst some Irish recruits in a public house. As I had supported my friend, we were both detained for want of means to pay for the damage done to the scene of the riot. Unfortunately, Sergeant Crooks (for that was our sergeant's name) did not have the means either[13], having only the allowance to carry the men to London. So we remained in the cage, which was in a very conspicuous part of the market-place.

My countrymen were not so plentifully scattered then as they are now, and the presence of an Irishman seemed to arouse all the little brats and blackguards of the neighbourhood. Every minute of the day, they would annoy us with:

The Pigeon House, Dublin. By William Sadler (1782-1839)

"I say Paddy, Hilloa Paddy, which way does the bull run?"

Taking both of us for Irish, the young devils kept twirling their fingers on their noses, even through the bars of the cage.

The poor sergeant, who was a mild and good fellow, eventually arranged matters with the magistrates: the money was to be sent to the injured parties as soon as we joined the regiment, and then deducted from our pay, which was done accordingly.

Wilkie, however, continued his pranks, and on a visit to St Paul's Cathedral in London, stopped the pendulum of the clock, and set the bells ringing. For this we were again imprisoned. This time we escaped by paying a fine of five shillings for being drunk. After this nothing occurred till we arrived at Colchester. Here I joined the 1st battalion, then under the command of Colonel Beckwith, afterwards known as General Sir Sidney Beckwith, and was attached to Captain Glasse's company[14].

Costello and Wilkie had joined the 95th Rifles, a regiment which, although new (having been formed in 1800 as the Rifle Corps), was building up a formidable reputation of being very effective in action. The men of the 95th were distinguished from their fellow infantrymen in several ways, one of which was their clothing: their jackets were green not red, and they wore no bright ornaments because they were often required to blend into the background. Although they were trained to fight in column or line as a battalion, like the infantry of other regiments, their primary function was to skirmish in extended order in advance of the army as it moved forward, and in the rear when it was in retreat. Skirmishing required them to act in small groups from whatever cover they could find, for which they received special training. Needing to manoeuvre quickly, the lightest and most active men were usually chosen, and they were given the weapon best suited to their function - the Baker rifle, which was far more accurate than the smooth-bore muskets used by the rest of the army. A musket would carry a ball straight for 100 yards, but was ineffective as a target weapon at 200 yards, whereas the rifle was accurate at nearly twice that distance. All British infantry were taught to fire accurately, but riflemen were marksmen who could pick off enemy officers and sergeants with their longer range weapons.

The concept of a regiment of light-infantrymen, armed with rifles, was a comparatively new one. There had been rifle corps attached to the British army before 1800, notably the 5th Battalion of the 60th Royal American Regiment, and the Duke of Brunswick Oels' Corps, but these soldiers were mostly foreigners, and their companies were spread around the various brigades. The 95th was the first British regiment of riflemen. It was the creation of Coote Manningham, who became its first Colonel, and Lt.-Col. Sir William Stewart, but the credit for their training must go to Sir John Moore, who gathered under his command at Shorncliffe in Kent in 1803, not only the 95th Regiment, but also the 43rd and 52nd. These three light infantry regiments were later to form the core of the Light Division, which fought in the Peninsular War from 1809 to 1814.

The Rifle Corps' first expedition was to Ferrol in 1800. In 1801 it was engaged in the battle of Copenhagen against the Danish fleet, when the riflemen acted as sharpshooters aboard Lord Nelson's ships. On 6 May 1806, a second battalion was raised, mostly through volunteering from the various militias, particularly in Ireland. Later that same year, three companies of that 2nd battalion were sent to South America to fight the Spanish, and in 1807 five companies of the 1st battalion followed. All eight companies were, in July 1807, involved in a failed attempt to recapture the city of Buenos Aires. A few months later, the whole expedition sailed back to England. The remaining companies of the 95th had been dispatched to Denmark with an expedition whose objective was to take possession of the Danish fleet before Napoleon could effect the same purpose, and in this they succeeded.

In the spring of 1808, part of the 1st battalion was sent to Sweden with an expedition commanded by Sir John Moore, but the troops did not disembark. Instead, they were redirected to Portugal to rendezvous with the army of Sir Arthur Wellesley (later the Duke of Wellington), which had been ordered to the Iberian Peninsula to fight against the French invaders of Portugal and Spain. This army, which sailed from Cork on 12 July 1808, included four companies of the 2nd battalion of the 95th. Within days of disembarking in Mondego Bay, they were fighting in the battles of Roliça and Vimeiro, and were therefore amongst the first British troops to become involved in what became known as the Peninsular War. The three companies of the 1st battalion with Sir John Moore, did not reach Portugal until 28 August, a week after the battle of Vimeiro had been fought. On landing they marched to Lisbon, where the rest of the regiment (and Wellesley's victorious army) was assembled.

The French army in Portugal , having been bettered by the British, quit Portugal, and Sir John Moore took over from Wellesley as the commander of the army. However, towards the end of the year, France threatened to invade the country again so, in November, the riflemen who were in Portugal marched into Spain with Moore's army to challenge them. At about the same time, most of the remaining companies of riflemen sailed from England for Corunna with orders to rendezvous with Moore's army in northern Spain. It is probably this last detachment which Costello now refers to.

> Shortly after my arrival, the campaign having commenced, the regiment was ordered to Spain. I was not perfect in my exercises, and as only time and practice could make me more proficient in light

infantry duty, I was left behind as depot. This was a necessary consequence of being a mere recruit, but I felt mortified at being prevented from sharing in the glory which I believed the regiment about to reap. But I had no great reason to complain, and I became an adept at my drill, and a tolerable shot, along with some other recruits[15].

The regiment returned in January 1809. We were at that time stationed in Hythe, the depot having moved from Colchester.

Sir John Moore's advance into Spain had turned into a retreat. The most graphic accounts of the riflemen's experiences during the Corunna campaign are in the *Recollections* of Benjamin Harris, who was with the 2nd battalion retreating toward the Spanish port of Vigo, and in the *Travels and Adventures* of William Green, who was with the 1st battalion retreating to Corunna. Before embarking at Corunna, Moore's army had to fight a battle with the French, during which he was killed.

The Rifle regiment distinguished itself, but suffered severely in the retreat to Corunna under the gallant Moore. The men embarked at Corunna for England where, on landing, they presented a most deplorable sight. Their appearance was squalid and miserable in the extreme. There was scarcely one amongst them who had not lost some of his appointments, and many, owing to the horrors of that celebrated retreat, were even without rifles. Their clothing was in tatters and in such an absolute state of filth as to swarm with vermin. New clothing was immediately served out and the old ordered to be burnt. This was put into execution at the back of our barracks amid the jests of the men, who congratulated each other on such an effective way of getting rid of the myriad of enemies which had proved a source of personal discomfort to them abroad[16].

CHAPTER 2

Hythe
March - May 1809

On 25 April 1809, Costello was drafted into the 3rd company of the 1st battalion, which included privates Thomas Bandle, James Brooks, Thomas Crawley, Robert Fairfoot, Patrick Fleming, Thomas Maher, John McCann and William Tidey, all of whom he later mentions. Also in the 3rd company was William Green.

Shortly after the return of the regiment, I was drafted into the company commanded by Captain Peter O'Hare, whose eccentric habits were equalled only by his extremely ugly countenance. Peter, for that was the name by which he was generally known to the men, was as brave as a lion. He had, it was said, risen from the ranks[1].

While in Hythe, he got in tow with a young lady whom he frequently escorted about the barracks and the neighbouring heights. This the men often took advantage of, and when he was arm-in-arm with the lady, they would throw themselves in his way and ask favours of him. These, Peter - who we presumed had an eye to the opinion of, and the future requital of his own wishes from, the fair one herself - would readily grant. Through the importunities of the men, he at last became awake to the scheme, and swore to flog the first man who made another attempt.

Through his servant, I learned of a rather humorous adventure which occurred here. One day, at a dinner party at Hythe at which the young lady was present, he unintentionally gave offence to a militia officer. The next morning, he was sitting shaving himself, when a note was delivered to him by his servant. Supposing it was a 'billet-doux', he dropped the razor to peruse it. To his surprise, it turned out to be a challenge. He called his man back.

"John," said he, "who brought this?"

"A gentleman, now waiting at the door."

"Then give him my compliments, and tell him to take this bit of paper back to the fool who sent it. Say that I am going to Spain, and that if he follows me, he'll not find me behind a hedge, for by Jove, captain's commissions are not to be got every day!"

Our commanding officer [Beckwith], was an excellent man, and well deserving of his fame. He was considered to be one of the most humane officers of the whole army. He seldom resorted to the 'cats', thinking, perhaps, that it was necessary only in extreme cases[2]. The plan of punishment generally adopted by him, was to put an offender on extra drill with all his accoutrements on. If the man was incorrigible, a six-pound shot, attached to a long chain, was affixed to the leg, and this he was obliged to trail about with him.

At this time, we had in our regiment one of those singular characters with which every regiment abounds. His name was Tom Crawley, and he was always getting into scrapes. To enormous strength, and great meekness of temper, was added an infinity of dry humour.

Tom first became known to me as one of the incorrigibles, but he made light of every punishment, and the six-pounder he would chuck under his arm as if it were a mere toy. To obviate this, our Colonel obliged him to wear a kind of long smock-frock, with a green cross painted on the back and front of it. Our barrack then was only temporary, and presented no outward wall to prevent our free intercourse with the town, where Tom was a general favourite. While under disgrace, therefore, he used to take advantage of the dusk to steal by the sentries into the town. There his strange dress elicited innumerable queries, to which Tom would reply with a suggestive side look, and say:

"Arrah and sure! And is it not the new regulation of the Duke of York[3]; and mustn't all the likes of me, that are Catholics in our regiment, wear the cross on their dress!"

Thomas Crawley was, of course, an Irishman. He had joined the 95th on 11 May 1805, at almost the same time as Tom Plunket, an even more famous character in the regiment.

I had, more than once, heard of a man of the name of Tom Plunket, and had heard him eulogised by the men for his courage. He was a smart, well-made fellow, about middle height and in the prime of manhood; with a clear grey eye and handsome countenance. He was a general favourite with both officers and men, besides being the best shot in the regiment[4].

Plunket, born in Newtown in County Wexford, had enlisted in Dublin on 10 May 1805 when he was about twenty years old. Costello here gives an account some of Plunket's deeds, to which he was *not* an eyewitness.

Plunket's first career in arms was in South America with General Whitelocke[5], where he acquired the reputation in his company of a good soldier. At the retreat of Corunna, he had an opportunity to distinguish himself. Despite the gallantry of some of our cavalry, the rear-guard of the British - which was partly composed of the Light Brigade - was exceedingly hard pressed by the French horse, who were vastly superior. In the neighbourhood of Astorga they made several determined charges, in which a French general named Colbert[6], conspicuous on a grey horse, was remarkably active. Although frequently aimed at by our men, he seemed to bear a charmed life, and invariably escaped. In one of the French charges headed by this daring officer, General Sir Edward Paget[7] rode up to the rifles and offered his purse to any man who would shoot him. Plunket immediately started from his company. He ran about a hundred yards nearer to the enemy, threw himself on his back on the road (which was covered with snow), placed his foot in the sling of his rifle, and taking deliberate aim, shot General Colbert[8]. Colbert's Trumpet-Major, who rode up to him, shared the same fate from Tom's unerring rifle. Our men, who had been anxiously watching, cheered, and Tom began running in upon the rearmost sections. He was just in time to escape some dozen troopers who had chased after him.

Our General immediately gave Tom the purse he had promised, with encomiums upon his gallantry. He promised to recommend him to his Colonel, which he did in high terms to Colonel Beckwith[9]. A few days afterwards, when the French attacked Sir John Moore's position at Corunna, Plunket was again noted for his cool bravery and daring, especially in making some admirable shots, by which they lost many officers.

By 23 April, Tom Plunket had been promoted to corporal in the 1st company. The event was recorded by Costello:

The first parade we had after our men had received their new equipment is imprinted upon my memory from a particular circumstance calculated to make an impression upon the mind of a youthful soldier, such as I then was. We were formed into hollow square, and ordered to face inwards. We knew it was not a punishment parade, so we naturally expected some address from the commanding officer. We were wondering what was coming, when Colonel Beckwith broke the silence by calling out:

"Private Thomas Plunket, step into the square."

All eyes were fixed upon Plunket, as he halted, in the finest position of military attention, with his rifle shouldered, within a few paces of his officer.

The commanding officer pointed to Plunket: "Here men, stands a pattern for the battalion!" Then addressing Tom, he added, "I have ordered a medal for you, in approval of your late gallant conduct at Corunna. Present yourself, sir, to the master tailor and get on a corporal's stripes, and I will see you do not want for higher promotion, as you continue to deserve it. I love to reward conduct such as yours!"

Making his salute, Tom retired, and we formed into column and marched back to our barracks, desiring the praise that had been bestowed on the fortunate Plunket.

I am convinced that the judicious conduct pursued by our Colonel in this instance was attended with the happiest effects among many of the men, and may have induced much of that spirit of personal gallantry and daring - that 'esprit de corps' which is absolutely essential in a regiment - for which our corps afterwards became celebrated.

However, the truth must be told. Like all heroes, Tom had his faults, and the destructive consequences of one in particular was, in a soldier, calculated to counterbalance a thousand virtues, for Tom was a thirsty soul, exceedingly fond of a 'drop'. This was his unfortunate failing through life, without which he would have got on in the service[10].

Our regiment was shortly afterwards raised to one thousand strong, chiefly through volunteers from the militia, our common medium of supply at the time. In the knowledge and exercise of their military duties during the war, the militia regiments were almost as good as the troops of the line, and the men who joined our battalion - chiefly the élite of the light companies of the different provincial corps - were, in general, a fine set of young fellows.

The Corunna campaign had so depleted the strength of the regiment that, in the spring of 1809, an order went out to fill up the ranks with volunteers from the militia. So successful was the call that a third battalion was formed, into which John Wilkie, Costello's friend, was transferred in April 1809.

At the time of the recruitment drive, the Lincoln Militia was barracked at Hythe. With them, as an assistant surgeon, was Yorkshireman George Simmons. As an inducement to join the regular army, militia officers were offered commissions in their chosen regiments if they could persuade a sufficient number of their men to join with them. This Simmons succeeded in doing and he became a second-lieutenant in the 1st battalion of the 95th. On 18 July 1809, a delighted Simmons wrote to his parents: *"My Colonel has treated me with every mark of respect, and has put me into a company under the patronage of an old warrior, whose bravery has often been shown to the regiment."*

This 'old warrior' was Peter O'Hare and Simmons' company was the 3rd, which included Costello and William Green.

Between 25 March and 24 April, the South Lincoln Militia supplied 80 volunteers for the 95th, and the North Lincoln Militia, 38. Some of these men may have succumbed to the persuasion of their officers, but that was not the only way they were induced to join, as Costello explains.

For his qualifications, Tom Plunket, with a few others, was selected to recruit from the Lincoln Militia, which lay at Hythe while we remained in temporary barracks on the heights.

While volunteering went on, the militia colonels were ordered to give their men liberty to do as they liked, and the better to obtain the object in view, the government ordered that barrels of beer, with the heads knocked in, should be placed in the different streets of the town. Those who chose to partake did so, consequently the butts were dipped into by every kind of person and with utensils of every description. This we must not wonder at, when we consider the double thirst those times gave rise to: 'Barclay'[11] as well as 'Glory'.

The Rifles, from the dark colour of their uniforms and the total absence of all ornament, had gained the nickname of 'Sweeps'. The pipe clay and button stick were hateful to the eyes of all soldiers, but particularly to riflemen, who regarded them as fit only for men less useful than themselves. This Tom took advantage of on all occasions. His manner of attack was singular, but very efficacious. He was the soul of every company he mixed in, and among his other accomplishments was an excellent dancer. One day, the better to attract the 'awkwards', and to the amusement of a very large crowd, he commenced a shuffle on the head of one of the barrels of beer. After a few steps, the head gave way and soused him up to his neck in the liquid. The whole crowd laughed uproariously as Tom, whose head only was to be seen, stared very gravely over the edge of the cask. Recovering himself suddenly, he bolted out of the butt, dashed to the public-house, and ascended some distance up its chimney. He then descended and as quickly reappeared amongst the crowd.

"There now," he exclaimed, giving himself a Newfoundland shake that, in a instance, opened a wide circle of militiamen; "damn your pipe clay - I'm ready for the grand parade!"

The IBERIAN PENINSULA

FRANCE

Bordeaux

Toulouse

Tarbes

Bayonne

San Sebastian

Santander

Bilbao

Vitoria

Pamplona

Zaragoza

Corunna

Burgos

Valladolid

Vigo

Salamanca

Madrid

Ciudad Rodrigo

Talavera

Porto

SPAIN

PORTUGAL

Badajoz

Lisbon

Cadiz

Miles

0   100   200   300

CHAPTER 3

To Talavera and Campo Maior
May - September 1809

The men recruited into the 95th were needed as reinforcements for the renewed military effort against the French in Portugal and Spain. After Moore's army embarked at Corunna, a French force under Marshal Nicolas Soult reinvaded Portugal, taking Oporto on 27 March 1809. There was a garrison of British troops in Lisbon, to which Sir Arthur Wellesley returned on 22 April as the commander of the army, which consisted of 29,000 men. The French were in an exposed position at Oporto so Wellesley moved against them, defeating Soult on 7 May.

Wellesley's next plan was to march into Spain to try to cut off the army of Marshal Claude Victor, so he requested reinforcements from England. In May, the 1st battalion 95th, having filled up its ranks with new recruits like Costello, and with transfers from the 2nd battalion like Captain Jonathan Leach, was ready for service, and was ordered to embark again for the Peninsula. The riflemen marched from Hythe on 25 May.

An order arrived for our immediate embarkation for Portugal, to join the army under Sir Arthur Wellesley. We went on board the transports lying for us at Dover in May 1809[1] in the best of spirits, like sportsmen anticipating the pleasures of the chase.

Simmons: *"At 2 o'clock this morning the battalion was formed in the barrack square, consisting of 1,000 as fine young fellows as were ever collected to fight their country's battles. For my part, my heart was as light as a feather when we marched off and, if I may judge from appearances, every person had the same feelings. Our destination is a profound secret, and as I am not inquisitive, it gives me little concern; I daresay I shall soon enough see some diversion; the rumour goes, Austria or Portugal. Our men are in very high spirits, and we have a most excellent band of music, and 30 bugle-horns, which through every country village strikes up the old tune, 'Over the hills and far away'... We entered Dover about 6 o'clock and marched through it. The windows were crowded with inhabitants; some greeted us, but in general the women seemed sorry to see us depart, knowing well that numbers must never return to their native land again."*

When the battalions of the 95th first set off for the Peninsula in 1808, six wives per company, selected by ballot, had been allowed to sail with them. At the retreat to Corunna, these women, their pregnancies, and their children, had proved such encumbrances that they were not allowed to go on the next expedition to Walcheren in the Netherlands. Nor, with one exception, were they allowed to embark with their husbands for the Peninsula in 1809. Lt. John Kincaid: *'They landed at Lisbon with 1,100 men and only one woman. By what particular virtues she had attained such a dignified position among them, I never clearly made out, further than that she had arrived at years of discretion, was what is commonly called a useful woman, and had seen some service."*

The other wives were left behind in Dover. Green: *'It was such a parting scene that I never wish to witness it again. The women clung round the necks of their husbands, so that the officers had much ado to part them. There was such a ringing of hands, tearing of hair, and crying, that I was glad to jump into the boat, thankful that I had no wife to bewail my loss!... A great many, very respectable, inhabitants of Dover stood around to witness our departure; and amongst the females many tears were shed, while they looked on to see a thousand fine young fellows push off in the boats from the harbour to the ship, which lay at anchor about a mile from the shore. Three cheers were given from the shore, which were responded to by us in the boats."*

Simmons: *'The battalion embarked in three transports, 'Fortune', 'Malabar', and 'Laurel', and sailed immediately for the Downs, where we came to anchor. The 1st battalion 43rd and the 52nd Light Infantry joined us here, which with ourselves formed a Light Brigade, under the command of Major-General Robert Craufurd, who took post on board the 'Nymph' frigate."*

Adverse winds detained them at St. Helen's on the Isle of Wight, but on 18 June, a fresh breeze enabled them to pass the Needles, and they were at last on their way to Lisbon.

> Shipboard, though not quite so forlorn as Doctor Johnson has portrayed it[2], soon becomes irksome and unpleasant to those not accustomed to it, especially when 300-400 men are crowded into a small vessel. Our officers, who were mostly a jolly set of fellows, had recourse to various expedients to while away the time. An extremely popular one was getting Plunket to dance a hornpipe upon the quarter-deck to the music of our band. Tom did so famously, and the beating of his feet in the 'double shuffle' drew the loudest plaudits from our men, and from the crew of the vessel. After a tolerably pleasant voyage we anchored off Lisbon.

They arrived in Portugal on 28 June. Simmons: *"Saw the Rock of Lisbon at daybreak. It is a bold mountain, whose sombre front*

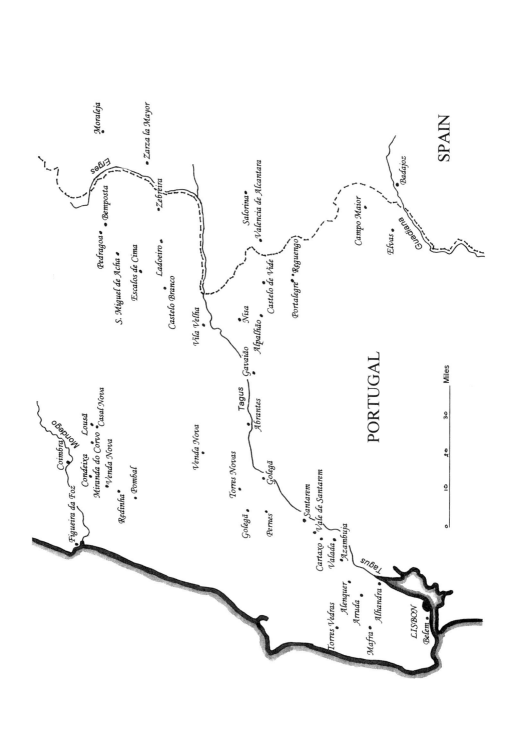

overhangs the sea. About noon we entered the Tagus, and our fleet came to anchor close to Lisbon, which from the sea appeared a most magnificent place indeed. On landing the charm ceased, as the streets are exceedingly filthy. The quays are built of stone, and very good along the river. The citadel is on a commanding eminence in the town, from whence in every direction you may observe churches, monasteries, convents, etc. The most magnificent church is that of S. Roche. The French under Junot robbed this church of many valuables, but the priests were fortunate enough to save some things by hiding them from the grasp of these rapacious plunderers. We remained on board for four days waiting for orders."

The new captain of the 2nd company was Jonathan Leach, who had been with the 2nd battalion at Roliça and Vimeiro. His memoirs were published in 1831:

"We were busily employed, from the moment of our arrival on the 28 June to 2 July, in purchasing horses, mules, donkeys, pack-saddles, cigars, and various other odds and ends indispensable in campaigning. We were to proceed, without delay, to join Sir Arthur Wellesley, who is at this time in Spanish Estremadura... At about midnight on 2 July, the tide serving to take us up the river, we were put into flat-bottomed boats and launches, and the tedious operation of towing us against the current commenced. After 24 hours spent in this bewitching manner, every man's legs terribly cramped by being crammed so tight into the boat, we reached Valada, near which place we bivouacked on the bank of the river."

They arrived at Valada at dusk on 3 July. Leach: "I never entertained the smallest doubt that all the frogs in the Peninsula had assembled, by common consent on this occasion, to welcome us to Portugal, for such an eternal croaking I never heard before or since."

From Lisbon, in a few days, we proceeded in open boats up the River Tagus, and landed about four miles from Santarem, where we encamped for the night.

Simmons: "For the first time in my life I was treated with a bivouac. Hungry, wet, and cold, and without any covering, we lay down by the side of the river. I put one hand in my pocket and the other in my bosom, and lay shivering, and thinking of the glorious life of a soldier, until I fell fast asleep."

They slept for only three hours before the bugles sounded on the morning of the 4 July. Simmons: "We fell in at daylight. I found the dew had wet me through, but the sun soon made his appearance and dried me."

On the following morning, we marched into the city of Santarem amid the cheers of its inhabitants, who welcomed us with loud cries of

"Long live the brave English!" Here we immediately became brigaded with the 43rd and 52nd regiments of light infantry, under the command of Major-General Craufurd[3].

Simmons: *'The town is surrounded with hills that are covered with innumerable olive-trees, a great source of wealth to the inhabitants. The place has a most respectable appearance, the ground very fertile, and plenty of wine, grapes, oranges, and vegetables of every description in the greatest abundance."*

Leach: *'Like all towns of any size in Portugal, it is full of churches and convents. With the fair inmates of the latter we had a deal of chit-chat, although the close iron gratings which separated us from our inamorata obscured them in great measure from view... These fair ladies presented us with preserved fruits, nosegays, and all sorts of fine things, in return for which certain little notes, or love-letters, written in villainously bad Portuguese, were transmitted by the same mode of conveyance to them."*

On 7 July, Craufurd's Brigade began its march to join up with Wellesley's army.

On the third day after our arrival at Santarem, we commenced a series of forced marches to join the main army under Sir Arthur Wellesley, at Talavera, then almost hourly expecting an engagement with the French corps commanded by Marshal Victor.

The route they took was through Golegã to Abrantes where, on the 10th, they crossed the Tagus by a bridge of boats, and bivouacked. Leach: *'Halted at Abrantes. Bathed in Tagus. A soldier of the 95th was drowned when bathing this morning. Brigadier General Robert Craufurd (damn him) issued this day to the Light Brigade an immensity of the most* <u>tyrannical</u> <u>and</u> <u>oppressive</u> <u>standing</u> <u>orders</u> *that were ever compiled by a British officer."* (Verner)

These orders were to regulate the conduct of the soldiers on the march. Leach did not like them, nor, at first, did the soldiers. The next day, which was exceedingly hot, they marched to Gavião and Nisa. On the 13th they reached, says Leach, *'the awfully grand and terrific pass of Vila Velha, leading down to the Tagus by a zig-zag mountainous road... We bivouacked on the right bank of the river, having passed it by a curious flying bridge, large enough to carry only a company or two at a time, which made a long and tedious process".*

The day's march usually began at 2am. Simmons: *"We continue marching every day in this manner, halting occasionally for half an hour, so that we manage to get to our destined place about 11 o'clock... generally upon a piece of ground shaded with trees. There we rest till one or two the next morning and start as before. Sometimes we met with stupendous mountains, whose summits were enveloped in the clouds.*

View of the pass of the Tagus at Vila Velha, 20 May 1811.
Painted by Major T. St. Clair. Engraved by C. Turner. Published 16 October 1812. ©British Museum

The villages in general were deserted by the unfortunate inhabitants, and houses, churches, and everything they possessed were one entire scene of ruin. Some towns were completely burnt to the ground, even the corn-fields... were generally laid waste by fire wherever the French had been... From such fatiguing marches, and often bad food and water, by day exposed to burning sun, and by night to the heavy dews, sleeping generally upon the ground, you will not wonder at the men becoming unhealthy, which daily obliged them to fall out on the march. Even the strongest in outward appearance would lie down, or rather fall down, and say positively they could not go any farther. The officers of our regiment - most of them rode on horses or mules - did not experience the fatigues so materially. As I had no money to spare, I was obliged to walk."

Our men suffered dreadfully on the route, chiefly from excessive fatigue and the heat of the weather. The brain fever soon commenced, making fearful ravages in our ranks, and many dropped by the road-side and died. I saw two men of the 52nd, unable to face the sufferings we daily endured, put a period to their existence by shooting themselves[4].

Riflemen were considered the lightest troops in our service, yet we each had to carry a great weight during this long and harassing march. There was knapsack and straps, two shirts, two pair of stockings, one pair of shoes, ditto soles and heels, three brushes, a box of blacking, razor, soap-box and strap, and also at the time, an extra pair of trousers. There was a mess-tin, centre-tin and lid, haversack and canteen, greatcoat and blanket, a powder-flask filled, a ball bag containing thirty loose balls, a small wooden mallet used to hammer the ball into the muzzle of our rifles, belt and pouch - the latter containing fifty rounds of ammunition - sword-belt and rifle, besides other odds and ends that at all times are required for a service-soldier. Also, each squad had to carry four bill-hooks, weighing 6lbs each, so that every other day each man had to carry it. Thus we were equipped with from 70-80lbs weight, in the melting month of July. Not content with the above, the General gave strict orders for each man to have his canteen filled with water every morning before commencing the day's march. Through being thus overloaded, 400 of the battalion died a few months after our arrival, without a single shot being fired[5]. The survivors soon found out the cause of this mortality, and five years after, before we left the country, I don't think there was a man in the regiment who could show a single shirt, or a pair of shoes, in his knapsack[6].

From Vila Velha, their march continued to Sarnadas, and on the 15th they reached Castelo Branco, where they halted for two days to allow the 43rd and 52nd Regiments to catch up.

With a major engagement between the British army and Marshal Victor expected, Craufurd redoubled his efforts to reach Wellesley before it took place, so the Light Brigade left Castelo Branco soon after midnight on the 18 July, and embarked on another series of marches to Ladoeiro to Zebreira, close to the Spanish frontier. On the 20th they entered Spain by crossing the river Erges, and encamped near Zarza la Mayor. They were soon on the move again, through Moraleja, Coria, Galisteo, and Malpartida, which they reached on the 25 July.

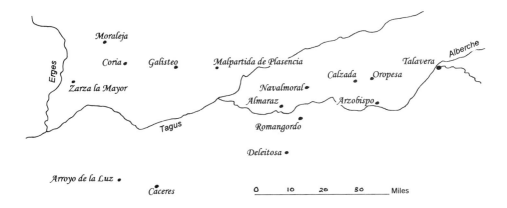

The greatest efforts were made by Major-General Craufurd to arrive in time to join the Commander-in-Chief before the battle was fought. The excellent orders our Brigadier issued for maintaining order and discipline on the line of march on this occasion, though exceedingly unpopular at first, have since become justly celebrated in the service. No man was allowed to fall out of the ranks on any pretext whatever, without a pass from the officer of his company. Thus it was that frequently, when almost dying of thirst, we were obliged to pass untasted, springs of the finest water. Fortunately for us, our longest halts took place during the heat of the day, and our longest marches at night.

This pass did not give complete security, for when the stragglers returned to camp, the orderly sergeants were compelled to parade them before their regimental-surgeons. If they were pronounced as skulkers, they were instantly tried by a drum-head court-martial, and punished accordingly. If the General found a man who had fallen out without a pass, he would take his ramrod and ride off. Often you would see him ride into camp with a dozen ramrods, and the adjutant of each regiment was then ordered to find the men who had none, each of whom would receive two dozen lashes. It was not unusual to see men who had been flogged with their knapsacks on their heads, and their bodies enveloped in loose greatcoats, to ease the wounds inflicted by the lash. Strange as it may appear, Craufurd maintained a popularity among the men who, on every other occasion, found him to be their best friend. We afterwards learnt that all this apparent severity was considered absolutely essential to the great purpose General Craufurd had in view - dispatch.

A few days before we reached Malpartida de Plasencia, we went through a small town, the name of which I forget. As we were passing the gaol, a man looking through one of the high barred windows of the building vociferated, in accents not to be mistaken:

"God's blood and 'ounds! Boys, are you English?"

Several of our men answered in the affirmative.

"Oh! by Jasus," the prisoner exclaimed, in a tone that set our men in a roar of laughter, "the Spaniards have poked me into this hole for getting a drop of wine. Get me out boys, pray."

We halted about half a mile on the other side of the town, and Colonel Beckwith sent for, and obtained, the man's release. He proved to be one of the 23rd Light Dragoons, who had been a prisoner of the French. He had escaped dressed as a peasant. Passing through this place, he had taken some wine from a man without paying for it, for which he had been incarcerated. Much merriment was excited by his appearance, and the droll and earnest manner in which he narrated his adventures.

They bivouacked at Malpartida on 25 July. Leach: *"On 26th and 27th, we continued our march, under a burning sun. In four days we passed from Coria to Navalmoral... Half a pound of bread was served out on the 27th, which was instantly consumed, as since our departure from Coria, we knew of such a thing only by name."*

Costello states that it was at Malpartida that they first received a report that a battle had been fought against the French, but Leach says that it was on the 27th at Navalmoral. The reports were carried by retreating Spanish soldiers who had been part of the army of General Gregorio García de la Cuesta (1740-1812), who had marched in support of Wellesley's army. Cuesta had been defeated by the French at Alcabon on the 27th.

On the following day, we bivouacked near Malpartida de Plasencia [Navalmoral?], when a report reached our corps that a battle had been fought at Talavera, and that the English had been beaten and dispersed. Few of us gave credit to the story, but it created some uneasiness among the men and officers. Its effect upon our Brigadier, however, was to make him hurry forward with increased speed. Our bivouac was immediately broken up, and we got under arms. We left the sick of the brigade behind us in the town, under charge of a subaltern from each regiment, and commenced one of the longest marches in the military records of any country, scarcely halting. To use the words of our admirable historian of the Peninsular War, we "passed over 62 miles and in the hottest season of the year in 26 hours"[7].

As we approached Talavera, we learned that a battle had been fought from the crowds of disorderly Spanish soldiery we met upon the road, a few of them wounded. These men were part of General Cuesta's army beaten by the French on the 27th. They chose to give the most disastrous account of the English army, saying it was completely destroyed. These Spaniards were a disorganised crew, but they had not forgotten to help themselves to plunder in their flight. Most of them carried some article or other, such as hams, cheese, and fowls, to which they could have little claim. Some, although they were infantrymen, rode on excellent horses, while others drove mules carrying sacks of flour, etc. There never was seen such a thoroughly demoralised wreck of an army.

Before the day dawned on the 28th, the brigade was on the march again, and soon, says Leach, "*something like a distant cannonade was heard. Our suspense and anxiety can easily be imagined, aware as we were of the proximity of the hostile armies to each other.*"

Simmons: "*Marched very early to the town of Calzada, where an express arrived from Sir Arthur Wellesley directing the brigade to make the least possible delay in joining the army. The brigade, after a short rest, marched to Oropesa, where it halted four hours to cook, having marched under a scorching sun.*"

Those men thought incapable of enduring the forced march which Craufurd was determined to make, were left at Oropesa. Leach: "*Having rested his brigade on this burning plain, where water was not to be procured, General Craufurd put it in motion towards Talavera de la Reina.*"

But Craufurd was too late for the battle which, on the morning of the 28th was already being fought. Leach:

"*I regret today, that stragglers from the British army, some without a wound, were also taking a similar direction to the rear. As they passed our columns they circulated all sorts and kind of reports of a most disheartening nature: 'the British army was utterly defeated, and in full retreat', 'Sir Arthur Wellesley was wounded', and by others, 'he was killed'. In short all was suspense and uncertainty. One thing was nevertheless certain - that the cannonade continued without cessation.*"

Simmons: "*We again commenced the march all night in very deep and sandy roads and arrived early upon the field of battle at Talavera de la Reina this morning.*"

As we advanced nearer to the scene of action the reports became less formidable, until the heights of Talavera burst upon our sight. With three loud huzzas, we hailed the news that in the action of the preceding day with the French, the British had been victorious.

It was early in the morning of 29 July, and our bugles struck up merrily as we crossed the field of battle. The scene, however, was appalling, especially to us young soldiers who, having taken no part in an encounter as yet, had here missed the interest which blunts the feelings of the men engaged. We 'raw ones' had scarcely seen the enemy, and could recognise no comrades among the fallen, although the experience of one engagement would effectively break the ice.

The field of action occupied an extensive valley, situated between two ranges of hills, on which the British and French armies were posted. It was strewn with the wreck of recent battle. The dead and dying, thousands of them, conquerors and conquered, lay in little heaps, interspersed with dismounted guns, and shattered ammunition waggons. Broken horse trappings, blood-stained shakos, and other torn paraphernalia of military pomp and distinction, completed the battle scene.

The long grass, which had taken fire during the action, was still burning, and added dreadfully to the sufferings of the wounded and dying of both armies. Their cries for assistance were horrifying, and hundreds, exerting the last remnant of their strength, were seen crawling to places of safety.

In the midst of this I saw, for the first time, our immortal chief, Sir Arthur Wellesley. I also beheld that deformed-looking lump of pride, ignorance and treachery, General Cuesta. He was the most murderous-looking old man I ever saw.

This was also the first time that Simmons had witnessed a scene of battle: *'The horrid sights were beyond anything I could have imagined. Thousands dead and dying in every direction, horses, men, French and English in whole lines, who had cut each other down, and, I am sorry to say, the Spaniards butchering the wounded Frenchmen at every opportunity, and stripping them naked, which gave admission to the attacks of myriads of pernicious flies, and the heat of a burning sun. You may be sure everything was done on our part, and the commanding officer's, to put a stop to such horrid brutality and give assistance, but the ground was covered for at least five miles with dead and dying.'*

Green: *"A solemn awe seemed to pervade every breast to hear the groans of the wounded. The poor fellows begged for water, and to be carried out of the field into the town for shelter from the heat of the sun; but we were not permitted to do these acts of kindness, for our orders were to take the advance post among some olive trees near the river, on the other side of it, away from the place of battle. The French artillery were all formed in parks, the infantry and cavalry covering the guns."*

Simmons: *'Expecting another attack, the army was drawn up in a line ready to receive the enemy. Our regiment was posted in front of the army, but the French thought proper to have no more of it at present, and retreated about three miles, and beyond a river, which secured their front.'*

On our arrival we were immediately ordered upon outpost duty and had to throw out a line of sentinels facing the French position. Another, more painful duty that devolved upon us, was to carry the wounded men into the town of Talavera. Many of these poor fellows were dreadfully burnt.

On 30 July, the day after their arrival, Simmons says: *"we were employed all this day in collecting dead bodies and putting them into large heaps mixed with faggots and burning them. The stench from so many dead bodies was volatile and offensive beyond conception, as the heat of the weather was very great."*

Another member of the 1st battalion was Lt. Harry Smith, whose autobiography was published in 1901: *"The soldiers were not satisfied with this mode of treating the bodies of their dead comrades, and the prosecution of the attempt was relinquished"*.

Before the battle, Sir Arthur Wellesley's army had consisted of nearly 20,000 able bodied men. Of those, he lost 33 officers and nearly 800 men killed, 195 officers and 3,700 men wounded. Nine officers and 650 men were missing. The French lost 900 men killed and 6,300 wounded; only 150 were made prisoners. The Spanish return indicated that 1,200 of their men had been killed or wounded. More Spaniards were to die because General Cuesta resolved to decimate those regiments which had given way in battle. Wellesley interceded on their behalf, but Cuesta still slew fifty of his own men.

Although the 95th took no part in the battle of Talavera, some of their riflemen did, as part of the 1st battalion of Embodied Detachments under Lt.-Col. Bunbury. This was one of two such battalions formed from the sick and wounded soldiers who had been left behind in Lisbon after their regiments had returned to England at the termination of the Corunna campaign. One of the six sergeants in the 1st battalion of Embodied Detachments was James Battersby, whom Costello mentions in Chapter 17. After the battle of Talavera, these two motley battalions were disbanded and the men rejoined their original regiments.

For several days, the Light Brigade stayed at Talavera, but the soldiers had very little to eat. Leach: *"The Spanish authorities had failed most shamefully in their promise of procuring supplies for the British army. I do not believe that more than a day's allowance of bread was issued from 29 July to the evening of 2 August, nor were the rations of wine, spirits, and meat, forthcoming. Dollars we had in our pockets, it is true; but they soon became totally useless."*

Simmons: *"Our army was nearly starving. There was no want of money in our camp, but our Spanish friends [Cuesta's soldiers] infested every road for miles and robbed the peasantry who were bringing bread and vegetables to us for sale... I rode several miles from our camp in search of bread, and luckily bought some from a peasant who had plenty hidden in his house, and would have gladly brought to our camp but durst not, from the dread of being robbed by the Spanish soldiers."*

Leach loaned his horse to a brother-officer who went to purchase food in Talavera, where it was stolen. It had carried everything Leach owned, none of which could be replaced therefore, when the army began to retreat from Talavera, he had to *"tramp it on foot from the Tagus to the Guadiana, no trifling distance either; and to stretch myself at the foot of a tree every night, with no covering but the sky and a green jacket."*

In consequence of the increasing weakness of the British army at this period - the ranks of which were daily thinned through the scantiness and wretched quality of the food with which they were supplied - and by the accession of strength which the French had received, Lord Wellington[8] was induced to retire.

The retreat began on 3 August; in twelve hours they were back in Oropesa. Craufurd's Light Brigade had been augmented by Donkin's Brigade, to create the 3rd Division, which formed the rear-guard in the retreat, and at the very rear of the rear-guard, there were always a couple of companies of riflemen and some dragoons.

On 4 August, they crossed the bridge of Arzobispo. Simmons: *"The only retreat open was by the bridge of Puente del Arzobispo. We passed it. The advanced guard of Soult's army, consisting of cavalry, was close to it. The bridge was secured by a body of infantry, and we had now the river between us."*

That evening, says Leach, *"as neither bread, meat, nor rations of any kind, were to be had, General Craufurd ordered that any animals in the shape of cattle, sheep, or pigs, which could be found in the extensive woods in which we halted for the evening, should forthwith be put in requisition for the troops. Never do I remember having seen orders so promptly obeyed. A most furious attack was instantly made on a large herd of pigs... It would be useless to attempt a description of the scene of noise and confusion which ensued. The screeches and cries of those ill-fated swine, as they met their death at the point of the bayonet, the sword, or sergeant's pike, and the rapidity with which they were cut up into junks, with the hair on, and fried on the lids of camp-kettles, or toasted at the fire on a pointed stick, to allay the cravings of hunger of some thousands of half-famished soldiers, was quite incredible, and, I must add, truly ludicrous... At midnight we resumed our march."*

Their orders were to reach the bridge at Almaraz without delay, so on the 5th, the Light Brigade marched for fourteen hours through a mountainous and barren countryside, in intense heat to the village of Romangordo, near to which they bivouacked.

We retraced our steps for a few days then the main army left our brigade encamped upon a rocky eminence, partly surrounded by wood, and overlooking the River Tagus. It was a wild and beautiful scene, with several corn fields in our immediate neighbourhood.

Here, says Simmons, they posted *'pickets on the bank of the Tagus and at the broken bridge of Almaraz. Marshal Soult's advanced posts were on the opposite bank of the river. Our brigade moved every evening after sunset near the river, and there remained all night with our arms ready in case the enemy should attempt to ford the river. This was a nasty damp place, and the exhalations from the vegetable matter which was corrupting from the heat of the sun, and the half-dried swamps that were swarming with vermin, laid the foundation of disease amongst our men. We called the place we occupied by day 'Dough Boy Hill', but a more appropriate name for it would have been 'Starvation Hill', as a small quantity of goat's flesh and a little coarse pea-flour was all we obtained here daily. The flour was made up into little cakes by each individual and put upon a thin stone over a fire until sufficiently done."*

Our living here became truly savage. Although we remained at this place for two or three weeks, we scarcely received half a dozen rations during that period[9], and existed by our own ingenuity. Fortunately, there were some droves of pigs that were taken into the woods to feed and fatten upon the acorns. To these animals, which were generally under the charge of some Spaniards, we were obliged to have recourse for food. For bread we took the corn from the fields. We had no proper means of winnowing and grinding it, so we rubbed out the ears between our hands, and then pounded them between stones to make into dough, such as it was. From this wretched practice, we christened the place 'Dough Boy Hill', a name by which it is well remembered by the men of our Division.

At midnight on 24 August, the Light Brigade withdrew from Dough Boy Hill and began to retreat back into Portugal through Deleitosa, Caceres, Arroyo del Puerco and Salorino to Valencia de Alcantara, where Craufurd flogged some of his men, earning another bitter reference in Leach's journal: *"27 August. The Division paraded at six this evening when we got a volley of <u>abusive</u> and <u>blasphemous</u> language from Brigadier-General Robert Craufurd. After him flogging half a dozen men for some very <u>frivolous offences</u> committed on our late harassing marches, we were dismissed."* (Verner)

They continued their march towards Campo Maior, and it was not until they reached Castelo de Vide on the 29 August that they had an opportunity to purchase bread, rice, chocolate and wine. Leach: *"Such good use was made of a certain fluid called 'confession wine', with which the cellars of Castelo de Vide abounded, that not a thoroughly sober individual could have been found in the whole Division by 9 o'clock that night."*

They remained at Castelo de Vide for about a week, then on 7 September, they marched to Portalegre and Arronches, arriving at Campo Maior on 11 September 1809.

CHAPTER 4

Campo Maior and Elvas
September 1809 - February 1810

From the preceding place [Dough Boy Hill] we marched to Campo Maior, where we remained three months.

Simmons: *"The town of Campo Maior is fortified, and has also a citadel. It stands on a plain abounding with corn. At about the distance of a league, a small river named the Caia flows. This river forms the boundary line between the two countries."*

During the winter there was no campaigning and the soldiers had more leisure time. When it was to be had, alcohol was part of the daily ration of a soldier, but some drank excessively.

I well remember a deplorable instance of insubordination, arising from this vice, which took place at Campo Maior after the battle of Talavera. Tom Plunket had been promoted to the rank of sergeant, and was in the Hon. Captain Stewart's company[1]. One morning, when the company was on private parade, Tom appeared quite tipsy. The officers had not yet arrived, and when he gave the words of command for inspection, he set the men laughing. The pay-sergeant, his superior in rank, ordered him to desist, but Tom refused. While an altercation was going on, Captain Stewart came up. Perceiving the state Tom was in, he ordered him to be put under arrest and confined to his quarters.

When sober, Tom was noted for his good humour and humanity, but now, left alone, and under the influence of intoxication, he felt that his treatment had been undignified, and wanted vengeance. He barricaded the door of the room, and loaded some ten or twelve rifles belonging to men then on fatigue duty. Taking up one of these, and cocking it, he placed himself at an open window for the purpose, as he stated to several of the men, of shooting Captain Stewart as he passed. Fortunately, the Captain was notified of the danger of going near the house. Meanwhile, several of the men, by coaxing and force alternatively, tried to get into the room Tom had barred. They were unsuccessful. Plunket was eventually induced to relent by the appearance of Lt. Johnston of the company, a great favourite of the men, among whom he was known by a very familiar nickname[2]. The door was eventually opened, and Tom was made a prisoner.

Although Tom's conduct had resulted from the madness of intoxication, his insubordination was too glaring to pass over, and he

41

was brought to a regimental court-martial. He was found guilty, and his sentence was to receive 300 lashes and be reduced to the ranks.

Plunket, having recovered his reason, experienced and expressed the most unfeigned contrition, so that when the sentence became known, sorrow was felt for him throughout the regiment, by the officers almost as much as the men. The bravest soldier of our battalion was to suffer the penalty of his crime in the presence of the very men before whom he had been held up as a pattern only a few months before.

The square was formed for punishment, with a tree in the centre to which the culprit was to be tied. Close to it, in front of his guards, stood Tom, with folded arms and downcast eyes. The surgeon stood by, while the buglers untangled the strings of the cats[3].

There was a solemn stillness on that parade. The pensiveness on the features of both officers and men was deeper than usual, as though the honour of the profession was to suffer in the person of the prisoner. Flogging is a disgusting subject of contemplation at all times, but in this instance it seemed doubly so now that a gallant, and until a few days previous, an honoured and respected man, was to suffer. Poor Tom had the commiseration of the whole regiment.

The adjutant read the sentence of the court-martial in a loud voice. Tom looked deadly pale. That countenance, which the brunt of the fiercest battle had been unable to turn from its ruddy hue, which the fear of death could not change, now blanched in dread of a worse fate.

"Buglers, do you duty," exclaimed Colonel Beckwith, in a voice husky with emotion.

The men seemed to hesitate in their business of stripping and binding the prisoner to the tree, but it was soon accomplished. Only once did Tom attempt to catch the eye of his colonel. With an imploring glance, and in a broken accent, he exclaimed:

"Colonel, you won't, will you? You won't... you cannot mean to... flog *me*!"

The appeal, although it went to the heart of every one present, was in vain, but Colonel Beckwith betrayed much uneasiness. At the commencement of the punishment, I beheld him give a slight start, but the moment he beheld the punishing bugler laying on rather lighter than was common, his sense of duty became paramount.

"Do your duty fairly, sir!" he uttered in a loud voice.

After the first man had bestowed his quantum of 25 lashes, he was succeeded by another who, determined that his reputation as a flogger should not suffer however his victim might, laid on like a hardened hand. Plunket's sufferings became intense. He bit his lip to stifle the utterance of his pangs, but nature was too strong for suppression. More than once, he gave way to a half-agonised cry that seemed to thrill through the blood in my veins. Happily, this wretched scene was destined for a brief termination when, at the 35th lash, the Colonel ordered the punishment to cease, and the prisoner to be taken down. When this was done, he addressed Plunket:

"You see now, sir, how very easy it is to commit a blackguard's crime, but how difficult it is to take his punishment."

So ended the most memorable punishment scene I have ever witnessed.

It has usually been contended by those averse to the system of flogging common in our army, that it destroys the pride and spirit of the man. Where the character of the soldier was not previously depraved, that effect I have in many instances myself witnessed, but Plunket appeared to get over the recollection of his former disgrace very quickly, and soon got into favour with his officers again. Notwithstanding his little fits of inebriety, he was made corporal, and went through the sanguinary scenes of the Peninsula, unscathed from shot or steel[4].

Campo Maior was in the Alentejo region of Portugal, close to the Spanish border. It was a very unhealthy place, and the soldiers began to fall sick in huge numbers.

Leach: *'The whole of Alentejo, and more particularly that part which approaches the sluggish and muddy waters of the Guadiana, is proverbially unhealthy, especially in summer and autumn. The natives of the northern provinces dread it as a West Indies or Sierra Leone, and they have a proverb to this effect, 'Once in Alentejo, never out of it again alive'. There proved to be too much truth in the adage, for during the three months our army was cantoned there, the mortality was frightful... one third of the army was in hospital, from fevers, agues and dysentery. The natives of Alentejo may be distinguished at once from those of the north of Portugal, fever and ague being legibly imprinted on their cadaverous faces and emaciated figures."*

The weakness of the men from heat, exhaustion and lack of food on their marches, must have made them more vulnerable to disease, which Leach called Alentejo fever but which Simmons, who had been a surgeon and himself fell ill from it, diagnosed as typhus fever. Typhus is an acute infection spread by the bite of infected fleas, ticks, mites or lice. The symptoms are severe fever, with shaking attacks, severe headache and muscular pains, followed by a spotted rash. The soldiers, who rarely had a change of clothes, and who slept in what they wore, would have been lousy. Leach remained unaffected, ascribing this to the fact that he took every opportunity for exercise by going hunting with gun and greyhound[5]. Costello was not so fortunate.

During this time a dreadful mortality took place. In our regiment alone, the flux and brain fever reigned to so frightful an extent that 300 men died in hospital. I myself was seized with the prevailing fever shortly after our arrival, and was sent to the Convent of St. Paul, the general hospital at Elvas.

Elvas was, says Simmons, *"a fortified town of Portugal, of considerable importance, and about four leagues from Badajoz. It is placed upon a rising piece of ground about a league from the Guadiana, and has two outworks to support the town... Elvas is supplied with water by an aqueduct. The water is brought a considerable distance."* **And** it was used liberally to help cure the soldiers:

> I could not help remarking the manner of cure adopted by our doctors, which consisted of throwing cold water from canteens or mess kettles, as often as possible over the bodies of the patients. In many cases this was effectual. I think it cured me.

One of those chosen to help with this cure was William Green. *"The hospital was soon filled with sick. The fever was so raging that many went in on the morning and at night were carried out to the graveyard. Our doctor used a very singular expedient, which was this: we were ordered, when off duty, to sit up with the sick in our turns, and about midnight to take each one out of bed - they all lay without shirts - lead them to a flight of steps, and pour two buckets of cold water on each. They were so deranged they knew nothing about it. I would put my finger into their hand, when they would jump out of bed, follow me, and sit quietly while we poured the contents of the buckets over them, and would be led by the finger back again to bed, and never utter one word. It was thought by the officers and doctors, that this mode of treatment had a good effect."*

Not all of those nursing the sick soldiers were as humane:

> I had a narrow squeak for my life, but fortunately recovered after an illness of nearly six weeks. This was thanks to my good constitution, but none to the brute of an orderly who, during the delirium of the fever, once beat me most furiously with a broom stick[6].
>
> When I left the hospital with other convalescents, I was sent to the Bomb Proof Barracks, where it frequently became our duty to see the dead interred. This was a horrible office, which obliged us to attend at the hospital to receive the bodies, which were conveyed away, cart-loads at a time, to the ground appropriated for their burial. This lay outside the town beneath the ramparts, and was so small that we had to get large, deep, oblong holes excavated. Two stout Portuguese were employed packing the bodies, heads and heels together, into these to save room. For this duty these two brutes seemed to have been born, for never before did I see two such ruffianly looking fellows[7].
>
> It was revolting to witness how the pair handed the bodies from the hospital to the cart. Each carried a skin of vinegar, with which they first soused themselves over the neck and face, then, with one jerk they jilted a single corpse, naked as it was born, across their shoulders and bolted off to the cart, into which it was pitched as if it had been a log of wood. Although the women who fell victims to the epidemic were

generally sewed in a wrapper of calico, or some such thing, they partook of the same hole as the opposite sex, and otherwise were as little privileged. Many were the scores of my poor comrades I thus saw committed to their first parent, and many were the coarse jests the gravediggers made over their obsequies[8].

According to Simmons, over 4,000 British soldiers died and were buried at Elvas. By the end of 1809, nearly a fifth of the 1st battalion 95th were either dead, missing, or had deserted. Many sick officers returned to England.

On 12 December 1809, after three months in Campo Maior, and in preparation for a new campaign, Wellington's army began the long march back to the northern frontier between Portugal and Spain. They went without Costello, who remained in hospital in Elvas. On 5 January, the Light Brigade marched into Pinhel, near Almeida, where they were cantoned for many weeks, and from where the riflemen made occasional advances into the villages on the other side of the River Coa.

On 22 February, a complete re-arrangement of brigades and divisions was ordered. The 3rd Division, with Donkin's Brigade, was given to General Thomas Picton, leaving Craufurd's Light Brigade separate, but augmented by the 1st Regiment of Hussars of the King's German Legion. The Legion had been raised in 1804 from Hanoverians, those who remained loyal to George III after Napoleon had seized their state. The German troopers soon won the respect of the men and officers of the 95th Rifles for their discipline and bravery in the field, and for the effectiveness of their reconnaissance.

On 27 February, a company of rifleman was ordered to the Spanish village of La Bouza to feel for the enemy, who were across the River Duas Casas at Barba del Puerco. Fired upon, the rifleman fell back, but two companies later occupied La Bouza, and a further two companies were established at Escarigo in support.

While I was confined in hospital, the brigade marched and took up their cantonments between Ciudad Rodrigo and Almeida. In the beginning of February, I was one of about 300 convalescents who were marched, under charge of an officer of the German Legion, to join their respective regiments. On this march, I narrowly escaped being provosted - in other words, flogged.

Some of the men, being from different regiments, and under the command of a foreigner, regarded it as a fair opportunity to pilfer from the country people as we pursued our march. I am sorry to say that drunkenness and robbery were not infrequent, and the German officer, as is usual under such circumstances, experienced great difficulty in keeping the skulkers and the disorderly from lingering in the rear. As a compliment to my steadiness, he made me an acting corporal, with strict orders to make the men at the rear of our detachment keep up.

Just before we arrived at the town of Viseu, which was the headquarters of the Commander-in-Chief and was occupied by the Foot, I came up to some our party, who were doing their best to empty a pig-skin of wine which they had stolen. I was dreadfully fatigued and thirsty, and did not have sufficient self-restraint to refuse their invitation to drink, which I did, and became a partner in the crime. I was taking the jug of wine from my lips, when a party of the 16th Light Dragoons rode up and made us prisoners: the peasant from whom the wine had been taken had made a complaint at headquarters. There were nine of us and we were imprisoned in Viseu.

The second day, the Honourable Captain Pakenham of the Adjutant-General's Department, paid us a visit. A brother-in-law to the Duke of Wellington, he belonged to my regiment[9], and was much beloved by us all because he was considerate. For example, on those occasions when the fresh arrival of necessaries (meat, wine, etc.) brought the men in crowds about the stores, he would abide his turn as though he were one of ourselves, and would oblige every newcomer, whatever his rank, to submit to the same. This was only fair, but for its rare occurrence with the other officers, it was never forgotten by the men.

Captain Pakenham now told us he had had great difficulty in saving us from being hanged. This was probably said to frighten us, but it was not altogether a joke, for a man called Maguire, of the 27th Regiment, who had been with me in hospital, was hung for stopping and robbing a Portuguese of a few *vintems*[10].

We left Viseu, but the German officer in charge of the detachment had orders to see that we received two dozen lashes each from the Provost Marshal every morning until we rejoined our regiments. This kind of breakfast I did not much relish, particularly as we had seven days' march to get through before reaching our battalion.

The following day, during a halt, myself and the eight other culprits were summoned to appear before the German. We expected to be punished, but were agreeably undeceived. The officer addressed us in broken English:

"I have been told to have you men flogged, for a crime dat is very bad and disgraceful to der soldier - robbing der people you come paid to fight for. But it is not the manner of my people to flog, so I shall not flog you. I shall give you all to your colonels; if they like to flog you, they may."

Relieved, we each saluted the kind man and retired. From that moment, I entertained a high respect for our Germans. This they deserved, not only on account of their humanity and general good feeling to us British, but from their determined bravery and discipline in the field. As cavalry, they were the finest and most efficient I ever saw in action, and I had many opportunities of judging, as some troops of them generally did duty with us during the war. The cavalry of the

German Legion cared for their horses with fondness. At night, a German soldier seldom thought of food or rest until his horse had been provided for. The noble animals seemed aware of this, and it amused me to see some of them run after their masters with all the playfulness of a dog. Because of this attention, their horses were in condition when those of our own cavalry - without wishing to be disparaging about our own countrymen - were either dying, or in a deplorable state[11]. If we saw a German vidette or express galloping furiously, we knew immediately that there was work for someone to do. While on outpost their vigilance was most admirable[12].

When Costello rejoined his battalion, it was at Barba del Puerco.

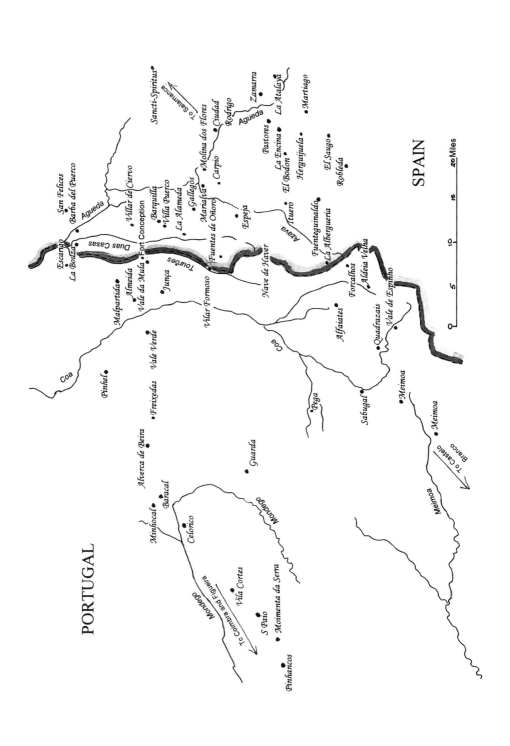

CHAPTER 5

Barba del Puerco and Gallegos
1 March - 9 July 1810

By early March, the riflemen were stationed in villages between the Coa and the Agueda, with the German hussars deployed along the Agueda to keep watch on the French movements on the other side. On 4 March, O'Hare's company was ordered from Reigada to Escarigo. The French, who were occupying Barba del Puerco, withdrew across the river Agueda to San Felices, and in such haste that they left as a breakfast for the riflemen, the bread they had been baking. Soon after, the rain fell heavily and the River Duas Casas, which was in the rear of the riflemen's position, and had no bridge, became so dangerously swollen that Craufurd ordered them back. By 11 March, the weather had improved and four companies were able to reoccupy the post.

> I rejoined my regiment at Barba del Puerco, a small village near the banks of the River Agueda[1], on the other side of which the enemy had taken up their position. Our regiment was cantoned in the surrounding villages, while nightly we mounted a captain's picket on a height facing a bridge, on the other side of which the French had thrown out their advanced sentry.

The bridge was in what Simmons describes as *"one of the most formidable passes I ever beheld. The river Agueda, which rises in the great Spanish mountains named Sierra de Gata, and runs furiously in the bottom of this deep chasm over rugged rocks, causing a continued noise, separated us. At the bottom of the zig-zag pass is the bridge over the river, 100 yards long and five yards wide. San Felices, in which the advance of the French army were lodged, under the command of General Baron de Ferey, is about half a league from the pass... The way to the bridge is very bad... These were the mountains we had to guard, and place our sentries in the different intricate pathways, and to post them in the dark in order to deceive our enemy, and take them off before daylight."*

Stationed at San Felices, a few miles away, was General Ferey, with a brigade of 3,000 Frenchmen. On the night of 19 March, he decided to take advantage of the bad weather, and make a surprise attack on the British post with six companies of light infantry - his best troops. That night, O'Hare's company, which was below strength

The bridge at Barba del Puerco today.

at 43 men, was on picket duty at the bridge. With it were George Simmons, William Green and Edward Costello.

On 19 March, the company to which I belonged was on picket. It was a fine night, though windy, with a fleecy scud occasionally obscuring the light of the moon. Two of our sentries were posted on the bridge, while a third was stationed half-way down the steep, to keep up communication with our picket above.

At about 8pm, O'Hare and Simmons placed their sentries: a sergeant and twelve men at a spot about fifty yards from the bridge, and a double sentry behind a rock fifteen yards from it. The latter two riflemen - Thomas Maher and John McCann - were told that, if attacked, they were to fire and retire back to the sergeant's picket. After surreptitiously reconnoitring the enemy position on the other side of the bridge, Simmons returned up the hillside to the officers' tent. The picket house, where the rest of the company was based, was a Catholic chapel, 300 yards from the bridge. At 9pm, O'Hare, feeling unwell, retired to bed, which may have been in the rear of his company's position.

At about the same time, William Green took up his sentry duty at the lodgings of Colonel Beckwith and his adjutant, Lt. Stewart, in the nearby village. Green was told that if there was an alarm, he was to tap at the window of the lower room where the two officers were sleeping. This information he passed to the sentry who relieved him at 11pm. Green then went to the chapel/picket house where his comrades, one of whom was Costello, were lying around a wood fire, sleeping. All was still and quiet; he lay down.

O'Hare's departure had left Lt. James Mercer[2] in charge of the pickets. With him were Simmons and Lt. Alexander Coane[3]. At 12 o'clock, they heard several shots fired.

Simmons: *The night was dark and stormy, and occasional rain had caused the river to make more noise in its passage over the rocky bed than usual, completely preventing our advanced sentinels hearing the approach of the enemy. Also from the obscurity of the night, it was not possible to see any object, and the enemy passed the bridge so rapidly, only one sentinel fired before they were both knocked down. Two men, Maher and McCann, were taken at the bridge. However, this gave the alarm, and a small party stationed amongst the rocks kept up a fire, but the sergeant being shot through the mouth, and the enemy being so numerous, they could not impede their progress."*

Both our sentries at the bridge were taken prisoners, one of them badly wounded. One, named Maher, returned to England in 1814 when an exchange of prisoners took place, and rejoined us at Dover[4].

As soon as the shots were heard, Lt. Coane was sent to fetch O'Hare, and the company in the chapel were ordered to fall in.

Our men were mostly asleep when, about 12 o'clock, we were suddenly woken by the rifle reports of our sentries, and by the French drums playing their advance of 'rub-a-dub-dub', which our men designated with the name of 'old trousers'[5]. The chilly hour of the night, and the inclination to sleep, had sunk my senses below zero, but I was soon startled out of my lethargy by the whizzing of the enemies' bullets. My astonishment gave place to perfect recollection, and in less than a minute we were all under arms. I was then but a young, sleepy-headed boy, scarcely aroused to a true sense of the profession I had embraced, and I felt an indescribable thrill, for never before had I been under the fire of a French musket.

Green: *'I was woken by the voice of the officers with the words, 'Be quick men, and load as you go to the brow of the hill!' I jumped up, got my rifle, and overtook them."*

The riflemen marched forward towards the bridge, to the alarm post, which was on the edge of the rocky chasm. There they found the French forming in line, yelling furiously and firing, with their drums beating.

The balls of the French whistled about us as a column came rushing over the bridge to force our position.

Simmons: *"In a moment, after the arrival of the main body of the picket, the French were literally scrambling up the rocky ground within ten yards of us.*

Green: *"About 500 big grenadiers, half drunk, had made a rush over, and extending themselves, were climbing the rocks, and out-flanking our little company, both right and left. We challenged them".*

At what point O'Hare arrived is not clear.

Captain O'Hare, with his characteristic coolness, immediately gave us the word to seek cover. We threw ourselves forward amongst the rocky and broken ground, from whence we kept up a galling fire upon those who had commenced storming our heights.

Simmons: *"We commenced firing at each other very spiritedly. Their drums beat a charge, and the French attempted to dislodge us, without effect. My friend, Lt. Mercer, who was putting on his spectacles, received a musket ball through his head, and fell dead close to my feet."*

The enemy were surrounding the riflemen in all directions. Simmons: *"Captain O'Hare called out, 'We shall never retire. Here we will stand. They shall not pass but over my body'. The shots flew round us thick as hailstones... They were advancing upon us, but we kept up a terrible fire... Several were now falling, and the moon for a few minutes shone brightly, then disappeared, and again at intervals let us see each other. We profited by this circumstance, as their belts were white and over their greatcoats, so that where they crossed upon the breast, combined with the glare of the breast-plate, they gave a grand mark for our rifles. Our men being in dark dresses, and from their small numbers obliged to keep close together, and the ground being exceedingly rugged, were all favourable circumstances."*

Green: *"Three of these big ugly fellows came within ten yards of me and my front-rank man. I had got my ball in my rifle, but had no time to return the ramrod, so both ball and ramrod went through one of them. My comrade fired, and the ball struck another in the breast. I threw my rifle down, as it was no use to me without a ramrod, and retired about 20 yards,"* where he borrowed the rifle of a wounded sergeant, and then went forward again to rejoin his comrade.

Simmons: *"I saw French officers beating their men with their swords to make them try to drive us from the rocks we occupied."*

O'Hare's little company were holding off 600 French infantrymen. Simmons: *"We fought in this way for at least half an hour, against fearful odds, when Lt.-Col. Beckwith brought up the three reserve companies from the village."*

We were exceedingly hard pressed when three companies of our regiment, under Colonel Beckwith, came up to our relief. During this brief conflict, Colonel Beckwith heaved large fragments of stone upon the French as they attempted to ascend the acclivity on which we were placed. While so engaged, he got a musket-shot through his cap[6]. And our adjutant, Lt. Stewart, a fine tall fellow, was engaged in a personal contest with two or three grenadiers, a number of whom had managed to ascend the hill on our right. At this critical moment, Ballard, one of our men[7], came to his aid and shot one of his assailants, at which the other instantly surrendered. The following year, this gallant officer fell on our advance from Santarem[8].

For a while the contest was doubtful and bloody, but after about half an hour's hard fighting, the enemy were obliged to retreat precipitately, and under a close and murderous fire from us. This was, I believe, the first and last time the French ever attempted to surprise a rifle picket.

All four companies suffered casualties, but O'Hare's suffered the most; some of his men were captured. Simmons: *"Lieutenant Mercer killed; 17 of our men killed and wounded. [Robert] Fairfoot was of the party taken; [Tuttle] Betts, the sergeant, wounded in the jaw; O'Gallagher wounded and died; William David, his skull blown off and his dura matter exposed."* David died two days later. The riflemen who survived were praised for their defence at the bridge. Leach: *'Lord Wellington sent a handsome letter of thanks to Colonel Beckwith, expressive of his approbation of the conduct of the regiment; and General Craufurd, never lavish of praise, issued an order complimentary to the corps."*

Expecting another attack at the bridge, two more companies of riflemen, two companies of the 52nd, and one of the 43rd, were drafted in as support, but they were not needed because it started raining again, the Duas Casas rose, and Craufurd was compelled to withdraw his infantry back across the river to Villar de Ciervo. He replaced them with a picket of the 1st German Hussars as a lookout.

General Craufurd was a notorious disciplinarian who frequently flogged his men for stealing food, so it is interesting to read in Napier's *History* that, after this affair, he was so incensed at the Spanish for not supplying food for his hungry men, he seized *"some church plate to purchase corn, a rash act which he was forced to redress; yet it convinced the priests that the distress was not feigned, and they procured some supplies."*

On 8 April, the 1st battalion marched from Villar de Ciervo to Vale da Mula and Malpartida, and on 11 April, having lost so many men, its ten companies were reduced to eight, the officers of the 9th and 10th companies of Captains Glasse and Balvaird being ordered to return to the depot in England. At the same time, Captain Hew Ross's troop of Horse Artillery - the A battery, known as the Chestnut Troop - became attached to the Light Brigade, which now became the Light Division.

On 21 April, the French, in considerable force, made an appearance in the vicinity of Ciudad Rodrigo, a strongly fortified town on the Agueda, which was held by the Spanish. The French prepared to besiege the town, therefore, on 29 April, as part of the British response, the 1st battalion 95th marched ten miles south to Espeja and Gallegos.

Shortly after the attempted surprise, we quitted Barba del Puerco for the town of Gallegos, five or six miles from Ciudad Rodrigo. While we lay here, I was employed as orderly to General Craufurd. I was acquainted with his private servant, a German, and at times, when an opportunity offered, we took a glass of wine together upon the most convivial terms. One morning, when I thought the brigadier had gone out, as was his usual custom, I went to his room to ask the valet to partake of some wine, which I had received from the patron of the house. I opened the door, went in unhesitatingly, and there beheld my servant friend, in a morning-gown and looking out of the window. As he had not been disturbed by my approach, it entered my head to surprise him. I stepped softly up to his rear, and with a sudden laugh, gave him a smart slap on the back. The gentleman in the dressing-gown started.

A distant view of Ciudad Rodrigo, from the oak wood near Espeja, with a troop of guerillas.
Published by C Turner, London, 24 May 1813. ©British Museum

"Who the devil is that?" he said, and turning round disclosed, not the merry phiz of the valet, but the stern features of General Craufurd himself. My consternation and surprise can be imagined. I wanted the ground to open and swallow me up, and I attempted, in a very humble way, to explain my mistake as I gradually retreated to the door.

The General, observing the fright I was in, said with a good-humoured smile: "And where did you get the wine from, sir?"

I told him.

"Well, you may go," he said; "but pray, sir, never again do me the honour to take me for my servant."

I vanished in a moment. The circumstance was circulated by the valet, and many were the laughs and jests afterwards created at my expense among the men.

On 30 April, two companies of the Rifles were posted as pickets upon the river Azava at the bridge of Marialva. A vidette of the German Hussars was posted on the other side of the river, from where he could see all the way to Ciudad Rodrigo. That same day, at Espeja, the Light Division was augmented by two regiments of brown-uniformed Portuguese light infantrymen.

We were here joined by the 1st and 3rd Regiments of the Portuguese Caçadores. These fellows I never had any opinion of from the very first moment I saw them. They were the dirtiest and noisiest brutes I ever came across. Historians have given them great credit, but during the whole of the Peninsular War, or at least the time they were with us, I never knew them to perform one gallant act. On the line of march they often reminded me of a band of strollers, and they were very fond of gambling. Every halt we made was sure to find them squatted, with cards in their hands[9].

One of these regiments was placed under the command of a captain of ours, named Elder, a brave officer, who was made Colonel of their 3rd Regiment. He was afterwards severely wounded at Badajoz, and returned to England[10]. At the same period, we were incorporated with the 14th and 16th Light Dragoons, together with the 1st regiment of German Hussars[11], and Captain Bull's troop of horse artillery.

The Light Division, now at full strength, was posted in advance of the army of Sir Arthur Wellesley - now Viscount Wellington - which consisted of about 36,000 British and Portuguese troops and 3,000 Spanish. They were only a few miles from Ciudad Rodrigo, which was being invested by Marshal André Massena's army of Portugal, numbering 47,000 men. Part of Massena's force was deployed to counter the threat, and it was the Rifles in particular, who had the task of watching for the French with pickets and patrols. It was a tense time, with the Spanish pressing Wellington to intervene more actively to help their countrymen besieged in Ciudad Rodrigo.

When the French commenced laying siege to Rodrigo, we were terribly harassed by the severity of our duty, being both day and night accoutred and under arms, expecting an attack.

Leach: *'From the beginning of March until 24 July, we were stationed so close to the outposts of the French, as to render it necessary for the soldiers and officers to sleep fully accoutred, with their clothes on, ready to get under arms in an instant... In short, the French cavalry were eternally in motion, in large bodies, towards our chain of posts, and we as often under arms waiting for them."*

On 10 June, the Agueda became fordable. This left the Light Division exposed, yet Craufurd held his ground in order to give moral support to the defenders of Ciudad Rodrigo, and to protect the surrounding villages from French foraging parties. A warning system had been set up for the Division:

A section of our Rifles, usually mounting picket with a troop of dragoons, occupied three different points - Carpio, Molina dos Flores and Marialva, all about two miles nearer to Rodrigo. Bull's troop of artillery always remained in the centre of the village of Gallegos, near a church, with a gun ready, loaded with blank carriage. A sentry was near it, watching a beacon, which had been erected on a hill, about a mile from the village. Placed near the beacon was a vidette and one of our riflemen who, if one of the pickets was attacked, was to give the alarm by discharging his piece into the combustibles to set it on fire. If it did not ignite, he was to ride round it three times, with his cap mounted on his sword, at which signal the gun was to be instantly fired, and the whole Division brought immediately under arms[12].

We had not yet established an understanding with the enemy at the outposts, which afterwards avoided unnecessary bloodshed and tended to humanise the war, so our pickets and the French were in the habit of firing at each other. Scarcely a day passed without some of the men being brought in killed, or wounded.

While the French besieged Rodrigo, the weather was intensely hot, so we delighted in bathing in a small river that flowed between the beacon-hill and the village. Many of us would also take the opportunity to wash our shirts in the running stream, laying them out to dry on the sand. Frequently, when thus employed, the alarm gun would be fired, and like so many water sprites, we would jump out of the stream and hurry on the wet shirts, wringing them and throwing them over our shoulders as we fell in with our comrades. I never felt any ill effects from these wet habiliments, but we had, from constant exposure, become as hardy as the soil itself.

The men preferred picket duty to any other because of its novelty, for we generally amused ourselves at night watching the shells exchanged between the besieged [in Ciudad Rodrigo] and the assailants. It was a very beautiful sight, and sometimes as many as 27 or 28 were seen crossing each other, like so many comets.

Leach: *"The French batteries opened on the 25th... the fire from the besiegers and the besieged was tremendous, and was kept up night and day with unremitting fury... Lord Wellington and General Spencer visited the outposts the day after the French batteries opened on the town."*

Once we were visited by the Duke himself, whose headquarters at the time were, I believe, at Viseu, about 20 leagues (50 miles) distant. His Grace came to our outlying pickets to reconnoitre while I was on sentry, and placed his telescope on my shoulder to take a view of the enemy's position. Our intelligence was chiefly derived from deserters, a number of whom daily came over to us; they said that Ciudad Rodrigo could not hold out much longer[13].

One day we were alarmed by an extraordinary bustle in the French camp. Being on the advanced picket, I could distinctly hear the cheering of men, and the firing of cannon. The whole of our Division was ordered to fall in. The following morning we learned the cause - it was news from Paris of the Emperor's marriage with the Archduchess Marie Louise of Austria[14].

We daily held ourselves in expectation of an attack, and were under arms every morning at one o'clock, five minutes only being allowed for the whole Division to fall in. We seldom took our accoutrements off, and used to cook and sleep with them on. The baggage was paraded every morning half a mile to the rear. With the French in our front in overwhelming force, and our Division scarcely more than 4,000 strong, every precaution was taken by the Brigadier for an orderly retreat.

On 30 June, Craufurd was compelled to withdraw his Division from Gallegos to the wood of Alameda after the French cavalry had closed on the Azava.

After several months of severe hardship at Gallegos, General Craufurd was at last obliged to change his ground. We retreated to Alameda, a little town about two miles in our rear, on the main road leading to the fortified town of Almeida. Here we remained a few days, and took a French spy. He had passed among us as a lemonade-merchant. His indifference and carelessness in accepting remuneration for his beverage, which was in constant request, together with his laughing very significantly when one or our men was swearing at the French for the trouble they caused, induced a sergeant to apprehend him. He was brought before General Craufurd and searched. Letters found upon him proved him to be a French Colonel. He was sent to the rear. How he managed to escape the doom he had rendered himself liable to, I know not.

On 3 July, in an attempt to deceive the French into thinking that his force was larger than it was, Craufurd marched his Division, formed in sections and opened out considerably, back to Gallegos.

One the General's stratagems was to make our small force appear more numerous in the eyes of the French, by drawing up the regiments up in rank entire.

However, at daylight on the 4th, the enemy appeared in force, and the Light Division had to retire over the Duas Casas.

A few mornings after this, the French came down in great force, and we were obliged to retire. This we did slowly, and with very little loss - covered by Captain Ross's guns and our Rifles, and assisted by a few troops of the 14th and 16th Dragoons and 1st German Hussars - for four or five miles to Fort Conception, in front of the little town of Vale da Mula, where we went into cantonments.

CHAPTER 6

Battle of the Coa
10 - 24 July 1810

Vale da Mula was a short distance from Almeida, a Portuguese fortress town where the garrison was commanded by Colonel Cox, a British officer in the Portuguese service.

> We were close on the border of Portugal, which was here divided from Spain by a stream [Turones or Tourões] so narrow that in some places it could be jumped over. We daily mounted a picket of two companies at the fort, which was a beautiful work, in the shape of a star[1].

At 7pm on 10 July 1810, Ciudad Rodrigo surrendered to the French. That same night, General Craufurd deployed some of his men to intercept one of the enemy patrols which sometimes crossed the Agueda River. Most eye witnesses record that the French patrol consisted of 200 infantrymen and a troop of cavalry.

> One or two French regiments nightly occupied an advanced position on our right, retiring every morning about daylight. A few days after our arrival at Vale da Mula, part of the Division formed a night expedition to surprise and cut them off. The Rifles got under arms at 10 o'clock at night, and were soon joined by several companies of the 43rd and 52nd regiment, one or two troops of the 14th Light Dragoons, and some of our favourite Germans[2]. We guessed that some secret enterprise was about to be undertaken because strict orders were issued to keep the men from talking, and from lighting their pipes, lest our approach should be noticed by the enemy. Even the wheels of two of Captain Ross's guns, which accompanied us, were muffled round with hay bands to prevent them creaking.
>
> We proceeded to the left of the enemy's position, which rested on Villa Puerco. A whispering order was given to enter a large field of standing corn and throw ourselves on the ground. Having loaded before marching, we expected an engagement, and waited anxiously for the dawn. At length the cold grey of the morning appeared faintly in the east. The commands were given, with scarcely a pause between 'fall in', 'double', and 'extend'. This was accomplished in a moment. We ran forward through the corn-field up to an eminence. Looking down we beheld a skirmish on the plain beneath.

That morning, at Barquilla, very close to Villa Puerco, a squadron of the 14th Dragoons successfully attacked the French patrol's cavalry, capturing one captain, one subaltern and 34 privates. The French infantry were then attacked by another squadron of the 14th Dragoons, led by Colonel Talbot:

> The 14th Dragoons were charging a body of French infantry, who had thrown themselves into square. The cavalry cheered forward in gallant style, but the French stood firm like veterans, and poured into them a close running fire that emptied many saddles. Lt.-Col. Talbot, who headed the charge, fell almost immediately. So did the quartermaster and 16-18 privates. After an unavailing attempt to shake the square, the cavalry was obliged to retire, which the enemy immediately imitated. An attempt was made to annoy them with our guns, but as they were only light field pieces the shots had little effect[3].

The rifle officers were full of admiration for the coolness and bravery of this small band of French infantry - led by a French captain called Gauche - and critical of Craufurd for not sending riflemen against them. Simmons: *'The French infantry were attacked by Colonel Talbot, though it was pretty evident that they would have had to surrender without firing a shot had he waited... During this sad affair we were not allowed to show ourselves, although a few infantry would have compelled them to lay down their arms... Our* *wise* *General had the 14th, 16th and German Hussars all to assist, also horse artillery and seven companies of infantry, but let this small party of Frenchmen slip through our fingers so shamefully."*

Leach: *'It appears incredible that 200 French infantry on a plain surrounded by nearly 1,000 British dragoons, and fully 800 British infantry not more than a mile distant, should escape without the loss of a man!"*

> The following day, we buried Colonel Talbot and the quartermaster close to the porch of the little chapel in the village we occupied, a somewhat romantic-looking spot for a soldier's grave. It was rumoured that the miscarriage of our enterprise had brought our General into bad odour at headquarters, and for some days after he wore a troubled look, as though he took our failure to heart.

Craufurd was not censured; Wellington ascribed his failure to bad luck rather than bad judgement.

Now that Ciudad Rodrigo had fallen, the French turned their attention to the Portuguese fortress of Almeida, which was the last impediment to their planned re-invasion of Portugal. In their way was the Light Division, now stationed at the poor village of Junça, a short distance from the town. The Division's infantry pickets, which consisted of two companies of Rifles, were at Fort Conception. Wellington instructed Craufurd to pull his Division back over the Coa, but Craufurd allowed his men to remain where they were.

Two of our companies alternately did duty in front of our position, at Fort Conception. The officer commanding the picket had an order to blow up the fort on the approach of the enemy. For this purpose, it was undermined in several places by the artillerymen, who were left to fire the mines when the order was given.

On the morning of 19 July, our company and another were on duty at this point. We were expecting to be attacked on the morrow, this intelligence, I think, being brought by a deserter. The fort contained a great quantity of good English rum and biscuit which Captain O'Hare allowed the men of both companies to help themselves to. He let them fill their canteens with rum, upon their promise, which they kept, not to get drunk.

The following morning, before it was scarcely light, the enemy advanced upon us in heavy columns, preceded by their light troops. The command was given to fire the mines, and we began to retire upon our Division. A few minutes later, the fort, whose beautiful proportions excited the admiration of many, was broken into a blackened heap of ruin, as if by the shock of an earthquake.

Fort Conception was blown up on the morning of 21 July. In camp, the explosion roused the rest of the riflemen from their sleep, and they gathered at the alarm post. When they learned the cause, and were assured that there was no immediate danger, they fell out and took breakfast.

Leach: *'On the 22nd, General Craufurd drew his whole force back near Almeida, observing with pickets of cavalry the different roads on the great plain in front.'*

We retreated to near the walls of Almeida, where we halted until the 23rd.

The retreat was in expectation of the French advancing to lay siege to Almeida. At about 8pm, the rain started to come down in torrents, and a storm of incredible violence commenced. Being outside the town, no-one in the Division could find shelter.

At night we experienced a storm that for violence exceeded anything I had ever beheld. The lightning, thunder, wind, and rain were absolutely awful. With a few other men, I sought shelter in the hollow of a rock, where we were not a little amazed to see numbers of snakes and lizards, which the occasional gleams of lightning exhibited to us, running about in all directions, as though the tempest had brought them all from their holes.

Green: *"There were neither bushes nor twigs to shelter us, so that our ammunition got wet. If we sat down, the water ran as a gutter either side of us."*

Simmons: *"I sat upon a stone like a drowned rat, looking at the heavens, amusing myself with their brilliancy, and longing for morning."*

Leach: *"General Craufurd placed his infantry in line amongst some rocky ground and stone walls, his left being within 700-800 yards of the walls of Almeida, and his right thrown back in a convex form towards the Coa.".*

Napier: *"His cavalry was on the plain in front, but his back was on the edge of a ravine forming the channel of the Coa. The bridge, more than a mile distant, was in the bottom of the chasm."*

That bridge was Craufurd's only avenue of retreat. The next morning, 24 July, 24,000 French infantry, 5,000 cavalry, and 30 pieces of artillery, were observed in march beyond the Turones. Craufurd had available to him only 4,000 infantry, 1,100 cavalry, and six guns.

Green: *"At daylight we were served out with fresh ammunition, good and dry, and it was well for us that we could have it, for our paymaster, early on the 24th, began to muster the regiment, but could only finish two companies before the French were upon us."*

Simmons: *"A little after daybreak, the enemy advanced against our pickets and drove them in."*

At break of day, intelligence of the enemy's advance was given by the cracking of the rifles of our outlying picket, which our company was immediately ordered to support. Captain O'Hare placed us behind some dilapidated walls, and we awaited the approach of the picket under the Hon. Captain Stewart, then engaged about half a mile in our front, and slowly retreating upon us. Several of their men had been killed, and Lieutenant McCullock[4] had been wounded and taken prisoner with a number of others. We could distinctly see the enemy's columns, which were in great force. But we had little time for observation, as our advance picket ran in upon us, followed by the French *tirailleurs* [sharpshooters], with whom we were soon hotly engaged.

Simmons: *"The enemy now advanced in vast bodies. The whole plain in our front was covered with horse and foot advancing towards us. The enemy's infantry formed line, and, with an innumerable multitude of skirmishers, attacked us fiercely. We repulsed them; they came on again, yelling, with drums beating. Frequently the drummers led, often in front of the line. French officers like mountebanks ran forward, placed their hats upon their swords, and capered about like madmen, saying, as they turned to their men, 'Come on, children of our country, the first that advances, Napoleon will recompense.' Numbers returned to the attack. We kept up a very brisk fire. Several guns began to play on us."*

In support of the riflemen during this action were several companies of infantry. Costello states that they belonged to the 52nd Regiment, whereas Simmons says it was the 43rd. The guns which played on them were fired by the Portuguese in Almeida - what is known today as 'friendly fire'.

> The right wing of the 52nd regiment [43rd?] was drawn up, behind a low wall, about 100 yards in our rear, when a shell, which with several others was thrown amongst us from the town, burst so near that it killed several of our men, and buried a sergeant so completely in mud - he was unhurt - that we were obliged to drag him out to prevent his being taken by the enemy. These shells were thrown at us by mistake because the town was in the possession of our friends the Portuguese, under the command of Colonel Cox, a British officer. They must have mistaken us for the French because of our green dress, and because of our nearness to the enemy. At this moment, Lieutenant Coane, who stood close to me, received a shot through the body. Captain O'Hare, who saw him roll his eyes and stagger, caught him by the arm.
>
> "Take that poor boy to the rear," he said in a rather soft tone to the men about him. "He does not know what is the matter with him."[5] And with characteristic coolness he continued his duties.

The French, with superior numbers, were attacking along the whole line of Craufurd's defence. Leach: *"It is not improbable that at this moment our brigadier began to think it would have been more prudent... had he implicitly obeyed the positive orders of the Commander-in-Chief, to withdraw his corps of observations behind the Coa... The baggage, artillery, cavalry, and the two Portuguese light battalions, were directed to retire instantly to the bridge over the Coa, and to gain the opposite bank without delay. Those who have seen and know this narrow and difficult defile, need not be informed that, to keep back as many thousand infantry as Marshal Ney might think proper to send forward, whilst the road was choked with troops, baggage, and artillery - which it was absolutely necessary should be covered and protected, during a retreat of a mile or more, and until they had crossed the bridge in safety - was no easy matter. The troops destined to cover the retreat consisted of our own battalion, and a considerable part, or the whole, of the 43rd and 52nd regiments...From the commencement of the action at the edge of the plain, until we reached the river, every inch of ground admitting of defence was obstinately contested by the rear-guard."*

Simmons: *"As the force kept increasing every moment in our front, and columns of infantry were also moving upon our right flank, we were* ordered to retire half the company. Captain O'Hare's retired, and the remainder, under Lieutenant Johnston, remained fighting for a few moments longer. I was with this party. We moved from the field into the road, our men falling all around us, when a body of hussars in bearskin caps and light-coloured pelisses got amongst the few remaining riflemen and began to sabre them. Several attempted to cut me down, but I avoided their kind intentions by stepping on one side. I had a large cloak rolled up and strapped across my body, and my haversack was filled with little necessary articles for immediate use; thus I got clear off."

Green and Costello were with this same group of riflemen.

Green: "We were surrounded by a troop of French hussars; they had come from behind a hill, and our company - only 80 men - were thus hemmed in by horse and foot, and were all made prisoners... Their infantry did not fire; if they had they would have killed their own hussars, who were cutting us down with their swords.'

The bridge over the Coa today

While hotly engaged with the French infantry in our front, one or two troops of their hussars, which from the similarity of uniform we had taken for our German hussars, whipped on our left flank between our company and the wing of the 52nd. A cry of "The French cavalry are upon us" came too late, and they charged in amongst us. Taken unprepared, we could offer little or no resistance, and our men were trampled down and sabred on every side.

A man of the name of Charity, of my own company, fell wounded in the head by a sabre. While on the ground, he received another severe sword slash on the seat of honour, and a shot through the arm, the latter, no doubt, from the 52nd. Yet after all this, he managed to escape, and clothed in scarlet lived to tell the tale, as a pensioner in Chelsea Hospital[6].

A French dragoon seized me by the collar, while several others aimed at me with their swords as they passed. The man who collared me had the point of his sabre at my breast, when a volley was fired from our rear by the 52nd.

Simmons: *"A volley was now fired by a party of the 43rd under Captain Wells, which brought several of the hussars to the ground. In the scuffle I took to my heels and ran to the 43rd, Wells calling out, 'Mind the rifleman! Do not hit him, for heaven's sake'."*

The volley had saved Costello's life:

This tumbled the horse of my captor and he fell heavily, dragging me down with him. The animal was on the dragoon's leg. Determined to have one brief struggle for liberty, I freed myself from his grasp, dealt him a severe blow on the head with the butt of my rifle, and rushed up to our 52nd. I was in the act of clearing the wall at a jump, when I received a shot under the cap of my right knee, and fell. With the Division in rapid retreat, there seemed every prospect that I would fall into the hands of the French, but a comrade of the name of Little dragged me over the wall. With me on his back, he proceeded as quickly as possible towards the bridge of the Coa, over which our men were fast pouring. Then he, poor fellow, also received a shot. It passed through his arm, smashing the bone, and finally lodged itself in my thigh, where it has ever since remained. Strange as it may appear, this ball may be this hour felt with as much ease as the first day it entered, 42 years back[7].

In this extremity, Little[8] had to abandon me. Urged by a strong desire to escape imprisonment, I made another desperate effort and managed to get over the bridge, from the other side of which Captain Ross's guns were in full roar, covering our retreat. In this crippled state, and faint through loss of blood, I made an appeal to another comrade, who assisted me to ascend a hill on the other side of the river[9].

Although Costello's part in the battle was over, it raged on fiercely. **Simmons:** *"The road to a small bridge across the Coa, which the Division would have to retire over, was very bad and rocky. Our gallant fellows disputed manfully every inch of ground and retired towards the river. Every place we left was covered with the enemy's light infantry in ten times our number. As we got near the river, the enemy made several attempts to cut us off."*

As the Division was retreating over the bridge, another mistake was made. Simmons: *"General Craufurd ordered a number of riflemen, who occupied a place that prevented the French from stopping our retreat over the bridge, to evacuate it before half the 52nd, who were on the right, had filed over. The enemy directly brought up their infantry to this hill, which commanded the bridge, and kept up a terrible fire. Colonel Beckwith, a most gallant and clever soldier, saw this frightful mistake and ordered us to retake the wall and hill instantly, which we did in good style, but suffered severely in men and officers."*

Major McLeod of the 43rd, distinguished himself with his command of this group of men, which consisted of four companies of his own regiment, and some riflemen and their officers (including Simmons, Lt. Pratt, Captain Leach, and Leach's two subalterns, Harry and Thomas Smith. Of these five men, only Leach, who was one of the last men over the bridge, escaped serious injury. The Division successfully prevented the French from crossing the bridge after them, and the river being so swollen, there was no other place for them to get over.

> On the summit [of the hill above the Coa], we found a chapel which had been converted into a temporary hospital, where some of the wounded were being taken to have their wounds dressed by the surgeons. Fortunately, I did not have to wait long for my turn because, with the French expected momentarily, everything was done with the greatest despatch.

A flag of truce from the French brought the action to a conclusion at about 5pm. The Light Division casualties (killed, wounded or missing) were 44 Portuguese and 272 British, of which 28 were officers. As at Barba del Puerco, it was O'Hare's company which suffered most:

> In this affair our company sustained a very severe loss. Our return was 'one officer, Lt. Coane, quite a youth, dangerously wounded, 11 file killed and wounded, and 45 taken prisoners'. Captain O'Hare had only eleven men on parade next day. This shows that skirmishes were more destructive to riflemen than general actions, although attended with little of their celebrity. For my own part, the only time I was nearer death was on the night we took Badajoz [6 April 1812].

Marshal Michel Ney, the French commander, lost 1,000 men at the Coa. At the bridge, the French slaughter had been fearful. It was literally piled with their dead for breastworks had been made of the bodies. Nevertheless, Ney had given the Light Division a severe trouncing. As usual, Leach was blistering in his condemnation of Craufurd. In a letter, written at the time, he told his correspondent:

"You will have heard how universally General Craufurd was hated and detested in the retreat from Corunna. If possible, he is still more abhorred now, and has been ever since we landed in Portugal. He is a damned tyrant and has proved himself totally unfit to command a company much less a Division. I understand he has just got into a scrape with Lord Wellington for pitching on ground for his position which the most uninstructed boy of one month's standing would have known better than to have taken up" (Verner). In his book, Leach's language was more measured: "The investment of Almeida was not retarded five minutes by our waiting under its walls for the approach of the besieging army."

What saved the day at the battle of the Coa was the courage and individual fighting qualities of the men of the Light Division, for which they were commended by Wellington. Again, he did not censure Craufurd. Had he done so, he would have had to censure Picton, who had failed to support Craufurd with his 3rd Division. Army politics, and the desire to tone down officer rivalries, influenced Wellington's response to the affair.

After the fighting at the Coa had subsided, the Light Division retired. Leach: "Soon after dark, General Craufurd retired with his whole force from the Coa to a wild rocky country, near the village of Vale Verde, where we bivouacked late that night amongst some granite rocks, drenched to the skin with the rains of the preceding day and night."

CHAPTER 7

Belem and Arruda
25 July - November 1810

When the Division retired from the Coa, the wounded in the chapel had to retire too.

> Having no mules nor waggons to accommodate us, the surgeons advised all who were capable of moving to get on as quick as they could to Pinhel. Our regiment had about 70 or 80 disabled, a number of whom hobbled onwards, assisting each other by turns. It was a slow and painful march, and with the help of a couple of rifles that served as crutches, I managed to reach the first village. Here the *juiz de fora*, or chief magistrate, selected the worst of our wounded and put them into bullock carts. Fortunately, I was one; and although crammed with six others into a wretched little vehicle scarcely capable of accommodating two, it was a blessing for which I could not feel sufficiently thankful.
>
> Among the officers wounded was Harry Smith, and his brother Tom. The former, being on the staff, had a sedan with two mules to carry him, but the latter was packed in the bullock carts with the men[1].

Simmons, wounded in the leg, had been carried from the Coa on the horse of a German hussar. He too was placed in a bullock cart, the motions of which tortured his injured limb. They reached Pinhel at 10pm that night.

> We were dragged along all night, and at daylight halted at another village. I felt so dreadfully faint from loss of blood, and from my confined position, that I could not move at all. While refreshing our parched lips with some water that had been eagerly demanded, Lord Wellington and some of his staff galloped up. He glanced at us, and seeing our crowded condition in the carts, ordered one of his aides-de-camp to obtain additional conveyance, bread, and wine, from the *juiz de fora*. He then rode off towards Almeida. Although neither bread nor wine made their appearance, a few additional carts were procured, into one of which I was transferred with four other men.

Simmons, along with three other rifle lieutenants - Tom Smith, M Pratt and Peter Reilly - was put into a spring wagon, which was even more painful for their wounds because of its bounce.

69

General Sir Harry Smith

One of my wounded comrades was shot through the body, and after driving some few miles further, his end seemed to be approaching. In his dying state, he relaxed his hold on the sides of the cart and fell across me as I lay at the bottom. Foam mixed with blood ran from his mouth which, with his glassy eyes fixed on mine, made me feel very uncomfortable. Being weak and wounded myself, I had no power to move him. Death put an end to his sufferings, and his struggles having ceased, I was able to recover myself a little. I called to the Portuguese driver to remove the body, but the scoundrel, who kept as much ahead of the bullocks as possible, was afraid of the French. All I could get from him was 'don't bother me', and a significant shrug of his shoulder, so it was some hours before I was granted any respite. The horrors of this situation survived in my mind for some time.

We arrived at Freixedas were I got rid of my dead comrade. The 1st Division were encamped outside the town, and as we had no men of our own to attend to us, 40 of the 1st Division's Guards, under an officer, were ordered to supply our wants until we arrived at Lisbon. We had our wounds dressed. I will never forget their kindness to us.

From Freixedas, we continued our journey to the Mondego.

On the morning of 26 July, they travelled to Celorico, and on the 27th to Vila Cortes. Costello's comrade was not the only wounded man to expire on the journey. Peter Reilly insisted on being left at Baracal to die rather than be tortured in his final hours by the motions of the wagon. Simmons: *"Several of our fellows died from the rough usage they suffered. Several soldiers had neglected to cover their wounds, which now became one frightful mass of maggots all over the surface; it really made me tremble to see them dressed. The flies and mosquitoes followed us in myriads. We had no means of keeping off the swarms of insects, and the slow pace that the bullocks went, made us feel the vertical rays of the sun with redoubled force. We had some salt meat as rations which, in the feverish state of our existence, we turned from with disgust. We seldom got bread, but generally biscuits, and that full of worms or mouldy. We were hurried away daily to the rear as fast as possible in order that our army, if pressed by the enemy, should not have us on the line of its march, to impede its progress to the rear. Halted for the night at Vila Cortes."*

From Vila Cortes, their route was through Pinhancos and Galizes to Lofrece on the river Mondego, which they reached on 31 July. The next day they embarked in boats to take them down the Mondego River to Coimbra.

We continued our march until we came to a stream of water [the Mondego?], where we halted. Here we lost Lt. Pratt, an excellent officer. Though wounded through the neck, he had appeared to be doing very well. He was seated on one of the men's knapsacks, conversing with some of his wounded brother officers, when he was seized by a violent fit of coughing, and started pumping a quantity of blood from the wound. I never saw so much come from any man. It appeared that the ball, which went through his neck, had passed close to the carotid artery, and the exertion of coughing had burst it. It was impossible to stop the haemorrhage and he bled to death. Warm as he was, they covered him in the sand and proceeded[2].

On the afternoon of 1 August, they arrived at Coimbra, where Pratt was buried. The next day they were rowed down the river to the seaport of Figueira.

We passed in boats down the river, through Coimbra, to the seaport of Figueira. Sick and ill as I was, I recollect the exquisite scenery on the banks of that beautiful river, as we floated over its surface to our destination.

The heat of the weather was intense and affected our wounds dreadfully. Doctors were scarce; fear of falling into the hands of the enemy had hurried everyone forward, so the surgeons had neither time nor opportunity to look after us. As a consequence of this neglect, maggots were engendered in the sores, and the bandages, when withdrawn, brought away on them lumps of putrid flesh and maggots. Many men died on board, and others were reduced to the necessity of amputation, but by care, and syringing sweet oil into my wounds, I managed to get rid of the maggots[3].

At Figueira, Simmons, Harry Smith, Tom Smith, and a Captain - Samuel Mitchell - were transferred to the *Nestor* transport, which lay outside the bar.

At Figueira, some transports were awaiting our arrival. We embarked on board them and sailed for Lisbon where, in a short time, we landed. Borne on stretchers by some men of the Ordenança, or Portuguese Militia, we were conveyed to the hospital[4] where, from regular and kind treatment, I soon recovered.

A few weeks after our arrival at Lisbon, I became sufficiently recovered to leave the hospital and was accordingly transferred to Belem, about two miles from Lisbon but contiguous to it, as are the suburbs of London to the city.

Wounded soldiers convalesced in Belem where, when recovered sufficiently, they might take on light duties as orderlies on the hospital wards, or help look after the stores. Most eventually returned to active service, but those who were reluctant to do so were called skulkers by their fellows soldiers.

The chief part of the 58th and 87th regiments were doing duty here, the latter, I believe, from the severe loss they had sustained at Talavera. It was a place noted for every species of skulk, better known to my fellow soldiers as the 'Belem Rangers'.

Here I was at my ease, and usually spent my time rambling about the quays. The port was thronged with shipping, bringing troops and stores from England, and ships of war - including I think, the *Hibernia*, the *Caledonia*, and the *Britannia* - lay in the bay. We constantly intermixed, and were mostly coupled, with the sailors. Some recognised old friends - town-mates, or nearer and dearer ties - or formed new links and acquaintances, which the peculiarity of our situations tended to strengthen, fighting as we were in the same cause though on different elements.

I was present at a row in a wine-house between an American and a Lancashire man. They belonged to the same ship, and from what I could understand, they were not only quarrelsome fellows, but also the most unfair fighters on board. The yankee was from Kentucky and had a precious knack of 'gouging', as they termed it - screwing his finger into the side locks of his opponent, and with his thumb poking his eye out. One or two on board had been 'jockied' in this way. 'Tummas', the Lancashire man, had nearly lost an eye to a splinter at Trafalgar, and seemed unwilling to risk the loss of the other in an encounter with the American.

"I tell you what, you cowardly sea serpent," he said, "if it warnt that I fear'd you fingering this 'ere solitary blinker o' mine, I'd dust your yankee jacket for you."

Despite this confession, the gouger, though ready for a scrimmage, also seemed to fear the contest, perhaps having some inward dread of being bitten, and kicked to a jelly.

The Englishman's friends came to a council of war, and it was agreed that, though ashore, they should thump it out 'ship fashion': that they should have it out on a barrel.

"I'll be damned if they can kick, scratch, gouge, or bite, when they hangs by their stern sheets," said a short, fat, big-whiskered, little sailor. He was, I believe, the boatswain, and he bolted to the boats to fetch large nails and a hammer.

A butt big enough to hold the rations of the whole Division, was soon procured from the patrone, and was rolled out to the centre of the quay where, to keep it steady, it was settled longways between two heaps of stone. While the boatswain was gone, the two combatants could scarcely be kept from each other.

"Clear the gangways!" shouted a voice from the crowd, and the boatswain bounded back, almost breathless, to the barrel. In a few minutes, the yankee and Tummas were seated, fronting one another, about two feet apart. The little man nailed one to the barrel edge by a bit of the bottom of his canvas trousers, and then the other. The two men balanced their fists, like rope dancers' poles, and fixed their eyes on each other, awaiting the signal to begin.

"Gentlemen, clear the decks," bellowed the boatswain. "Now Tummas, for the honour of your mess-mates, let's have no shamming afore these 'ere Portugals and boiled lobsters [sun-baked soldiers?]. When you sees me put my quid [of tobacco] into my jaws" - the two men looked at each other - "heave on your broadsides."

The words were scarcely out, when in flopped the quid, and the combatants commenced hammering away at each other. After a few rounds Tummas fell. Caught by his breech, he remained hanging over the barrel edge until he was re-seated. Then at it they went again until the yankee fell, and hung in the same manner.

"Excellent!" roared the boatswain, "excellent preventative, or my old aunt warn't a virgin!"

The yankee was soon himself, and they closed again, round after round, until the two champions hung powerless at the same moment.

"Drawn fight!" bellowed the little man again. "Both tough ones!" and, while the crowd was convulsed with laughter, he proceeded to separate the fixtures at their trousers with an enormous clasp knife, which increased the hole in each of the combatant's trousers to a size almost large enough to admit the barrel. The two sailors, having recovered themselves, tucked back the blue check and, with a growl, steered away to the wine house.

Belem was a place of convalescence for officers too, including George Simmons, Harry Smith, and Samuel Mitchell. Meanwhile, the war continued unabated. On 27 August, Almeida had fallen to the French after a brief siege during which the citadel's magazine ignited, causing a huge explosion which destroyed the town and killed 500 of its defenders. Massena, intending to expel the English from Portugal, engaged Wellington in battle at Busaco on 27 September.

During my convalescence, the battle of Busaco was fought. Lord Wellington, finding his numbers greatly unequal to the enemy, was obliged to retreat, and the British army retired towards Lisbon[5]. This he directed in a very skilful manner. Having long before anticipated the probability of such an event, he had erected the lines of Torres Vedras. During the retreat, his Lordship ordered the people of the country to accompany the troops, and to destroy all those things which they could not carry with them. By this precaution, Massena's army, on the track of the British and Portuguese, through want of food and necessaries, was reduced to the greatest privations, of which the Marshal bitterly complained in his dispatches of that period.

At the beginning of October, Simmons and Smith, anxious to return to their battalion, sought permission to do so from Colonel Tucker of the 29th Regiment, who was in command of the convalescent department at Belem. This he granted on the condition that they marched a detachment of men back with them, and took responsibility for their subsistence. Reluctantly, the two officers agreed.

Simmons: *"The detachment was formed at Belem under the command of Major Murphy of the 88th Regiment. He had men belonging to every regiment in the country, amongst whom were several who had much rather have remained at Belem than parade their bodies in a field to be shot at... The men of the Light Division who had been wounded with us and were well again, formed the rear-guard, and I travelled with it. In spite of all my precautions, several men skulked away unobserved, slipping into houses and other places."*

Among the officers of our battalion wounded at Almeida [the battle of the Coa], was Captain Mitchell[6]. Shot through the arm, he had been transferred with us to Lisbon. One morning, when he was sufficiently recovered, he came to the convalescent barrack to muster those who were willing and able to rejoin their regiments. Amongst those selected was Billy McNabb of our corps, who was a Methodist and a notorious skulker. He had scarcely ever done duty with his company, but had remained sneaking about the hospital as an orderly, occasionally preaching and praying to the drunken soldiers in the streets of Lisbon. Captain Mitchell made up his mind that McNabb should see the enemy before he returned to England. Billy violently resisted the summons, so was tied to a bullock cart, and amid the jeers of the soldiers, conveyed back to his regiment. But it was only for a short period because Billy got tired of the 'sight', and took the earliest opportunity to decamp. He disappeared suddenly from among us, and had I not seen him since, preaching in the streets of London, I should have been inclined to think he never returned home at all[7].

The destination of the convalescents was the Torres Vedras region of Portugal, north of Lisbon, to which the British Army was retiring. Simmons' detachment set out from Belem on 7 October 1810. It would appear that Costello was with a detachment which left a few days later.

On the morning the convalescents fell in to start for the main army, we were joined by a batch of recruits, chiefly intended for the 68th and 85th regiments. They were a squad of rosy-cheeked, smart-looking fellows who, like ourselves, had each had been provided with five days' rations. This consisted of salt pork, biscuits, and rum, the first of which they cooked ready for the march.

The officer in command I shall never forget. He was an astonishing man, nearly seven feet tall, and with high cheek bones. He had such a dark complexion that I took him at first to be a foreigner, but as soon as he spoke, his broad accent declared him to be a North Briton, and from as far north as could be [ie Scotland]. On the march, he placed himself at the head of the men in order to direct their movements. His shoulders were so broad, and yet so skinny and square, that he looked like a kite, with the files of short men after him being the tail. His height was so convenient, that without stirring a peg from the front section, he could look over their heads down the ranks and see every manoeuvre.

He seemed well acquainted with every theory, and in accordance with the regulations of Dundas[8], then Commander-in-Chief, ordered his men, at the end of every three miles, to halt and rest for ten minutes or a quarter of an hour.

"Come, men," he would say, pulling out his gold watch, "yer three miles is up, set ye down and eat a pound. The more ye take into yer stomachs, the less ye'll carry on yer backs."

This over, the watch would be out again, and it would be: "Come men, yer quarter of an hour is nearly up, ye must be going again".

And the men, of course, would fall in. By thus halting every three miles, and eating a pound, at the end of the second day's march, before we reached Jafra [Mafra?] the men had 'pounded' the whole of their five days' rations. Some of them began to growl most confoundedly from the want of provisions, and wishing to learn the cause, the colonel had them fall in and lectured them for consuming all their rations in only two days!

Amongst the convalescents was a Cockney named Josias Hetherington. This fellow was one of the queerest I ever met. I believe he had seen service before, but amongst gypsies, prigs [thieves], gaol-birds, and travelling showmen. He was up to everything, and was such a good ventriloquist that, as we went along, when occasion offered, he would terrify the inhabitants.

On the third day's march, we stopped for the night in a small village. Josh and I got billeted together in the same house, where we started to cook our rations. In front of the house was a small square - every town, village and pig-sty in Portugal had one - in the middle of which the inhabitants commenced a fandango, which is usual in Portugal on Sundays. Attracted by the whistle, and by the small drum, beaten by a short, dumpy, ugly-looking Portuguese, Josh and myself left our pots beside the patrone's wood fire, as close as we could to the red embers, and ran down to join in. When we came back to see how well they were boiling, we found our utensils moved aside, and the contents as cold as charity. Josh looked at me, and I at Josh. Who the blazes had moved our meat about so? Hearing footsteps on the stairs, Josh popped me, and then himself, into a kind of pantry, and stood watching through the partially closed door.

In came the old patrone, or lady of the house. She looked about her, then bounced to our little utensils, muttering to herself. She was just about to purloin the meat, when a voice, apparently from the pot, told her, in Portuguese, 'to wait a little'. The old woman frisked up. Looking doubtful, she crossed herself, and with the courage this afforded, again attacked the pots, but the same words, quick now, and smart as a rifle shot, sent her reeling and screeching to the corner of the kitchen.

"*Oh Santa Maria! Oh Jesu!*" she cried, and thinking the devil was in the pot, she went off in a Portuguese fit.

Josh and I, scarcely able to contain our mirth, rushed out of the house and joined the crowd, which her screams were collecting about the doorway. In a twinkling, she was off to the priest and the alcalde [mayor], but in vain, for the billet could not be changed. She left her domicile, and as the whole village feared the devil, we held quiet possession till the next morning. We might have carried away the house for all the old patrone cared, for she never returned till we marched out of the place[9].

The Lines of Torres Vedras, into which Wellington withdrew his army early in October, were formidable defensive fortifications, which he had ordered to be built a year earlier. They consisted, said Napier: *"of three distinct ranges of defence. The first, extending from Alhandra on the Tagus to the mouth of the Sizandro on the sea-coast, followed the inflections of the hills, 29 miles long. The second, traced at a distance, varying from 6 to 10 miles, in rear of the first, stretched from Quintella on the Tagus to the mouth of S. Lourenço, being 24 miles in length. The third, intended to cover a forced embarkation, extended from Passo d'Arcos on the Tagus, to the tower of Junquera on the coast."* Massena, who pursued Wellington towards Lisbon, did not know the Lines were there. When he saw them, he came to an abrupt halt and settled his army into encampments opposite.

The Light Division had retired with the rest of Wellington's army. The 1st battalion 95th was directed to take up a position at Arruda, on the first line of defence. Simmons, travelling up from Belem, learned of the battalion's destination and, having delivered his convalescents and recruits to their regiments, reached Arruda at about 8pm on 9 October, before it arrived. He took possession of a good house for O'Hare and his officers, and by midnight, when they appeared, he had a good fire going for them.

Only a week of so earlier, the battalion had received a reinforcement in the form of Captain Charles Beckwith and his company, one of whom was a six-foot Scotsman called John Kincaid. Kincaid had joined the 95th as a lieutenant in the spring of 1809, but had fallen victim to malaria at Walcheren that same year. He made a good recovery, and on 15 September 1810, arrived with his company at Lisbon. They travelled by boat to Figueira, and then marched to Coimbra for a rendezvous with Wellington's army, then retreating to the Lines of Torres Vedras.

Kincaid: *"Our long retreat ended at midnight... at the handsome little town of Arruda, which was destined to be the picket post of our Division, in front of the fortified lines... Like all other places in the line of march, we found Arruda totally deserted. Its inhabitants had fled in such a hurry that the keys of their house doors were the only things they carried away, so that when we got admission through our usual key - transmitting a rifle-ball through the key-hole, which opens every lock - we were not a little gratified to find that the houses were not only regularly furnished, but most of them had some food in the larder, and a plentiful supply of good wines in the cellar. In short, they only required a few lodgers capable of appreciating the good things which the gods had provided, and the deuce is in it if we were not the very folks who could!"*

Leach: *"The inhabitants, dreading the approach of the French, had taken flight to Lisbon, leaving their houses, many of which were magnificently furnished, without a human being in them. The chairs and tables were subsequently carried up to the camp, which was formed on the fortified ridge of hills running from the Tagus to the sea... and they proved highly useful to us in our canvas habitations."*

Costello did not reach Arruda until 12 October, the day after he and Josh Hetherington had been teasing the old Portuguese lady. His comrades were already in residence. One, William Green, had, on 25 September, become a bugler in the company.

On 12 October 1810, I rejoined my regiment, which was encamped near Arruda, a small village on the lines of Torres Vedras. There I found my old captain [O'Hare]. Despite his severe loss, he had scraped together a snug company, partly from men who had made their escape from the French after the affair at Almeida [the battle of the Coa], but chiefly from a batch of recruits that joined our 1st battalion while I was in hospital. They had come from England with the 3rd battalion of our regiment[10].

Arruda was a pretty little place, but when we mounted our pickets, the men defaced it dreadfully, perhaps from a belief that the French might enter it. The inhabitants, whose fears had been enhanced by its exposed situation, had nearly all evacuated the place, taking with them only the most portable and valuable of their effects, and leaving the houses, as it were, furnished and tenantless. The change was the more extraordinary from the circumstances of its pleasant site, having for many years been a country resort for the rich citizens of Lisbon[11]. However, a few days after our arrival, it presented a picture of most wanton desolation. Furniture of a most splendid description was, in many instances, laid open to the spoliation of the soldiery. Elegant looking-glasses, wrenched from mantelpieces, were wantonly broken to obtain bits to shave by, and their frames - with chairs, tables, etc - were used as common firewood for the pickets. These proceedings unravel the secret of spending half a crown out of sixpence a day. I suppose you could say that if we had not done this, the French would have done it for us, but that event, though expected, was never realised.

Tom Crawley was pre-eminent in this havoc, his enormous strength and length fitting him especially for the pulling down and breaking up department. He loved exploring the houses of the village, his favourite amusement being to look for wine. One evening, while our company was on picket at Arruda, we made a blazing fire close to the stable of a large house, as we usually did. After several chairs had been consumed by the fire to keep it alive, we found it necessary to obtain fresh fuel. That morning we had noticed that the stable contained a very handsome carriage, the only one I had ever seen in Portugal, and while we were consulting where the wood was to come from, one man, with an oath, proposed to burn this coach. The novelty of this idea among our thoughtless fellows was received with acclamations and, with our officers absent in a house close by, several of them got to their feet. The stable doors were immediately opened, and the coach wheeled backwards into the large blazing fire.

"This will make a jolly roast!" exclaimed several of the men.

In the heat, the paint and panelling began to crack, and flames began to curl up around the devoted vehicle, while our scamps laughed, enjoying what they called a capital joke.

Suddenly, a roar like a bull came from the interior. We were thrown into consternation. One of the glasses was dashed out, and Tom Crawley's big head was thrust through the window. The men shouted with laughter.

"Oh, bad luck to your souls!" he cried out. "Are you going to burn me alive?"

He made the most violent efforts to open the door, but the handle was hot, and it was a difficult and painful operation. We had trouble extricating the poor fellow, and he got severely scorched. He had gone to the carriage half tipsy. He was having a snooze when he was so warmly awoken. After this, Crawley used to boast of sleeping with one eye open.

At this period, the French soldiers and ourselves, apart from duty in the field, began to establish amicable feelings with each other. Every day, when both parties were in search of wine and food, we would meet in the houses between our lines[12]. I remember once finding Crawley in a drunken state in one of these houses, in company with a couple of French soldiers. His appearance excited some merriment, and it was only with difficulty that I got him away, because he stripped and offered to fight all three of us for laughing at him.

By the end of October, Massena's men began to desert, bringing with them reports that he had exhausted the forage in the area he controlled, and that his soldiers were suffering from lack of food and disease.

Perhaps few events in the Peninsular War reflect more credit upon Lord Wellington as a commander than the admirable manner in which he drew an overwhelming force of the French into famine, in front of works that afforded security and plenty to his own comparatively small force.

CHAPTER 8

Winter Quarters before Santarem
November 1810 - February 1811

Massena clung to his position in front of the lines of Torres Vedras until 14 November, when he withdrew towards Santarem. This was not discovered until the next morning. At 3pm, the Light Division followed, through Alenquer, Vila Nova and Azambuja to Cartaxo, which they reached on the 17th, and where they spent the night.

At daybreak, says Simmons, the Light Division *"advanced across a plain in considerable force, with the enemy retiring before them, and crossed a causeway and bridge over the Rio Maior, the whole country in the neighbourhood of the river being a boggy impassable swamp."* At the bridge, the French had left a strong rear-guard.

> About the middle of November the enemy retired, and we followed them to Santarem, which they immediately occupied and strongly fortified. As soon as we came in sight of their works, our battalion received orders to cross the Rio Maior, which discharged itself into the Tagus about half a mile lower down on our right. However, we met with rather a warm reception. It became more intense as we attempted to get a peep into their position, and we were obliged to retreat.

The Light Division spent the night by the river. Dawn revealed that the French had been busy cutting down olive-trees and forming abattis on a defensive and commanding position on heights about a mile in front of Santarem. Massena obviously intended to stay, and the town became his headquarters for the whole of the winter.

The Light Division took possession of Valle [Vale de Santarem], a straggling sort of village near the bridge over the Rio Maior. Leach: *"In various half-ruined hovels and stables near the bridge, the Division was stowed away pretty close."*

> We finally took up our cantonments at a place called Valle. The regiment was distributed in companies on the houses on both sides of the main road. That to which I was attached was an old wine-store near the bridge crossing the Maior. On this bridge we had double sentries and abattis of fallen trees, and in order to foil the incursions of the enemy, the arches were undermined. The powder was secured from the wet by bullocks' hides, trained ready for explosion. About 200 yards in

Santarem from the British advanced post in front of Valle, March 1811.
Published by Edward Orme, 25 March 1811. ©British Museum

front of this were the French outlying sentries, and a little in their rear, on a slight eminence, their camp ground, on which they had built ranges of huts. About three or four miles to our left, divided from us by the Rio Maior, rose the pretty town of Santarem, its towers and steeples peering up from the summit of a hill, which was studded on all sides with groves of olive-trees. The prospect from Santarem must have been very 'soul-stirring', as the two armies lay within shell range. We were flanked on the left and right by the 43rd and 52nd regiments.

In his *Random Shots*, Kincaid describes in some detail the deserted farming establishment at Valle in which his company, and another, were quartered. There are so many similarities between his and Costello's accommodation, that there is a strong likelihood that it was O'Hare's company with which Kincaid's shared:

'It was situated on a slope of the hill overlooking the bridge of Santarem, and within range of the enemies' sentries... Our mansion was a long range of common thatched building. One end was a kitchen, next to it a parlour, which became also the drawing and sleeping room of two captains, with their six jolly subs. A doorway communicated from thence to the barn, which constituted the greater part of the range, and lodged our 200 men. In a small apartment at the other extremity, which was fitted up for a wine-press, lodged our non-commissioned officers."

Leach says that they slept *"fully accoutred throughout the winter; being so near the enemy, that a few minutes would have sufficed to bring us into contact. The sentries of the two armies were so near each other on the bridge, and the videttes of the cavalry so closely advanced on the marsh on the right, that they might have conversed without exalting their voices much."*

While they were at Valle, they had a daily routine. Kincaid: *'It was our practice to dress for sleep: we saddled our horses, buckled on our armour, and lay down, with the bare floor for a bed and a stone for a pillow, ready for anything... We stood to arms every morning at an hour before daybreak, and remained there until a 'grey horse' could be seen a mile off (which is the military criterion by which daylight is acknowledged, and the hour of surprise past), when we proceeded to unharness, and to indulge in such luxuries as our toilet and our table afforded.*

'The Maior, as far as the bridge of Valle, was navigable for the small craft from Lisbon, so that our tables, while we remained there, cut as respectable a figure as regular supplies of rice, salt, fish and potatoes could make it; not to mention that our pigskin was, at all times, at least three parts full of a common red wine, which used to be dignified by the name of blackstrap. We had the utmost difficulty, however, in keeping up appearances in the way of dress. The jacket, in spite of shreds and patches, always maintained something of the original about it; but woe befell the regimental small-clothes, as they could only be replaced by

very extraordinary apologies, of which I remember that I had two pair at this period, one of a common brown Portuguese cloth, and the other - or Sunday's pair - of black velvet.

"We had no women with the regiment, and the ceremony of washing a shirt amounted to my servant's taking it by the collar, giving it a couple of shakes in the water, and then hanging it up to dry. Smoothing irons were not the fashion of the times. If a fresh well-dressed aide-de-camp did occasionally come from England, we used to stare at him."

For the whole of the four or five months that we were there, the armies never interfered with each other. We enjoyed the most uninterrupted repose, almost our sole employment being to watch the French movements.

For want of a better pastime, some of the men succeeded in constructing a still, and using a quantity of dried grapes found in the old wine-house, managed to make spirits. However, much to our chagrin, a discovery soon took place, and the still was destroyed by our captain, Peter O'Hare.

One laughable circumstance that made the time pass gaily was a ghost story in which Tom Crawley was conspicuous. Our company had turned into quarters - accoutred, as was our custom before laying down for the night's repose - when in rushed Tom Crawley like a distracted man.

"Bring me some salt and water, for the love of God, boys!" he demanded; "I have seen a ghost." (According to a vulgar superstition in Ireland, those who have seen a phantom, in order to avoid evil influence, should drink salt before seeing a light.)

"What sort of ghost, Crawley?" sung out a dozen voices from the men, immediately alive to the fun.

"Oh a Portuguese ghost, as sure as the Lord," replied Crawley. "Give me a little water with some salt in it."

A tin measure, filled not with salt and water but, I am sorry to say, with a much more objectionable liquid, was brought to the agitated Tom. He drank it as if his future salvation depended on it, making many wry faces, which were sufficiently accounted for by the potion he had swallowed. The men were convulsed with laughter at his credulity. When something like silence was restored, he took a seat and told us, in a very solemn manner, that he had distinctly seen the semblance of a man of Colonel Elder's regiment, a caçadore who used to sell us rum on the retreat from Almeida, and who had been killed at the battle of Busaco.

"Did you speak to it?" enquired Jack Murphy[1].

"You know I can't talk Portuguese," replied Crawley.

"A ghost can talk any language; he would have spoken English to you if you had talked to him," observed another.

"But I was in too great a fright to talk, and then he vanished away among the trees."

Poor Tom Crawley! His ghost story afforded us ample amusement for many weeks afterwards, but his grog was stopped because the noise he created with his spiritual narration woke the captain of our company, in an adjoining room.

Nothing dampens the spirit of a service-soldier more - particularly a man of Crawley's temperament - than stopping his grog. Like his renowned prototype, Nautical Jack, if granted three wishes, his first would be for all the rum in the world, the second for all the tobacco, and the third for more rum. One day, a number of our men were employed baking bread in the ovens our commissary had had made. The bread was like our quartern loaf, one of which was allowed each man every four days. On this occasion, the company was being served out with its rations: salt beef, and a hot four-pound loaf each. As the quarter-master called over the name of each man, the commissary served out rum from a barrel, which had been turned on the end with the head knocked in. When Crawley's name was called, the answer came: "Stopped by order of Captain O'Hare."

Had sentence of death been pronounced, it could not have sounded more harsh, but Tom had a little philosophy and this trial put it to the test. While he was peeping over the men's shoulders, anxiously watching each man receive his portion of rum, I observed him poking his thumb into different parts of his hot loaf. He edged himself through the men, got close to the barrel, and put the loaf under his arm, then, when the commissary turned round to speak to one of the men, Tom raised his arm and the loaf dropped into the rum-barrel. Lustily, he damned some awkward fellows for pushing and causing the accident, wishing, no doubt, for the loaf to remain soaking in the barrel as long as possible. The commissary was about to take it out, when Crawley delved his arm into the barrel, and shoved it to the bottom, before drawing it out himself. It was dripping, and so was his coat-sleeve. He regarded the commissary with a serious face, and begun cursing his misfortune:

"Faith sir, I'll have a hot meal for the next four days, anyhow. If salt junk and hot rum don't blister a poor devil's guts, I don't know what will."

The good-natured commissary looked upon it as a pure accident, and handed Tom an extra half loaf, which he instantly squeezed against the wet one, lest a drop of the precious liquor should fall to the ground. And then he walked away, humming as he went: "Oh, love is the soul of a neat Irishman..."

If O'Hare was in the same accommodation as Kincaid, it was no wonder that Crawley's exclamations should have woken him, for the doorway separating the officers from the men was so inadequate that Kincaid could hear nearly all that went on in the soldiers' living area:

'I know not what degree of amusement the soldiers derived from the proceedings on our side of the wall, but I know that the jests, the tales,

and the songs from their side, constituted our greatest enjoyment during the many long winter nights that it was our fate to remain here. The early part of their evenings was generally spent in witticism and tales; and in conclusion, by way of a lullaby, some long-winded fellow commenced one of those everlasting ditties in which soldiers and sailors delight so much. They are all to the same tune, and the subject (if one may judge by the tenor of the first 98 verses!) was battle, murder, or sudden death; but I never yet survived until the catastrophe, although I have often, to attain that end, stretched my waking capacities to the utmost. I have heard a fresh arrival from England endeavour to astonish their unpolished ears with 'the white blossomed sloe' or some such refined melody, but it was coughed down as instantaneously as if it had been the sole voice of a conservative amidst a select meeting or radicals. The wit and the humour of the rascals were amusing beyond anything - and to see them next morning drawn up as mute as mice, and as stiff as lamp-posts, it was a regular puzzler to discover on which post the light had shone during the bygone night."

The officers had their own pastimes. Leach and a few others would hunt for quails, snipe and golden plovers, or go coursing for hares[2]. They even had a horse-race, but the animals were such nags that the end result was horses and riders floundering on the ground in one big heap. Hearing that the French were having theatricals in Santarem, the riflemen were not to be outdone. Leach:

"Accordingly, the soldiers of a certain company of our battalion... converted an old house, in which olive oil had formerly been made, into a theatre. The blankets and greatcoats of the soldiers made capital side-scenes; and had not too much wine and grog found their way behind them, no doubt the piece would have gone off with great éclat. But, as the truth must be told, they all forgot their parts, and it was a toss-up whether our attempt at horse-racing, or at play-acting, was the most ludicrous."

During that winter, Wellington's men were quite well supplied from Lisbon, but Massena's had very little to eat.

For a great part of the time we were quartered here, a very friendly intercourse was carried on between the French and ourselves. We frequently met them bathing in the Rio Maior, and would often have swimming and jumping matches. In these games we mostly beat them. This was probably due to their distressed and half-starved condition, which our stolen intercourses soon made us more awake to. Touched with pity, our men shared with them the ration biscuits with which we were occasionally supplied by our shipping from England.

All national hostility was buried in our anxiety to assist and relieve them. Tobacco was in great request. We used to carry some of ours to them, while they in return would bring us a little brandy. Their reveille was our summons as well, although our captain seldom troubled us to fall in. However, it was not unusual to find the rear of our army under arms, expecting an attack. Our captain knew his customers, for though playful as lambs, we were as watchful as leopards.

Spanish guerillas were very active against the French, raiding the the supplies being transported through Spain to the army in Portugal. Massena's men foraged in the Portuguese villages under their control, but found little to eat, and left none for the local people, who starved. The sufferings of Portuguese and Spanish peasants at their hands led to brutal reprisals against French soldiers.

The French provision and ammunition resources depended entirely on their communications with France, which was separated from them by the Pyrenees. Such long distances made the transport of their supplies exceedingly precarious, and were it not for the contributions levied by the French generals on the inhabitants, they would have found themselves caught more often between hunger, and the bayonets of their enemies.

The two armies [French and British] were contending on a soil to which both were aliens. The French were fighting in support of the usurpation of the Spanish throne by Joseph Bonaparte, and therefore had to contend with the Spanish people as well as with the Portuguese. Night and day, the French troops were not only open to attacks from the British, but in constant alarm from the natives, whose animosity made them alive to the slightest opportunity of doing them mischief. No Frenchman, however fatigued, dared to straggle or fall back because it was instant death to him. At this time the Spanish guerillas wore their own peasant dress, not uniform, so the French could not recognise friend from foe. The guerillas and the peasantry watched with the thirst of wolves, and slaughtered all who fell into their hands.

With us it was different. We were received everywhere with open arms, and were well backed, if not by the courage of the local people, then by their best provision resources. We could safely leave behind us hospitals which were full, whilst the sick and wounded of our opponents were sometimes slaughtered wholesale by the citizens. Nevertheless, the natives were not always to be relied on, and though drawn up with us on most occasions, they generally left the British to bear the brunt of action, thus showing that a weak friend can be more dangerous than a determined enemy.

The sanguinary nature of the Portuguese during the whole period of the war was notorious. When crossed or excited, nothing but the shedding of blood could allay their passion. It was very difficult to prevent them butchering our French prisoners in cold blood. They would hang upon the rear of a detachment of prisoners like so many carrion birds, awaiting an opportunity to satiate their love of vengeance, and it required all the firmness and vigilance of our troops to keep them in check. In stepping between the Portuguese, and the French they had marked out as victims, our men sometimes fell, and suffered the consequences of their ferocity.

While at Valle, I myself had a narrow escape when I crossed the hills to purchase some necessaries at the quarters of the 52nd regiment. On my return, I fell in with several of the soldiers of the 3rd Caçadores. One of them was a fierce-looking scoundrel, and perceiving that I was unarmed and alone, he evinced a great inclination to quarrel. He cast some abuse upon the English. I replied rather sharply by reflecting on his countrymen in return, and he flew into a rage, drew his bayonet, and made a rush at me. I avoided it by stepping aside, and tripped him head foremost on the ground. I was in the act of seizing his bayonet, when a number of his comrades came up. To them he related, in exaggerated terms, the cause of our disagreement, and before he had half concluded, a general cry arose of 'kill the English dog!' They all drew their bayonets, and were advancing upon me, when a party of the 52nd came up. The tables were turned, and the caçadores fled in all directions.

The Portuguese civilians who had chosen to remain in areas controlled by Massena, suffered great want, but so did those who sought protection inside the Lines of Torres Vedras. According to Verner, there were 100,000 troops (including Portuguese irregulars) inside the lines, and a huge number of civilians.

Leach: *'Thousands of the unfortunate inhabitants of the provinces through which our army had recently retreated, had abandoned their homes, and were endeavouring to exist between Lisbon and the lines. There was, therefore, an immense population hemmed up in a small space of country, hundreds of them without a house to cover them, or food to eat, except what was afforded by the bounty of the rich at Lisbon, and by the liberal subscriptions raised for them in England. In the course of the winter, the number of Portuguese who actually died of want was quite dreadful. It was not unusual to see hordes of these poor wretches, old and young, male and female, in rags, the very pictures of death, seated in despair on the wet ground, round a miserable fire, on which was placed an earthen vessel, full of such herbs as could be gathered in the fields and hedges. Thousands contrived to drag on a miserable existence on this vile sustenance. Their death-like, emaciated faces were sufficient to have touched the heart of the most callous and unfeeling. The British soldiers assisted them by every means in their power; and in the Light Division (as well as, I conclude, in every other), soup was made from the heads and offal of the cattle killed for the troops, and distributed among the starving inhabitants."* According to Napier, at least 40,000 civilians died within the Lines that winter.

Desertion was a problem for both armies, and the soldiers in the Duke of Brunswick Oels' corps of infantry, which joined the Light

Division on 13 November, the day before Massena retreated to Santarem, were noted for it.

About this period we had a regiment of Brunswickers sent to join our Division. We used to call them the 'death and glory men', because their badge, worn on their shakos and accoutrements, was of the skull and cross-bones. They were dressed in dark green, which all too frequently enabled them to steal past our guards to join the French, with whom many of their connections were. One of our least amusing duties consisted of watching them to prevent them deserting to the enemy.

Among their other attributes, they had a *canine* appetite, and would kill and eat any dog they could privately lay hold of. The different dogs of the Division disappeared before the Germans with a celerity that is truly astonishing, and we were ignorant of their fate until the fact became openly acknowledged. Among those 'potted for consumption' was Rifle, a dog which had attached itself to our regiment, and which could never be induced to leave us. We lost him on one or two occasions, but he always managed to rejoin us. We used to joke among ourselves at Rifle's antipathy to a red coat, for he had a decided preference for green. The poor fellow survived many of our skirmishes, in which he used to run about barking and expressing his delight as much as a dog could, only to be devoured by the insatiable jaws of the Brunswickers.

In our company was a sergeant of the name of Fleming, a tall, athletic, brave fellow from the Lake of Killarney. One night, being posted on picket, he collided with one of the Brunswick officers. Thinking he intended to bolt to the enemy, Fleming knocked him down with his rifle, and maltreated him. For this assault, he was tried by a brigade court-martial and convicted. He was sentenced to be reduced to the ranks and to receive a corporal punishment of 500 lashes. This put us all on the alert; the officers too, by whom Fleming was very much liked. The Division was formed by order of General Craufurd, and the prisoner brought to the centre of the square. The minutes of the court-martial were read aloud and Fleming proceeded to strip. The men stood attentive, but sullen. Then the General spoke.

"Prisoner Fleming, the offence which you are guilty of is of so heinous a nature, that could it be proved to have been wilfully committed, it would be unpardonable. However, the excellent character for gallantry and honourable conduct, given of you by your officers, is such that I take the responsibility on myself not to flog you. But your stripes will be cut off, and I trust your future conduct will testify that the discretion I now use is not misplaced. And I here," the General went on, turning round to the Division, "take the opportunity of declaring, that if any of those gentlemen (meaning the Brunswickers), have a wish to go over to the enemy, then let them express it, for I give my word of honour that I will grant them a pass to that effect instantly, for we are better off without them."

The Brunswickers had such a propensity for desertion, that Lord Wellington was eventually induced to distribute their force among the different divisions of the army[3].

Fleming was shortly afterwards reinstated. The poor fellow was destined for an honourable fate - he fell leading on the ladder party, in the forlorn hope at Badajoz[4].

Route of Massena's
Retreat through Portugal

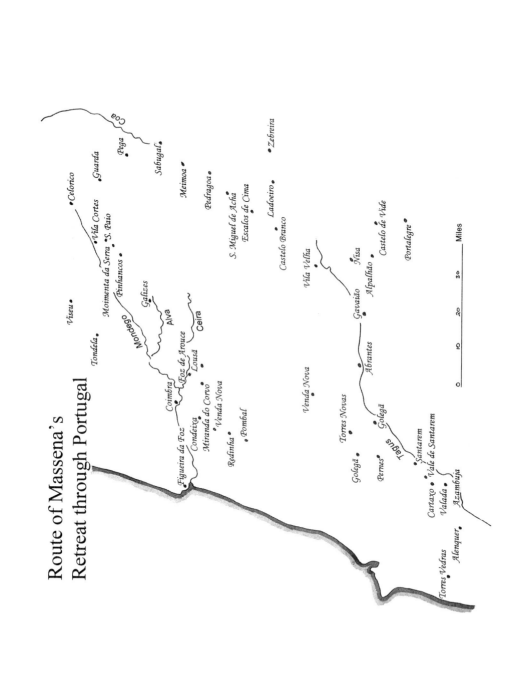

Coa

Pega

Sabugal

Guarda

Celorico

Vila Cortes

S. Paio

Zebreira

Meimoa

Pedragoa

Moimenta da Serra

Pinhancos

S. Miguel de Acha

Escalos de Cima

Ladoeiro

Castelo Branco

Castelo de Vide

Portalegre

Viseu

Tondela

Mondego

Galizes

Alva

Ceira

Coimbra

Foz de Arouce

Lousã

Miranda do Corvo

Venda Nova

Redinha

Pombal

Figueira da Foz

Condeixa

Vila Velha

Nisa

Alpalhão

Gavião

Abrantes

Venda Nova

Torres Novas

Golegã

Golegã

Tagus

Santarem

Vale de Santarem

Permes

Cartaxo

Valada

Azambuja

Torres Vedras

Alenquer

Miles

0   10   20   30

CHAPTER 9

In Pursuit of Massena
February - 13 March 1811

In February, General Craufurd went to England on leave. During his absence, the command of the Light Division devolved upon Major-General Sir William Erskine.

On 6 February, Simmons transferred out of O'Hare's company and joined Kincaid in Captain Beckwith's. Within days, French deserters were saying that Massena was likely to move off his ground at Santarem because disease amongst his men was reducing the strength of his army, and because his line of communication had been cut. No longer sure of receiving the reinforcements he needed to carry out his plan to attack the allies dug in around Lisbon, Massena decided to retreat. On 4 March his men began burning everything they could not take with them. Then, at 2am on 6 March 1811, they moved quietly out of Santarem. Information of their departure was brought to the British by a peasant sent by the town's chief magistrate. At daybreak, the Light Division followed.

> On the night of 5 March we were suddenly ordered to fall in, as intelligence had reached us that the French were evacuating Santarem. This was ascertained to be the fact, and we immediately commenced an advance, crossing the bridge in our front at 3 o'clock on the morning of the 6th.
>
> Our captain being the senior of the regiment, our company was in the advance as usual. Suddenly, some of the front files came within a few yards of what appeared to be a French sentinel leaning against a wall that ran along from the bridge. One of our fellows fired. Perceiving no movement, we all rushed up and discovered him to be what our money-changers at home have so great a horror of: a man of straw. It was a piece of sacking, stuffed and accoutred.

William Green: *"I was on an outlying picket with my company to the bridge... We perceived their camp fires almost burnt out. They had a sentinel at the foot of the bridge... an officer and six men made a rush towards him. To our surprise, it was a mawkin [scarecrow] stuffed with straw, with jacket and trousers, and cap, a long stick for a firelock, and for cross-belts, pieces of English newspapers."*

This afforded a fit theme for joking, and we carried our prisoner with us to Santarem. Our march, which was uninterrupted, was over a bold, thickly wooded country, much cut up by the retreating enemy. About midday we entered Santarem, where a most horrifying sight offered itself. The streets and houses presented a mass of desolation and filth, which contaminated the air around.

Simmons: *"How different this town now appeared. When I last was in it all was gaiety and happiness, and the shops abounding with every luxury, and a smile upon every one's face; but now the houses are torn and dilapidated, and the few miserable inhabitants, moving skeletons. The streets were strewn with every description of household furniture, half-burnt and destroyed, and many streets were quite impassable with filth and rubbish, with an occasional man, mule, or donkey rotting and corrupting and filling the air with pestilential vapours."*

Numbers of half-starved Frenchmen were grouped about in knots, exhibiting the loathsome appearance of disease. Without enough transport for all his sick, Massena had been obliged to leave these to their fate, which would have been soon decided had the Portuguese come up with them first. The faces of many of these poor fellows were dreadfully swollen and white, and our men, moved to pity, threw them biscuits as we passed through the town.

At every mile on their retreat, the enemy had fixed finger posts with directions to the road the French had taken, and they directed us also: straggling groups of the unfortunate enemy which strewed the road as we advanced over it. At first, the poor fellows would greet the English with a faint hope of protection. They would turn up their swollen and pallid countenances to us with expressions that needed no words to explain them, but we were obliged to pass on, and for aught I know, they were butchered by the inhabitants, who retaliated fearfully for all the scenes we had witnessed.

At night we encamped on the outskirts of a small village whose name I do not recollect, but the sights within it I can never forget.

Kincaid: *"We halted for the night near Pernes... The streets were strewed with broken furniture, intermixed with the putrid carcases of murdered peasants, mules, and donkeys, and every description of filth."*

In searching for a stream from which I might procure water, I found a small fountain. Close to it lay two or three murdered Portuguese, whose brains and blood had oozed from their mangled remains and had even streamed into the spring. I turned away from the water with disgust.

Proceeding onward, I observed a gaunt, ghastly figure in a cloak, stealing towards a group of cadaverous-looking Frenchmen. When he got a little nearer, he spat in his hands, threw his cloak aside, and produced a heavy club, with which he was going to beat their brains out. Struck with horror, I seized the stick from his half-famished grasp and drove him away. Assisted by one or two comrades, I got the poor men into a house, and pursued my search[1].

As I approached the plaza, the desolation thickened. All the havoc that can possibly be imagined in so small a compass lay before me - murdered and violated women, shrieking and dying children. All in the village that had possessed life, lay quivering in the last agony of slaughter and awful vengeance[2].

To Leach, the sights at Pernes *"presented objects of misery and disgust at every step, sufficient to raise feelings of the highest indignation against Massena and his followers, to whose name indelible disgrace will be attached for their atrocious and wanton cruelties."*

These became everyday scenes until we overtook the French rear-guard at Pombal on the 11th.

On 7 March, the Light Division followed the enemy's rear-guard to Torres Novas, and on the 8th to Venda Nova. The road, says **Simmons**, *"was often covered with dead Frenchmen, gun-carriages, waggons, and pieces of different military equipment."*

On the night of 10 March, the Light Division bivouacked in a pine wood a few miles from Pombal. Before daylight on the 11th, the enemy moved off. The Light Division's cavalry went in pursuit. Mounted behind some of the dragoons were the riflemen of O'Hare's company:

My company was hurried forward by the cavalry, each dragoon carrying a rifleman behind him on his horse. During the war, we frequently experienced this method of riding, but it was galling to us because the men's mess tins could become shaken off by the jolting, and lost. Also, the friction produced on the legs and seat by the dragoon's saddle-bags, meant that it was some time before we could move with anything like despatch when placed on our feet again. Most of our men preferred marching twice the distance on foot to being thus carried[3].

We first got sight of the enemy about two miles from the town of Pombal. They had possession of a wood, from which we managed to drive them.

Green: *"We came in sight of the enemy near to a place called Pombal. Here was a river and a bridge. Captain Ross, with his troop of horse artillery, came up and said 'A thousand pounds for a gun here!' He gave the word 'unlimber', fired three rounds of grapeshot, gave the words 'limber up', and galloped forward. We were running in front of the guns, the grapeshot flying over our heads. On our way we had to scour a wood. I was walking near him when our lieutenant [John*

Pombal in flames as evacuated by Massena's army, and the advance of the Allied troops, 11 March 1811.
By Major T St. Clair, Published by C Turner, November 1814. ©British Museum

Hopwood?] said 'I don't think there are any of the enemy in this wood'. The words were scarcely out of his mouth when a musket ball passed between his head and mine; we were in extended order. He bid me sound the 'double-quick'; and we rushed into the wood and cleared it of its sharpshooters."

They retired in great disorder in the direction of the town. The long straight road that led to Pombal became filled for some hundred yards with the confused masses of the French, and their distress was increased by the arrival of Brigade-Major Mellish, who came up with a couple of Ross's guns and commenced playing upon them. It soon became a complete rout with the enemy pressing pell-mell over the river bridge, which was between us and the town. We followed.

Green: *'The artillery played their shot over our heads. The French rear-guard could not get over the bridge fast enough; many of them took to the river."*

During our approach to the bridge, Palmer and Treacy[4], two men of known daring, saw a French sergeant fall and ran up to claim the meed of conquest by relieving him of any valuable he might possess. They quarrelled as to the appropriation of the spoil. Palmer, who was an excellent shot, claimed to have shot the sergeant and told Treacy to go and 'kill a Frenchman for himself'. That was the first time I heard the phrase, which afterwards became common in our regiment. It gave birth to a little gasconade [boasting] that every rifleman ought to kill a Frenchman in action.

Palmer's nick-name became the 'man-killer', until the siege of Badajoz [April 1812] gave him another. While relieving pickets in the trenches at Badajoz, many of our men, instead of going quietly through the trenches, or parallels, in front of the walls of the town, used to show their contempt of danger by jumping out of them and running across in the face of the enemy's fire. One day, Palmer was executing this feat with some others, when a cannon-shot fired by the French, struck the ground and hit him on the back. He fell. We thought he had been killed, but to our surprise, a moment later he jumped up unhurt. The ball had glanced off his knapsack. In commemoration of this event, he became known as the 'bomb-proof man'.

The French suffered considerably at Pombal and the ground was strewed with their dead. At the bridge, we found several poor fellows badly wounded by the Rifles. There were many disssevered legs and arms, caused, no doubt, by Ross's two pieces.

Green: *"When we came to the bridge, they lay in heaps both killed and wounded, some with both legs shot off."*

Only my own company were present here, and we were at a great disadvantage, having to sustain a smart fire from the different houses, which were occupied by the rear-guard of the enemy. As soon as we crossed the bridge, we took possession of the houses opposite them, and kept up a brisk fire out of the windows. Tired with this cross work, several of our men dashed into one of the French holds. They found it crowded with 30-40 of the enemy, who quietly surrendered themselves as prisoners. Sergeant Fleming[5], who was the first to mount the stairs, bundled them neck and crop over the staircase. When Lieutenant Hopwood entered the house, he fell, severely wounded in the thigh[6]. We maintained the conflict until the remainder of the regiment came up, and then drove the enemy entirely out of their cover.

In the eagerness of pursuit, our men followed the enemy a considerable distance out of the town. We were galling them terribly in the street when, perceiving how few our numbers were, and that we were supported by only a single troop of our German hussars, they turned round and made it a hard matter for us to escape the consequences of our temerity.

Green: *'They were in full retreat. We followed them to the other end of the town and were within twenty paces, when their officers gave the word for them to wheel into line. They then faced us and poured a volley into our ranks, wounding several of our men, and an officer in the leg (Lt. Hopwood). One man near me fell when he had a ball pass through the upper lip, the roof of his mouth, and out the back of his neck. Those of us thus close to the French column had to retire to the bridge."*

Several of the men were outflanked and taken prisoners. For myself, I had to run a great risk, and should certainly have been killed or captured, but for the gallantry of a German dragoon, who rode up, dragged me behind him, and galloped away amidst a volley of shots. We were unhurt.

The company casualties that day were five - one officer and four men wounded. Green: *"We kept possession of one end of the town all night, and the French rear-guard the other end."*

The French posted themselves partly under cover of a wood. At night, they threw shells into the town of Pombal, of which we had possession, and succeeded in setting in on fire in several places. Nevertheless, we remained for the night.

We had taken some baggage, snugly packed on a grey horse, and this we auctioned among the officers and men. It had belonged to a General, and among other valuables, there were two beautiful gold medals, which one of the purchasers sent off to England. By the desire of our old captain [O'Hare], we divided the proceeds, which amounted to six dollars to each man of the company[7].

When Wellington was sure of the route of Massena's retreat (via Coimbra), he concentrated his resources to force it. He had 43,000 men to Massena's 46,000. His first move was to attack Marshal Ney, who fell back to Redinha.

In the morning, the French continued their retreat, and we were again in pursuit. After crossing a well-wooded hill, we came up with them at Redinha, a small town situated in the hollow of rather a difficult pass. The company ascended a pine-covered hill on the right of our battalion.

Green was with him: *'Our company, being relieved of outlying picket, formed a reserve, and were posted on a hill. The enemy formed two good lines for a grand attack, and we of the reserve party had nothing to do but look on. It was a very grand sight to see the British and Portuguese armies march on the plain, with colours flying, bands playing (horse and foot), and with horse and foot artillery.'*

Simmons: *'It was a sunshiny morning, and the red coats and pipe-clayed belts, and glittering of men's arms in the sun, looked beautiful. I felt a pleasure which none but a soldier can feel.'*

From this eminence, I remember to have seen one of the finest views of the two armies I ever witnessed. The rifles were extended for perhaps two miles, and rapidly on the advance to the enemy's position. These were followed by our heavy columns, whose heads were just emerging from a wood about a quarter of a mile in our rear. Everything seemed conducted with the order and regularity of a field day[8].

Simmons: *'The wooded heights were attacked by a wing of the 1st battalion, commanded by Major Stewart, who carried them in gallant style. The other wing attacked the left, the Light Division acting in unison with these attacks, our columns moving rapidly into the plain, forming line and moving on, and also the cavalry.'*

Green: *'The French sharpshooters were sent out in front of their lines, and their cavalry on their two flanks appeared very warlike, but when the charge was made by the British, their front line gave way, and they retreated!'*

The rear columns of the French were slowly retiring, but a few minutes later, the scene became exceedingly animated when our artillery opened their fire upon the retreating forces. This was the signal for us to set to work. We moved down from our lofty station and were soon engaged in skirmishing, endeavouring to outflank and drive in their light troops. This we accomplished after a hard struggle, and many men fell on both sides. Although they slowly retired, the enemy continually turned, and made temporary stands whenever the ground seemed favourable.

97

In this action, a French officer, who was conspicuously cheering on his men, fell by a rifle-shot through the thigh. Two of our buglers ran forward for the purpose of easing him of his money, which the French generally kept concealed in a kind of belt round their waists. In order to disencumber him of this belt, both buglers fell to their knees over the poor man. They immediately commenced quarrelling as to which of them should possess his property. One had drawn a knife to cut the strap that secured the hoped-for treasure, and when the other endeavoured to restrain him, there was a scuffle, and the knife entered the body of the wounded man. I arrived in time to see this happen. He expired on the spot, and it was with difficulty that I restrained myself from shooting the owner of the knife; but then he told me it was an accident.

With the men fighting in companies, the buglers closest to Costello would have been those of his own company, of which there were no more than three, and William Green was one of them. Was he one of these two buglers?

While pursuing the French at Redinha, Simmons and Kincaid had a narrow escape.

Simmons: *'Lieutenant Kincaid passed with me through a gap in a hedge. We jumped from it at the same moment that a Portuguese grenadier, who was following, received a cannon shot through his body and came tumbling after us. Very likely during the day a person might have a thousand much more narrow escapes... but seeing the body of a brave fellow so shockingly mutilated in an instant, stamps impressions upon one's mind in a manner that time can never efface."*

Kincaid: *'Just as Mr Simmons and myself had crossed the river, and were talking over the events of the day, not a yard asunder, there was a Portuguese soldier in the act of passing between us, when a cannon-ball plunged into his belly. His head doubled down to his feet, and he stood for a moment in that posture before he rolled over a lifeless lump."*

We pursued the enemy through the town, and in a water-mill we found a number of prisoners. Among them were some of my own company, taken the day before[9].

We encamped at night on the side of an extensive hill. The country here was well wooded and watered, and exceedingly picturesque, as was the position occupied by the enemy. We were on a range of heights, while the French lay below in a beautiful valley. The outlying sentries of the armies were not more than 200 yards apart.

The combat at Redinha left four Rifleman dead and 11 wounded.

In action, the care of the wounded devolved upon the buglers and bandsmen alone. At first, it was a common excuse for a soldier to get out from under fire, but the braver men regarded it with such indignation that, during the latter part of the campaign, no good soldier would venture to expose himself to the scorn of his comrades under so frivolous a pretence, other than in extreme cases.

This night our company, with Captain Balvaird's[10], formed the outlying picket. Having had no rations for two days, we were busily employed cooking what we had taken from the prisoners, when a man of the name of Humphrey Allen - a tall, powerful fellow whom we had nick-named Long Tom of Lincoln - came up from the rear where, during the skirmish, he had been employed taking the wounded. He asked to be allowed to join one of the messes, but was refused because he had gone out of action with the wounded. Allen now proved himself more daring than humane. He coolly observed that, if a Frenchman had something to eat, he would get it. Taking up his rifle, he walked quietly down to our outlying pickets, took deliberate aim, and shot one of the French sentries on the spot. He then ran across the field to where the man had fallen, hoisted him on his shoulders, and started to bear him back to our line. Perceiving this, the French fired, and pursued him, compelling him to drop his prize. This firing occasioned a general alarm, and before it could be checked, Colonel Beckwith came down. Having traced its origin, he sent for Allen and made enquiries.

"Why, sir," replied Tom, "I arn't had nought to eat these two days, and thought as how I might find summut in the Frencher's knapsack."

Although he had been guilty of a cruelty which no law of arms could justify, he managed to escape with a severe reprimand[11].

An hour later, I was on sentry at our advance posts. It was just at the close of the evening, and between the lights. Leisurely, I sauntered up and down, occasionally looking about me, and stooping to cull some flowers that grew in the field which divided us from the enemy. The French sentry advanced occasionally, seemingly for the same purpose. At last, he came so near that I feared he was up to some manoeuvre. Thinking he was about to fire at me, I cocked my rifle, and awaited his approach. Suddenly, he rushed towards me, bellowing out in French, "Deserter! Deserter!". I allowed him to approach. He did so.

"*Je suis allemand!*" [I am German], he exclaimed, and turning on his former comrades, he fired into them.

The report of his fire caused the pickets of both parties to fall in, and the whole line of sentries were again engaged. He stuck by me all the time, shaking his fist at them, and leading and firing with all the jaw-breaking oaths that French, and his native German, could supply him with.

Colonel Beckwith, alarmed for a second time, was soon amongst us, swearing at what he supposed to be another Lincoln job; but he returned rather pleased, leading the deserter.

The French got under arms before the dawn. As usual, we followed. keeping them well on before us.

CHAPTER 10

Casal Nova, Foz de Arouce, and Sabugal
13 March - 7 April 1811

On the morning of 13 March, the Light Division followed the French to Condeixa. Kincaid: *"Arrived on the hill above Condeixa in time to see that handsome little town in flames. Every species of barbarity continued to mark the enemy's retreating step. They burnt every town or village through which they passed, and if we entered a church which by accident had been spared, it was to see the murdered bodies of the peasantry on the altar."*

> At noon we passed through the pretty little town of Condeixa. The enemy had fired it in several places, and the main street was blocked by flames darting across the road from the houses. To enable the troops to pass, we had to break a way through some dry walls, which caused a temporary halt, during which the chief part of the Division gallantly employed themselves extricating the unfortunate inhabitants from the burning houses[1]. Tom Crawley, forgetting his experience in the coach, made use of his great strength, and brought forth on his shoulders some five or six old people. He chucked them over a wall where, he supposed, they would be out of immediate danger, but he should have 'looked' before he made the old ones 'leap', because close to their descent was a large well, into which the terrified and screeching sufferers nearly dropped.
>
> Having cleared the houses, we proceeded to Casal Nova, where we came up with the incendiaries, whom we found perfectly prepared to receive us.

The morning of 14 March was foggy. When it cleared, the French could be seen very strongly posted at the village of Casal Nova, which they were obliged to hold in order to give their columns time to retire. The countryside for miles in their rear had a series of good defensive positions.

> The country all about was greatly intercepted by old walls, and afforded excellent facilities for skirmishing. In a few seconds, some of our Division were observed moving upon our right. We were ordered instantly to extend, and at it we went.

Simmons: *"The heights and village of Casal Nova were spiritedly attacked by Major Stewart with the left wing of the 95th Rifles."*

After several hours' hard fighting, kept up with great spirit on both sides, we compelled the enemy to retire, but not before we had lost an excellent officer in the person of Major Stewart, who received a shot through the body. I was close at hand, and caught the reins of his horse to prevent him from falling. Blood and foam were oozing from his

Major John Stewart, as a lieutenant in the 79th Regiment

mouth. Two buglers led him to the rear, where he died shortly after[2]. The death of this officer gave a step to my old Captain, O'Hare, who obtained the majority[3].

When O'Hare became a major, command of his company passed to Captain John Uniacke, another brave Irishman.

Lieutenant Strode also received a severe wound. This officer always carried a rifle, for the skilful use of which he was celebrated[4]. It is surprising that, in general, our officers do not carry a rifle into action. Superior to the sword and pistol, which are mere toys in the field, the defence it would afford them should carry its own argument. It would give additional efficiency and strength to the regiments generally, from the number (50 to a regiment) that it would add to each volley. It would inspire confidence in the officer, without preventing him from keeping his eye on his riflemen who, while in action, use their own judgement by getting under cover, and are consequently out of sight[5].

Also at Casal Nova, a man of our company, named Pat Mahone, received three balls in the hip at the same instant, and so close together that a dollar might have covered the holes they made[6].

The Light Division's casualties that day were heavy. They lost nine officers and over 80 men killed or wounded, for which some of the rifle officers blamed their commander, Sir William Erskine. Kincaid: *"At Casal Nova on the 14th, we breakfasted, dined and supped on powder and ball... We were the whole day battering our brains against stone walls at a great sacrifice to life, whereas had we waited with common prudence until a proper period, when the flank movements going on under the direction of our illustrious chief had begun to take effect, the whole of the loss would have been on the other side. As it was, I am afraid that although we carried our point, we were the greatest sufferers... We drove them from one stronghold to another over a large tract of very difficult country, mountainous and rocky, and thickly intersected with stone walls, and were involved in one continued hard skirmish from daylight until dark. This was the most harassing day's fighting that I ever experienced."*

The enemy continued to retreat. Their skirmishers made short stands to keep our Rifles in check, and a few of their rear sections occasionally poured a running fire into us.

We drove them through the village of Casal Nova where, for a few minutes, some of the French availed themselves of the dilapidated walls. As soon as we commenced outflanking them, they retreated, with the exception of one man who remained loading and firing as if he had a whole division to back him. This poor fellow was alone, and exposed to at least twenty shots. My blood was up because he once aimed at me, his ball whizzing close by as I approached, so when I got within fifty yards of him, I fired. I was beside him in an instant. He had fallen in the act of loading, the shot having entered his head. The fusil [a light flintlock musket] was tightly grasped in his left hand, while his right clutched his ramrod. A few quick turns of his eyes as they rolled their dying glances on mine turned my whole blood within me. An indescribable uneasiness came over me, and I reproached myself as his destroyer. I felt like a criminal, and knelt to give him a little wine from a small calabash, which hung at my waist.

I was wiping the foam from his lips when a heavy groan attracted my attention. Turning my head I beheld, stretched out nearby, close to the wall, another wounded Frenchman, a stout, heavy sergeant whose thigh had been broken by a shot. Big tears suddenly gushed down his sun-burnt countenance, and he pointed to my victim.

"You have killed my poor brother," he said in French, and indeed such was the melancholy fact. The younger brother, unable to carry him off the field, had remained, apparently with the intention of perishing by his side.

When we halted for the night on an adjacent hill about a mile in advance, I took advantage of a few moments' leisure to return to the French sergeant. I found him and his brother as naked as they were born, perforated with innumerable wounds, no doubt administered by the Portuguese. I turned back to the camp in a very poor humour with myself. Even so, I could not close my eyes to the magnificent scene around me. The French had taken up their position opposite, and a beautiful ravine sloped between us, which the pickets of both armies occupied. The sun had set, its light supplanted by burning villages, and by the fires that on vale and mountain pointed out where the hostile divisions were extended.

That night, Simmons and Kincaid were on picket duty at the entrance of Lousã. Kincaid: *'Our post that night was one of terrific grandeur. The hills behind were in a blaze of light with the British camp-fires, as were those in our front with the French ones. Both hills were abrupt and lofty, not above 800 yards asunder, and we were in the burning village in the valley in between. The roofs of houses were every instant falling in, and the sparks and flames ascended to the clouds. The streets were strewed with the dying and the dead - some had been murdered and some killed in action - which, together with the half-famished wretches whom we had saved from burning, contributed in making it a scene which was well calculated to shake a stout heart."*

The following morning, the French continued their march of havoc, and we closed after them, village after village giving flaming proofs of their continued atrocities.

The next was Miranda do Corvo. Simmons: *'The rascally French had even plundered this place, and committed every sort of wanton atrocity upon the inhabitants, and then left many of their helpless countrymen for the infuriated inhabitants to wreak their vengeance upon. Luckily for these poor wretches, we followed the French so rapidly that they fell into our hands, and were put in charge of British soldiers, or they would have been butchered indiscriminately."*

Passing through one, which we were informed had been the quarters of Marshal Ney and staff [Miranda do Corvo], an appalling instance of vengeance occurred. The parents of one of our caçadores lived in this village, and as soon as we entered he rushed to their house. The door was open, and stretched across the threshold were the mangled bodies of his father and mother, their blood still warm and reeking from bayonet stabs. His only sister lay breathing her last, and exhibiting dreadful proofs of the brutality with which she had been violated. Frenzied with grief, the unhappy man staggered. He stared wildly around him, then rushed forth from what had once been a happy home towards some French prisoners nearby, who were being guarded by some of our dragoons. Burying all other feelings in the maddening passion of revenge, he attacked them with the fury of a madman. He shot one and wounded another, and would have sacrificed a third had not the guard made him prisoner. On the circumstances being made known to the General, he was liberated.

Outside the village, on a gentle slope, we came to the enemy's camp ground. This they had been obliged to quit so precipitately that they left their fires lighted. A goat was frisking and jumping about - the pet, I suppose, of some French officer - and whenever we went near, it would step aside. Some of the men levelled their rifles and shot it. Swords were out in a moment, and the little animal was dissected, skin and all. I was just apportioning the hind quarter, when who should ride near but Lord Wellington with his staff. I could feel the noose around my neck; but then the Colonel [Beckwith] came up and congratulated us on our lucky chance, which re-established my serenity.

We had suffered dreadfully throughout the previous week, and through weakness and want of rations, many of our men had been unable to keep up with their regiments[7]. In the hearing of many of us, Colonel Beckwith took the opportunity to make this known to the Commander-in-Chief, who promised we should have the first rations that came up. We then marched to some high ground, from whence we could distinctly see the French camp at Foz de Arouce. That night, for his kindness, we shared our goat with Colonel Beckwith.

The French had retreated to a position on the river Ceira but, says Leach, *"Marshal Ney's corps, which formed the rear-guard, had not crossed, and was near Foz de Arouce, having at its back the rocky bed of the Ceira, which was passable only by a bridge, heavy rains having rendered the fords impracticable."*

The situation of Ney's corps at the Ceira was identical to that of the Light Division at the Coa the previous year, ie they were the wrong side of an unfordable river over which there was only one bridge. Leach: *"Lord Wellington, ever alert, took immediate advantage."*

The French had lit their fires preparatory to passing the night there, but it was determined that they should not enjoy it so easily, and our battalion was instantly ordered to attack.

The order was so unexpected that some riflemen were cooking their meals when it was given. Simmons: *"We were all hungry and tired. I was frying some beef and anxiously watching the savoury morsel, when an order was given by Lord Wellington himself to Colonel Beckwith: 'Fall in your battalion and attack the enemy; drive in their skirmishers, and I will turn their flank with the 3rd and 1st Divisions'."*

A few evenings before, we had been reinforced by a fresh batch of recruits from England, a number of whom had been drafted into our company. These fellows' rosy cheeks and plump appearance formed a bright relief, and an amusing contrast, to our fierce, brown visages, covered with whiskers and mustachios. Their dresses were new, whereas our clothing was patched, and of all colours. They were about to go through the ordeal of fire for the first time, and as it was such a momentous occasion, Major O'Hare thought proper to give them a few words of advice.

"Recruits to the front!" he commanded.

Some ten or twelve immediately stepped forward, wondering, no doubt, what they were wanted for.

"Do you see those men on that plain?" said the Major, pointing to the French camp.

"Yes, sir!' several of the men answered.

"Well then," said Major O'Hare, with a dry laugh, "those are the French, and our enemies. You must kill them, and not allow them to kill you. You must learn to do as these old birds do," - here he pointed to us - "and get cover where you can. And remember: if you don't kill those fellows, they'll kill you."

"Yes, sir!"

The Major's logic elicited roars of laughter from the old soldiers, but it had a powerful effect on the recruits. Immediately after this, out went our muzzle stoppers, and we sallied down the slope on which we had been drawn up. At the enemy we went.

The attack on the French at Foz de Arouce commenced at about 5pm. Simmons: *"The whole of the Light Division were smartly engaged. The enemy opposed to the company I was with (Captain Beckwith's), were behind a low wall, The approach was through a pine wood, and the branches were rattling about our ears from the enemy's bullets. Lt.*

Kincaid got shot through his cap, which grazed the top of his head. He fell as if a sledge hammer had hit him." The musket ball rendered Kincaid unconscious, but only for a short while.

Our battalion was soon hotly engaged; we were assisted by some light companies of the Guards, belonging to the 1st Division. The night was fast setting in, but we succeeded in beating the enemy out of their camp ground.

During the skirmish, and while very closely engaged, I saw a horse, gaily bedizened with French trappings, galloping about as though looking for an owner. I managed to catch it by the bridle, but a minute afterwards, my prize received a shot - probably intended for me - which stretched the poor animal dead beside me.

We dashed at the enemy as they were retiring with precipitation over a bridge, which crossed the river in their rear. The bridge was crowded, and before two-thirds of their force were over, it was, by some irregularity, blown up. Great numbers were drowned in attempting to ford the stream.

Leach: *"At length they were forced back, in utter confusion, on the narrow bridge, which their comrades on the opposite side blew up, thus leaving on the same side of the river with the British, many of their countrymen, who were drowned in the Ceira by attempting to flounder through its rapid stream. Some hundred perished in this manner; they threw two of their eagles into the river to prevent them becoming trophies of the victors."*

Simmons: *"The enemy so little dreamt of being disturbed this night that their cooking utensils were left upon their fires for strangers to enjoy their contents."*

At their camp ground, many of our men came in for a bit of a windfall, as the French, in their hurry to place the river between us and them, had left their meat and pots on the fires. This afforded a happy regale to our hungry stomachs, and food thus come by was eaten with a sense of having been fairly earned[8].

Simmons: *"The men looked about and found several knapsacks. They emptied them at the fireside to see their contents and added to their kits, shoes and shirts of better quality than their own. In every packet I observed twenty biscuits nicely rolled up, or deposited in a bag; they were to last each man so many days, and he must, unless he got anything else, be his own commissary. We had been very ill-off for some days for bread, so some of them proved a great luxury."*

Kincaid: *"It ever after became a saying among the soldiers, whenever they were on short allowance, 'Well, damn my eyes, we must either fall in with the French or the commissary today, I don't care which'."*

The night was passed on the French camp ground. At the fire round which we thronged were two wounded Frenchmen, and it was satisfying to mark the care and attention which they received at the hands of our men. One of the prisoners was a very intelligent fellow, who gave me interesting accounts of the state and proceedings of Massena's troops:

"When Massena and his troops lay at Santarem, we hoped to drive the English into Lisbon, or the sea, but this was given up in despair, and at about the beginning of the spring of 1811, the army prepared to retire back through the country into Spain.

"The batteries and other works, which for several months our men had been erecting, were destroyed. Leaving behind a great number of our sick, whom we had no means of conveying away, we shared out the last of our provisions and prepared to retreat. These provisions consisted of about ten biscuits to each man, each biscuit with a hole in the centre to fit them for carriage, for they were generally slung on a string appended to the knapsack.

"The troops, whose numbers had been reduced by half, were in a distressed state, almost naked and without provisions, for most consumed in a few days the whole of their scanty allowance. They could not expect aid from any of their comrades for all were without, the country around us having been devastated by both parties. Our wants urged us to plunder, and we wandered from the regiment in strong parties. Meeting with every species of resistance, we gave blow for blow.

"The guerillas followed us everywhere, harassing us in the front and on our flanks. To save our lives, we were obliged to be alert always, and out of this arose every cruelty which ensued, and which made our retreat almost unparalleled for devastation and bloodshed. Meanwhile, the British troops came on in our rear, their light divisions harassing us night and day, and completing the wreck that will not be forgotten while Portugal retains its name."

Simmons: *"At 2 o'clock this morning [16 March], the enemy had the arches of the bridge more effectually blown up. The weather began to clear at daylight and we saw numbers of the enemy dead in the river, and lying about near the bushes as the water had left them. It was judged about 700-800 had been drowned, and the 39th Regiment lost their Eagles in the water. A great quantity of baggage must have been destroyed or thrown into the water, as there were a great many mules and donkeys close to the river-side hamstrung in the hind leg. These poor animals looked so wretched that one could not help feeling for them, and disgusted with the barbarous cruelty of the French. To have killed and put them out of their misery at once would have been far better. We remained in bivouac."*

Just before the River Ceira, the waters of which flowed over the body of many an unfortunate French soldier, was a sight which was enough to make the Humane Society declare eternal war against the men of the wooden shoes[9]. Some 200-300 donkeys and mules, which the enemy were unable to drive off, had been maimed and hamstrung. The poor animals looked up to us as if for vengeance. Every mute appeal was sternly fulfilled, for they struck home to the feelings of us all[10].

Leach: *"Having out-marched the commissariat, and the country being so thoroughly ransacked and plundered as to afford provisions of no kind, Lord Wellington was unable to proceed far in pursuit of the French on the 16th."*

We continued to occupy the same spot the whole of the following day, waiting very anxiously for the promised supply of rations. That evening, to our exceeding joy, one day's rations made their appearance. The following morning, it being St. Patrick's Day, the whole of our battalion, English and Irish, celebrated the event by a proper attention to greens. We had no shamrocks, so leaves, grass and boughs of trees were substituted. Thus ornamented we commenced our march.

It was a short march; they spent the night in a nearby pine wood. Early the next morning, the 18th, they advanced, says Simmons, *"to the river Alva, found the bridge blown up, and the enemy in position on very strong ground at Ponte de Murcella, with some guns in position commanding the approach to the river.*

After about two leagues [5 miles], the battalion halted upon a hill covered with pine-trees. At the bottom, and near our advanced posts, flowed the River Alva, on the opposite side of which the retreating army lay encamped. We halted and refreshed ourselves, thinking we should spend the night there quietly, but we were miserably undeceived, as a fresh order was given for us to fall in. The artillery came up and commenced playing on the enemy's masses.

Simmons: *"We formed opposite the enemy and had a fine view of a large body of them. Some nine-pounders were soon got up, and commenced pounding their columns. I never saw Johnny go off in such confusion. The cavalry followed for some distance. The Light Division went into bivouac in the pine woods for the night."* During the night a wooden bridge was thrown across the Alva.

Lord Wellington was determined to allow the French no rest if possible and, in truth, ourselves as little, for our Division was ordered to cross the river over which a pontoon had been thrown, while others forded the stream a little higher up on our right. The enemy retired in excellent order, and we pursued them until we both halted for the night.

108

This pattern was repeated for the next four days, as the Light Division pursued the French through Galizes, Moimenta da Serra and S. Paio, a similar route, but in the opposite direction, to that which the wounded Costello had taken in the bullock cart only seven months earlier. All of the villages exhibited evidence of the murderous savagery of the French soldiers.

On 23 March, the Light Division lodged in the town of Mello, and the next night bivouacked in a wood nearby to wait for supplies, having again completely outmarched the commissary in pursuit of the enemy.

The place we occupied was a little village called Mello. Here we remained during the following day, having had one ration only for the last four days. Never let is be said that John Bull cannot fight upon an empty stomach. If ever a Division proved this more than another, it was certainly the Light one for Heaven knows we were light enough at this, and at other periods. We growled sadly at not providing ourselves with a bit from the donkeys, and impelled by hunger, myself and Wilkie searched about for something to devour. Proceeding down a lane, we came upon the body of an elderly woman lying in the middle of the road. She was dressed in white and, from the general appearance of the corpse, had been taken out for the purpose of burial, it being the custom in that country to inter them in full dress, without a coffin. No doubt, the arrival of the French had obliged her attendants to abandon her. The corpse had round its neck a set of beads with a gold cross at the end. This Wilkie very 'piously' put into his pocket[11].

We continued our prowling and stumbled on a small cottage, which we entered, hoping we had made a substantial discovery. An old, emaciated, half-starved hag was squatting by some extinguished embers. She was the only living inhabitant we had seen in the village. She was like the last survivor of a universal wreck, whose only privilege was permission to recount her tale. Wilkie, suspecting something, pressed her to move.

"There is nothing!" screamed the old lady in Portuguese. "There is nothing!"

"Oh, but there is," replied my comrade.

Growing furious, he upset the old woman from her position, and a loaf of bread rolled out from under her as natural as an egg from under a hen. Wilkie pounced on it, and the miserable old creature burst into tears. She screamed herself almost into fits, and in a few seconds her cries brought in her daughter, who rushed forward to her parent's assistance, unable to remain concealed at the sound of her agonising appeal. Never before did I see such a pitiful pair. They were almost cadaverous with want, and begged hard for the loaf, but we were all of us half starved. At last, Wilkie and myself, unable to contain ourselves any longer, willingly shared it with them[12].

On 26 March, the Light Division marched from Mello to Celorico and bivouacked for two days. On the 28th they crossed the Mondego and occupied the villages of Baracal and Minhocal. A party of 100 rifleman under Captain Beckwith was sent to dislodge a body of the enemy from a mill in the front of Freixedas, where they were grinding flour. The attack was successful, but as he was riding into the town, Lt. James Stewart, adjutant of the Rifles, who was acting as Brigade-Major to Colonel Beckwith, was shot in the head and killed.

> We were engaged daily with the enemy until we came to Freixedas on the 28 March, on which day we lost our gallant adjutant, Lt. Stewart, who fell by a musket shot[13].

The next day, Stewart's body, wrapped in his cloak, was buried in a chest in front of Beckwith's headquarters in the village of Alverca. A quarter of an hour later, the Light Division followed the French towards Guarda. On 1 April they marched to Pega and halted at the River Coa, Opposite them, in Sabugal, a body of the enemy, under General Jean Reynier, was gathered in great force. Wellington decided to attack.

> On 1 April, we again came up with the enemy, who held possession of the town of Sabugal, situated partly upon a hill, with some woodland interspersed about. The rapid River Coa wound between it and the Lisbon side of the country. Here they seemed inclined to make a final stand. On the 3rd, an attack was commenced by our battalions.

The Light Division was in two brigades; the one commanded by Colonel Beckwith was ordered forward by Erskine. It was led by four companies of the 95th with Costello, Kincaid and Simmons. Because of fog, the riflemen missed their direction and crossed the Coa a mile below the ford which had been assigned to them.

Simmons: *"Colonel Beckwith's brigade crossed the river Coa; the sides steep; the 95th led. It was deep and came up to my arm-pits. The officer commanding the French picket ordered his men to fire a few shots and retire."*

> After crossing the river, we advanced up the hill on the other side. Under a fleecy shower of rain, we soon became hotly engaged with the French.

Simmons: *"As soon as the riflemen crossed, they extended and moved up the steep hills, covered with mountain heath and brushwood. On approaching the first chain of heights, the enemy commenced skirmishing. By this time the 43rd Light Infantry and Caçadores had joined us. The enemy were driven from one chain of hills to another for*

Sabugal on the River Coa.
By Major T St. Clair. Published by C Turner, 19 August 1815. ©British Museum

two miles, when suddenly, on gaining the top of a third chain of hills, our whole line in skirmishing order came in contact with seven columns of French. The company I was leading on... owing to the situation of the ground, came literally within twenty yards of a column before we could see it. Guess my astonishment! The most hideous yelling assailed my ears, the French drumming, shaking their bayonets, and calling out 'Long life to the Emperor Napoleon'."

Sabugal today. The French positions were on the slope to the right.

Kincaid: *"A thick drizzling rain now came on, in consequence of which the 3rd Division, which was to have made a simultaneous attack to our left, missed their way, and a brigade of dragoons under Sir William Erskine, who were to have covered our right, went Lord knows where but certainly not into the fight, although they started at the same time that we did and had the music of our rifles to guide them; and, even the 2nd Brigade of our Division could not afford us any support for nearly an hour, so that we were thus unconsciously left with about fifteen hundred men, in the very impertinent attempt to carry a formidable position, on which stood as many thousands."*

Through some mistake, we were left almost unsupported. The enemy were at least four or five times our number, and they compelled us to retire twice before their overwhelming masses.

Simmons: *'Luckily, the ground was thinly patched with stout trees, which afforded our men good shelter in retiring... Nothing could intimidate our brave fellows, retiring and keeping up a hot and destructive fire upon the enemy's close column, so as to annoy them very materially... Colonel Beckwith rode along the line in the most cool and gallant style, cautioning the men to be steady, knowing well that if we maintained our ground for one hour or so, we should have two or three divisions of our army to our support, and that if we did not keep our ground the whole brigade would be drowned or bayoneted... Finding the enemy did not advance farther, the Colonel formed part of the 43rd Regiment, our little line of skirmishers moving up at the same time and making a desperate attack upon a gun that was keeping up a very destructive fire. Every one near the gun was bayoneted or shot. We were driven back, and we attacked again, but were obliged to retire, when luckily the other part of our Division moved up, and the gun was ours.*

Led on by our gallant Colonel, we fixed swords, came to the charge and drove them up the hill before us. There a strong reserve was prepared for our reception. A third time we were obliged to give ground, then our 2nd Brigade came to our aid. We again dashed at them, carried the position, and after a hard contest, obliged the enemy to retreat with the utmost precipitation, leaving behind them a howitzer, which had been twice taken and retaken. No one that day could have observed our Colonel during the heat of the action, and not have admired his cool and soldier-like bearing.

"Steady lads; show no hurry," was his cheering exhortation when we were obliged to retreat. And it was accompanied by a smile, although the blood flowed copiously from a wound he had received across his forehead.

Never, perhaps, in any action, did the Rifles display more consummate tact and resolution than in this. Lord Wellington was too just to pass over their services on this occasion, and in general orders passed a high encomium upon the gallantry of Colonel Beckwith and the brigade under his command. But we lost a fine young lieutenant in the Honourable Duncan Arbuthnot, whose head was smashed by a round-shot[14].

Simmons: *'From the enemy's numbers being very much superior, the combat was kept up very warmly until General Picton's 3rd Division came up and pushed out its light companies on their flank. The 5th Division, under General Dunlop, soon crossed the bridge and passed through Sabugal. The enemy gave way and went off in confusion. The rain now fell in torrents and materially assisted their retreat."*

At the conclusion of the battle the rain poured down in torrents, and obliged us to take such shelter as the walls and trees around afforded. The enemy were in rapid retreat, and we should, in all probability, have continued in pursuit, but for the exhausted state of the men.

While endeavouring to obtain shelter, Lord Wellington rode up. Knowing the chief business of the day had fallen upon our brigade, he ordered us into the town. We arrived just in time to prevent the 5th Division from supplanting us. They were obliged to retrace their steps, which they did with much grumbling and discontent.

It was dark before we got into the house appropriated for us. Myself and one or two others turned into a small square room, the floor of which was covered with straw. Though wetted through to the skin I soon fell into a sound sleep, but was quickly awakened by a hurried exclamation from a man who had just entered the room with a light. On looking around for the cause of his surprise, I beheld a stiff and naked corpse, brutally defaced, placed upright against the wall of the room. At the same moment, in the act of turning, I placed my hand on the clammy features of another body, partly concealed under the straw, and across which I had actually been sleeping. We found four bodies altogether, evidently Portuguese, and all of them bearing the usual proofs of French retaliation.

The next morning (4 April), the Light Division marched from Sabugal to Quadrazais, Vale de Espinho, and through Alfaiates to the village of Forcalhos, close to the Spanish border. During this march, they saw neither the enemy nor their own commissariat. Harry Smith: *"We were literally starving. That old rogue Picton had seized the supplies of the Light Division for his 3rd."*

On the 5th, they marched across the border to Albergueria, where they were able to get something to eat. The enemy withdrew across the Agueda.

The next day [6 April], Massena evacuated Portugal, with the exception of Almeida. In a short time, we took up our old quarters at Gallegos, where we found many of our acquaintances of the preceding year. The enemy retired upon Ciudad Rodrigo, and we were suffered for a while to recruit our strength.

The French army retired towards Salamanca leaving a garrison of 1,000 men in Almeida.

CHAPTER 11

Fuentes de Oñoro
8 April - 10 May 1811

On 8 April, the Light Division entered Fuentes de Oñoro. Kincaid: *"Fuentes, which was our first resting-place, was a very handsome village, and every family so well known to the Light Division, that no matter into which quarter the billet fell, the individual was received as an old and approved friend."*

The riflemen took up their old line of outposts upon the Agueda, some of them occupying the villages of Gallegos and Espeja. Meanwhile, the fortress of Almeida was being blockaded by General Pack's Portuguese brigade, and some British battalions. On 10 April, two companies of the 95th were dispatched to Almeida to try to shoot the enemy's cattle as they grazed outside the walls, but it was such a hazardous venture, inviting cannon-shot from the town, that they were withdrawn. About 16 April, the Light Division was ordered to move forward to intercept a French convoy travelling along the road from Salamanca to Ciudad Rodrigo.

Some weeks after our arrival at Gallegos, on afternoon parade, Colonel Beckwith issued orders that we were to prepare for marching in an hour without our knapsacks. A forced march was to be undertaken to prevent the French throwing supplies into Rodrigo, and he therefore desired those who were sick or weakly to fall out. On hearing this, several skulkers in the regiment fell out of the ranks, but were obliged to fall in again. Passing down the regiment, Colonel Beckwith noticed that a man named Burke, who was noted for his daring courage, did not look well.

"You look very ill, Burke," said the Colonel, and advised him to remain behind.

"No sir," replied Burke, casting a look of contempt on the skulkers, "I am certainly not well, but I still have the heart of a man, and will keep up with my comrades as long as my legs will carry me."

The Colonel evinced a melancholy satisfaction at this reply. "I am sorry that the sneaking propensities of others should compel a brave man to act against himself," he said.

Burke was afterwards one of the forlorn hope at Ciudad Rodrigo, Badajoz and San Sebastian, through the successive horrors of which he lived, only to fall mortally wounded at Quatre Bras, previous to the battle of Waterloo[1].

Early in the morning, our expeditionary party marched in the direction of Rodrigo, fording the River Agueda on our way. But the enemy convoy had escaped us and, harassed to death, we had the pleasure of retracing our steps not a whit wiser than we went. In re-crossing the river, a poor fellow of our company, spent with fatigue, was carried off his legs and drowned. Another man would have shared the same fate but for Brigade-Major Mellish, who swam his horse to his assistance and saved him.

Towards the end of April, Wellington learned that Massena was advancing from Salamanca with a view to relieving Almeida. Kincaid: *"The French army began to assemble on the opposite bank of the Agueda to attempt the relief of the garrison, while ours began to assemble in position at Fuentes de Oñoro to dispute it... As a general action seemed now to be inevitable, we anxiously longed for the return of Lord Wellington, who had been suddenly called to the corps of the army under Marshal Beresford near Badajoz, as we would rather see his long nose in the fight than a reinforcement of 10,000 men any day."*

On 1 May, Massena's forces started massing in the vicinity of Almeida, intent on pushing Wellington's army back across the Coa. They moved forward, forcing the Light Division to retire from the villages of Gallegos and Espeja onto Fuentes de Oñoro, where the British and Portuguese troops were already in position for the battle. Don Julian Sanchez's guerillas were also present, ready to act upon the enemy's flank. The centre of the allied position was behind Fuentes de Oñoro, the left upon Fort Conception, and the right upon the Portuguese village of Nave de Haver, a distance of seven miles. The Light Division was posted in reserve as a flying corps ready to be despatched to any point in this extended position.

On 2 May, amid the granite built houses and walls of the village of Fuentes de Oñoro, the fighting began between Massena's light troops and the 3rd Division. It escalated to involve reinforcements on both sides. The firing did not cease until daybreak on the 3rd. Being in the reserve, the Light Division took no part, but the battle was not over.

On 4 May, about 9.30am, our advance videttes were observed circling at a trot, one to the right, and the other to the left, which meant that bodies of infantry and cavalry were advancing. The bugle immediately sounded the assemblée, and our Division quickly assembled on its alarm post on the Gallegos road.

My company was attached to the 14th Light Dragoons, then under the orders of General Slade, who commanded the cavalry brigade. He ordered them to take ground to the right, and deploy into line in the rear of a rivulet, which flowed between us and the French. In a few minutes the enemy's cavalry emerged from a wood in our front, where they had formed in close columns and halted, throwing out strong bodies of skirmishers.

A sharp conflict ensued betwixt the cavalries, but the enemy were evidently awaiting the concentration of their advancing columns from Ciudad Rodrigo. General Slade ordered all of us to retire. This was quietly effected by the cavalry in echelons of squadrons, with them covering us on the road towards Nave de Haver. The enemy retained their old position near the wood.

One squadron of the 14th was stationed on the verge of another wood, on the right of Fuentes, as an advanced picket, but was withdrawn at the close of evening. It joined the regiments in bivouac within some stone wall enclosures, near Vilar Formoso. During the night, some of the dragoons discovered the resting-place of a sutler, who had just arrived from Abrantes with a string of mules laden with rum, wine, aguardiente and sardines, a species of red-herring which was then considered a great luxury. Through the camp, news of such a neighbour flew on eagle wings, but in low whispers, lest the slumbers of the chief should be disturbed to check the merry-making. But the secret was soon discovered, no doubt occasioned by the uproarious burst of merriment and songs which pealed from fire to fire. These were the general characteristics of the British soldier on the eve of a battle, but on this occasion they were heightened by the liquor, and were louder than usual.

The officers, awakened from their slumbers, could not for some moments conceive the cause of what they heard, so General Slade, with lungs that roused the camp as effectively as a thirteen-inch shell exploding amongst them, called for the regimental Sergeant-Major, Sharp. When Sharp made his appearance, it was discovered that he had partaken too freely of the sutler's strong waters, and was immediately placed under arrest. A non-commissioned officer was ordered to bundle off the sutler and his mules to a safe distance, and place a line of sentries so that no one might come in or go out of the camp. The noise and hilarity soon ceased and the merry-makers dispersed. In a few minutes they were outstretched and asleep under the cover of the dry walls.

On 4 May, Massena, having gained no advantage in three days of fighting, had reconnoitred Wellington's position. That same day, Craufurd resumed command of the Light Division.

Early on the morning of the 5th, our company was ordered to join the battalion. We did so, and took up our position to the left of the ruins of Fort Conception, which lay near the main road to Almeida, the siege of which place the French seemed anxious to raise.

At an early hour, General Craufurd made his reappearance amongst us from England, and was welcomed with much enthusiasm by the Division. Although a strict disciplinarian, the men knew his value in the field too well not to testify their satisfaction at his return. The Caçadores caused much laughter among us, for the moment they caught sight of him, they shouted out in Portuguese, "Long live General Craufurd, who takes care of our bellies!" In other words, while under his command, they got their rations regularly! The General seemed highly pleased, and bowed repeatedly with his hat off as he rode down the ranks.

The whole of the British were under arms at daybreak expecting an attack. The suspense was short, for very soon a heavy cannonading was heard on our right, in which direction we were immediately ordered.

Simmons: *"This morning we observed that the enemy had concentrated a large force of all arms in the vicinity of Fuentes de Oñoro. The Light Division was moved to the right and also some distance to its front, and entered a large wood, throwing out skirmishers to our front, as it was expected.... that a large force was concentrating there under cover. Their skirmishers kept up a fire, but did not attempt to drive us out until a large body of cavalry had debouched some distance to our right. When clear of the wood, they wheeled to their right so as to intercept our retrograde movement. The enemy's skirmishers then followed us up, keeping up a smart fire until we left the wood. We formed column at quarter-distance ready to form square at any moment if charged by cavalry, and in this way we marched to that part of the position where the Guards were formed in line. A body of cavalry hovered about us, but from our formidable appearance and the steady manner with which the movement was conducted, the enemy did not charge us. A company of Guards wheeled back, their battalion being in line; we passed through and then halted in column and became a support for that part of our line."*

Soon afterwards, O'Hare took four or five companies of riflemen to occupy some rugged ground on the Turones river between the 1st and the 7th Divisions. Simmons: *"The enemy attempted to penetrate this valley, but were kept in check by our men, and some light companies of the 1st Division."* Simmons and Leach do not appear to have been part of this group, but Costello probably was.

We passed the Guards of the 1st Division, entrenched behind the town of Fuentes. We immediately occupied some old dry walls considerably in advance, and facing the enemy's left. A fine extended plain lay between us, with a wood on the French side, of which the enemy had possession. In front of this a regiment of cavalry was conspicuously formed, a troop of which came trotting leisurely towards us to reconnoitre our position.

This movement induced a corresponding one from some of our dragoons. Both parties threw out their videttes, and remained halted with some 400 yards of ground between them.

One of their videttes, after being posted facing an English dragoon, of the 14th or 16th (for we had only those two light dragoon regiments, and the German Hussars, with us at the time), displayed an instance of individual gallantry in which the French, to do them justice, were seldom wanting. Waving his long straight sword, the Frenchman rode within sixty yards of our dragoon, and challenged him to single combat. We expected to see our cavalry man engage his opponent, sword in hand, but instead he unslung his carbine and fired at the Frenchman Not a whit dismayed, the Frenchman shouted out so that everyone could hear him:

"*Venez avec le sabre: je suis prêt pour Napoleon a la belle France.*"

In vain did he endeavour to induce the Englishman to a personal conflict, and after having endured two or three shots from his carbine, the Frenchman rode proudly back to his ground, cheered even by our own men. We were much amused by his gallantry, and hissed our own dragoon who, it was afterwards stated to the credit of the gallant regiment he belonged to, was a recruit.

Just after this, a smart action commenced in the wood, and our company was ordered to take ground to the front, where the 85th Regiment, in their conspicuous red dresses, were being very roughly handled by the enemy in this their first engagement since arriving in the country. They were opposed to the well-trained and veteran French *tirailleurs* [sharpshooters], so it is no wonder that this gallant regiment should suffer so severely. When we came up, our practised fellows in their dark clothing, soon turned back the advancing French with the murderous nature of our arms. They retreated gradually before us, and through the wood on the plain that leads to Nave de Haver. Then a loud cheering to the right attracted our attention, and we saw our 1st Heavy Dragoons charge a French cavalry regiment. This was the first charge of cavalry most of us had ever seen and we were all much interested in it. The French skirmishers extended against us seemed to feel the same, and by general consent both parties suspended firing while the affair of dragoons was going on.

The English and French cavalry met in the most gallant manner, and with the greatest show of resolution. The shock of the first collision seemed terrific, and many men and horses fell on both sides. Having ridden through and past each other, they now wheeled round again and a second charge followed, accompanied by some very pretty sabre-practice, by which many saddles were emptied. English and French chargers galloped about the field without riders. These occupied our attention, and the French skirmishers and ourselves were soon engaged in pursuing them, each nation endeavouring to secure the chargers of the opposite one as legal spoil. While engaged in this chase we frequently became intermixed, and laughed at the different accidents that occurred in our pursuit.

119

I secured a very splendid charger when, chancing to turn my head, I perceived that the French were playing a deep game and had moved a regiment of infantry, and some cavalry, through the wood in our rear. The alarm was immediately given. I was obliged to part with my horse as our company, which was foremost, had to run for our lives into a square formed by the 52nd, who were close to the foot guards. The cavalry did not pursue us, but their artillery opened up on the 52nd's square, and did some execution.

Such incidents were very enlivening for our enemy was a noble one, never permitting us to flag for want of stimuli, and keeping us always on the look out. We anticipated little terror from capture, and although they were our roughest antagonists, they were such a chivalrous and generous opposition, that our men even had a kind of respect for a wound inflicted by a Frenchman.

Our next attempt was upon the left of Fuentes, where one company was detached while the remainder of the regiment was ordered to take possession of the town. The section to which I belonged was posted near the banks of the River Duas Casas. The 79th Highlanders had suffered very severely here, and the place was strewn about with their bodies. The poor fellows were unused to skirmishing, and instead of occupying the houses in the neighbourhood, and firing from the windows, I heard they had exposed themselves by firing in sections. The French, who still occupied part of the town, had not escaped a rough handling, as their dead also evinced.

During the latter part of the day, the enemy had made some prisoners, who we saw as they were marched among their lines. As a party was going over a small bridge that crossed the Duas Casas near a mill, one prisoner, who was loitering in the rear, turning suddenly upon the Frenchman behind him, and threw him into the water. He made a dash for our position in a determined attempt to obtain his liberty, but there were several of the French between him and us, and we had the mortification of seeing the poor fellow recaptured, without being able to render him any assistance. We could see by his kilt that he belonged to the 79th regiment.

Simmons: *"Night put a stop to further havoc, and the British soldiers rested upon the field of battle with that proud feeling which a man only can have under such circumstances - of having fulfilled his duty to his country by repulsing a much larger force of cavalry and infantry at all points."*

They had done more than that; they had thwarted Massena's attempts to throw them back over the Coa, and had prevented him from relieving Almeida. But there was a cost. Verner reports that the British casualties were 9 officers and 189 men killed, 59 officers and 971 wounded, and 6 officers and 287 men missing. The French lost 2,192 men. The losses in the Light Division were few: the lst battalion Rifles had one sergeant and 6 men wounded.

The old stone bridge over the Duas Casas at Fuentes de Oñoro.

That same evening, the enemy evacuated the town, and a flag of truce was sent to us to bury the dead. Some idea may be formed of the loss sustained by the 79th alone when you hear that, while occupied in this melancholy duty, a man of our company had his arms full of sable plumes taken from their bonnets, which were strewn about the town.

The British Casualties were 9 officers and 189 men killed, 59 officers and 971 wounded, and 6 officers and 287 men missing. The French lost 2,192 men. The 1st battalion 95th had only one sergeant and 6 men wounded.

That night, the Light Division supplied the pickets.

Our company was on picket one side of a mill dam. Tidey[2], a blacksmith of ours, had erected his forge in the old mill close by, and was at work shoeing the officers' horses. The opposing lines of sentries were very close to each other, the French divided from us only by a narrow plank thrown across the mill-dam. The French sentry, who had crossed the plank to light his pipe, was standing carelessly chatting with me, when who should I see approaching but General Craufurd. He had come to inquire if Tidey had shod his horse. The Frenchman's red wings [shoulder epaulettes] soon attracted the notice of the General, who glanced sternly at him.

"Who the devil are you talking with, rifleman?" he enquired.

I informed him that it was a French sentry, who had come over for a light for his pipe.

"Indeed. Let him go about his business for he has no right here," replied Craufurd. "Nor we either," he added in a low whisper to his aide-de-camp, and away he walked.

It was expected that the fight would be renewed the next morning, but, says Simmons, "the enemy we found, when visible, to be not inclined to fight us. They had been busily occupied in getting their wounded and heavy guns away to the rear, as well as encumbrances, in order to be able, if pressed, to make a clean start and be off."

The British army remained in the neighbourhood of Fuentes de Oñoro for a few days, which was very unpleasant for them. On 8 May, Simmons wrote: "The weather is very warm, and great numbers of dead, all stripped naked, were spread in every direction and swollen in a disgusting manner from putrefaction, and exhaling most offensive smells. Such is the general result of a hard-fought battle when the dead are not buried."

Two days later, the enemy moved off, and the Light Division again went into quarters at Gallegos and Espeja.

Our battalion remained in the suburbs of Fuentes a few days. The enemy, who had desisted from their attempt to relieve Almeida, retired. We followed them and took up our quarters at Gallegos.

Immediately on our arrival, anxious to know the fate of Sergeant-Major Sharp of the 14th Light Dragoons, I called on Corporal Henley of the same regiment, who was an old friend. This veteran soldier was afterwards promoted to the rank of Sergeant-Major, and through the interest of his old commander, Sir Hussey Vivian, now [ie in 1841] holds a situation in the Tower, where we frequently meet. Henley gave me the following particulars of that gallant and highly distinguished regiment:

"On the 5th, early in the morning, after you left us, we assembled on our respective alarm posts, which at daylight we found to be none other than the position so gloriously contested and known as Fuentes de Oñoro. The regiment formed in close columns and dismounted. The commissariat arrived with their mules, and rations were issued to both man and horse: to many it proved to be their last. During the distribution of corn, the horses of Lieutenant Shields were forgotten, and in order to make good the deficiency, it was necessary to make a collection from each dragoon. One of these, named Trowers, under the influence of the preceding night's liquor, refused to allow any of his corn to be taken. Drawing his sword, he declared with an oath, that he would cut down the first man who dared to take a grain from his horse. He was placed under arrest, and a drum-head court-martial instantly summoned, at which was also arraigned the unfortunate Sergeant-Major Sharp.

"Meanwhile, the action was becoming general along the lines, and Captain Bull's troop of artillery, then on our right, marked with accurate skill the movements of the enemy who, in their turn, did not allow us to remain silent spectators: their round shot measured with equal exactness the standing of our columns. The court-martial being closed, the troops stood to their horses, and the proceedings were read. The Sergeant-Major was reduced to the rank and pay of a private sentinel, and his bars were immediately cut off. The dragoon was sentenced to receive 300 lashes, and a gun from Captain Bull's train was brought to the flank of the regiment for him to be tied to. As this was being done, one of the staff came galloping up, his horse covered with foam, bearing orders for the regiment to take ground to the right and charge to cover our flank, which was falling back harassed by the enemy's cavalry. The words 'Stand to your horses. Mount. Three right. Gallop,' followed in quick succession, and like a shot from a six-pounder, we left the scene of military discipline.

"In the confusion, the prisoner, half accoutred, made a leap into his saddle. He drew his sword, and giving his horse a spur, rushed into the ranks. Unable to prevent him, the non-commissioned officer, in whose charge he had been left, galloped after him and mixed in the attack. This occurrence saved the poor fellow from the disgrace of the lash, but his good fortune did not continue because he was one of the brave men who fell a short time afterwards, in the gallant charge made by a squadron of ours, on two of the enemy's guns.

"On our arrival on the right, our infantry had formed square and were falling back, menaced by numerous cavalry, and our right flank was turned. Our guns opened between the interval of squares, upon their advancing columns, when one squadron of 1st Royal Dragoons, and one of our regiments, led by Major Mills, charged. Their cavalry were driven back, and many prisoners taken. The infantry continued to fall back with as much steadiness and order as if in review.

"I must here relate," continued Henley, with deep emotion, "an event which at the time filled all who were present with sorrow, and which I shall never forget. General Slade, observing the numerous cavalry against which his brigade had to contend, advised the officer in command not to allow their ranks to be weakened by conducting prisoners to the rear. After disarming them, they were to let them proceed of their own accord. It was not uncommon therefore to observe groups of French dragoons riding quietly to the rear, looking for someone to take them in charge. A hussar of the 3rd [1st?] Germans, having taken a prisoner, ordered him to fall back. The latter, having ridden some little distance as directed, suddenly applied both spurs to his horse and made a detour to his regiment. Seeing this, the German was quickly in pursuit, and upon closing with him, fired his pistol. The dragoon fell dead from his horse.

"The hussar having secured the Frenchman's rein conveyed him some little distance to the rear, and proceeded to take off his valise. Overhauling the contents, he discovered a letter and read it. He was stupefied with horror: it was from his father, for it was his own brother he had killed. He sat on his horse for some minutes, motionless and speechless, then big tears rolled down his veteran cheek. 'The king has commanded, and my God will forgive me,' he exclaimed, and applying his spurs, he rushed headlong into the battle.

"A few days later we met a patrol of his regiment near Gallegos, and enquired after the unfortunate hussar. We were informed that he too numbered among the dead that day, not far from the corpse of his brother."[3]

CHAPTER 12

Almeida and El Bodon
10 May 1811 - January 1812

The Light Division returned to its quarters in Gallegos on 10 May.

Almeida was being closely invested by the 5th Division, while we in
front watched the main army. Early on the morning of 10 May [11
May?] we were ordered to get under arms and march towards Barba del
Puerco, the scene of the skirmish the year before. Near the town we
heard some smart firing and halted. We were informed that the French
garrison at Almeida, after blowing up the walls at night, had evacuated
the town, and cut their way through the blockading force.

The French garrison at Almeida, consisting of 1,400 men under
General Brenier, had mined the works, broken out, and escaped
across the bridge at Barba del Puerco, losing 360 men in skirmishes
on the way.

I believe that the brigades of the 5th Division had been doing duty
by turns, and that the brigade containing the 2nd Regiment (whose
badge was a lamb), and the 4th Regiment (whose badge was a lion),
happened to be on picket when the French made their way through the
investing force. This gave rise to a verse that became very common
amongst the troops. The lines were as follows:

> "The lion went to sleep,
> And the lambs were at play;
> The eagle spread her wings,
> And from Almeida flew away."

Although these regiments were rendered somewhat unpopular from
this circumstance, there were not two finer in the service. While they
were quartered at Colchester, our battalion had become particularly
fond of the 4th, who christened us the 'young 4th'. The death of their
Colonel [Bevan] who, from an oversensitive feeling of honour, shot
himself shortly after this unlucky affair, was generally regretted[1].

In April 1812, after the siege of Badajoz in which he was wounded,
Costello was sent into hospital, where the English and French
wounded were intermingled. In the next bed was a Frenchman who

could speak English. He was one of the garrison which broke out from Almeida, and he related his experiences to Costello:

"A few evenings before the evacuation of the fortress, an officer from Massena entered the town in the guise of a peasant. His gave orders to the governor to undermine and blow up the walls, and with the garrison, to cut his way through the British lines. The message was received with delight because the distresses of the besieged were excessive. We had seen and felt innumerable hardships and were so reduced by famine that, for food, we had to slaughter the horses and mules.

"General Brenier was in command. He had been a prisoner of the English some years before, but had broken his parole and escaped, so he was more anxious about capture than us because he knew that if he was retaken, he would in all probability be shot. On receipt of the order, he drew from us an oath to die or effect our purpose, and for several days, as a first step, we were employed undermining the walls. These were soon hollowed and loaded in fourteen different places, linked by trains of gunpowder.

"The evening of the evacuation, after destroying the stores and spiking the guns, the whole garrison of 700-800 men assembled in one of the squares. At about midnight, we slowly moved through the gates. The first to oppose our progress was a picket of Portuguese who we bayoneted in an instant. Just then the mines began exploding. There was a low grumbling, as if of an earthquake, and a few seconds later, the whole citadel rose in the air, and descended in shivering and blackened masses.

"The noise of the explosion brought the British divisions to their arms, and our forlorn body dashed through your closing columns. It was a desperate moment for we were starved, but we gained new strength from each reverse, and despite the numbers of well-fed British opposed to us, cut our way through the living wall. We gained the approach to San Felices. Here the inequalities of the ground fortunately and effectually kept off your cavalry, and after a few more trifling encounters, we reached the grand army. We had no sooner arrived within hail of our comrades than the whole location rung with one universal shout of enthusiasm. Our General was carried about on the men's shoulders, and the day became one of joy throughout the camp."

This was related in the most spirited manner, as you would expect from a soldier of the Emperor, whose very name took the place of every other feeling. He spoke also of Marshal Ney, who in his estimation, was second only to Napoleon.

Soon after the escape of the garrison at Almeida, Massena was relieved of his command and replaced by Marshal Auguste Marmont who, at 36, was twenty years younger.

*Serra de Estrella. The march of the baggage following the army, 16 May 1811
By Major T St. Clair. Published by C Turner, 28 August 1815. ©British Museum*

Troops bivouacked near Vila Velha on the evening of 19 May 1811
By Major T St. Clair. Published by C Turner, 12 June 1813. ©British Museum

The evacuation of the fortress of Almeida rendered the presence of our Division thereabouts unnecessary, so another movement was made to the southward of General Hill[2], who commanded the 2nd Division, at this time menaced by a very superior force of the French.

Wellington had sent an army to the Alentejo region of Spain. It was commanded by William Carr Beresford, the Marshal of the Portuguese Army, and he was besieging the Spanish citadel of Badajoz, then occupied by the French. On 10 May, Marshal Soult, who had assembled 25,000 men in Seville, marched against Beresford to relieve Badajoz, and on 16 May, a very bloody battle was fought between them at Albuera. The outcome was indecisive but Soult was unable to relieve Badajoz, to which Wellington now sent his 3rd and 7th Divisions to invest. Ordered to follow them, the Light Division retired from Gallegos and Espeja on 6 June. On the second night of their march (7 June), there was an alarm in the camp:

On the first day's march we passed through Sabugal, crossed the Coa, and encamped in a chestnut wood, close to our former scene of action. Here a very strange panic occurred, which could have been disastrous. About midnight, I was stretched on my back under some boughs of a tree, admiring the comet that was creating such a sensation in Europe from its nearness to the earth[3], when a general outcry was raised in the Division that the French were upon us. I started up, and seized my rifle. The different regiments were assembling in the greatest disorder, and the general cries of alarm on all sides, induced a terror that was never felt in battle. I observed General Craufurd, desiring all whom he met to fall in and load.

In a short while the panic ceased, and we all looked foolish at such a great ado about nothing. Some attributed the cause to French spies having got among us, others to bullocks knocking down several stands of arms while grazing by. Some blamed the comet. Among the latter was that worthy, Tom Crawley, who stoutly contended that the comet would shortly drop down and burn up that part of Europe, and that it was a sign we ought to leave the country. (It was shrewdly suspected that, at this time, Tom had a great desire to turn his steps homewards.)

Kincaid confirms that the incident was caused by bullocks: *"In the course of this very dark night, we had one of those ridiculous false alarms which will sometimes happen in the best organised body. Some bullocks strayed by accident amongst the piles of arms, the falling clatter of which frightened them so much that they went galloping over the sleeping soldiers. The officers' baggage-horses broke from their moorings, and joined in the general charge, and a cry immediately arose that it was the French cavalry. The different regiments stood to their arms and formed squares, looking as sharp as thunder for something to fire at, and it was a considerable time before the cause of the row could be traced. The different followers of the army, in the meantime, were scampering off to the rear, spreading the most frightful reports."*

Simmons does not mention the alarm, but refers instead to the graves of some of his comrades, who fell at Sabugal two months before. *"We bivouacked in a wood of chestnut-trees, where several of our brave fellows had been buried, and whose bones had been dug by wolves and were strewn above their graves."*

Over the next two weeks, their marches, which owing to the heat of the day were usually undertaken at night, took them through Meimoa, São Miguel de Acha, Escalos de Cima, Castelo Branco, Nisa, Alpalhão, and Portalegre, to an encampment upon the River Caia.

> We continued our march through Castelo Branco, Portalegre, and encamped on a low ground called Monte Reguengo, on the right of the road leading to Campo Maior.

Their encampment was about three miles in the rear of Campo Maior. Kincaid: *"This was a sandy, unsheltered district; and the weather was so excessively hot, that we had no enjoyment but that of living three parts of the day up to the neck in a pool of water."*

The region was just as unhealthy as it had been when they camped there in the autumn of 1809.

> We called it the furnace camp, and were here about six weeks, during which time we suffered dreadfully for want of rations, and from the oppressive heat of the weather.
>
> While we were at Reguengo, Tom Crawley imagined himself poisoned. He gorged himself on some pork and caravançes (a sort of pulse), and was suddenly seized with violent paroxysms of pain. Old Doctor Burke[4] was sent for. He found Crawley on the ground groaning most piteously. He had swelled to an enormous size, and two of his comrades were busy rubbing the lower part of his belly. The Doctor, who fancied that two years in Spain had brought Tom's stomach to suit the convenience of the commissary, commenced a volley of abuse:
>
> "You cannibal, what garbage have you been swallowing to leave you in this condition!"
>
> "Oh, murther, do you hear him, boys," roared Tom, as he turned his eyes towards his tormentor. "By the mother of God, sir, this infernal country will kill us all. May a curse fall on it. When I came into it I had a stomach like any other Christian, but now? Oh God, have mercy on me poor stomach! For want of Christian food, it is turning into a scavenger's cart, obliged to take in every rubbish."
>
> The Doctor, who seldom did anything by halves, gave him an emetic sufficient to physic a dromedary. Crawley, who never feared death on the field, hesitated meeting him in quarters and so, between the groans he uttered, he made the most vehement promises, if spared, to mend

his sinful life. Never did such a pious scene appear more ludicrous; our men were in convulsed with laughter[5].

On 20 July, after several weeks encamped around Badajoz, and in response to the movement of the French troops on the northern frontier, the soldiers of the Light Division began retracing their steps towards Ciudad Rodrigo. That same day, John Cooke, a junior officer in 43rd Regiment, saw them for the first time. On 28 June, he had landed in Lisbon from which he marched to join them:

"On 20 July we descended into the valley and, at the edge of a wood, awaited the coming of the Division from an advanced camp on their way to Castelo de Vide. Every eye was on the stretch. In the distance we descried a cloud of dust rolling towards us, the bright sparkling rays of the sunbeams playing on the soldiers' breast plates, when suddenly the leading regiment of the Light Division burst forth. Their bronzed countenances and light knapsacks, and their order of march, all united to inspire a conviction that their early discipline had not only been maintained amidst privations, battles, and camps, but had become matured by experience. They had traversed mountains, and forded rivers; the grim and icy hand of death had grasped many in the unhealthy marshes of the Alentejo, and with sure effect had scattered balls amidst their ranks without distinction, yet the remainder of these veterans were still bent onwards, to gather fresh laurels in the rugged and uncertain paths of fortune. Seven regiments of light infantry and riflemen defiled before us with their thread-bare jackets, their brawny necks loosened from the stocks, their wide and patched trousers of various colours, and brown-barrelled arms slung over their shoulders, or carelessly held in their hands, whilst a joyous buzz ran through the cross-belted ranks, as their soldier-like faces glanced towards us to greet many of their old comrades now about to join in their arduous toils after a long separation. A cloud of dust alone marked their further progress as they receded from our view. Following in succession, we brought up the rear."

The Division marched at night, sometimes bivouacking on the same ground on which they had bivouacked only a month before. On 22 July, they reached Portalegre, and on 23rd Castelo de Vide, where they remained for six days in cantonments. On 30 July, they crossed the Tagus at Vila Velha and marched via Castelo Branco, Bemposta and Quadrazais to Fuenteguinaldo, where they arrived on 10 August.

On 11 August, the French outposts south of Ciudad Rodrigo were driven in, and the Light Division occupied the villages of Martiago, El Saugo, Lariquella [Herguijuela?] and Villarego, thus blockading the fortress on that side. Costello's battalion encamped at Martiago and Lariquella.

On 21 August, four companies of the 3rd battalion of the 95th, under Lt.-Col. Barnard, arrived from Cadiz where they had been stationed. With them was John Wilkie, Costello's friend. They were placed in Colonel Beckwith's Brigade, and on 29 August, the right wing of the 1st battalion, and four companies of the 3rd battalion, marched to Atalaya, in front of the River Vadilla. Within weeks, the 3rd battalion riflemen began to fall sick. Many were hospitalised, including John Wilkie.

In July, we returned to assist in the blockade of Ciudad Rodrigo, and took up a position at a village called Atalaya, at the base of the Sierra de Gata, a range of mountains. Here we were joined by our 3rd battalion under the command of Colonel Barnard, a gallant and very distinguished officer, now known as General Sir Andrew Barnard. Colonel Beckwith had to retire through ill health[6].

Here also Lord Wellington's staff frequently went out hunting. The place abounded in wolves and wild boars so a great deal of amusement was experienced in this sport. They generally had five or six riflemen to assist. Along with others of our battalion, I often had the good fortune to be selected to attend his Lordship's staff in these excursions. The chase was very exciting, particularly from the ferocious nature of the game we sought. The first wild boar I saw was a huge fellow, with tusks of a most alarming size. We fired several shots, and the hounds pursued him, but he escaped. One day we came upon three young wolf cubs, the old ones having abandoned them on our approach. These we presented to one of our officers. They remained in his possession for a long time, and became as docile and playful as kittens.

We were also reinforced by a batch of recruits from England. One, Tommy Searchfield, was a character well known to all the Light Brigade. This gentleman was a squat, square little fellow who had formerly been a 'middy' in the Royal Navy, but had come over to us as a cadet. Tommy's lessons had been learned under the immortal Nelson and he was accustomed to meeting his enemies 'muzzle to muzzle', so whenever we were given the least intimation of the presence of the French, he would imagine them almost passing through the loopholes, or our 'ports' as he termed them. On one occasion he bawled aloud, 'to quarters', and to our surprise, and that of the inhabitants, he seized hold of a bell-rope suspended outside the church of the village, and ran up it like a cat to keep a look-out for the enemy, although we were some distance from them.

For want of better employment, the officers occupied their own and our time erecting sham fortifications in the woods in order to turn Tom's peculiarities to their amusement. Searchfield, however, became awake to them. His original good-natured simplicity gave way to experience, and he gently informed his tormentors that he kept a clean brace of pistols about him, at any time at their service. This unexpected show of pluck made his teasers less gibing. Tommy took his proper position and, I believe, became as respectable as any of them. He subsequently obtained a lieutenancy[7].

At Atalaya, we were very much in the advance of the main army, and the distance made it difficult for the commissariat to forward our rations regularly. As a consequence, we suffered dreadfully through want, and I underwent more privations than at any other place in Spain, except Dough Boy Hill. We had to make up for the deficiency of bread with roasted or boiled chestnuts, of which we were allowed a quart a day each. We eventually had to make an incursion into the mountains, to press the alcaldes of the different villages to supply us.

Kincaid: *"The neighbourhood had been so long the theatre of war, and alternatively forced to supply both armies, that the inhabitants, at length, began to dread starvation themselves, and concealed for their private use, all that remained to them so that, although they were bountiful in their assurances of good wishes, it was impossible to extract a loaf of their good bread. We were so wildly in want that we were obliged to conceal patrols on the different roads and footpaths, for many miles around, to search the peasants passing between the different villages, giving them an order on the commissary for whatever we took from them; and we were not too proud to take even a few potatoes out of an old woman's basket."*

On one of these expeditions, under charge of a quartermaster, we observed two persons mounted on mules, riding towards us. We remarked to one another about the light-haired appearance of one, upon the singularity of a 'fair-complexioned Spaniard', when the fellow suddenly stopped his mule and jumped toward us.

"Oh, by the merciful God, are ye English?" he exclaimed, and was answered in the affirmative by a dozen voices. We discovered that he was one of our cavalrymen, who had been captured by the French at Talavera, and had since escaped[8]. His short stay among the Spaniards had not spoilt his brogue, and he gave us a full account of his adventures in the real Irish accent,

When the enemy took him, he had a slight wound and could not keep up with his captors. Having no mules, the French pressed the strongest and most robust of the inhabitants into carrying the English prisoners on their backs, keeping up their stamina by pricking their hindquarters with bayonets now and then. Our cavalier found himself mounted in this manner. Such close contact brought him into whispering range of the ears of his bearers, and the Spaniards, no doubt as tired of their burden as the burden was of the French, slipped him into a house on the wayside. Having quickly shaved the top of his sconce, they passed him as a priest, and he escaped with them into the mountains. Here he got amongst the guerillas under Don Julian Sanchez, of whom he gave us many amusing anecdotes. They passed him on till he reached us.

As soon as we returned to the village, he reported himself to General Craufurd, who laughed heartily at the details he gave of himself. The General ordered his servant to give him a coat to supply his almost naked condition until he could rejoin his regiment. Meanwhile he was ordered to stop with our company; he took up his quarters in the house with me.

Pigs were kept in great numbers by the farmers of the village, and although they belonged to different owners, they all obeyed one master who, with the alcalde, held absolute sway over man and beast. Early in the morning the animals were assembled by the sounding of a horn, and taken by the master into the woods to feed on acorns. At night, they were driven home again in like manner. The swine-herd's only deputy was a short iron on the end of a long stick, like that used by our shepherds. The response of the animals to the tones of his horn was immediate and remarkable, and if they chanced to be confined at the time, their screams and grunts were so vociferous that they could be heard a mile off. The herdsman could tune up at any time of the day and they would come to him instantly. Seldom were any missing, except now and then when they chanced to fall into the clutches of our riflemen.

Kincaid: *"I know not whether any process was resorted to in the mornings to entice them from their homes to grub up the falling acorns from the beautiful little evergreen oaks which adorned the hills above, but it was a great scene every evening at sunset to go to the top of the village and see about 500 of them coming thundering down the face of the mountain at full speed, and each galloping in to his own door."*

Among other amusements, we used to get up jumping, wrestling, and cuffing-matches with the peasantry, who generally joined most heartily in the fun. One day, a Spaniard of theirs, being overmatched, became exceedingly nettled and commenced quarrelling with Kitchen, one of our sergeants[9]. The result was that they came to blows. After two or three slight cuffs, the peasant fell suddenly and expired. The village became a scene of uproar, and to satisfy the inhabitants, we were obliged to hold a kind of inquest upon him. To their extreme mortification, the barber, or 'Sangrado'[10] of the place, together with our own surgeon, declared that the man had injured the spleen of his stomach, and had died of spite.

Ciudad Rodrigo had been isolated by the retreat of the French army, and about 21 September, Marshal Marmont sent from Salamanca a convoy of provisions to help try to relieve it. To counter this, Wellington assembled his forces at El Bodon where, on 25 September, a battle took place between the two armies. The Light Division, whose troops were deployed in Atalaya and other forward positions in the mountains, was not involved.

About this period Marmont, who had succeeded Massena in command of the French army, concentrated his force, relieved Rodrigo, and made a forward movement, which caused us to retire. This we did at an hour's notice, having heard that the enemy were stirring to beat up our quarters. We fell in at dead of night, and after making a semi-circular march - for there were some fears of the enemy cutting us off - we arrived at El Bodon. There we found the greater part of the army assembled under Lord Wellington, together with the remainder of our Light Division. We were loudly cheered when we appeared because a report had arisen amongst the troops that a battalion had been captured.

After our arrival, most of us were occupied gleaning accounts of the battle of El Bodon, which had been fought the day before. We heard that the 5th and 77th regiments had distinguished themselves resisting the desperate charges made upon them by the Polish Lancers in the French service.

The non-arrival of the Light Division for the battle of El Bodon was blamed on Craufurd's obstinacy in not obeying Wellington's order to join him. Wellington was extremely displeased because he had held his position at El Bodon with extreme difficulty.

After dark, Wellington withdrew his forces to Alfaiates, leaving the Light Division and the 1st German Hussars to hold the heights at Fuenteguinaldo as a rear-guard.

From El Bodon, where we remained some time, we retreated[11] and returned to Fuenteguinaldo.

Marmont, having succeeded in protecting the convoy for Rodrigo, and despite the fact that he was reputed to have 60,000 men at his disposal, did not then wish to engage in a full scale battle with Wellington's army and therefore, at the end of September, he retired into the Spanish interior.

On 1 October, the Light Division marched to Aldeia Velha and moved into cantonments in the adjacent villages. The divisional headquarters was at Alfaiates. By 21 November, in order to more effectively blockade Ciudad Rodrigo, the Division occupied the villages of El Bodon, Martiago, Zamarra, and Atalaya. By 20 December, Ciudad Rodrigo was blockaded completely.

While in these winter quarters on the line of the Agueda, there was little for the soldiers to do, and scant means for the officers to occupy their time, cigars being about their only consolation. However, weather permitting, the officers went hunting, and their evenings were commonly spent dancing with the village girls, who taught Spanish dancing in return for instruction in Irish jigs!

Kincaid: *"In every interval between our active services, we indulged in all manner of childish tricks and amusement, with an avidity and delight of which it is impossible to convey an adequate idea... We invited the villagers every evening, to a dance at our quarters alternately. A Spanish peasant girl has an address about her which I have never met with in the same class of any other country; she at once enters into society with the ease and confidence of one who has been accustomed to it all her life. We used to flourish away at the bolero, fandango, and waltz, and wound up early in the evening with a supper of roasted chestnuts. Our village 'belles', as already stated, made themselves perfectly at home in our society, and we too should have enjoyed theirs for a season but, when month after month, and year after year, continued to roll along, without producing any change, we found that the cherry cheek and sparkling eye of rustic beauty furnished but a very poor apology for the illuminated portion of Nature's fairest works, and ardently longed for an opportunity of once more feasting our eyes on a lady."*

During 1811, the overall strength of the eight companies of the 1st battalion, through casualties and desertion, dwindled from 791 rank and file in January, to 702 in December. Between 17 November and 10 December 1811, four men of the 1st battalion deserted. They were Joseph Almond, William Mills, Malcolm McInnes and Miles Hodgson.

CHAPTER 13

Ciudad Rodrigo
4 - 20 January 1812

In January, having received reinforcements, Wellington had 38,000 British and 22,000 Portuguese troops fit for duty. On the 4th, his army was on the move again, their supplies carried by 10,000 commissariat mules and hundreds of bullock carts. It re-deployed around Ciudad Rodrigo, which was garrisoned by 2,000 French soldiers. The day of the march was cold and stormy, with incessant rain. To get to their new quarters at El Bodon, La Encina and Pastores, the Light Division had to ford the Agueda, which was so swollen that it came up to Simmons' shoulders:

'The men were obliged to put their pouches upon their knapsacks, and lay hold of each other to prevent being forced down with the current. Some time exposed before there was any possibility of getting lodged. Officers, men, and all huddled together. Got our men better regulated, and had three houses for the company."

On 8 January, the Light Division were ordered to a position close to Ciudad Rodrigo, nine miles from their quarters. To get to it, they had to cross the Agueda again - at a ford above the convent of La Caridad - and then march around the city.

> In the beginning of January 1812, our Division commenced investing Ciudad. The first day, our brigade crossed the Agueda, about three miles up the river from the city, round which we marched, keeping always at a most respectful distance on account of their round-shot. From this survey of Rodrigo, most of our men were aware of the great strength of the fortress and outworks, but it afforded only a subject for jest. Such was the confidence that filled the ranks of our Division, it would have been difficult to persuade the men that they could not beat the French under any odds.

Wellington ordered the Light Division to furnish a party under Lt.-Col. Colbourne to take the Renaud redoubt on top of a ridge known as Great Teson, close to the citadel.

> The same evening, Colonel Colbourne, with less than 200 men of the 43rd, 52nd, and Rifles, carried in the most gallant manner a strong fort of the enemy[1].

CIUDAD RODRIGO

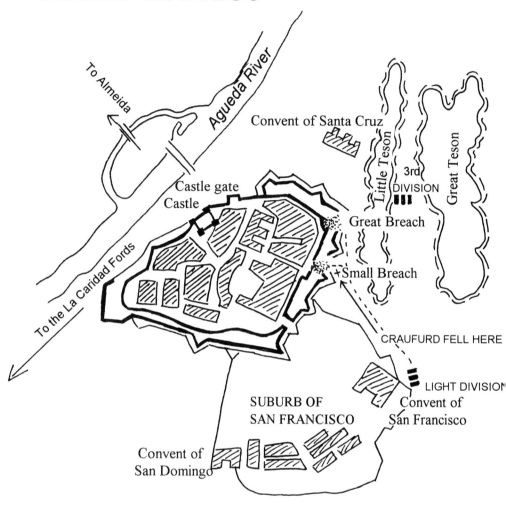

Simmons: *'Three pieces of cannon, two captains, and 48 men were made prisoners, besides what fell by the bayonet in the assault.'*

A number of caçadores were ordered to take blankets to convey away the wounded, French as well as the British. Most employed in this duty stripped the 50 prisoners, whom they left almost as naked as they were born, exposed to all the rigours of the January weather. I was near the tent of General Craufurd when a talkative, smart little French officer was brought before him. The poor fellow had nothing on but his trousers, and due to the blows he had received, was bleeding profusely from the nose and mouth. The General was chagrined at the sight, and lamented his inability to give the Frenchman clothes because his own baggage was so distant, whereupon Tom Crawley, who had been actively employed hunting the Portuguese from them[2], immediately stepped forward, touched his hat, and said:

"Yer honour, I'll lend him my greatcoat, if ye'll allow me." His eyes sparkled at being able to assist.

Craufurd was much pleased by his frank offer. "You are very good, rifleman; let him have it." And Tom proceeded to strip.

Meanwhile, more of the Frenchmen were marched in, many worse off than their officer. One was a sergeant, and as soon as he saw the officer, he ran to embrace him. Leaning his head on his shoulder, he burst into tears over their mutual misery. Captain Smith (now Sir Harry), the General's aide-de-camp, was present. He pulled forth his pocket-handkerchief and generously wrapped it round the sergeant's totally naked person, till further covering could be obtained.

After this, we expected to be marched back to our quarters at El Bodon, but instead were ordered to break ground, and we commenced the task of throwing up entrenchments in the face of the city. Being unsheltered from the enemy's shot, their grape and canister occasionally played among us, so although the night was remarkably cold - it was freezing at the time - we had no reason to complain of not having a good fire!

Now was the time to cure a skulker, or teach a man to work for his life. There we were, in twos, each provided with a pick-axe and shovel, digging with a vengeance into the frozen mould, and watching for the glances of the shot and shell. We stuck to our work like devils, sometimes pitching ourselves on our bellies to avoid their being purged with grape or canister.

Simmons: *"Began immediately to break ground, and before morning dawned, we had commenced our first parallel and completely covered ourselves. The enemy kept up a most tremendous fire all night, and I became perfectly familiar with the difference of sound between the two missiles, shot and shell, long before day."* At the end of the day, the Light Division were relieved.

The following day, we were relieved by the 1st Division[3] and marched back to our quarters, cold, hungry, and fatigued. It was very annoying to have to cross the Agueda going to the trenches, and returning from them. Pieces of ice were constantly carried down this rapid stream, and they bruised our men so much that the cavalry were ordered to form four deep across the ford, under the lee of whom we crossed comparatively unharmed. Nevertheless, by the time we reached our quarters, our clothes were frozen and icy[4].

On the night of 12 January, it was again the turn of the riflemen to go in the trenches. The fire from the fort had been so bad for the troops they were relieving that, says Simmons, 30 riflemen were ordered to *"get as close as possible, dig holes sufficiently deep to cover themselves, and take deliberate aim at the enemy's embrasures, which a good marksman could easily do by observing the flashes of their cannon, although it was dark."*

That same night, Kincaid was given command of the battalion's 'Highland Company' which contained a strong Scottish element, and was told to take up a position which would protect the working parties from a sortie from the town. The working parties were, says Leach *"employed all day in completing some batteries, and at night in laying the platforms for the battering artillery"*. And all the time shells rained on them. Simmons: *"The enemy had got the range to such a nicety that their shells were literally dropped into our works."* The Division was relieved at 10am the next morning (13 January).

There were several convents on the outskirts of Ciudad Rodrigo, all held by the French; one by one, they were captured. Simmons: *"The convent of Santa Cruz was taken by surprise by General Graham with the King's German Legion on the night of the 13th, and on the night of the 14th, the convent of San Francisco and Santa Clara and suburbs were in our hands."* The convent of San Francisco was stormed by 300 men of the 40th Regiment, one of whom was William Lawrence, who left an account in his autobiography.

On the night of 16 January, after two day' rest, the Light Division was back in the trenches. Simmons: *"I had charge of a party to carry earth in gabions [wicker baskets] and plant them upon the advanced saps in places where the ground was an entire rock and could not be penetrated. The enemy fired grape, and consequently numbers fell to rise no more from the effects of it. I ran the gauntlet here several times, and brought gabions of earth, always leaving some of my poor fellows behind when I returned for more. Glad enough I was when the Engineer said 'We have now sufficient'."*

> Our divisions continued relieving each other in the trenches for some days, until two breaches were considered practicable for an assault.
>
> At night on the 18th, an order came that we were to proceed to the works the next morning. As this took us out of our turn of duty, we guessed that something unusual was to be done. At daylight we joined the 3rd Division in the works, and heard that the city was to be stormed.

At Ciudad Rodrigo, the 3rd Division was assigned to storm the right breach and the Light Division the left, or small breach. Major George Napier of the 52d Regiment was given command of the storming party, and went to the three Light Division regiments to ask for volunteers. Half the men stepped forward.

On the eve of the storming of a fortress, when the breaches were ready, captains of companies, on private parade, would inform the men that the place was to be taken. Those men volunteering to head the stormers would step forward to the front and have their names taken down by the officer. If none offered themselves, the first men for duty were selected. With our regiment this latter alternative was never required, as a sufficient number were always ready. The forlorn hope, designated by the French in the equally appropriate term *les enfants perdus*, or 'lost children', always leads in the first attack.

Volunteers were now required from the different regiments of our Division, and many of our men came forward with alacrity for this deadly service. With three others from my company I had, as I then considered, the good fortune to be chosen. This was a momentous occasion in the life of a soldier, and so we considered it.

At the time, we were in the trenches in front of the city, from whence came a very smart fire of shot and shell, which gave us an idea of the warm reception we might expect on our visit that night. The entire company gathered round our little party, each pressing us to have a sup from his canteen. We shook hands with friendly sincerity, and speculated on whether we would outlive the assault. If truth must be told, we also speculated on the chances of plunder in the town. I gave my father's address to my comrade before starting, in case of accident.

In our regiment, there were four or five volunteers from each company, and we were led by Captain Mitchell and Lieutenants Johnston and Kincaid[5]. The storming division was commanded by Major George Napier of the 52nd Regiment.

Darkness closed over the city, and our imaginations became awake to the horrors of the coming scene. The stormers - in all about 120 men - were ordered to 'fall in' and 'form', and we moved to a convent occupied by the 40th, the walls of which protected us from the enemy's shot.

The forlorn hope and storming parties moved on at about 7pm, the head of the Light Division column following close behind. They formed up behind the convent of San Francisco.

Kincaid: *"First, four companies of our battalion, under Colonel Cameron, to line the crest of the glacis and fire upon the ramparts. Second, some companies of Portuguese carrying bags filled with hay and straw, for throwing into the ditch to facilitate the passage of the storming party. Third, the forlorn hope, consisting of an officer [Lt. Gurwood of the 52nd] and 25 volunteers. Fourth, the storming party, consisting of three officers and 100 volunteers from each regiment; the officers from ours were Captain Mitchell, Mr Johnston and myself... Fifth, the main body of the Division under General Craufurd, with one brigade, under Maj.-Gen. Vandeleur, and the other under Colonel Barnard."*

According to Verner, there were about 160 Portuguese caçadores who carred twelve-foot ladders, axes and haybags. Wellington's orders stated that *"the men with the ladders, and axes, and bags must not have arms; those who storm must not fire,"* their duty being to prepare the way for the troops who followed.

> General Craufurd led us in person. While we stood formed under the wall, he addressed us upon the nature of the duty assigned us. On this memorable occasion his voice was more than ordinarily clear and distinct:
> "Soldiers! the eyes of your country are upon you. Be steady, be cool, be firm in the assault. The town must be yours this night. Once masters of the wall, let your first duty be to clear the ramparts, and in doing this keep together."
> With hearts beating, we waited watchfully for the signal, with our Division formed immediately in our rear, ready to second the effort. We were on the brink of being dashed into eternity, and among the men there was a solemnity and silence deeper than I ever witnessed before.

William Lawrence of the 40th Regiment, was watching from the Convent of San Francisco: *"The business those men were about to undertake was about the worst a soldier can undertake, for scarcely anything but death stares him in the face. They were silent, watching with intense anxiety for what, to many, would be the fatal signal."*

> The expected signal, a rocket, went up from one of our batteries.
> "Now lads, for the breach!" General Craufurd called out, and led the way. We started off in double time, and in turning the left corner of the wall, came under fire. As we neared the breach, the shot of the enemy swept our men away fast. Canister, grape, round-shot, and shell, with fireballs to show our ground, and a regular hailstorm of bullets, came pouring on and around us. General Craufurd fell almost immediately, mortally wounded.
> Without a pause we dashed onwards to the town, and precipitated ourselves into the ditch before the walls. We did not wait for the ladders for they were carried by the Portuguese, who ran away. The ladders did not make an appearance until their use had been superseded by a series of jumps made by our men into a trench 16' deep. When one or two ladders were procured, they were instantly placed against the scarp of the trench, and up we mounted to attack the breach. There the fire was constant and most deadly, and for some minutes, small bodies of men were swept away as they appeared. But they persevered, and gradually formed a lodgment. On our right, where the 3rd Division were storming the second breach, we heard a loud cheering. This had a magical effect: regardless of the enemy's fire, and every other impediment, the men dashed in over the breach, carrying everything before them.

I had got up among the first, and with a crowd of our fellows, struggled to push over the splintered and broken wall that formed the breach. Major Napier was by my side encouraging on the men, when he received a shot and staggered back. He would have fallen into the trench had I not caught him. His arm hung shattered by his side. To my brief inquiry if he was badly hurt, he squeezed my hand and said "Never mind me. Push on, my lads; the town is ours!"

And so it was; our men were entering it pell-mell. I mounted the ramparts, and although it was dark I saw my own Captain, Uniacke[6], rushing along with a few men to the right of the breach. Though not on the forlorn-hope, this gallant soldier was determined to be first in the town. It was the last time he was to be at our head for a few moments afterwards, the French sprung a mine, and the whole party were killed or maimed[7].

Harry Smith *'ran on with poor Uniacke's company to meet the 3rd Division, or rather clear the ramparts to aid them, when the horrid explosion took place which killed General Mackinnon of the 3rd Division on the spot, and many soldiers, awfully scorching others. I and Uniacke were much scorched, but some splinters of an ammunition chest lacerated him and caused his death three days after the storm. Tom, my brother, was not hurt. I shall never forget the concussion when it struck me, throwing me back many feet."*

With a few others I took a direction to the left. As they retired, the French kept up an occasional fire along the ramparts. Running forward, I came up against a howitzer with such force that it tumbled me over and I found myself prostrate across the body of a wounded French officer. Beside him was a *cannonier* [gunner], who was assisting him. The *cannonier* seized me, and a fearful struggle ensured, till I was bent almost double by the height and weight the heavy Frenchman. After all my escapes, I thought my game was over. At this crisis a few of our men came rushing up, one of which was my old 'chum' Wilkie.

William Green: *"Some of us got to the gun; it was loaded again, and the French gunner was in the act of applying the match, when one of our men knocked him down with the butt of his rifle. If we had been one moment later, many of us would have been sent into eternity, as we were close up to the muzzle."*

The *cannonier* was instantly fastened on, and tripped by the side of his master. But poor Wilkie! The next minute, he himself staggered against the howitzer, mortally wounded. I flew to his support. He seized me hastily by the hand, and gave it a deadly squeeze,

"Ned," he articulated, "it's all up with me." Relaxing his grasp, he fell back and expired.

The castle at Ciudad Rodrigo today. It is now a parador, ie a state-run hotel.

The officer, perceiving my agitation, and fearful of me retaliating, handed me his gold watch.

There is no doubt that Wilkie, Major Napier, and several others in the advance fell by the fire of the Portuguese who, panic-stricken by the first volley they received from the town, lay down on the glacis and commenced firing on the breach. A random shot through the embrasure deprived my friend of life[8]. Our Division was fast entering the breach, and finding I could be of little use to my comrade, I proceeded with the stormers, clearing the walls of the enemy as we went[9].

Turning to the right, we entered a large square or plaza, where we were soon joined by some of every regiment in the two divisions. Like ourselves, they were all helter-skelter, subject to everything but order.

The combat was over. It had lasted only half an hour. Kincaid, in the first street he came to, accepted the surrender of a French officer, whom he escorted to the great square, where the soldiers were streaming.

Green: *"I ran down the main street with some men; we met one of our officers with the French commander... A little further in the street we met a sergeant of ours with one of our men, who had deserted to the enemy. In this place the enemy had all given themselves up as prisoners of war, and among them were about 40 who had deserted from the British."*

On one side of the square, some of the garrison were lined up on one side as prisoners, the rest was filled with British and Portuguese soldiers.

In a short time, a regiment of the 3rd Division entered the square and, commanded by their officer, something like order prevailed. When the British colours were planted in the centre, proclaiming the town to be taken, three cheers were given by the whole. When this was over, they commenced firing in the air, as well as at windows where any light appeared[10].

Seeing the confusion, a number broke into squads, which went in different directions and entered different streets according to the fancy of their leaders. Myself and about a score of others took a large street to the right. The night was dark and as the city was not lit, we had to grope our way along. We had not gone far when we got mixed up with a quantity of French muskets, which had been thrown on the ground with their bayonets fixed. These pricked the legs one or two of the men, who swore they had come to a *chevaux-de-frise*[11].

Groping about we came across a wounded French soldier, who told us in Spanish that we were close to the barracks. Knowing the French would not resign their liberty without a struggle, I expected a volley to be sent amongst us from the barracks, and began retracing my steps towards the square. However, I had only gone a short distance when I saw another party advancing towards me with a lighted candled. Hearing the noise of the first party in their front, they commenced firing as they advanced. Squeezing myself edgeways against a door, I awaited their arrival then I begged them to desist from firing because there were some of their own men lower down. I then went with them and joined the first party.

The wounded French soldiers pointed to a large gateway, and told us it was the barracks. Having a light we entered, and mounted a large stone staircase. We found ourselves in a French hospital, full of sick and wounded. Those who were able to sit up in bed did so, supplicating mercy, but they had no occasion to do so for our fellows were kind to them, and wrapped the bedclothes round them. Shortly afterwards a third party came down. Seeing a light in our window they commenced firing. The poor fellow who held the candle was shot through the head, and one or two others were wounded. The rest lay down while the firing continued, but then one man, more daring that the rest, flew to the window and cried out that they were firing on their own men.

When this panic was over, I came downstairs, anxious to meet some of my own company to know how things were. I found a few outside, and we started in another direction, to a place with a large white house that had been used as a commissary's store by the French. Here a crowd had assembled to break it open. They were warned off by a sentinel, a German, who was posted to guard the premises. Not heeding his threat, the throng rushed at the door. The poor sentry, true to his trust, attempted to oppose their entrance, and was run through the body by a bayonet.

The house contained several puncheons[12] of spirits, which the men present immediately tapped by striking in the heads. Some became madly drunk. Several wretches, who mounted the steps that had been placed against the butts to enable them to obtain the rum, fell into the liquor head first and, unnoticed by the crowd, perished. Several fights took place, and it was only the drunkenness of the parties which prevented mischief being done. To crown the whole, a light fell into one of the barrels of spirits and the place was set on fire. Many poor wretches, incapable of moving from the quantity of liquor they had swallowed, were consumed in the flames.

Hardened though I then was, I turned from this scene of horrors and went with a comrade to look for a house where we might obtain refreshment, and take up our quarters for the night. After a search, we found the domicile of a doctor, who we took from under a bed clasped in the arms of a very pretty girl whom he called his niece. Like himself, she was shivering with fear. This we soon dispelled, and were rewarded with a good supper crowned by a bowl of excellent punch which, at the time, seemed to compensate us for all the sufferings we had endured in the trenches during the siege.

Kincaid: *We succeeded in getting a great portion of our battalion together by one o'clock in the morning, and withdrew with them to the ramparts, where we lay until daylight."*

Simmons: *"My battalion formed up upon the ramparts and made fires, as the night was a clear and frosty one. Some men brought me wine, ham, and eggs. I soon made a hearty meal, and washed it down with some good French burgundy, put my feet to the fire, and enjoyed as calm a sleep as I ever did in my life before, for three or four hours."*

The next morning, I was anxious to visit the left breach to look for the body of Wilkie. At length, I found him, cold and stiff. He was stripped, but I easily distinguished him by the likeness he bore to his sister. The bullet had entered his breast close under the left shoulder. As I stood over his prostrate remains, vivid recollections burst into my mind of all the scenes in which he had been so active. My fellow recruit, bed-fellow, and pot companion, lay stretched before me clotted and besmeared with blood, a single drop of which was, at one time, more valuable to me than the whole of my own lucky current. The remembrance of his sister, which my profession had wiped from my mind, now resumed its almost pristine freshness. My eyes dimmed for a second. One solitary tear, proof of my weakness, might have left its scalding course behind, but as a soldier I felt only a momentary sorrow. I held my life in my own hand, and was ready to part with it at a moment's notice, and I presumed as much of all that belonged to me.

A few half-drunken soldiers staggered near me, staring stupidly at my anxiety. With the proceeds of the storming business, I gained them over, and we buried Wilkie in the glacis, near the breach. The wreck around us was a true monument to the memory of a soldier[8].

I now proceeded to the right breach, which had been carried by the 3rd Division, and where the mine had been sprung. The sight was heart-rendering in the extreme. The dead lay in heaps, numbers of them stripped. They displayed the most ghastly wounds. Here and there, half-buried under the blackened fragments of the wall, or reeking on the surface of the ruin, lay those who had been blown up in the explosions, their remains dreadfully mangled and discoloured. Strewed about were dissevered arms and legs[13].

The 88th, or Connaught Rangers, had suffered most severely at this spot, and I observed a number of poor Irish women hopelessly endeavouring to distinguish the burnt features of their husbands.

Though heartily sick of the morning's mournful perambulation, I was anxious to see Captain Uniacke, who lay in the suburbs, in a house next to that in which our brave old General were stretched out, for this was the last enterprise General Craufurd's gallant spirit was destined to direct. Several of the men of Captain Uniacke's company crowded about his person, hoping - for he was still living, and sensible - that he might yet return amongst us, but his arm had been torn from the socket[14], and he died some few days afterwards.

Uniacke died in agony. Green, who was in his company, described him as: *"an Irish gentleman, the best runner in the regiment... He said, just before he died, 'Remember, I was the first man that entered the breach'."*

> Here let me pay a brief but sincere tribute to his memory. Though young in years, he was gallant, daring, and just to all whom he commanded. During the Peninsular War our men divided the officers into two classes, the 'come on' and the 'go on'. In action, Tom Plunket once observed to an officer, "the words 'go on' don't befit a leader, sir" and to the honour of the Rifles, with us the latter were exceedingly few in numbers. Amongst the former, none were seen so often in the van as Uniacke, whose affability and personal courage rendered him the idol of the men of his company.

During the storming of the town, one rifleman of the 1st battalion was killed, and one sergeant and 15 rank and file wounded. A total of 553 allied soldiers had been killed or wounded during the siege, and a further 568 during the storming of the town. About 8 French officers were killed and 21 wounded, and about 500 French soldiers were either killed or wounded. The Governor, 78 French officers and 1,700 French soldiers were taken prisoner.

On the morning of 20 January, the Light Division was ordered to return to their cantonments because, says Simmons, *"the men who have stormed a town are seldom fit for anything but vice and irregularity."* They were replaced by the 5th Division, which had not been employed in the siege.

> A very small portion only of the troops that had taken Rodrigo were allowed to remain in the city, and our battalion, among others, were ordered back to their former quarters. The next morning, we marched over the bridge dressed in all variety of clothes imaginable. Some had jack-boots on, others wore frock-coats, or had epaulettes, and some even had monkeys on their shoulders. The 5th Division, who we met on their way to repair the breach, immediately formed up on the left of the road, presented arms, and cheered us as we went along.
>
> I was afterwards told by several of our men that the Duke of Wellington, who saw us on our march, inquired of his staff: "Who the devil are those fellows?"

As the riflemen were marching out, Wellington happened to be riding in. Kincaid says he had to *"ask the officer of the leading company what regiment it was, for there was scarcely a vestige of uniform among the men, some of whom were dressed in Frenchmen's coats, some in white breeches and huge jack-boots, some with cocked hats and queues; most of their swords were fixed on the rifles and stuck full of hams, tongues, and loaves of bread, and not a few were carrying bird-cages. There never was a better masked corps!"*

We entered El Bodon, with songs, and were welcomed by the *vivas* of the inhabitants.

CHAPTER 14

Burials and Executions
20 January - 17 March 1812

The second day after the storming of Rodrigo, our brave General Craufurd died of his wound. The chief part of the officers of the Rifles went to pay the last tribute to the remains of this gallant veteran, and the Duke of Wellington attended the funeral [20 January]. General Craufurd was borne to the grave by four sergeant-majors of his own Division, and was buried in the breach where he fell. Though most strict in discipline, he was averse to punishment, and was beloved by the men for his justice, and for his care for them, as well as for his bravery. I was an eyewitness to an event which shows his character:

I was on guard one day when he came riding in from the front with his orderly dragoon, as he usually did. Two of our men, one of them a corporal, came running out of a house with some bread, pursued by a Spanish woman. *"Ladrone ! Ladrone* [thief]*!"* she cried lustily.

They were immediately pursued by the General and his orderly. The bread was given back to the woman, and the men were placed in the guard-house. The next day they were tried by a brigade court-martial, and brought out to a wood near the town for punishment. The poor corporal, whose name was Miles, was to be reduced to the pay and rank of a private soldier, and to receive 150 lashes; the other man was to receive 200.

When the brigade was formed, and the Brigade-Major had finished reading the proceedings of the court-martial, General Craufurd lectured both men and officers on the nature of their cruelty to the harmless inhabitants, as he called the Spaniards, laying particular stress on our regiment, which, be said, committed more crimes than the whole of the British Army.

"You think that because you are riflemen, and more exposed to the enemy's fire than other regiments, that you are to rob the inhabitants with impunity, but while I command you, you shall not." Then turning round to Miles, who stood in the centre of the square, he said, with a stern voice, "Strip, Sir."

Miles never said a word until he was tied up to a tree, then he turned his head round as far as his situation would allow, towards the General, who was pacing up and down the square.

"General Craufurd," he said, "I hope you will forgive me."

"No sir, your crime is too great."

"Do you recollect, sir," said Miles in a mild and respectful tone, "when you and I were under the command of General Whitelocke, and we were taken prisoners in Buenos Aires? With a number of others, we were marched to a sort of pound surrounded by a wall. There was a well in the centre, out of which I drew water with my mess-tin by means of canteen straps collected from the men, who were prisoners too. You sat on my knapsack, and I shared my last biscuit with you. You then told me you would never forget my kindness to you. It is now in your power sir, for you know we have been short of rations for some time."

The General was affected by this, as was the whole square. The bugler, who stood close to the corporal, waiting to commence the punishment, received the usual nod from the bugle-major to begin. When the corporal received the first lash, the General started and turned hurriedly round.

"What's that! Who taught that bugler to flog? Send him to drill! He cannot flog. He cannot flog! Stop! Take him down. Take him down! I remember it well." And he paced up and down the square, muttering to himself words I could not catch, blowing his nose, and wiping his face with his handkerchief, trying to hide the emotion that was evident to the whole square. A dead silence prevailed as the corporal was untied, and our gallant General recovered a little of his noble feeling

"Why does a brave soldier like you commit these crimes?" he said with a broken accent. Beckoning to his orderly to bring his horse, he mounted and rode off. Needless to say the other man also was pardoned, and in a few days the corporal was restored to his rank[1].

On the death of Captain Uniacke, Captain Smith, now the celebrated Sir Harry Smith. was appointed captain of my company, but being on the staff, his brother Lt. Thomas Smith, now Barrack Master at Chatham, took command[2].

On the fourth day after we had taken the town, the company received orders to pay a last tribute to our captain, Uniacke. We marched under the command of Lt. Smith, and arrived at Gallegos about 12 o'clock.

The men, who had obtained plenty of money at Rodrigo, got drinking, and while conveying the body to the grave, they stumbled under the weight of the coffin. The lid had not been nailed down so out rolled the mangled remains of our brave Captain. This caused consternation among a number of French officers from Rodrigo, who were on parole. They were the ugliest set I ever saw, with a very undersized appearance, more like Italians than Frenchmen; they seemed to be the refuse of their army. One, more careless than the rest, viewed the occurrence with a malicious sneer, which so enraged our men that one of them took the tawny-looking little Italian by the nape of the neck, and kicked his hind-quarters soundly for it[3].

Uniacke's pay sergeant, Robert Fairfoot, another Irishman, was anxious that Uniacke be buried in consecrated ground, but the Spanish priests objected because they thought he was a Protestant and a heretic. Fairfoot assured them that Uniacke was Irish, which implied that he was also a Roman Catholic, and he was laid to rest at the foot of the finest tree in the churchyard of Gallegos by his company, led by his subaltern, Thomas Smith.

Lt. Thomas Smith

On 31 January, the Light Division marched to Fuenteguinaldo where they remained until 26 February. Marmont, who had not expected Ciudad Rodrigo to fall, had given up the idea of further advance for the time being.

> On our return to El Bodon, one of the men, overpowered by liquor, lay down to sleep in the wood that separates the road from Gallegos. It was his last, poor fellow. On the roll being called, a party was sent in search of him, and they discovered his body under a tree, torn to pieces by the wolves which infested that part of Spain.
>
> Another melancholy incident occurred while we remained at El Bodon. Ten men, who had deserted from our Division and had been recaptured when we took Rodrigo, were condemned to be shot.

A general court-martial was held at Nave de Haver on 12 February 1812. Arraigned before it for desertion were William Mills, Miles Hodgson and Malcolm McInnes (95th); Corporal Robert Fuller, and privates James Cummins, William Robinson, Patrick O'Neil and John Maloney (52nd); Thomas Price (43rd); George Cameron (Royal Horse Artillery); John Curtan and Luke McGann (88th); Thomas Jones (23rd Welsh Fusiliers); Joseph Lambrecht, Conrad Eylich and John Engle (5th batt. 60th); Charles Knierim (1st line batt, King's German Legion); and Joseph Ball (7th Royal Fusileers). They were all found guilty and each was sentenced to be shot in the presence of their division. The first ten were from the Light Division, and their place of execution was to be the village of Ituero, on the banks of the Azava river.

William Surtees, who had been in the 95th Regiment since 1802, was the 3rd battalion's quartermaster. His memoir *Twenty-Five Years in the Rifle Brigade* was published in 1833. Having rejoined his regiment just before the siege of Ciudad Rodrigo, Surtees was present at the executions. According to him, the deserters *"never attempted to plead not guilty, but said in palliation of their heinous crime, that they were forced to desert from want of food and clothing; indeed the army had not been so well supplied for a short time previously."*

> The place of execution was a plain near Ituero, where our Division was drawn up, forming three sides of a square. As was usual, the culprits were placed on the vacant side, in front of a large trench, dug as a grave for the wretched men.
>
> Two of the deserters were pardoned on the ground. One was Hodgson, of my company, a very handsome fellow, who had allowed himself to be persuaded into rash step of deserting[4]. The other was a corporal of the 52nd regiment, named Cummins, who had been placed on the fatal ground in a wounded state. He had, I believe, been mainly instrumental in getting the others to desert with him[5]. He had been particularly noticed in one of the breaches at Rodrigo, actively

employed opposing our entrance, and cheering on the besieged to resist us. He was pardoned also, but why I cannot say.

As this was the first military execution I had witnessed, I felt not a little curiosity to see the forms pursued[6].

Those forms were described very well by Surtees: *'The Division was formed into three sides of the square, on a plain in front of the village, the graves of the hapless beings occupying a part of the fourth face of the square. When all was ready, and a firing party from each regiment had been formed in the centre, the provost marshal went to the guard tent, where the prisoners were waiting, to conduct them to the place of execution. They soon after appeared, poor wretches, moving towards the square, with faces pale and wan, and with all the dejection such a situation is calculated to produce. Their arms had been pinioned one by one as they came out from the guard tent, and all being ready, the melancholy procession advanced towards the centre of the square.*

'The proceedings of the court which tried them, together with the sentence, and the approval of the Commander of the Forces, was read by the Assistant Adjutant-General, in the hearing of the whole Division. Being concluded, the prisoners were marched round in front of every regiment, that all might see and avoid their unhappy fate. They were then moved towards their graves. I ought to observe that the chaplain of the Division had been with them in the guard tent some little time previously to their leaving it, and when they quitted it as above described, he followed them at a considerable distance, apparently ashamed of his peculiar calling, and the duty incumbent on him in such a conjuncture. They were led... towards their graves; and when they reached the bank of earth in front of each, they were made to kneel down with their faces fronting the square. Being one after another blindfolded, they were left for a few moments to their own reflections, or their prayers.'

Along the summit of the little heap of mould that had been thrown up from the pit, the deserters were placed in a row, with their eyes bandaged, so that on receiving the fatal volley they should fall forward into the trench. Some of the poor fellows, from debility, were unable to kneel, and lay at their length, or crouched up into an attitude of despair, upon the loose earth.

Surtees: *'The provost marshal proceeded to the firing party, who had been previously loaded, directed the men of each regiment to fire at their own prisoner, and advanced them to within about ten or twelve paces of the wretched men. Giving the signals by motion for their making ready and firing, the whole fired at once, and plunged the unhappy criminals into eternity.'*

The signal to the firing party was given by the motion of the provost's cane, when the culprits were all hurried together into eternity. There was one exception. Strange to say, a man of the 52nd remained standing and untouched. His countenance, that before had been deadly pale, now exhibited a bright flush. If he imagined himself pardoned, he was doomed to be miserably deceived, as the following minute two men of the reserve came up and fired their pieces into his bosom. He gave a loud scream, that had a very horrible effect upon those near, and sprang forward into his grave.

Surtees says the man who remained untouched was from the horse artillery (ie George Cameron): *'One of the prisoners belonged to the troop of horse artillery attached to the Division, and it seems the provost, in giving his orders for the soldiers of each regiment to fire at their own man, had not recollected that the artillery had no men there to fire. He was thus left sitting on his knees, when the others had fallen all around him. What his feelings must have been it is in vain to guess but, poor fellow, he was not suffered long to remain in suspense, for a reserve party immediately approached and fired, stretching him along with his companions in crime and misery. In such of the others as they perceived life still remaining, they immediately put an end to their sufferings by placing their muskets close to the body, and firing into them. One poor man, when he received his death wound, sprung to a considerable height, and giving a loud shriek, fell and instantly expired.'*

To prevent unnecessary suffering, a reserve firing party was brought up, who continued to fire wherever the slightest sign of life exhibited itself in the bodies, the provost himself winding up the tragedy by discharging a pistol shot through the head of each corpse.

Harry Smith: *"It was an awful ceremony, a military execution. I was Major of Brigade on that day... Some prisoners were fortunate enough to be killed, others were only wounded, some untouched. I galloped up. An unfortunate rifleman called to me by name - he was awfully wounded - 'Oh, Mr Smith, put me out of my misery', and I literally ordered the firing-party, when reloaded, to run up and shoot the poor wretches. It was an awful scene."*

Surtees: *"When all was finished, the Division was formed into column and marched round in front of the bodies, where each soldier might distinctly perceive the sad and melancholy effects of such a fatal dereliction of duty. They were then, without more ado, thrown into their graves, which were filled up without delay, and the Division separating, each regiment marches to its quarters."*

After this very solemn and impressive scene, we were marched in column of companies round the dead, so that the spectacle might be witnessed by every man in the Division[7].

With Ciudad Rodrigo captured, Wellington turned his attention to the other French-held Spanish citadel of Badajoz. On 26 February 1812, the works at Ciudad Rodrigo having been put in order, and the town garrisoned with Spaniards, the Light Division (along with the rest of the army) left their cantonments and marched towards Badajoz again.

On 26 February we broke up our cantonments in the environs of Ciudad Rodrigo, crossed the Tagus, and marched southward for six or seven days, at the expiration of which our Division took up their quarters in and about the town of Castelo de Vide. The country around the town was the most fruitful and luxuriant I had ever beheld. It was bounded with the most delightful hills and valleys, that produced in abundance the finest fruits, such as grapes, pomegranates, oranges, and lemons. As may be supposed, the men were delighted with such a paradise, and the wine was so plentiful that, while they remained here, our fellows invariably boiled their meat in it.

Here, another unhappy deserter was captured. His name was Almond[8], and he had been a corporal in our battalion. When we took Rodrigo, he escaped from the town, but was captured by some Spanish troops on his way to join the French at Salamanca, and brought back to the regiment a prisoner.

The fate of this man excited much commiseration. I knew him well. He was an exceedingly fine-looking fellow, and up to the period of his unhappy departure from duty, had been noted for possessing the best qualities of a soldier. Some harshness on the part of an officer was the cause of Almond's desertion, and because of his previous good character, and the fact that he had marched as a prisoner for many days, it was commonly thought he would be pardoned.

Joseph Almond, who was in Balvaird's 5th company, had deserted on 17 November 1811. He was arraigned for desertion at Pedrogão on 7 March 1812. He pleaded not guilty. He was found guilty and was ordered to be shot at Castelo de Vide on 10 March. He was not pardoned.

I was on guard over him the night before his execution. That evening, while he was playing at cards with some of the men, the provost of the Division entered the guard room, and gave him the intelligence that he was doomed to suffer at 10 o'clock the next morning. Sudden and unexpected as the announcement was, Almond's face showed scarcely any emotion.

"Well," he remarked to those around him, "I am quite ready."

He sent for the pay-sergeant of the company he belonged to, from whom he received his arrears of pay[9]. This he spent on wine, which he distributed among the men of the guard. Seeing that one man had very bad shoes, and as his own were better, Almond took them off and exchanged them.

"They will last me as long as I shall require them," he said.

The morning turned out showery. The Division formed on three sides of a square and the guard, headed by the band with Almond in front, slowly marched round to the muffled drum beat, in dull time, of the 'Dead March'. The swell of its solemn harmony filled the eyes of every man present, but only seemed to strengthen the glance of the doomed man. He led the van of his funeral procession, like one who was to live for ever. His step was so firm and correct that I thought at the time there never had been a finer soldier.

Poor Almond. We halted at his own grave, which the heavy rains had half filled with water. This he noticed, and gave a faint smile.

"Although a watery one, I shall sleep sound enough in it."

He then stood upright in a fine military position as the Brigade-Major read aloud the proceedings of the court-martial. The provost came to tie the handkerchief round his eyes.

"There is no occasion," he coolly remarked; "I shall not flinch," but he was told that it was customary.

"Very well," he said, "do you duty."

Before this last office was performed, he turned round and, calling most of the guard by name, bade them farewell. As I nodded to him in return, I fancied it was to a dead man. And in two minutes he was no more. The intrepid and cool manner in which he met his fate drew forth a general feeling of admiration.

A few days after the execution we marched for Badajoz, in the environs of which we arrived on 17 March.

Badajoz, as approached from Elvas. Coloured aquatint by J H Clark and M Dubourg, after Captain Wilmot RHA. Pub. E Orme, 1 Mar 1813. ©British Museum

CHAPTER 15

The Siege of Badajoz
17 March - 5 April 1812

On 14 March, the Light Division was ordered to quit Castelo de Vide for Elvas, a march of ten miles. They arrived on the 16th.

Harry Smith: *"We Light, 3rd and 4th Divisions thought, as we had taken Ciudad Rodrigo, others would have the pleasure of the trenches of Badajoz, but on our reaching Elvas we were soon undeceived. We were destined for the duty, to our mortification, for soldiers hate sieges and working-parties."* At dawn the next day, the Division marched out of Elvas to the tune of St. Patrick's Day, in commemoration of the same.

> The celebrated city of Badajoz stands on an extended plain ten miles from Elvas. The Guadiana, which hereabouts forms the boundary between Spain and Portugal, flows on one side of the fortification, and a bridge over its surface connects with one or two forts on the opposite bank. The fortress was surrounded on all sides by strong bastions, to the number of 13 or 14, and what with trenches and other forts and outworks, was almost impregnable. In addition, the Rivillas, a tributary stream of the Guadiana, flowed round and through the trenches in our front.

Green says that to reach their position at Badajoz, they *"had to cross a river called the Guadiana; the bridge was composed of boats chained together"*. When they arrived, they found the 3rd and 4th Divisions already there.

> When we arrived, our battalion took up its encampment on the Spanish side of the river, where we occupied a small hill. Here, for the first time during our campaign, we made use of small square tents, belonging to the Portuguese.
> The first night of our arrival we commenced laying siege, by breaking ground within 300-400 yards of the town. Fort San Roque and Fort Picurina, were rather on our left.

Harry Smith: *"On the night of 17 March, St Patrick's Day, the Light Division broke ground under a deluge of rain, which swelled the Guadiana so as to threaten our bridge of boats."*

159

BADAJOZ

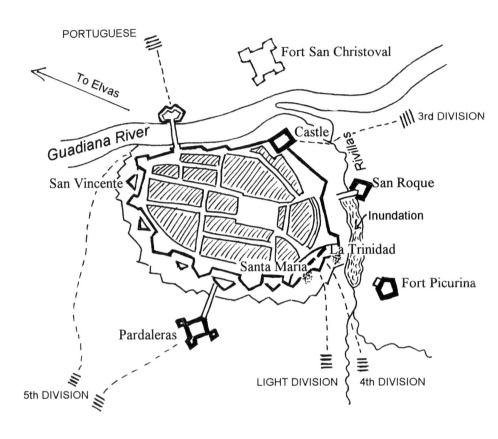

Breaches

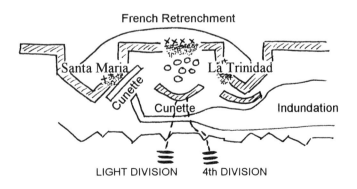

⁰°ₒᵒ Holes
x x x Chevaux de frise

Green: *"We had to break ground in open daylight. Each man had to carry a skip and a spade. We set our skips about three paces apart, and began to fill them with earth to make a cover for us from the enemy's fire. Their musket balls reached us; we had two or three men wounded, and one officer, but no one killed. Other skips were brought to fill up the intervals and set one upon another and filled with earth, so that we soon had a good shelter from the enemy's balls."*

The French garrison inside Badajoz numbered about 5,000 men, and the scale of siege operation was much greater than at Rodrigo. Kincaid: *"It required every man to be actually in the trenches digging for six hours every day, and the same length of time every night which, with the time required to march to and from them, through fields more than ankle deep in a stiff mud, left us never more than 8 hours out of the 24 in camp, and we never were dry the whole time."* It was, he said, *"like serving an apprenticeship to the double-calling of grave-digger and gamekeeper, for we found ample employment both for the spade and the rifle."*

On 19 March, the visibility was poor due to the rainy weather and this allowed a French force to make a sortie from the town.

Simmons: *"The enemy collected a body of horse and foot and made a sortie upon our works. They had a number of men to take away our tools and fill up the trenches. They drew back very soon. At the moment of the attack, our different parties were relieving, and the weather being very dull, accompanied with drizzling rain, the enemy got very close before they were observed. The enemy's cavalry dashed through our camp, and at the spot where the engineers were engaged in carrying on the work for the siege, captured an officer: a dragoon tried to drag him away with him. Our people in the camp fancied they were the Portuguese cavalry, but soon were undeceived, and a number took up arms and ran forward to attack them. They made their way back as rapidly as they had moved forward."*

All the while the soldiers worked in the trenches, shot and shell was fired at them from the town, causing many casualties.

A man named Brooks, for three or four nights successively, dreamt he saw the body of a rifleman without a head. Some days after we had taken one of the forts from the enemy, our battalion was relieved in the trenches and, as was customary with some of us, Brooks, Treacy, and myself jumped out of the trench, exposing ourselves to a fire from the walls of the town, and ran to the next parallel, or trench. A little ahead of my comrades, I heard the rush of a cannon-ball, and felt my jacket splashed by something. I jumped into the next trench, turned round, and beheld the body of Brooks, headless, but quivering with life for a few seconds before it fell. His dream, poor fellow, had singularly augured the conclusion of his own career. The shot had smashed and carried away the whole of his head. My jacket was bespattered with the brains, and Treacy was materially injured by a splinter of the skull being driven deep through the skin behind his ear. This circumstance is well known to several now living in London[1].

The greatest annoyance we experienced during the siege arose from shells thrown at us from the town. Our works screened us from the round-shot; but these dangerous missiles, falling into the trenches where we worked and exploding, frequently did great mischief. Immediately a shell fell, every man threw himself flat upon the ground until it had burst.

Tom Crawley, though tolerably fearless of other shot, had an inveterate dislike of these deadly visitors, and believed that more were thrown where he chanced to be than in any other part of the trenches. At night, in particular, he was always on the look out. As soon as he beheld a shell coming he would call out, "Here's another brute! Look out!" and dive head first into a mud-heap, which he would always manage to have at hand. This did not always protect us, for the head was no sooner in the mud than its presence was again required outside, to watch for falling splinters which, being composed of large portions of metal from the missile, descended with great violence, and were of themselves sometimes sufficient to crush a man into the earth.

Occasionally, Lord Wellington would pay us a visit during the work, to make observations and examine the trenches. One day, when Crawley and myself were working near each other, a shell fell inconveniently close to us. Tom was instantly half buried in mud, awaiting the explosion. The shell had sunk itself deep into the earth because the fuse was too long, so I decided to play a trick upon Crawley - when the shell exploded, I was going to throw a large lump of clay on his head to make him believe himself wounded. To obtain the clod I sprang at the other side of the trench, and in doing so exposed myself to a grape-shot. It splashed me from head to foot with mud, and I had to throw myself back into the trench upon Crawley who, believing that a shell had fixed itself upon his rear, roared like bull. In an instant, however, the sunken missile burst, and when the smoke dispersed, I beheld the Duke, crouched down, his head half averted, dryly smiling at us.

Like his renowned contemporary [Napoleon], the Duke had a remarkable cast of feature, which distinguished him at an almost incredible distance. Shot and shell pay no respect to persons, but the enemy did, so whenever the Duke came amongst us, they poured in shells, grape, and canister, and other delicacies of the kind, with unusual liberality.

Sometimes parties of men were sent out in independent files to pick up the dismembered legs, arms, etc, which the bursting shells had scattered about. This was to prevent the ill-effects of their appearance upon the courage of the Portuguese, who were as likely to put their heels in motion as their heads. I remember observing some of these gentlemen carrying the body of a wounded officer of theirs, wrapped in a blanket, from the trenches, intending to cross the fields to their camp ground. They got only a few yards when a ball fired from the town came bounding along the ground, half spent. The Portuguese, unconscious of its approach, crossed the line of its progress, and the shot glanced between them and cut the unlucky officer in two. The terrified bearers took to their heels, leaving the blanket behind them, and one of our fellows, who had been watching, shook the body out and took possession of it.

"It's an ill wind that does nobody any good," he said.

About 22 March, a party was ordered to proceed to Elvas for the purpose of conducting some heavy artillery from that fortress to use against the walls of Badajoz. The weather was exceedingly wet, and we had to place six or eight large guns on things resembling sledges. It took twelve bullocks to draw each gun. When we arrived at the pontoon bridge crossing the Guadiana River, which was between Elvas and Badajoz, it was so damaged the guns could not pass over. We were obliged to bivouac for the night amongst a party of sappers who were stationed there to repair the pontoons.

The bullocks were unharnessed and they began jumping and frisking about. This amused our men, but it proved dangerous because the French saw the bullocks grazing and started firing on them. Our little party was stationed on a rising ground, and they occasionally sent a 24-pounder hopping about amongst us.

At night we placed our advanced picket near the town, and the remainder of the party turned into the tents of the sappers for the night. But their slumbers were not so sound as they anticipated because at the dead, but not silent, hour of night, a round-shot came whirling through one of the tents, struck the pole and brought it down on those within. Their cries awoke those of the adjoining tent, who immediately flew to their assistance. Having been relieved from this new-fashioned man-trap, the poor sappers flew from their lair like rats. I could not help laughing, even although one man had his thigh broken, and another had his leg taken off at the calf. These poor fellows were comrades, one named Green, and the other Gea. They were natives of Coventry[2].

When we were helping to raise the tents again, every eye was intent on looking about for another 24-pounder, but a droll countryman of mine, instead of bolting like the rest, said: "Where the devil are you all scampering to? Sure you don't think the French took aim? I wished they did, for by Jasus! they wouldn't hit our tent in a week. You may be easy then, for they never hit twice in the same place."

The next morning the sappers put the pontoons to rights, the guns passed over, and we arrived safe at our own camp.

We were on private parade one morning [25 March?], when a party of convalescents from hospital came up. Among them was Sergeant Jackson, who had been absent from our company for two years, chiefly in employment as a hospital-sergeant at Belem, near Lisbon. The Major's [O'Hare] aversion to absentees from the regiment was well known, and we anticipated a scene. We were not deceived.

"Is that you, Mr. Sergeant Jackson?" exclaimed the Major, as soon as the party came up. "And pray where, in God's name, have you been for the last two years? The company have seen a little fighting during that period."

"The doctors would not allow me to leave the hospital, sir," replied Jackson.

"I am sorry for that," the major observed dryly, "because all I can do is give you the choice of a court-martial for absenting yourself from duty without leave, or I can have your stripes taken off."

The sergeant, after a little hesitation, preferred to surrender his non-commissioned dignity quietly than stand an inquiry into his conduct.

Turning round to the men, the Major remarked aloud, "By God, I will not have these brave fellows commanded by skulkers." Then taking the sash and stripes that were cut off by the Sergeant-Major, he handed them to Corporal Ballard.

"You will not disgrace them," he said[3].

There were two outworks at Badajoz, Fort Picurina and the San Roque Lunette, both of which had to be taken before the main assault. A little after dark on the 25 March, a storming party from the 3rd Division, under the command of General Sir James Kempt, was ordered to take Fort Picurina, and 100 men of the Light Division, under Lt. J M Stokes of the Rifles, were assigned to carry the ladders for them. It was a duty with which the riflemen were not content.

Harry Smith: *'The working party were sent to the engineer park for the ladders. When they arrived, General Kempt ordered them to be planted... The boys of the 3rd Division said to our fellows, 'Come, stand out of the way,' to which our fellows replied, 'Damn your eyes, do you think we Light Division fetch ladders for such chaps as you to climb up? Follow us', and springing on the ladders, many of them were knocked over. A notorious fellow, Sergeant Brotherwood, a noble fellow on duty, told me this anecdote. The siege was prosecuted with the same vigour from without with which it was repelled from within.'*

Simmons says that Stokes, after placing the ladders, was the first man into the fort. This was a severe action in which the British losses were four officers and 50 men killed, 15 officers and 250 men wounded. As soon as Fort Picurina was taken, the riflemen began breaking ground in front of it.

Simmons: *'I knew well, as soon as the enemy were aware of the place being in our possession, that they would commence a fire of grape, so I made my men work hard to cover themselves. About midnight a most furious fire of shot, shell, and grape went over us, and did us no harm. Before daylight our trench was perfect."*

On 30 March, the allied batteries began to play upon the walls of Badajoz with great effect.

One very disagreeable duty, that usually fell upon a few of the best shots of the battalion, was having to run out in independent files to occupy a number of holes, that had been dug at night between our batteries and the walls of the town. Each man had a pit to himself, and our particular business was to pick off any of the enemy gunners who exposed themselves through the embrasures on the walls. Many a Frenchman was thus knocked off by us, but in their holes, our men too were killed or wounded. When this happened, it was doubly dangerous for the man of the relieving party who, instead of finding a ready covering, perceived his pit occupied by a wounded or dead man, and he therefore stood a great chance of being shot before he could remove the body and get shelter.

The artillery in front and rear made such a tremendous noise that it destroyed the sense of hearing for some hours after leaving the trenches.

It was amusing to watch our artillerymen, who were employed almost incessantly in their duties, which were most arduous. The batteries were the chief object for the aim of the enemy's shot and shells, so an artilleryman was always stationed as a sort of signal-man, to give notice of the appearance of either of these missiles. It was remarkable how quickly, on the word 'shell', the men at the guns would throw themselves on the ground for protection.

Kincaid: *'The Portuguese artillery, under British officers, was uncommonly good. I used to be much amused in looking at a 12-gun breaching-battery of theirs. They knew the position of all the enemy's guns which could bear upon them, and had one man posted to watch them, to give notice of what was coming, whether a shot or a shell. He accordingly kept calling out 'Bomba, balla, balla, bomba'; and they would duck their heads until the missile passed. But sometimes he would see a general discharge from all arms, when he threw himself down, screaming out, 'Jesus! Todos, todos!' meaning 'everything!'.'*

On 4 April, says Simmons, *'I was with a party of men behind the advanced sap, and had an opportunity of doing some mischief. Three or four heavy cannon that the enemy were working were doing frightful execution amongst our artillermen in their advance batteries, so I selected several good shots and fired into the embrasures. In half an hour I found the guns did not go off so frequently... and soon after, gabions were stuffed into each embrasure to prevent our rifle balls from entering. They withdrew them to fire, which was my signal for firing steadily at the embrasures. The gabions were replaced without firing a shot. I was so delighted with the good practice I was making against Johnny, that I kept it up from daylight till dark with forty as prime fellows as ever pulled trigger. These guns were literally silenced.'*

By 5 April, the weather having improved, the engineers pronounced the breaches practicable.

The effect of our 24-pound shot upon the wall gave notice that the breaches would soon be practicable. On the 5 April, a storming party was selected for the assault on the following night.

CHAPTER 16

The Storming of Badajoz
6 - 9 April 1812

It was decided that, on the night of 6 April, Badajoz would be stormed. The 3rd Division were allotted the castle, the 5th Division the Olivença Gate, and the 4th and Light Divisions the great breach at Santa Maria and La Trinidad. Colonel Barnard commanded the Light Division. Volunteers for the forlorn hope were again required.

William Green: *'The forlorn hope was composed of 350 men of the 43rd, 52nd, and Rifles, all volunteers, and two buglers from each regiment. Our bugle-major made us cast lots which two of us would go on this momentous errand. The lot fell on me and another young lad, but one of the buglers, who had been on the forlorn hope at Ciudad Rodrigo, offered the bugle-major two dollars to let him go in my stead."* Green reported the bugle-major to the adjutant for taking bribes, and his place on the forlorn hope was restored. *'Those who composed this forlorn hope were free from duty that day, so I went to the river and had a good bathe. I thought I would have a clean skin whether killed or wounded, for all who go on this errand expect one or the other. At 9 o'clock at night, we were paraded - it was then dark - and half a pound of bread and a gill of rum were served out to each man on parade."*

For the second time I volunteered on the forlorn-hope. After having received a double allowance of grog, we fell in about 8 o'clock in the evening, 6 April 1812. The stormers were composed of men from the different regiments of the Light Division. I happened to be on the right of the front section when my old captain, Major O'Hare, who commanded the wing to which my company belonged, came up with Captain Jones of the 52nd regiment. They were in command of the storming party. There never was a pair of uglier men, but a brace of better soldiers never stood before the muzzle of a Frenchman's gun.

"Well, O'Hare," said the Captain, "what do you think of tonight's work?"

The Major seemed in rather low spirits. "I don't know. Tonight, I think, will be my last."

"Tut, tut, man! I have the same sort of feeling, but I keep it down with a drop of this," and he handed his calabash to the Major.

Sergeant Fleming, a brave soldier who I have mentioned before, came up and informed Major O'Hare that a ladder party was wanted.

"Take the right files of the leading sections," was the Major's prompt order.

It was no sooner said than done, and I and my front-rank men were immediately tapped on the shoulder for the ladder party, and I gave up all hope of ever returning. At Rodrigo we had fatigue parties for the ladders, but now the case was altered, and the ladders being prepared were much longer than those employed at that fortress.

To keep down the fire from the ramparts, the Light Division was to have a covering-party of four companies of the 1st battalion 95th (including Kincaid), and it was they who led the way towards the breach followed, says Kincaid, by Lt. William Johnston and six volunteers from the same battalion, *"carrying ropes, prepared with nooses, to throw over the sword-blades [of the chevaux-de-frise], as the most likely method of displacing them was to drag them down the breach."* Next came the forlorn hope and the storming party of 100 men under the command of Major O'Hare, followed by the rest of the Division, which included Harry Smith, George Simmons, and John Cooke of the 43rd.

Green: *"We were told to go as still as possible, and every word of command was given in a whisper. I had been engaged in the field about 26 times, and had never got a wound. We had about a mile to go to the place of attack, so off we went with palpitating hearts. I never feared nor saw danger till this night. As I walked at the head of the column, the thought struck me forcibly - you will be in hell before daylight! Such a feeling of horror I never experienced before. On our way to the wide ditch that surrounded the wall of the town were laid small bags, filled with grass, for each man to take up as he passed along, to throw into the ditch to jump on, that we might not hurt or break our legs, as the ditch was eight or nine feet deep. A party were in the rear with short ladders to be put into the ditch, and to be carried across for the men to ascend to the surface near the wall."*

The word was now given to the ladder party to move forward. There were six of us supporting the ladder allotted to me, and I contrived to carry my grass-bag before me. We were accompanied at each side by two men with hatchets to cut down any obstacle, such as *chevaux-de-frise*, that might oppose us[1]. We had gone only a short distance when we heard the sound of voices on our right. Supposing they were enemies, we halted, and I disengaged myself from the ladder, and cocked my rifle ready for action. Then one of our party cried "Take care! 'tis the stormers of the 4th Division coming to join us." So it was[2]. This brief alarm over, we continued advancing towards the walls, the Rifles, as before, keeping in front.

Green: *"We had to pass between our batteries and the town. The artillery fired blank cartridges while we passed the guns; this we were apprised of as being designed to keep the enemy from suspecting that we were to storm that night. There was no firing from the enemy until we arrived at the ditch."*

Harry Smith: *"When the head of the Light Division arrived at the ditch of the place, it was a beautiful moonlight night... The breach and the works were full of the enemy, looking quietly at us, but not 50 yards off and most prepared, although not firing a shot."*

The assault was scheduled for 10pm, but began about 20 minutes earlier.

We had to pass Fort San Roque on our left, near to the town. As we approached it, the French sentry challenged[3]. This was instantly followed by a shot from the fort and another from the walls of the town. A moment afterwards, a fire-ball was thrown out. It threw a bright red glare of light around us. Instantly a volley of grape-shot, canister, and small arms poured in among us as we stood on the glacis about thirty yards from the walls[4].

William Green: *"All had been still so far, but as the bags were thrown and the men descended, the enemy threw up blue lights; we could see their heads, and they poured a volley down upon us. I was in the act of throwing my bag, when a ball went through the thick part of my thigh, and having my bugle in my left hand, it entered my left wrist and I dropped, so I did not get into the ditch."*

Lt. Johnston and his small party were struck down. So were the men with the ladders:

Three of the men carrying the ladder with me were shot dead in a breath, and its weight fell upon me. I fell backwards with the grass-bag on my breast. Our men were falling fast. The remainder of the stormers rushed up, disregarding my cries, and those of the wounded men around me. Many were shot and fell upon me, so that I was drenched in blood.

Green: *Our men were in the ditch, while the enemy had shells loaded on the top of the wall about two yards apart. As they were fired they rolled into the ditch, and when they burst, 10 or 12 men were blown up in every direction! Some of them arrived at the breach, but a great many, both killed and wounded, lay around me. The balls came very thick about us, and we were not able to move. At length the whole of the Light Division came past me... and made for the breach."[5]*

Simmons: *"Our storming party was soon hotly engaged. Our columns moved on under a most dreadful fire of grape that mowed down our men like grass. We tore down the palisading and got upon the glacis. The havoc now became dreadful. My captain (Gray) was shot in the mouth. Eight or ten officers, and men innumerable, fell to rise no more."*

The weight I had to sustain became intolerable. The grass-bag in some measure protected me, otherwise I might have suffocated. By a strong effort, I managed to extricate myself, but left my rifle behind. Drawing my sword, I rushed toward the breach, where I found four men putting a ladder down the ditch. Fresh lights were being thrown from the town and there was a continual discharge of musketry. Not daring to pause, I slid quickly down the ladder, but before I could recover my footing, I was knocked down again by the bodies of men shot in attempting the descent.

Simmons: *Ladders were resting against the counterscarp from within the ditch. Down these we hurried, and as fast as we got down, rushed forward to the breaches, where a most frightful scene of carnage was going on."*

Kincaid: *"We were entirely excluded from the right breach by an inundation which the heavy rains had enabled the enemy to form."*

I succeeded in extricating myself from underneath the dead, and rushed forward to the right, but to my surprise found myself immersed to my neck in water. Until then I was tolerably composed, but now all reflection left me. Diving through the water - I was a good swimmer - I gained the other side, but in doing so I lost my sword.

I now attempted to get to the breach, which the blaze of musketry from the walls clearly showed me. Without rifle, sword, or any other weapon, I succeeded in clambering up a part of the breach where there was a *chevaux-de-frise*, consisting of a piece of heavy timber studded with sword-blades, turning on an axis. Just before I reached it, I received a stroke on the breast. Whether it was from a grenade, or a stone, or the butt-end of a musket, I cannot say, but down I rolled senseless, drenched with water and human gore.

Smith: *'The breach was covered by a breastwork from behind, and ably defended on the top by chevaux-de-frises of sword blades, sharp as razors, chained to the ground. The ascent to the top of the breach was covered with planks with sharp nails in them... and most difficult and steep. A rifleman stood among the sword-blades on the top of one of the chevaux-de-frises. We made a glorious rush to follow, but in vain - he was knocked over."*

I could not have laid long in this plight, and when my senses started to return, I saw our gallant fellows still rushing forward, each seeming to meet a fate more deadly than my own. The fire continued in one horrible and incessant peal, as if the mouth of the infernal regions had opened to vomit forth destruction upon all around us. Even more appalling were the fearful shouts of the combatants, and cries of the wounded that mingled in the uproar.

The Light Division struggled at the breaches for hours. Kincaid: *"The five succeeding hours were passed in the most gallant and hopeless attempts on the part of individual officers, forming up 50 or a 100 men at a time at the foot of the breach, and endeavouring to carry it by desperate bravery; and fatal as it proved to each gallant band in succession, as fast as one dissolved, another was formed."*

Simmons on the fighting at the breaches: *"Fifty times they were stormed, and as often without effect, the French cannon sweeping the ditches with a most destructive fire. Lights were thrown amongst us from the town that burnt most brilliantly, and made us easier to be shot at. In this way we remained for a considerable time... The ditch now, from the place where we entered to near the top of the breaches, was covered with dead and dying soldiers. If a man fell wounded, ten to one that he ever rose again, for the volleys of musketry and grape shot that were incessantly poured amongst us made our situation too horrid for description. I had seen some fighting, but nothing like this. We remained passively here to be slaughtered, as we could do the besieged little injury from the ditch."*

Strange to say, I now began to feel my arms and legs were entire. At such moments, a man is not always aware of his wounds. I had lost all the frenzy of courage that had first possessed me and felt weak, my spirit prostrate. Among the dead and wounded bodies around me, I endeavoured to screen myself from the enemy's shot. While I lay in this position, the fire continued to blaze over me in all its horrors, accompanied by screams, groans, and shouts, the crashing of stones and the falling of timbers. For the first time for many years, I uttered something like a prayer.

William Lawrence of the 40th who, like Green and Costello, had been wounded in that first volley, reached the breach, and even cut his hands trying to remove the swords from the *chevaux-de-frise*, but then his comrades persuaded him to go the rear. Crawling on his hands and knees, he succeeded in getting beyond the reach of the enemy's musketry, where he encountered Wellington and his staff. Wellington enquired whether any of the men had got into the town. Lawrence told him they had not, and that he did not think they would because the defences were so strong.

Kincaid: *"I was near Colonel Barnard after midnight, when he received repeated messages from Lord Wellington to withdraw from the breach, and to form the Division for a renewal of the attack at daylight but, as fresh attempts continued to be made, and the troops were still pressing forward into the ditch, it went against his gallant soul to order a retreat while yet a chance remained. However, after heading repeated attempts himself, he saw that it was hopeless, and the order was reluctantly given about 2 o'clock in the morning. We fell back about 300 yards and reformed all that remained to us."*

Simmons: *"We were ordered to leave the ditch and move away from the works. The Light Division formed up on the plain at some distance from the town. Here we observed the 3rd Division assailing the castle and escalading its walls."*

Costello did not withdraw with the Division.

> After the horrible scene of carnage had lasted some time, the fire gradually slackened from the breach and I heard a cheering come from within the town. Shortly afterwards there was a cry of "Blood and 'ounds! Where's the Light Division? The town's our own, hurrah!" It was, no doubt, from some of the 3rd Division.

The 3rd Division had succeeded in getting into the town via the castle, and the 5th Division by the Olivença gate.

Simmons: *"I was lying upon the grass by my comrades, having the most gloomy thoughts of the termination of this sad affair, when a staff officer rode up and said, 'Lord Wellington orders the Light Division to return immediately and attack the breaches,' and we moved back to this bloody work as if nothing had happened. Never were braver men congregated together for such a purpose. We entered the ditches."*

Kincaid: *"We stole down into the ditch with the same silence which marked our first advance. An occasional explosion, or a discharge of musketry, continued to be heard in distant parts of the works, but in the awful charnel pit we were then traversing to reach the foot of the breach, the only sounds that disturbed the night were the moans of the dying, with an occasional screech from others suffering under acute agony. A third class lying there disabled, and live to passing events, on hearing the movement of troops (though too dark to distinguish them), began proclaiming their names and regiments, and appealing to individual officers and soldiers of the different corps, on whose friendly aid they seemed to feel that they could rely if they happened to be within hearing. It was a heart-rending moment to be obliged to leave such appeals unheeded."* Costello was one of these men.

> I now attempted to rise, but found myself unable to stand because I had received a wound, although I know not when. A musket-ball had passed through the lower part of my right leg, and two others had perforated my cap, which I should have lost had I not taken the precaution to secure it with a cord under my chin before starting. I saw two or three men moving towards me and was glad to find they belonged to the Rifles. One of them, O'Brien[6], of the same company as

myself, immediately exclaimed, "What! Is that you, Ned?, We thought you ladder-men all done for." He then assisted me to rise.

Kincaid: *"On our arrival [at the breaches], we found them entirely evacuated, and had no occasion to fire another shot; but we found the utmost difficulty, and even danger, in getting in in the dark, even without opposition."*

The *chevaux-de-frise* remained above the breach, and we could not proceed over it until more men arrived to remove its fastenings. Meanwhile, the 3rd Division had entered the town on our right by the castle, where there was no breach.

I moved with great difficulty, even although being partly supported by O'Brien. At the top of the breach we found another trench with a plank of wood lain across, leading into the town. It was then that I felt drops of blood trickling down my face - one of the balls, in passing through my cap, had torn the skin on my head. I was in a crippled state and had to lean upon my comrade, and use his rifle as a crutch. Accompanied by a few of our rifleman, we entered the town that had been so gloriously won.

We hurried from the breach as quick as possible lest the enemy should spring a mine, as they did at Ciudad Rodrigo. We heard occasional firing and cheering from one end of the town, and imagined the fire was till raging, but we soon afterward learnt that the chief part of the French had retired to the fort, where they surrendered on the following morning[7]. When we turned the corner of a street, we saw some men. A light shone from a window opposite, so we could see from their uniforms they were French. The moment they saw us they disappeared, except one man, who seemed to make a rush at us with his musket. O'Brien sprang forward and wrested the firelock from his grasp.

"O'Brien," I exclaimed, angry and irritated from the pain occasioned by the wound; "let me have the pleasure of shooting this rascal; he may be the man who had brought me to the state I am now in!"

I then presented the rifle close to Frenchman's breast, intending to shoot him through the body, but as my finger was about to press the trigger, he fell upon his knees and implored mercy. The rifle dropped from my hand. I felt ashamed. My feeling of irritation had nearly betrayed me into the commission of a crime for which I could never have forgiven myself. The Frenchman immediately started from his knees and threw his arms around my neck, wanting to kiss my cheek to show his gratitude. He followed me, and I took him under my protection.

Simmons: *"Firing was now going on in several parts of the town, and we were not long in chiming in with the rest of them. The prisoners were secured and the place was given up to be plundered and pillaged.*

I am sorry to say our soldiers were now nearly as great adepts as any continental soldiers in this work of destruction."

Harry Smith: *"Now comes a scene of horror I would willingly bury in oblivion. The atrocities committed by our soldiers on the poor, innocent, and defenceless inhabitants of the city, no words suffice to depict. Civilized man, when let loose, and the bonds of morality relaxed, is a far greater beast than the savage, more refined in his cruelty, more fiend-like in every act; and oh, too truly did our heretofore noble soldiers disgrace themselves."*

We now looked around for a house where we could obtain refreshment and, if truth must be told, a little money, for wounded though I was, I had made up my mind to gain by our victory. At the first house we knocked at, no notice was taken of the summons, so we fired a rifle-ball at the key-hole, our usual method of forcing locks. It sent the door flying open. As soon as we entered the house, we found a young Spanish woman crying bitterly and praying for mercy. She said she was the wife of a French officer. When O'Brien, demanded refreshment, she said there was nothing in the house but her poor self. However, she produced some spirits and chocolate, and being very hungry and faint, I partook of them with much relish. But the house looked poor, so we soon quitted it in quest of a better and went in the direction of the market-place, O'Brien and the Frenchman supporting me.

It was a dark night, and confusion and uproar prevailed in the town. The shouts and oaths of drunken soldiers in quest of liquor, the reports of fire-arms, the crashing in of doors, and the appalling shrieks of hapless women, made you think you were in the regions of the damned.

When we arrived at the market-place, a number of Spanish prisoners were rushing out of a gaol, many still bearing the chains they had not had time to free themselves from. The were like a set of savages suddenly let loose. Among them were men of the 5th and 88th regiments holding lighted candles. We turned down a street opposite, and entered a house which was occupied by a number of men of the 3rd Division. Seeing that I was wounded, one of them struck the neck off a bottle of wine with his bayonet, and presented it to me. For a while, the wine relieved me from the faintness I felt.

I sat at the fire, which was blazing up the chimney, fed by mahogany chairs broken up for the purpose. Then I heard screams for mercy from an adjoining room. I hobbled in and found an old man, the proprietor of the house, on his knees, imploring mercy of a soldier who had levelled his musket at him. With difficulty, I prevented him from being shot. The soldier complained that the Spaniard would not give up his money, so I immediately informed the wretched landlord in Spanish, as well as I was able, that he could only save his life by surrendering his cash. Upon hearing this, and with trembling hands, he brought out from under the mattress of the bed, a large bag of dollars enveloped in a night-cap. The treasure must have amounted to 100-150 dollars. By common consent, it was divided among us. The dollars were piled on the table in small heaps according to the number of men present, and called out the same as messes in a barrack-room. I confess that I participated in the plunder, receiving about 26 dollars for my own share[8].

As soon as I had resumed my seat at the fire, a number of Portuguese soldiers entered. One of them took me for a Frenchman and snapped his piece at me. Luckily it hung fire. Forgetful of my wound, I rushed at him, and a regular scuffle ensued between our men and the Portuguese, until one of the latter was stabbed by a bayonet, and they retired, dragging the wounded man with them. After ejecting the Portuguese, the victors, who by this time were tolerably drunk, proceeded to ransack the house and, unhappily, discovered the patrone's two daughters concealed upstairs. They were young and very pretty. Shortly afterwards, the mother too was dragged from her hiding-place.

Without dwelling on the frightful scene that followed, I will just add that our men, more infuriated by drink than before, again seized upon the old man and insisted upon a fresh supply of liquor. His protestations that he possessed no more were in vain, as were all attempts to restrain them from ill-using him.

The scenes of wickedness that soldiers are guilty of on capturing a town are often truly diabolical, and I shudder at the memory. Our men were prejudiced against the inhabitants of Badajoz because they had submitted so tamely to the French. It was different at Ciudad Rodrigo, where the Spaniards had defended themselves gallantly.

It is to be lamented that the memory of an old soldier should be disturbed by such painful reflections, but it has to be considered that the men who besiege a town in the face of such dangers generally become desperate from their own privations and sufferings. Once they get a footing within its walls, they are flushed by victory. Hurried on by the desire for liquor, and eventually maddened by drink, they will stop at nothing. They are literally mad, hardly conscious of what they are doing in such a state of excitement. I do not seek to justify it; I only remark what I have observed human nature to be on these occasions[9].

Sick of the scene of horrors, and attended by my French prisoner, I left the house for one on the other side of the street. It was occupied by men of the 3rd Division, who were drinking chocolate made not with water, but with wine. They seemed rather more sober and peaceable than those we had just left, but here also, as in most of the houses in Badajoz, the greatest outrages were being committed.

I passed a wretched night, and the next morning was determined to rejoin what remained of my regiment, for I did not know what number we had lost. I left the house and, accompanied by my Frenchman who rendered what assistance he could, proceeded through the crowds.

The town was still in great confusion and uproar, although every available means had been taken to suppress it. In one of the streets I saw the Duke of Wellington. He was surrounded by British soldiers who, holding up bottles of wine and spirits, with their heads knocked off, cried out a phrase then familiarly applied to him by the men of the army:

"Old boy! will you drink? The town's our own - hurrah!"

That day, 7 April, Wellington issued the following general order to the British and Portuguese troops: *'It is now full time that the plunder of Badajoz should cease, and the Commander of the Forces requests that one officer and six steady non-commissioned officers of each regiment be sent into the town at 5am next morning to bring away any stragglers."* He also ordered *"the Provost Marshal into the town, and he has orders to execute any men he may find in the act of plunder after he shall arrive there."*

In another street I observed a sort of gallows erected, with three nooses hanging ready for service. Johnny Castles, a man of our company, a quiet, inoffensive little fellow, had a near escape[10]. He was rather fond of a drop, but not that distilled by Jack Ketch[11] & Co. He was brought under the gallows in a cart, and the rope placed round his neck, but his life was spared. Whether this was done to frighten him or not I cannot say, but the circumstance had such an effect on him that he took ill, and was a little deranged for some time after. I am not aware that a single execution took place, notwithstanding the known severity of the Duke in matters of plunder and outrage.

Some officers believed that if soldiers took a town by siege, then they had the right to plunder it. Kincaid was with the four companies of 1st battalion riflemen who had acted as a covering party for the stormers:

'Once established within the walls we felt satisfied that the town was ours. Profiting by his experience at Ciudad, our commandant (Colonel Cameron) took the necessary measure to keep his battalion together so long as the safety of the place could in any way be compromised. Knowing the barbarous licence which soldiers employed in that desperate service claim, and which they will not be denied, he addressed them, and promised that they should have the same indulgence as others, and that he should not insist upon keeping them together longer than was absolutely necessary; but he assured them that if any man quitted the ranks until he gave permission, he would cause him to be put to death on the spot. That had the desired effect until between 9 and 10 o'clock in the morning, when, seeing that the whole of the late garrison had been secured and marched off to Elvas, he again addressed the battalion... 'Now my men, you may fall out and enjoy

yourselves for the remainder of the day, but I shall expect to see you all in camp at the usual roll-call in the evening.' When evening came, however, in place of the usual tattoo report of all present, it was all absent, and it could have been wished that the irregularities had ended with that evening's report."

About the time that these riflemen were let loose on the town, others were on their way out. Surtees: *"Some of them had dressed themselves in priests' or friars' garments, and some appeared in female dresses, as nuns, etc. In short, all the whimsical and fantastical figures imaginable almost were to be seen coming reeling out of the town, for by this time they were nearly all drunk. I penetrated no farther into the town that day than to a house a little beyond the breach, where I had deposited the wounded, but I saw enough in this short trip to disgust me with the doings in Badajoz at this time."*

It may appear strange, but I did not wish to remain in Badajoz. I was suffering from my wound, and preferred the quiet of the camp. On my way there, I felt fatigued and sat down with my prisoner on a bench opposite the bridge which leads to Fort St. Christoval. We had not been there long when I was noticed a large baboon. It was surrounded by a number of soldiers, who were tormenting him. The poor animal had been wounded in the foot, probably by one of our men, and by his chattering, grinning, and droll gesticulations, he showed as much aversion to red coats as a Frenchman. A servant told the soldiers that it belonged to a colonel of the 4th regiment, who was wounded, and he attempted to take the beast away, but the party was divided in their sentiments and a scuffle ensued, in which several men were wounded with bayonets.

We got up to leave and saw a number of Frenchmen, guarded by our soldiers, coming over the bridge. They were the prisoners taken in Fort St. Christoval, which had surrendered only an hour or two previously. They were soon surrounded by our men, who began examining their knapsacks, from whence a number of watches, dollars, etc, were quickly extracted. A short distance further on we came up with a mule, which was tied to a door. In my crippled state, and wishing to relieve my poor prisoner, I appropriated it for my own use. I afterwards sold it to Lieutenant Jackson of the 83rd regiment.

Mounted on the animal, led by the Frenchman, we continued. Near the gates that led to the camp, I saw a rather affecting scene. A little fellow, a drummer-boy belonging to the 88th regiment, was lying wounded, his leg broken by a shot. He was crying bitterly and I said that, if he wished, the Frenchman would carry him.

"No," said the boy, "I don't care for myself, but look at my poor father!"

He pointed. There lay a man shot through the head, weltering in gore and blood. The poor little fellow! I gave him a couple of dollars, and called some men to his assistance, then I was compelled to leave him.

Simmons spent the night in Badajoz in a house where the previous incumbent had been the French Quartermaster-General: *"When the day dawned I went to see the breaches... the Governor had done everything to make the place as defensible as possible, and displayed a great deal of ability and judgement in his masterly arrangement."*[12]

Surtees: *"Within the space of less than an acre of ground, I should imagine not less than 1,200-1,500 men were lying: it was a heart-rending sight."*

John Cooke of the 43rd: *"One man only was at the top of the left breach (the heaps of dead had, as a matter of course, rolled to the bottom), and that was one of the rifle corps who had succeeded in getting under the chevaux-de-frise. His head was battered to pieces, and his arms and shoulders torn asunder with bayonet wounds."*

Simmons: *I saw my poor friend Major O'Hare lying dead upon the breach. Two or three musket balls had passed through his breast. A gallant fellow, Sergeant Fleming, a man who had always been with him, was also dead by his side. I called to remembrance O'Hare's last words just before he marched off to lead the advance. He shook me by the hand saying, 'a lieutenant-colonel or cold meat in a few hours'. I was now gazing upon his body lying stretched and naked amongst thousands more. Our loss was very severe, but principally fell upon the young officers. The 43rd and 52nd Light Infantry lost about the same number as ourselves. I am only astonished how anyone escaped, but I was not touched in any part of me. I went away from the town to the camp as soon as possible."*

The British casualties at Badajoz were terrible. The number killed during the siege and storming was 4,670. The Light Division lost 62 officers and 744 men killed, and 251 officers and 2,604 men wounded. The 1st batt. 95th lost 3 officers. 3 sergeants and 24 riflemen killed, and 9 officers, 15 sergeants, 3 buglers and 136 riflemen wounded. The French losses were comparatively small. General Phillipon, the commander of the garrison, told Wellington that during the whole course of the siege he had lost 1,200 men killed and wounded out of 5,000.

> We soon arrived at the camp ground of the 3rd Division. I dismounted and sat on one of the men's knapsacks. A soldier of the 83rd regiment was engaged in cleaning his firelock when the piece went off, shooting a corporal through the head, and wounding the hand of another man. As the corporal fell dead at his side, the Frenchman turned pale as marble thinking, perhaps, that the shot was aimed at him. This accident struck me forcibly for the poor corporal had survived the dangers of the preceding night only to lose his life by a clumsy hand cleaning a firelock.

We had no sooner arrived at the camp than I was obliged to part with my faithful Frenchman, who was sent to join the other prisoners. I gave him a few dollars. which he was most likely deprived of before he got many yards. He left me with many expressions of gratitude for the protection I had afforded him.

I have been in many actions, but I never witnessed such a complication of horrors as surrounded me on the forlorn-hope at Badajoz. It was one of the most sanguinary and awful engagements on the records of any country.

Despite the general order of the 7th, the disorder in Badajoz continued. Kincaid: *"We went into the town on the morning of the 8th, to endeavour to collect our men, but only succeeded in part, as the same extraordinary scene of plunder and rioting still continued."*

On 8 April, at 11pm, there were further orders: *'The Commander of Forces is sorry to learn that the Brigade in Badajoz, instead of being a protection to the people, plunder them more than those who stormed the town. The Commander of the Forces calls upon the staff officers of the army, and other officers of regiments to assist him in putting an end to the disgraceful scenes of drunkenness and plunder which are still going on in Badajoz."* Guards were to be *'placed at the gates of the town to prevent soldiers entering, and from quitting it with bundles."*

Surtees: *'The different camps of our army were for several days after more like rag-fairs than military encampments, such quantities of wearing apparel of all kinds were disposed of by one set of plunderers to the others."*

The soldiers, says Simmons, were *'in possession of all sort of things brought from the town, and crowds of country people bartered with them for clothes and other articles. These two sieges [Ciudad Rodrigo and Badajoz] had demoralised the men very much, and coercion was necessary on many occasions (with men that had never behaved ill before). The men were made to throw away a quantity of things, and to prevent them secreting any of the articles, their packs were examined, and the plunder that had not been made away with was collected into heaps and burnt. A garrison of Spaniards were put into Badajoz, and the place was put in order."*

Kincaid: *'Lord Wellington found that, to restore order, severe measures must be resorted to. On the third day, he caused a Portuguese brigade to be marched in, and kept standing to their arms in the great square, where the provost marshal erected a gallows, and proceeded to suspend a few of the delinquents, which very quickly cleared the town of the remainder, and enabled us to give a more satisfactory account of our battalion than we had hitherto been able to do."* It would appear that, despite the threat, no soldier was actually executed at Badajoz.

The men's experience of unrestrained plunder made them unmanageable. Surtees: *'they had now got such relish for plunder, that they could not leave it off when driven out of the town. A night or two after the surrender of the place, they stole no less than eight horses and mules belonging to my battalion [3rd], and took them to some other division, where they sold them as animals captured from the enemy."*

I remained three days in camp before there was a possibility of my being conveyed into the hospital at Badajoz[13]. During this time, I had an opportunity of hearing of the casualties that occurred. The number of men killed, wounded, and absent was such that the company could not muster a dozen men on parade for three days afterwards. Parties were sent to the breaches to bury the dead, which began to smell most dreadfully, but we could not collect enough men to perform that duty. My poor old captain, Major O'Hare, was amongst the slain, and had received not less than ten or a dozen balls through his body[14]. His presentiments, and those of Captain Jones, were fatally realised, for in less than twenty minutes after their conversation, they had both fallen riddled with balls.

While in hospital, here as in other places, we were intermingled with the French prisoners who, sick and wounded, were placed indiscriminately in the wards with the British. In the bed next to me was a Frenchman, a smart young fellow with whom I became intimately acquainted. He could speak a little English, which he had acquired during a short stay as a prisoner in England. He had been exchanged, only to be captured again. He was recovering fast from a gunshot wound in his shoulder.

During one of our evening chats, he gave me an account of his escape from Almeida, which he had helped to defend, blow up and evacuate [recounted in Chapter 12]. This account, and many others equally entertaining, but which the years have blotted from my memory, he related to me, generally finishing with:

"Well, it is all the same; the pupils are worthy of their teachers. The French have taught you some terrible lessons, and you understand at last the art of making war as it is, as it should be".

The plunder of Badajoz had unfortunate consequences for the British army. A general order of 10 June notes *"that recent outrages and plunder at Badajoz had turned the local people into enemies instead of friends."*

Advances to Salamanca, Burgos, and Madrid

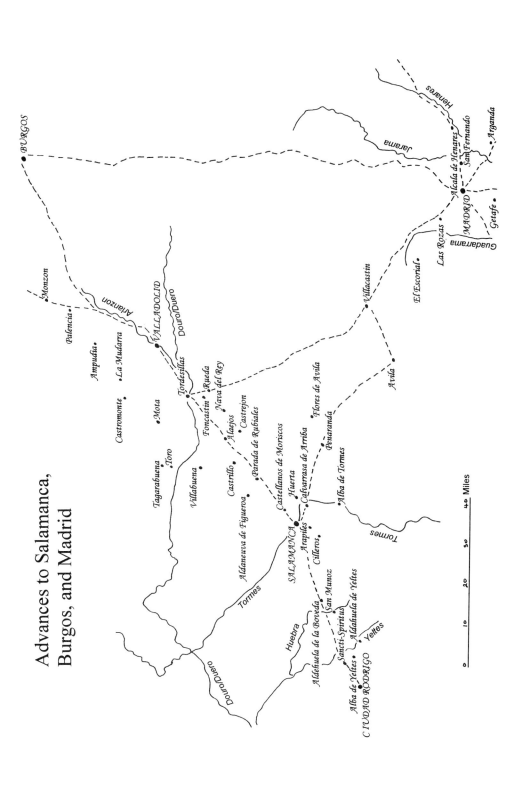

CHAPTER 17

Advance to Salamanca and Rueda
10 April - 21 July 1812

While Costello was in hospital, and in response to the movements of the French - Marmont was stationed at Salamanca - Wellington's army left Badajoz and returned, yet again, to the environs of Ciudad Rodrigo. The Light Division, now under the command of Baron Charles Alten, reached Campo Maior on 12 April, and Ituero on the 24th. They moved into quarters near the river Agueda, and prepared for a new campaign by filling the gaps in their ranks caused by their losses at Rodrigo and Badajoz. Each regiment was ordered to enlist 50 Spaniards, and between 25 May and 20 June, eight were recruited into the 1st battalion 95th. By the beginning of June, the strength of Wellington's army was 47,000 men: 28,000 British and German, 15,000 Portuguese, and 3,000 Spaniards.

> Having recovered from my wounds, I left the hospital and rejoined my regiment at Ituero, near Ciudad Rodrigo. Here, one of our men had an unfortunate accident. With several comrades, he was playing at a game called nine-holes. Instead of a wooden ball, he was rolling along the ground a grenade, which he believed to be filled with earth only. A spark from his pipe fell into the hole, and it exploded, wounding him dreadfully. The poor fellow never recovered from his injuries[1]. A short time after I rejoined, our Division marched for Salamanca.

The Light Division was the advanced guard, and on 11 June they camped in front of Ciudad Rodrigo.

> On our first day's march we encamped in a wood, principally composed of cork-trees, on the right side of the road leading to Salamanca. The evening was beautiful and the sun, having lost its meridian heat, imparted a refreshing warmth to the weary soldiers. The camp was all astir for some time with everyone busily engaged cooking and preparing for the night's comfort. When completed, the evening found us mostly seated and scattered about in small groups, intent on enjoyment of some sort.
>
> I finished my evening's meal, and sat drinking a tot of wine with Battersby, a sergeant of ours. A few days previously, he had rejoined us from Belem, where he had been a hospital-sergeant[2]. He had brought

with him a very pretty English woman, who passed for his wife, and she was doing much to keep up the spirit of our conversation.

We had been seated for some time under the branches of a clump of cork trees, when we were interrupted by some of the men calling for Battersby. A moment later, up marched a tall, fine-looking grenadier of the 61st Regiment of Foot from the 6th Division, which lay encamped some two or three miles in our rear. As he approached, he cast sundry anguished glances about him. From the moment he made his appearance, the woman seemed wondrously confused, changing colour several times. He drew near, seated himself on a knapsack near her, and fixed her with a firm and deliberate look.

"Nelly," he said, and with such emotion that his voice was scarcely articulate; "why do you treat me so. How can you stoop" - and here he cast a contemptuous glance at Battersby - "how can you stoop to such a disgraceful, dishonourable, protection?"

"I am with those who know better how to treat me than you do," she replied rather snappishly,

"That may be your opinion, but why leave the child? It is but three years old; what can I do with it?"

To this she made no answer.

"Do not think that I wish you return to me," he continued. "That is impossible, but I cannot help my feelings!"

This was replied to with reproaches, which I did not listen to. As it was no business of mine, I turned to converse with my companions.

At last, the grenadier made a move to take his departure. His wife - for such she was - agreed to accompany him a little of the way, and they walked together. I do not know why, but I felt a bit uneasy, which kept me on their trail, and Battersby and myself followed in their rear. They proceeded a few hundred yards, and were some distance in advance, when she turned to wish him goodnight. The poor fellow paused again, as if in deep thought, then fixed on her that same cool, deliberate look. 'So you are determined, Nelly, to continue this way of living?"

"Yes," she said, and extended her hand for him to shake.

Holding her firmly by his left hand, he drew his bayonet with his right, "Well then, take that," he exclaimed, and drove the bayonet right through her body. The poor woman gave a convulsive scream. So forceful was the blow that he actually tripped over her, and they both fell, the bayonet sticking in her side. In a moment, she expired. The grenadier bounded instantly to his feet, and stamping one foot on the body of his victim, jerked forth the bayonet, reeking with her blood. Wheeling himself round on his heel, the fatal weapon tightly clutched in his right hand, his eyes sought Battersby, whom he flew after with the speed and countenance of a fiend, to wreak a second vengeance.

Fortunately, Battersby arrived in the camp in time to call out the rear-guard, and the grenadier, seeing that Battersby was safe, halted. He cast a half-contemptuous smile towards the body of his dead wife, wiped the bayonet through his fingers, and returned it to the scabbard.

Drawing himself to his full height, he calmly awaited the approach of the guard. When brought before the Colonel, he extended his arm towards his wife, and said in a rough and manly tone of voice:

"I have done the deed, but I am sorry her seducer has escaped."

He was afterwards brought to a court-martial, and sentenced to three months' solitary confinement, but I suppose, in consideration of his case, he suffered for one month only then was ordered to return to his regiment. I have since been informed that he was shot in one of the actions on the Pyrenees. His name was Bryen [Farrell]; he certainly was a fine-looking fellow[3].

As for Nelly, we buried her that very night near the spot where she fell, having dug her grave with the same kind of weapon as that by which she had been deprived of life. It was rather strange, but Battersby was not noticed, and still held his rank. He was the second man I saw fall at the battle of Quatre Bras on 16 June 1815. He was shot through the head by a musket-ball [4].

They remained bivouacked in the wood for two days, then on 13 June marched to Alba de Yeltes. By 16 June they were within five miles of Salamanca. On the 17th, says Simmons, they: *'marched and forded the Rio Tormes above the town [Salamanca]; bivouacked in a wood for the night... The enemy retired from Salamanca as the British army approached, merely skirmishing with our dragoons as they made a forward movement."*

On our arrival at Salamanca, we took up our position to the right of that city, near the River Tormes. Here we remained for some days, our chief having completely outmanoeuvred Marmont.

For several days, the Light Division were, says Simmons *'in bivouac near Rio Seco with the whole army is position, and the French under Marshal Marmont concentrating his force in front of us"*

John Cooke said that the French had left *'800 men to garrison the three forts of St. Vincent, Cajetano and La Merced, that were constructed with the masonry extracted from different handsome convents, monasteries, colleges, which had been pulled down to be converted into bastions. The 6th Division took possession of Salamanca and invested the forts."*

On the evening of the 4 July[5], stormers were required from our Division, to lead in the assault on Fort St. Vincent, the strongest of the three forts the enemy had constructed in the city, and which commanded the other two. Two men from each company of our regiment were selected, the first for duty[6]. The men were marched down close to the fort, but while they were awaiting the signal for attack, the orders were countermanded. A few days afterwards this fort was set on fire by red-hot shot from our artillery, when it immediately surrendered, along with the two others.

The forts at Salamanca surrendered on 27 June, and Marmont retreated to Toro and Tordesillas, with Wellington's soldiers in pursuit. On 28 June, says Simmons, *"the army moved forward towards the Douro. As our movements had been confined between the northern frontier of Portugal and the banks of the Guadiana for so long a time, it gave us great delight to be entering the very heart of Spain to offer battle to the French army, each day seeing towns and villages we had never entered before. Marched to Castellanos de Moriscos and bivouacked."*

Over the next two days they marched to Parada de Rubiales, Castrillo, Alaejos and Nava del Rey. Simmons described how he slept: *"My usual bed was two blankets stitched together and made into the shape of a sack, into which I crawled; and if I rolled about, the clothes never left me until I took a fancy to crawl out again. My pillow was a good sod and a smooth stone, and if before I lay down, I could obtain some wild lavender, which generally was in plenty, I then had a splendid bed, exhaling the most agreeable perfumes, with the canopy of heaven over one's head... Often, before daylight, I have been well soused with rain, with many thousands more in the same predicament, and in spite of the elements, have not been much disturbed. It is astonishing what habit will produce in a man of strong and robust health."*

On 2 July, they marched to Rueda, and halted close to it. Kincaid describes it as a handsome little town on the left bank of the Douro.

> The enemy, baffled in their views on Salamanca, slowly retreated. Our army followed until we arrived near Rueda where our light troops had a smart brush with their rear-guard. This ended in the capture of some few French prisoners. A party of the Rifles brought in a very fine-looking man, a French sergeant, who seemed inconsolable at his capture, and lamented the circumstance by actually shedding tears. However, the following day, to his infinite joy, he was exchanged for a sergeant of our cavalry, who had been made prisoner a few days before[7].

The prisoners were taken on 2 July at Rueda where the Light Division remained for the next two weeks, occupying the town during the day, and moving out every night into bivouac about a mile in front of it.

> After this skirmish, our regiment advanced to the neighbourhood of Rueda, where we occupied a hill close to the town. It was completely covered with vines. The country thereabouts abounded in grapes, from

which an immense quantity of wine was made every year. In this part of Spain, the places used for making wine are very singular for they are subterranean, and of such immense extent, they sometimes undermine many acres of ground. Chimneys are constructed over them to admit the air and light. The vats, into which the juice of the grape is pressed, are in proportion to the size of the vaults, and would entirely put to shame the same description of receptacle used for beer by Barclay and Perkins[8].

Simmons: *'The country round abounds in corn and wine. The latter is kept under ground in vast excavated cellars, with high chimneys above ground to ventilate them. The casks containing this wine, which is white, and of a pleasant and agreeably sharp flavour, are of immense magnitude, and must have been introduced piecemeal and then afterwards formed. They contain many thousands of gallons.'*

Leach: *'Descending, after a long day's march under a roasting sun, into those deep cellars, where the air and wine were both like ice, was no trifling luxury, the transition being nearly as great as from the equator to the pole. This, however pleasant, might be supposed to have been an unsafe experiment, but the only inconvenience complained of was that the wine was so cool and delicious, as to render it no easy matter to ascend the long flight of steps to regain our billets above ground.'*

The officers appear to have entered these vaults by the front door, but the soldiers took to going in by 'back' door:

Although the French had ransacked the 'wine-houses', our fellows, always alive to the value of good liquor, frequently used to find something to reward them for their search of these cellars. Our usual method was to let one or two of our men down the chimneys using a rope.

One evening, three or four comrades and myself assembled over the chimney of one of these wine vaults, and it was proposed that one of us should descend to bring up some wine. This was no comfortable task because the proprietors below were usually on the look-out, and would scarcely hesitate to greet an intruder with a cuchillo, or long knife. After some deliberation, and plenty of peeping, it was at last decided that I should take the first chance. A rope, obtained from one of the muleteers, was secured round my waist, along with a number of canteens and with these clinking enough to wake the dead, I was gradually lowered.

The vaults could be as deep as a three-storied building, and half way down, I was left dangling in the air with the canteens chinking enough to hail a knife the moment I arrived in the lower region. Eventually, I touched the ground, but the place was so dark I could scarcely see a couple of yards before me, and was obliged to grope my way to the vats. The canteens, which formed a kind of breastwork for my approach, came in contact with something, and I put my hand forward... upon the cold clammy face of a corpse. My whole body tingled, and the canteens responded. By now I could see, and I could tell from his red wings that this was a French soldier. He exhibited the most frightful gashes, evidently inflicted by the same kind of weapon which, at every turn, I was expecting. I shook with terror, the canteens clattering most awfully. With no weapon to defend myself, I kept looking for the arm of some concealed assassin, who I felt must be watching my movements. Afraid to call out, I tugged at the rope, which was the signal to pull me up. From above came a voice expressing doubt that the canteens should have been filled so soon, and damning my eyes and limbs for me. This only made me shake the rope more violently and, to my great satisfaction, I found myself again dangling and ascending. I came up blowing with agitation, and with hollow tins, and my comrades burst into roars of laughter, which the adventure I related only increased. Their mirth rallied us all, and one more daring that the rest, loaded his rifle and, with an oath, suffered himself to be lowered. Shortly afterwards, he brought up the canteens filled with excellent wine[9]. I shall never forget the terror I experienced in this adventure.

In Rueda, as in other places, the rifle officers organised dances to which the local women were invited. Leach and Kincaid were always at the forefront of such amusements.

Kincaid: *'Our usual evening dances began there to be graced by a superior class of females to what we had hitherto been accustomed. I remember that, in passing the house of the sexton one evening, I saw his daughter baking a loaf of bread. Falling desperately in love with both her and the loaf, I carried the one to the ball and the other to my quarters. A woman was a woman in those days, and every officer made it a point of duty to marshal as many as he could to the general assembly, no matter whether they were countesses or sextonesses. In consequence, we frequently incurred the most indelible disgrace among the better orders or our indiscriminate collection, some of whom would retire in disgust; yet, as a sufficient number generally remained for our evening's amusement, and we were only birds of passage, it was a matter of the most perfect indifference to us what they thought. We followed the same course wherever we went."*

The two weeks at Rueda were spent in relative peace because Marmont did not wish to attack Wellington without reinforcements, and Wellington declined to attack Marmont.

> After remaining here for some time, we left Rueda at 12 o'clock at night on the 16th [July] because the enemy, who had concentrated their forces at Tordesillas, were on the advance.

The Light Division marched to Castrejon where, at daylight on the 18th, the enemy advanced on them in great force. This was the first day of several where the two armies manoeuvred as Marmont tried to separate Wellington from his line of communication through Salamanca and Ciudad Rodrigo.

The following morning the sun rose unclouded, and we had a distinct view of the two armies moving in parallel lines along a ridge of low hills, separated only by the intervening valley and a river, which was fordable in most places. The French columns appeared in such beautiful order they called forth the plaudits of our own men.

Leach: *"A furious cannonade soon commenced. As the country was quite open, and every way favourable to cavalry, the infantry were ordered to form close columns or squares of battalions. In this manner we remained stationary for a length of time, under a heavy fire of artillery, whilst the cavalry, and some companies which had been thrown out in front, were engaged in a sharp skirmish."* Kincaid was one of the skirmishers but Costello, apparently, was not.

Skirmishing soon commenced between some of the cavalry and light troops. One or two companies of our Rifles, seconded by a troop of the 14th Dragoons, became partially engaged with a corresponding number of the enemy, who would occasionally dash through the little river and attempt to take up a position to annoy our skirmishers.

This day, our riflemen were delighted with several little cavalry brushes that occurred between our dragoons and the French. One, which most of us saw, was particularly exciting. A kind of half charge was made by sections of French and English cavalry, and one of the Frenchmen dashed alone through some of our dragoons. His own party retired, leaving at least a dozen of our dragoons between him and his section, and there seemed every prospect of him being killed or taken prisoner. We thought he would surrender. Not so. The gallant Frenchman wheeled round and gently trotted his horse for about 20 yards then, giving spurs to his steed, and engaging in several hand-to-hand conflicts with our dragoons in passing, he succeeded in reaching his party. He was, I believe, unhurt, and he was cheered by our own men, who were never insensible to intrepidity, even of an enemy.

Leach: *'Lord Wellington now ordered the infantry to retire in columns, covered by the cavalry and horse artillery. No man who was present can possibly have forgotten that magnificent sight, nor the steadiness and extreme regularity with which the columns fell back over this extensive plain, followed and assailed in flanks and rear by overwhelming numbers of cavalry and artillery... Nor was the steadiness and gallantry displayed by the cavalry and artillery less worthy of admiration."*

As a consequence of another incident, I gained a new pair of trousers. Pratt, a fine, strapping young fellow of the 14th Dragoons, and a townsman of mine, brought in a French dragoon on his horse. The poor Frenchman, who had lost his helmet and had a severe cut on his cheek, seemed exceedingly chop-fallen, but declared with much vehemence that the Englishman could not have taken him had he possessed a better horse. Lieutenant Gardiner of our company[10] who spoke excellent French, repeated this to Pratt.

"Then by Jasus, sir," Pratt answered; "tell him if he had the best horse in France, I would bring him prisoner - if he stood to fight me."

The words caused roars of laughter from all but the prisoner who, patting the goaded and smoking steed exclaimed affectionately, "My poor beast has not had his saddle off for the last week."

And such appeared to be the case because, before the horse was sold, the saddle was removed and part of the flesh that had become a sore, came away with the saddle-cloth. In this condition, the animal was sold to Lt. Gardiner for five dollars. Pratt opened the valise of the unfortunate prisoner, who looked on with folded arms and mournful eyes, and came upon a pair of trousers, which he threw to me. It was an exceedingly welcome gift, as my own were worn to rags.

The action on 18 July ended with the British upon the high ground, still facing the French. The next day, Marmont threw some shot and shell at the British columns; the cannonade did not cease until dark. By daylight on the 20th, the French had moved position.

The following day, after some slight skirmishes with the advance of the enemy, we retreated upon Salamanca.

Wellington realised that he could not carry on his offensive campaign, but would have to devote his energies to securing the route of his retreat to Portugal.

At 2am on the 21 July, the Light Division halted near Castellanos de Moriscos. A little after dark, they crossed the River Tormes above Salamanca by a ford. Simmons: *The river was very much swollen from the rain, which made it very deep, Everybody got wet up to near their shoulders in crossing. Luckily we got over before the rain, which immediately afterwards began to fall in torrents.*

Kincaid: *Before reaching our ground, we experienced one of the most tremendous thunderstorms that I ever witnessed. A sheet of lightning struck the head of our column, where I happened to be riding, and deprived me of the use of my optics for at least ten minutes. A great many of our dragoon horses broke from their picketing during the storm, and galloped past us into the French lines. We lay by our arms on the banks of the river, and it continued to rain in torrents the whole of the night.*

The night previous to the battle [of Salamanca], which was fought on 22 July 1812, was the most stormy, I think, I ever witnessed. The thunder, lightning, and rain strove to excel, and their united effect was terrible. As we lay, without covering, in an open field close to the River Tormes, not a man that night had on a dry shred.

It has, I believe, been previously remarked, by military and other writers, that rain has been the forerunner of almost all our general battles. From my own recollection, the truth of this assertion is singularly supported by facts.

CHAPTER 18

Battle of Salamanca; Retreat from Burgos
22 July - 26 November 1812

Despite the terrible storm the night before, the morning of 22 June was fine. Wellington's force numbered 50,000, and he had 60 guns. Marmont had 47,000 men and 78 guns. The Light Division was ordered to hold the ground west of Calvarrasa de Arriba, with the 7th Division in support, and Bock's German Hussars on its flank.

The battle of Salamanca - in which the Rifles were less engaged than in any other action fought during the war - commenced on rising ground upon our right at about 10 or 12 o'clock. Our position was first disturbed by some cannon shot of the enemy, which came very near without doing any harm.

Simmons: *"A brisk cannonade commenced on both sides, and about 11am, the columns on our right moved to the attack."*

Although every moment expecting to be sent into the thick of it, we kept undisturbed possession of our ground, from whence we could see the column of the enemy on the heights, engaged in attempting to repel the advance of our troops.

Simmons: *"The high ground and tops or elevated points were crowded with Frenchmen, and in the afternoon these hills, the Arapiles, were lost and won often, but ultimately the French were completely driven off them. About 5 o'clock, the Light Division were ordered to move forward."*

When the 'glad sound of victory' reached us, a general feeling of pleasure pervaded our ranks, mixed perhaps with some regret that we had not taken a more active share in the battle. But all we could do we did, which was to pepper the French well in their hurried retreat from the field. In fact, it seemed to me as if the whole French army might have been cut off by a little promptitude[1].

The action had taken only 40 minutes. Simmons: *'The French were routed at all points, and darkness came on, which enabled many to escape that would otherwise have fallen into our hands... The pursuit*

The Battle of Vitoria, 21 June 1813. Painted by W Heath. Engraved by T Sutherland. Published by J Jenkins, 4 June 1815. ©British Museum

was continued through a wooded country until 11 o'clock at night, when we bivouacked near the village of Huerta."

We halted at Huerta, and the following morning our Division crossed the River Tormes in pursuit of the enemy. We came up with their rear strongly posted on the side of a hill on the left of the road. Cavalry charges seldom succeed against well-trained infantry, but here we beheld one that did: Major-General Bock, at the head of his heavy German cavalry, charged the French squares and broke them, taking the men prisoners almost to a man. It was the most gallant dash of cavalry ever witnessed.

Simmons: *"A brigade of heavy German cavalry, commanded by Major-General Bock, that had only recently joined our army from England, was in advance of the Light Division, and came up with the French rear-guard. The officer commanding the latter formed three squares. The Germans made a most brilliant and dashing charge at two squares, and succeeding in breaking them, slaughtering numbers. The French had 1,500 killed and taken."*

Kincaid described the German dead: *"I saw there many fine fellows lying dead along with their horses, on which they were still astride, with the sword firmly grasped in the hand as they had fought the instant before, and several of them still wearing a look of fierce defiance, which death itself had been unable to quench."*

This day I began to feel the ill effects of the wound I had received at Badajoz, which the fatigue of marching and the warmth of the weather had caused to break out again. Our surgeon inspected the sore and immediately recommended that I go into hospital at Salamanca for a few days of medical treatment and rest. I set out with the guard appointed to escort the prisoners taken by our German cavalry. Their wounded, who were carried in waggons, were extremely numerous, and it was painful, even to an old soldier, to hear their groans and incessant cries for water. There were very few gunshot wounds among them, but many had sabre-cuts, the severest I had ever seen. Several men had both eyes cut out, and numbers had lost both ears.

The escort consisted chiefly of the Germans who had taken them prisoners, and it was pleasing to behold these gallant fellows paying the greatest attention to the wants of the wounded. Water was in particular request due to the loss of blood, and one prisoner, who had his arm hanging - probably wounded in endeavouring to defend his head from a sword cut - was very frequent in his demands for *eau*. When none could be obtained, he imagined himself neglected and suddenly called out in English, "For the love of Jesus, give me something to quench my thirst; I am a fellow countryman of your own."

This surprised us not a little, and I entered into conversation with him. I found that he formerly belonged to the 9th Regiment of Foot.

With a number of others of his regiment, he had been taken prisoner some time previous, while on board ship, and in preference to being kept in close confinement, he had been prevailed upon to enter the French service. At Salamanca a sentry was placed over him. What became of him I know not.

On arriving at Salamanca, the wounded prisoners, and myself and some other invalids, were immediately taken into hospital. There French and English were laid up together, and I saw sufficient daily practice in the use of the surgeon's knife to become perfectly familiar with every form attendant upon amputation.

Costello was in hospital and convalescent in Salamanca for over two months.

While lying in hospital - at all times a wretched place, from the groans of the numerous sufferers - I was placed under the immediate attendance of Sergeant Michael Connelly who, having recovered sufficiently from a slight wound, had been appointed sergeant to the hospital, and was in charge of our ward. He was one of the most singular characters I ever met with. If an awkward person and uncouth face had gained him the preferment, then his match could not be found anywhere.

Mike was exceedingly attentive to the sick, and particularly anxious that the dying British soldier should hold out a pattern of firmness to the Frenchmen, who lay intermixed with us. "Hold your tongue, ye blathering devil," he would say, in a low tone. "Don't be after disgracing your country in the teeth of these 'ere furriners by dying hard. You are not at Elvas to be thrown into a hole like dog. You'll be buried in a shroud and coffin; you'll have the company at your burial, won't you? You'll have the drums beatingm and the guns firing over you, won't you? Marciful God! what more do you want? For God's sake, die like a man before these 'ere Frenchers."

Mike, however, had a great failing - he drank like a whale, and as he did not scruple to adopt as gifts or legacies, the wine rations of the dying and the dead, he drank himself out of the world. As his patients remarked, *he* died like a beast.

The news of Mike's death spread like wildfire, and all his old friends, and the convalescents, crowded around to do honour to his remains. The funeral of the Duke himself could not have made a greater stir. The coffin carrying the deceased sergeant, borne by four bearers, and with the usual complement of soldiers with the arms reversed, slowly wound its way through the city of Salamanca. Cavalier and foot soldier, drum boy and trumpeter, and all the women, children and camp followers in the locality, flocked to follow his remains. The town became unusually alive with the variegated throng, and many a jest made the streets ring with laughter. They reached the burial-ground, near the French battery, which had been taken by us some time previously. The bearers were about to enter the gateway, when they were suddenly aroused by a slight cry. It came from within the coffin, and was accompanied by a kind of scraping noise. They halted, paused, and listened. Surely it was Mike scraping! On they moved again doubtfully, but for a second time they heard the voice.

"Whist!" ejaculated the bearers, their caps moving almost off their heads.

"Oh blood and ouns!" said the voice. "Where am I? Oh, bad luck to yer souls! Let me out, won't you? Oh, merciful Jasus, I'm smothered."

The bearers bolted out from under the coffin, and in an instant a dozen bayonets were sunk under the lid to lift it. The crowd crushed forward to take a look. There lay Sergeant Michael Connelly, as stiff as a fugleman[2], but somewhat colder. One of the bearers was that blackguard Josh Hetherington, the cockney ventriloquist, and he joined in the astonishment as 'innocent' as you please! He winked at me, and I winked back.

"Ned," he said, "I'm blessed if I think he's dead. Why don't some of them there chaps go for a doctor?"

"To be sure," cried the crowd, "send for the doctor."

Meanwhile a regular rush was made to press Mike to swallow some of his favourite liquor, but his teeth so obstinately opposed the draught, that when the doctor arrive, they pronounced that poor Mike was 'not himself'.[3]

While here, I became acquainted with a pleasant and intelligent man who belonged to the 13th Light Dragoons. He was fast recovering from a shoulder wound, and we used to alleviate the unpleasantness of our situation with a little conversation. His history amused and interested me.

While serving in General Hill's division, he had been taken prisoner by the French near Badajoz. Shortly afterwards, between Vitoria and Pamplona, he managed to make his escape, and the following morning fell in with a party of General Mina's Guerillas[4] who, as soon as they found him to be an Englishman, wished him to enlist in their band until he could regain his regiment. This offer he was glad to accept. After giving me a very amusing account of the manners of the guerillas, their rich, picturesque dresses and arms, and their wild military life in the mountains, he proceeded to detail several anecdotes of their cruelty and ferocity, one of which, though he related it simply, left a strong impression on my mind:

Mina's information of the movements of the French seemed unerring, and one morning, having united several of his guerilla bands in the neighbourhood of Vitoria, he surprised and captured a number of waggons filled with stores, which had been sent from Madrid for the army at Vitoria. The waggons were escorted by gendarmes, all of whom were either killed or captured. There were about 20 prisoners and they were marched into the mountains, but not before they had time to draw a dark augury of their own fate by seeing all their wounded comrades brutally stabbed to death on the ground where the skirmish had taken place.

The prisoners were stripped of nearly every article of clothing, even to their boots, and then confined in a space of ground encircled by hurdles - a cattle pen - around which were planted many sentries. In the evening, the ferocious mountaineers were joined by a number of females - their sweethearts and wives. Elated with the day's success, they made merry with drinking wine and dancing to the music of several guitars. During this merriment both men and women frequently taunted their wretched prisoners, recapitulating the wrongs the Spaniards had suffered at the hands of the French. Having thus excited their passions to a partial state of frenzy, a signal was given by one of their number, and they rushed in among their hapless prisoners and commenced a general massacre. As they gave each blow, they drowned the cries and supplications for mercy of their victims, by enumerating the different losses each had sustained in his family during the war: "Take that for my father you shot", "that for my son", "this for my brother", etc, until the work of death was complete. The most inhuman, and perhaps most revolting trait in the general murder, was that some of the women actively assisted in the slaughter. This sanguinary feeling of revenge peculiarly characterised the guerillas during the war.

On 24 July, the day after Costello was taken to hospital, the Light Division quit Salamanca with the rest of Wellington's army and marched towards Valladolid in pursuit of Marmont, who retreated so fast that he outdistanced them. On 30 July, when the British were about six miles from Valladolid, Wellington decided to march south upon Madrid to eject King Joseph Bonaparte from the Spanish capital. Joseph, learning of his advance, left Madrid on 10 August for Aranjuez, leaving a small garrison to hold the Retiro, and man the defensive wall around it. On the 11th, the Light Division, which was marching in the rear of the army, bivouacked in the park of El Escorial, a palace near Madrid, while Wellington himself entered the city to an ecstatic welcome from the citizens. On the night of the 13 August, the Retiro fortification in Madrid was stormed, and on the 14th, the French commander surrendered.

On 20 August, the Light Division marched to Getafe eight miles from Madrid, where they remained while Wellington, with most of the rest of his army, proceeded north to Burgos, the principal depot of the French Army of Portugal. Burgos barred the route to France and Wellington was determined to take it. With him, he had 23,000 men, having left 7,000 in and around Madrid.

The Light Division remained at Getafe for three months, and it was there that Costello rejoined the 1st battalion. The companies were reorganised again: the 3rd and 4th were disbanded and the men from them spread around the remaining six companies. Costello, and many of his 3rd company comrades, were transferred into Captain Jonathan

Leach's 2nd Company. Between 22 August and 22 September another 13 Spaniards joined the battalion.

Captain Jonathan Leach in about 1806, the year he joined the Rifles.

I rejoined my regiment at Getafe, a little village about three leagues from Madrid. In the farmhouse, where the greater part of our company were quartered, was a very pretty Spanish girl, who seemed much attached to me. With her I spent many a moonlight night serenading to the Spanish guitar, and she taught me to use the castanets in the Spanish dance[5].

One hot summer evening, several comrades and myself were sitting on a bench outside the door, joking with the girl, when a swarthy, savage-looking Spaniard came up. He was armed to the teeth with pistols, daggers, and a long gun which, together with his crimson sash and free bearing, at once proclaimed him as a guerilla. He was welcomed with much joy by the girl and her parents. The girl had a brother serving with the guerillas and, at first, that was who we imagined him to be, but we soon perceived that another, equally dear tie cemented their affection: he was her lover, or suitor.

While engaged in conversation with his sweetheart and her parents, he ostentatiously took from his side a long heavy-looking silk purse and emptied the contents into the lap of his mistress. The Spaniard's eyes sparkled with pleasure, but in general, my comrades and myself felt only disgust, for what we beheld was a number of human ears and fingers, glistening with the golden rings they retained. With an air of bravado, the Spaniard told us that he had cut them from the bodies of the French who he himself had slain in battle.

"Napoleon," he observed, in his native dialect, and with a grim smile; "Napoleon loves his soldiers, and so do the ravens."

He pointed to several of those carrion birds perched on the ivy-covered walls of an old convent.

"We find them plenty of food. They shall never want, so long as a Frenchman remains in Spain."

Such were the men were considered the greatest patriots attached to the Spanish army during the war.

Wellington reached Burgos on 18 September, but by then the French Army of Portugal had received reinforcements, and Marmont had been replaced by General Joseph Souham. Wellington's attack against Burgos failed.

The chief business of the British at this time was laying siege to Burgos. The enemy assembled in great numbers betwixt it and Vitoria and Lord Wellington, thinking he was not able to oppose their force, ordered the whole of the divisions to retire on Salamanca. We of the Light Division received orders to the same effect and left Madrid on 22 October. The contempt with which the inhabitants treated us for leaving them once more to the mercy of the French, cannot easily be forgotten. What the men said gave us little concern, but to be taxed and taunted for cowardice by the Spanish ladies was most galling. Even my handsome, dark-eyed Clementeria, even she with all her pretended love, refused me a buss at our last moment of parting. I used all my eloquence, welding the Spanish, French, and English together, in pleading my cause, but it had no effect on the hard-hearted girl. Her last words were:

"Begone, you cowardly English; you don't have the courage to fight the enemy of our country, those who have butchered my dear father and brother."

The Light Division left Getafe on 21 October and embarked on a march east of Madrid as far as Alcala de Henares, before retreating back to Madrid via Arganda and San Fernando. They continued westward through the city to Las Rozas and bivouacked on the River Guadarrama. The people of Madrid were unhappy about the British withdrawal because it left them again exposed to the advancing French.

Simmons: *'I was truly glad to get away from this unfortunate place, as we could not do the people any good, and pity is at best (under the circumstances) a sorry way of showing good wishes. It would have delighted me, as well as thousands more, if our noble commander could have risked a battle, but that was impossible. He was in full retreat from Burgos, having failed in an assault of it, owing to the guns used on this occasion being too light to make a sufficient breach in its walls; also a very powerful French army was ready to attack him under Marshal Soult, and a large force was moving upon Madrid to attack us."*

King Joseph, with a large army consisting of most of the French troops which had been fighting in other parts of Spain, was advancing upon Madrid.

At the latter end of October, the whole of our army began retracing their steps towards Salamanca, and we had several days of tiresome and harassing marches through mountainous country.

On 2 November, the Light Division reach the camp of El Escorial and the next day crossed the Sierra de Guadarrama to Villacastin. From there they marched to Alba de Tormes, which they reached on the 7th. Here they were joined by the four divisions retreating from Burgos. On 10 November, the army marched into Salamanca and the troops were put into various large buildings. The Light Division were placed in the Irish College.

We arrived at Salamanca where we joined the remainder of our army, and took up our quarters in a convent, which exhibited such a loathsome picture of filth as to be almost unendurable. We were there for a few days. Some of our men tore up a part of the balustrade for firing. As a consequence, a young officer of the 3rd battalion fell down a height of 50 feet, and was killed on the spot.

This happened on 13 November. The officer was Walter Firman who had joined the 95th as a second lieutenant only 6 months before. Simmons: *"In the evening, being orderly officer, I went at 8 o'clock to see the lights out and that the men were present. I met Lieutenant Firman, who was upon the same duty for our 3rd battalion. Finding the stairs very slippery and the place very dark, I observed, 'If you will wait, I will go in search of a candle', as I knew there were open spaces in the balusters which a person in the dark might walk through. I left him, got a candle from a neighbouring house, and returned. I went up three or four stairs, when I heard a slip and in a moment, poor Firman fell through. In his progress downwards his feet repeatedly struck one side, and his head the other. He came with tremendous force to the bottom, which was a flagged pavement in the cellar. I directly retraced my steps and found him almost dashed to pieces, his skull frightfully fractured and several ribs broken. I had him removed to his billet. He remained for two days in a state of insensibility and died. It was odd enough that a soldier of the 43rd and his Portuguese wife were sleeping together close to the place where he fell, and never were awakened by the noise until I came to the place."*

The next day, 14 November, the Light Division crossed the Tormes and took up a position on the heights of the Arapiles, where the army was concentrated. Wellington had about 52,000 British and Portuguese troops, and 16,000 Spaniards, and was being threatened by the combined armies of King Joseph and General Souham (100,000 men). As a consequence, says Simmons, on the evening of the 15th, *"the army began to retreat from Salamanca upon Ciudad Rodrigo. Weather very bad and the roads excessively deep... The enemy moving upon our right flank in large bodies."*

> On the second morning after our arrival, we again proceeded towards Rodrigo. The rain fell in torrents, and the roads were so heavy - one or two feet deep in mud in many places - most of our men lost their shoes, and were obliged to march barefooted. Unfortunately, I was one of them[6].

Simmons: *"Marched and bivouacked in a wood near Cilleros. Very ill off for provisions... every step I was up to the knees in mud. Small rills, which it was necessary during the day's march to cross, frequently became rivulets from the continued rain."*

> When we reached our halting-ground for the night, our prospect was most desolate for we were wet to the skin, and without fire or shelter. The first thing I did was take off my jacket and shirt and wring out about half a gallon of water. I placed them upon my back to dry as they might. Most of our men cut down boughs of trees to keep themselves out of the mud, but it was some hours before we could

obtain that greatest of luxuries, a good fire. It had been a fatiguing day, and although possessed of a ravenous appetite, we had nothing to satisfy it. We had not a morsel to eat, no rations having been issued, so our men suffered from pangs of cold, and hunger.

Hunger, incessant duty, and fatigue were the disagreeable things attendant upon our life in the Peninsula, and I am convinced that it was these sufferings that so often rendered our men callous to death. At different periods during the war, some men, from the privations they endured, wished to be shot, and exposed themselves in action for that purpose.

Simmons: *'The Light Division, being the rear-guard upon this retreat, were the first under arms in the morning, and the last in bivouac at night, which was generally some time after dark. Our poor fellows lit fires, and then, being nearly starved, went about in search of something to eat. Some lean and half-starved bullocks were here and there lying dead in the mud in the deep parts of the road, yoked to carts laden with baggage. From these the hungry soldiers sliced off a delightful repast, which was grilled - half-smoked and half-roasted - and as tough as a shoe sole; but severe hardship and hunger made this an agreeable substitute for better food. Other soldiers would be groping about upon their hands and knees under a bastard description of oak and cork trees for acorns. These trees yield them in abundance, and at this time of year they are to be found in plenty. Although hard and bitter, such food was found better than none.*

The next day, 16 November, the weather was just as bad, added to which, towards evening, there was a cannonade. Kincaid: *'We cut down some boughs of trees to keep us out of the mud, and lay down to sleep on them, wet to the skin; but the cannonade of the afternoon had been succeeded after dark by a continued firing of musketry, which led us to believe that our pickets were attacked, and in momentary expectation of an order to stand to our arms, we kept ourselves awake the whole night. We were not a little provoked when we found, next morning, that it had been occasioned by numerous stragglers from the different regiments, shooting at the pigs belonging to the peasantry, which were grazing in the wood.'*

According to Costello, the shooting had a different cause:

Fortune favoured a few of us when, towards the middle of the night, one or two of our men brought intelligence that several cars laden with spirits and biscuit for the Spanish army were stuck fast in the road. The temptation to our hungry maws could not be resisted. We left our fires, and screened by the darkness of the night, got up to the cars and managed to get a portion of both biscuit and aguardiente. But the Spanish guard discovered our fellows and commenced firing on them. This was quickly returned and several were, I believe, shot. The firing continued all night, which alarmed the chief part of our army. Had the offenders been discovered, it would not have been difficult to have foretold their fate, as the Duke's orders were particularly strict against plunder, even although all the carts, unable to be moved, fell into the hands of the French next morning. Such were my feelings this night that, were it not for the liquor I drank, I believe I should have expired.

In a general order issued from Aldeheula on 16 November 1812, Wellington asked that measures be taken to stop soldiers shooting pigs in the woods close to the columns of marching, as the previous night two dragoons were shot, which had led him to believe that flank patrols were skirmishing with the enemy. Notice was also given that two men caught in the act of shooting pigs had been ordered to be hanged. Surprisingly, they were not named, and none of the autobiographers who were present recall witnessing hangings at this time.

Food was so scarce on this march that even the officers had to scrabble around for acorns. Kincaid: *"We again passed the night in a wood. I was very industriously employed during the early part of it, feeling in the dark for acorns, as a substitute for bread."*

> Despite their hunger, the men had sympathy for the officers which, considering their distance, was remarkable. Several of the most haughty gladly received little kindnesses from the soldiers. On this retreat, Lord Charles Spencer, a youth about 18 years of age, suffered dreadfully from hunger and fatigue. Trembling with cold and weakness, he stood perched upon some branches that had been cut down for fuel, anxiously watching a few acorns which, to stay the pangs of hunger, he had placed in the embers to roast. I dare say that, til then, his Lordship had never known the joys of poverty, and through the pain he experienced while thus sharing the common lot, the tears started silently from his eyes. He will not, I expect, forget how willingly the rough soldiers flew to offer him biscuits, which they could not withhold from one so tenderly and delicately reared. His Lordship was very much liked by us. No doubt, it did many a veteran's heart good to hear his thanks, and see the eagerness with which he devoured the offering, for these are times when Lords find that they are men, and men that they are comrades[7]
>
> Before daylight we pursued our route, the rain continuing to fall in torrents. The state of our regiment was pitiable. To add to our discomfort, the enemy were close upon our heels. This night we spent something like the last - wet, cold and hungry.
>
> On the following morning [17 November], the shots of the French came rattling in among us and we were obliged to continue our retreat rather precipitately. During the morning, the enemy's cavalry succeeded in getting through a wood, and they cut off the baggage of the 7th Division, then in front of ours. Their captives included several

children in panniers carried by donkeys; one grief-stricken Irishwoman in particular, seemed inconsolable at the loss of her child. However, the French desired to be as little encumbered with children as ourselves, and a few days later sent them back with a flag of truce. The scene that followed was most interesting as the different mothers rushed forward to clasp their darlings in their arms.

Simmons on events on 17 November: *'The enemy were very superior in force, consequently the Division retired leisurely before their cavalry. Some French cavalry dashed across the road our baggage was upon, took some, and had momentary possession of Lt. Cameron, who commanded the baggage guard, when the head of the column made its appearance. The officer was let go. Riflemen were sent into the wood near the road and fired a few shots, which made the dragoons scamper off... Numbers of men were left behind, and several died. The road was covered with carcases of all description, and at every deep slough we found horses, mules, donkeys, and bullocks mingled together, some dead, others dying, all laden with baggage. It is a most disagreeable sight to a soldier to see everything going to rack and ruin without being able to prevent it.'*

Cooke, of the 43rd: *'The Marquis of Wellington at this time joined us, and continued riding on the left flank quite close to our column, for he could not well join the main body of his army, as the enemy's horse scoured the road and all our cavalry had retired... As we emerged from the forest, to our surprise we were saluted on the left by a number of the enemy's cannon, posted on a high hill just above San Munoz. The Division broke into double time across the plain, about half a mile, and made for the ford of the river Huebra. The second brigade branched off to the right to cross elsewhere to extend a line of defence behind its banks.'*

Simmons: *'Our company extended, and were the last to retire down the inclined plane towards the river Huebra, followed a short distance by the enemy's skirmishers. The high ground was covered with masses of infantry and cavalry, which was fun for them, but death to us. The enemy got up guns and infantry, and as the Light Division descended to pass the ford, which was rapid and breast-high, their guns cannonaded us and killed several men and some officers.'*

This day we were hard pressed by the enemy's advanced guard, and I was in one of the two companies of ours which were ordered to cover the retreat of our Division. The French, confident in their numbers, pressed us vigorously, and we had difficulty checking their advance. Hotly engaged in skirmishing, I was about to take possession of a tree, when I beheld at the foot of it a poor woman. Unable to keep up with the regiment, she had sunk down exhausted. Poor soul! She seized my hands, and begged me to assist her; the enemy's balls were rapping into the tree that only partially screened us. I was obliged to leave her as there seemed every prospect of most of us being cut off. The assembly sounded, and away we dashed, 'devil take the hindmost', in upon the battalion.

Our illustrious chief [Wellington], who was generally to be found where danger was most apparent, saw us come puffing and blowing up to our column and called out to us in a cheering voice: "Be cool, my lads; don't be in a hurry!" But, in faith, with all possible respect for his Lordship, we were in no greater haste that the occasion demanded, as the French were upon us. We were obliged to dash down the sides of the hill, where we halted for a moment - and his Lordship also - and then ford a river. The stream was much swollen by the late rains, and while we were crossing, a round-shot from the enemy, who were now peppering away at us, took off the head of Sergeant Fotheringham, of our battalion[8], and smashed the thigh of another man. On gaining the other side of the stream we turned to give a salute in return, but owing to the wet, our rifles were unserviceable.

Simmons: *"On getting through this ford we faced about and formed columns of battalions."* The French tried to cross after them but met opposition from the Rifles and from some men of the 52nd, who were posted on picket at that point. Not a Frenchman got across. That night, the Light Division bivouacked amid the cork trees on the steep bank of the river in miserable weather. The rain that had held off all day, started to fall heavily again after dark. Beef was served out, but there was no biscuit.

Kincaid: *"We received the usual order 'to make ourselves comfortable for the night', and I never remember an instance in which we had so much difficulty in obeying it, for the ground we occupied was a perfect flat, flooded more than ankle deep with water, excepting here and there where the higher ground around the roots of trees presented circles of a few feet of visible earth, upon which we grouped ourselves. Some few fires were kindled, at which we roasted some bits of raw beef on the points of our swords, and eat them by way of a dinner."*

We remained that night stationary on the banks of the river, exposed to all the delights of cold, hunger and fatigue. These feelings were not improved by a course of shelling that the enemy indulged in at our expense. As I have remarked, the sufferings of our men were such at this period that many of them considered death a happy relief.

The morning at length dawned upon our half-famished persons, but brought no alleviation to our miseries for the rain still continued to come down in torrents.

According to other witnesses, the next morning (18 November), the sun began to shine. The French army, apparently in want of provisions themselves, and suffering equally from the bad weather, no longer pressed so hard.

Simmons: *This was very good news. The day was very fine, but the road extremely bad, and we were obliged to wade for miles in slush and water, which made the feet extremely tender. Also, not being able to see where to place them, made one hit the stumps of small trees, which gave great pain. I do not know when I suffered so much from a day's march, which was a very long one. Bivouacked upon the side of a mountain near Sancti-Spiritus... The enemy followed us on the 19th. Most of us walking barefooted, my shoes also having no bottoms, as well as my friends'. My legs and feet much frostbitten so could hardly crawl. Halted near Ciudad Rodrigo. Three days' bread served to us upon the spot."*

Pursuing our route, we arrived at Ciudad Rodrigo. In this manner we ended the Burgos retreat. We took shelter under its walls, where we found some sheds used as stables for the Spanish cavalry. The moment I entered, the first thing that caught my eye was some Indian corn-leaves. I considered this a lucky chance. Wet as I was, I threw myself on them and soon fell into a sound sleep, the only rest I had had since we left Salamanca. However, in the morning when I awoke, I found myself in a glow of heat, and covered with perspiration. I attempted to rise but was unable to move, as if paralysed. Calling some of the men to assist, they were astonished at the steam being emitted from under me; it was like smoke. I then found that my bed had been hot horse-dung, slightly covered by the Indian corn-leaves. The doctor was sent for. He ordered me to be carried into the town where I was given hot baths. In a few weeks, I was able to join my regiment.

The retreat from Burgos ended the campaign of 1812. During the retreat, the 1st battalion 95th lost one sergeant and one riflemen killed, and five wounded; several were missing.

As a consequence of irregularities on the retreat, Wellington issued an order which conveyed a sweeping censure of the conduct of the whole army. This upset Kincaid and Leach who felt that the riflemen, although suffering greatly from want, had continued to behave in a soldierly manner in the rearguard. Leach: *'The Commander in Chief sent a circular letter to the officers commanding regiments, expressing his highest disapprobation of the conduct of the army at large during the late retreat, which we found as difficult to digest as the acorns in the woods of San Munoz."*

On 25 November, the battalion marched to Alameda where, says Simmons, *"the people were glad to see us return. We had begun to look upon the villages near the Agueda as our homes. Formed a regimental mess; we got wine from Lamego upon the Duero, and passed the winter comfortably and happily."*

CHAPTER 19

Winter Quarters in Alameda;
Advance to Vitoria
26 November 1812 - 20 June 1813

During the winter of 1812-1813 there was a lull in the fighting on the border between Spain and Portugal as the French and allied armies rested and prepared for a new campaign.

Towards the end of November our battalion became stationed at its old quarters in the little village of Alameda. Here we obtained fresh clothing, and not before it was wanted, green having become the least conspicuous colour in the regiment. So various had been the expedients resorted to as a substitute for shoes, that the fresh supply from England was welcomed with no common joy. It was amusing to see our fellows enjoying their clothing by strutting about as proud as peacocks among the Spanish peasant girls, in whose estimation they doubtless conceived they should be advanced.

They were inactive in winter quarters for over five months. As there were no libraries in Portugal and Spain, there was little for those who could read to read, other than a bible belonging to a rifle sergeant and carried in the mess-kettle of a comrade (Green), a novel carried in the pocket of an officer (Cooke), or the newspapers which occasionally reached them from England (Leach). But they found other ways to amuse themselves.

Surtees: *"While we remained here, every sort of innocent amusement - at least generally innocent - we had recourse to, both by officers and men... We accordingly had races, balls, plays, and every other description of pastime our situation admitted of. We in Espeja established what was termed a 'trigger' club, each one in turn giving an entertainment at his house, and at which, as the name would imply, as much game was produced as our sportsmen could procure... A 'walking' club was established in our 1st battalion, which was quartered at Alameda. We were of course frequently favoured with the company of its members, for they thought nothing of setting out, each with a long pole in his hand, and walking 20 or more miles to dinner. Thus harmony, and a brotherly feeling, was promoted amongst the officers of the*

Division... *Some of our people also occasionally had a wolf-hunt, for these animals were quite numerous in this part of the country.*"

Hunting was a major pastime for the officers. Surtees went fishing in the Asava and the Agueda, and Jonathan Leach was a keen duck-hunter. Kincaid, *"Lord Wellington kept a pack of fox-hounds, and the Hon. Captain Stewart of ours, a pack of harriers, so that these, in addition to our old 'bolero' meetings, enabled us to pass a very tolerable winter.*"

The bolero meetings were the dances organised by the officers, but Simmons was less enthusiastic about them than Kincaid.

"We usually gave a ball once a week to the ladies of the village, who did us the honour to attend it... They dress in short brown jackets, and petticoats of the same, very coarse, figured with ridiculous patches of red cloth. These delicate ladies feed so grossly and eat so much garlic, that it is enough to suffocate a person being in the room with 20 or 30 of them. I am only giving you a description of the women in the villages on this mountainous frontier. In large towns there are beautiful women, and something like the English (but not so fair), who dress splendidly in black satin."

As at Valle in 1811, the Light Division officers tried their hands at putting on a play - *The Rivals*. A small disused chapel at Gallegos was loaned to them for the purpose. Scenery and costumes had to be improvised. A copy of the handbill has survived and is on display at the Royal Green Jackets Museum (see next page).

Leach: *"It is impossible to imagine anything more truly ludicrous than to see Lydia Languish and Julia (which characters were performed by two young and good-looking men, dressed uncommonly well, and looking somewhat feminine on the stage), drinking punch and smoking cigars behind the scenes at a furious rate, between the acts.*"

Wellington rode twenty miles from his headquarters to see the performance, and then rode back again afterwards.

Headquarters were at Guinaldo [Fuenteguinaldo], some miles distant from where we lay. A company of our regiment occasionally did duty over the Duke, whose quarters were in the house of the alcalde. We had strict orders to admit no-one inside the gates leading to the house, unless it was a particular dispatch from the front, or from Don Julian Sanchez, the guerilla chieftain. At the time, a report arose amongst us that his Grace was not altogether right in his head, but this was mere fiction. I used to observe him walking through the market place, leading by the hand a little Spanish girl some five or six years old. He would be humming a short tune, or whistling drily and, at the child's request, would occasionally purchase little sweets from the paysannes of the stalls.

Here, for the first time, linked arm in arm with the Duke, I saw Don Julian Sanchez, the noted guerilla leader. He had a square well-set

LIGHT DIVISION THEATRE

GALLEGOS

on Thursday the 4 *February* 1813
Will be performed the COMEDY of
THE RIVALS

MEN

Sir ANTHONY ABSOLUTE	Lieut. TYLDEN-PATTENSON, 43rd Regt
Capt. ABSOLUTE	Capt. BECKWITH, 95th Regt.
FAULKLAND	Lieut. PEMBERTON, 95th Regt
Sir LUCIUS O'TRIGGER	Lieut. COX, 95th Regt
ACRES	Capt. CATOR, Royal Artillery
DAVID	Lieut. HENNEL, 43rd Regt
FAG	Lieut. HAVELOCK, 43rd Regt
COACHMAN	Lieut. HAMILTON, 95th Regt.

WOMEN

Mrs MALAPROP	Capt. HOBKIRK, 43rd Regt
LYDIA LANGUISH	Lieut. Honble C. GORE, 43rd Regt
JULIA	Lieut. Lord C. SPENCER, 95th Regt
LUCY	Lieut. FREER, 43rd Regt

After which a Variety of Comic Songs

VIVAT WELLINGTON

Printed at Freneda

figure, dark scowl, and flashing eyes. His humble birth-place I afterwards visited in a small village between Rodrigo and Salamanca, an instance of obscure merit rising of its own impulse to an equality with the greatest man of the age.

I had been informed that the guerilla first began his career as a pig-boy, but owing to some cruelties exercised on a branch of his family, took an inveterate hatred to the French, which he exemplified by surprising and slaughtering two or three of their soldiers whom he found asleep in a wood. Accompanied by one or two others, he continued his sanguinary feats, and increased them, collecting first a small band, then a body of men. He eventually commanded upwards of 20,000 guerillas. They were well-armed and, equipped with British arms and accoutrements, rendered more assistance to the cause of the British than all the Spanish troops beside[1].

At the beginning of 1812, the 1st battalion had had 694 men. During the year 116 had died, 58 were invalided home, and 10 had been transferred. Although it had been augmented by one sergeant and 88 rank and file from England, and 46 Spanish recruits, by the end of 1812, the total strength of the battalion was down to 620.

Our regiments, by constant collision with the French, had got exceedingly thin, and as recruits from England came but slowly, we found it necessary to incorporate some of the Spaniards. For this purpose, several non-commissioned officers and men were sent into the adjacent villages recruiting. In the course of a short time, we were joined by a sufficient number of Spaniards to give 10 or 12 men to each company in the battalion. This we found surprising. The mystery was soon unravelled by the recruits themselves, who gave us to understand that they had had but three alternatives: to enter the British service, Don Julian's service, or be hanged! The despotic sway of Sanchez so disjointed their inclination for the guerillas, that they hastily fled their native woods (for fear of finding themselves noosed up in them), and gladly joined the British regiments. Many proved themselves worthy of their new comrades, whom they rivalled in courage and determination in every undertaking; some were even made corporals. The gallantry of the Spaniards of our regiments make me believe that had their countrymen during the war been more properly commanded, they would have made excellent soldiers[2].

The sound of cats was seldom heard in our battalion, and in the six years I served in Spain, I can safely say that, to my recollection, not more than six men in our battalion were punished, yet I cannot brag of our fellows being the most honest branch in the British army.

Our regiment's opinion of flogging is shown through the following anecdote. At the time, we had a man in our regiment of the name of Stratton who, after robbing several of his comrades of trifling articles, deserted to the enemy. The vigilant guerillas detected him in a wood that leads from Rodrigo to Salamanca, and brought him back to our cantonments a prisoner. He was tried by regimental court-martial, and sentenced to receive 400 lashes. The regiment was formed for the punishment in a wood near the village, and the proceedings of the court-martial were read by the adjutant, Major Cameron[3], who commanded us at the time.

The Major was not only a brave and gallant soldier, but a shrewd man. He knew that the men were better judges of each other's qualities than the officers could possibly be, so he devised the following plan to find out the true character of the prisoner.

"Stratton," he said. "I ought to have had you tried by general court-martial - in which case you would have been shot - but the high character the regiment has borne in the army prevents me from having it mentioned in general orders that a man of the Rifles could be guilty of the heinous crime of desertion to the enemy. Even now I am willing to show you kindness, so if the men of the battalion will be answerable for your future good conduct, I shall pardon you." Major Cameron was standing in the square. He turned round and looked the men in the face, as if waiting for an answer. There was a pause, but none was given.

"Strip, sir," the Major told Stratton.

Stratton was tied to a tree, and received 25 lashes. The second bugler was preparing to commence, when the Major said, "Will you not be answerable, men, for Stratton's conduct? If his own company will be answerable for his good behaviour, I shall forgive him."

The prisoner looked round as far as his position would allow, towards his own company. He eye was imploring. "Do speak for me, men," he said. "I will not act so in future."

I recollect well that each man was leaning on the muzzle of his rifle with his left hand, while his right covered his face. All were silent. Not a man spoke.

"Go on," said the major, and the culprit received 25 lashes more. "Now, sir, if only one man in the regiment will speak in your behalf, I shall take you down."

Still silence, so the third bugler commenced. When the prisoner had received about 16 lashes, a voice from the square cried out, "Forgive him, sir!"

"Stop bugler, stop!" said the major. "Who was the man that spoke?"

"I did, sir!" was the answer.

"Step into the square."

A man of the prisoner's own company came forward.

"Oh! is it you, Robinson[4]?" said Major Cameron. "I thought as much. You are as good-for-nothing a fellow as he is; but take him down."

The prisoner was conducted out of the square, and the Major addressed the men: "Your conduct in the field is well known by the

British army; but your moral worth I have not known before. Not a man would speak in that fellow's behalf except the man who did, whom you know as well as I do."

This served to show that however soldiers dislike this mode of punishment, they still like to see a rascal punished. Nothing destroys the feeling of pity for his sufferings more than his having been guilty of an act of cowardice, or of robbing his comrades[5].

Some months before our sojourn at Alameda, Napoleon had had a disastrous campaign in Russia, when Moscow was burnt. The circumstance was now brought to our notice by a general order, soliciting a day's pay towards defraying the losses sustained by the Russians. This was most cheerfully bestowed by every man in our battalion except two - Stratton, and a man of the name of Frost. To crown the occurrence, the day was made one of jollity and fun, and country dances were struck up by the band. It was laughable to behold everyone - officers as well as private soldiers - kicking about their heels to the tune of 'The Downfall of Paris'.

The year 1812 had been a turning point in the military fortunes of the French. In June, Napoleon Bonaparte had led an army against Russia and in September had reached Moscow, which was burned by the Russians. He tarried in the city for a month before retreating, by which time the Russian winter was upon him. Over the next two months his retiring army, harassed by the Russians and severely hindered by snow and freezing temperatures, was nearly destroyed. Meanwhile, in Spain, his armies were more insecure because he had withdrawn troops from them for his Russian campaign, and at a time when the guerilla bands (about 40,000 strong and well supplied by the British), were becoming more organised and more formidable. And now Wellington's army was receiving reinforcements.

The arrival in May 1813 of 5,000 troops necessitated the reorganisation of the divisions, which numbered seven, but totalled eight with the Light Division, commanded now by Baron Charles Alten. The fighting strength of the 1st battalion 95th was 573 in six companies. It was placed in the First Brigade of the Light Division, under the command of Major General Sir James Kempt, with five companies of 3rd battalion 95th (including Surtees), the 1st battalion 43rd, and the 17th Portuguese Regiment. The Second Brigade of the Light Division was commanded by Major-General Vandeleur, and was formed by the 1st battalion 52nd, 1st and 3rd Portuguese Caçadores, and the six companies of 2nd battalion 95th Rifles. As usual, Major Hew Ross's troop of Horse Artillery was attached to the Division, as was the 14th Light Dragoons, and the 1st Regiment of Hussars of the King's German Legion, under Lt.-Col. von Arentschildt.

Our Division was cantoned in and about Alameda during the

winter, and the men of our battalion, soldier-like and ever sighing after a change of scene, generally began to grow tired of their monotonous and inactive life.

At the beginning of May, Wellington reviewed the Light Division. Kincaid: *"I certainly never saw a body of troops in a more highly efficient state. It did one's heart good to look at our battalion that day, seeing each company standing a hundred strong, and the intelligence of several campaigns stamped on each daring, bronzed countenance, which looked you so boldly in the face, in the fullness of vigour and confidence, as if it cared neither for man nor devil."*

Soon afterwards, the army began to assemble for the new campaign. Kincaid: *"An army which has seen some campaigns in the field, affords a great deal of amusement in its assembling after winter quarters. There is not only the greeting of long-parted friends and acquaintances in the same walks of life, but among the different divisions, which the nature of the service generally threw a good deal together, there was not so much as a mule or donkey that was not known to each individual, and its absence noticed; not a scamp of a boy, or a common Portuguese trull [prostitute], who was not as particularly inquired after, as if the fate of the campaign depended on their presence."*

About the middle of May, we received orders for marching, and we commenced the campaign of 1813. Notwithstanding past sufferings, s spirit of enterprise extended itself throughout the Light Division[6]. We left Alameda in high spirits.

Wellington's plan for the new campaign was to use the combined forces available to him to drive the French through Spain and over the Pyrenees into France. His first target was their base in Salamanca to which, on 21 May, the Light Division began its march through Sancti-Spiritus and San Munoz, crossing the Huebra by the same ford at which they had been cannonaded six months earlier. On 26 May, they reached the ford at Villamayor upon the left bank of the Tormes, where they pitched their tents.

On the third day's march, our battalion encamped in a wood near Salamanca, where we were joined by the Life Guards and Oxford Blues, that had just come out from England. We beheld them drawn up at the side of the road, and their fresh, well-fed appearance gave rise to many jests at the 'householders' expense[7]. I learnt that because of our dark clothing and embrowned visages, they took us for a foreign regiment.

They were only a short distance from Salamanca, from which the French retired and began to retreat towards Burgos. On 28 May, the

Advance to Vitoria and Pamplona

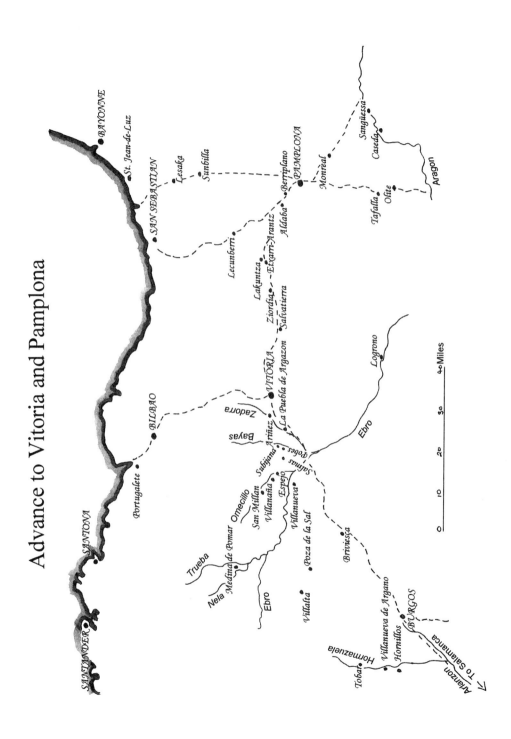

Light Division forded the Tormes and followed them up through Aldeanueva de Figueroa and Villabuena to Toro, which they reached on 2 June. At Toro, the principal arch of the bridge over the river Duero had been blown up and the soldiers could cross only by moving Indian file over planks laid across it; the guns and baggage passed through a deep ford. About midday, the Light Division marched through Toro and encamped at Tagarabeuna, where they remained for two days.

> The first peep we got of the enemy was at a place called Toro, on the road towards Burgos. There our hussars had a sharp skirmish, in which they took some prisoners. Continuing our advance, we overtook the enemy's rear-guard the following day, and after a little skirmishing and cannonading, they continued their retreat to Burgos.

Pursuing the French towards Burgos, the Light Division passed through many small villages, including La Mota, Castromonte, La Mudarra, Ampudia, Palencia and Monzon. Simmons: *"The villagers everywhere as we passed, hurried together. The men greeted us with vivas and the women danced, some of them in the most ridiculous and droll manner, to the great amusement of the soldiers, who although labouring under a heavy load and marching rapidly, often forgot their hardships and partook in the general mirth and hilarity."*
On the evening of 12 June, they camped at Hornillos on the Hormazuela River. On the 13th they began their march very early.

> The next morning we were startled by a tremendous explosion. At first many of our men thought it was an earthquake, then we ascertained that it arose from a mine, with which the French destroyed the castle at Burgos, and some of the works of the town.

Simmons was relieved that Burgos did not have to be besieged: *"I would much sooner have a fair field to fight on, than storm a town. I was convinced that the enemy had evacuated the place, which soon proved to be the case. The castle had been blown up, and some of the outworks destroyed. We passed through Argano to Tobar, where we encamped."*
On 14 June the Light Division marched through Quintana to Poza, in a wood near to which they encamped. On the 15th they marched through Villalta and entered the vale of the Ebro. Kincaid: *"we found ourselves, all at once, looking down upon the valley of the Ebro, near the village of Areñas, one of the richest, loveliest, and most romantic spots that I ever beheld. Five minutes before we were as lively as stones, but in a moment, we were all fruits and flowers; and many a pair of legs that one would have thought had not a kick left in them, were, in five minutes after, seen dancing across the bridge, to the tune of the*

'Downfall of Paris', which struck up from the bands of the different regiments."

Simmons: *"We were much amused at their wit on this occasion, and we had it followed by a national tune or two to remind us of Old England and absent friends. Encamped close to the village of Areñas. The banks of the river here are low, and from its appearance it must rise and fall very considerably, as the country in mountainous. The villages about here are very numerous."*

On 16 June they crossed the river Nela and encamped at Medina de Pomar on the river Trueba.

On 16 June we passed through the pretty little town of Medina de Pomar, and encamped on the other side of it close to the banks of a fine river.

On this march we suffered much from a deficiency of supplies from the commissariat. As we seldom received any rations, myself and one or two others, having a few pence, determined to start off - on the sly, as we were not allowed to move from our camp ground - and purchase bread at a little village we beheld at the other side of the river[8]. We forded the river unobserved and entered the village. Our appearance alarmed the people. Apparently they did not wish to have any dealings with us, and asked an immense price for the bread. Irritated by this, and urged by hunger, every man seized a loaf and threw down the usual price in the country. An immediate outcry was raised against us by the people and, carrying our loaves with us, we had to run for safety. We were overtaken by some of the swift-footed peasantry, who came up to us with knives and clubs. The dearly-obtained bread put our lives in jeopardy because we were all totally unarmed. Being without even our side-arms; our party had recourse to stones for defence.

"Kill the English dogs," the Spaniards cried as they brandished their long knives. They were about to make a rush in among us - by which my own personal adventures, and those of my comrades, would in all probability have ended on the spot - when several men of the 43rd and 52nd regiments, which belonged to our Division and who were foraging like ourselves, came running up. It was now the turn of the Spaniards to retreat, which they did in a hurry.

Having escaped the attack of the Spaniards, we arrived at the bank of the river, when General Sir Lowry Cole came galloping up to us with some of the staff, which might be termed the police of the army.

"Halt, you plundering rascals of the Light Division! Halt!" the General commanded, pulling his spectacles up.

We plunged into the river - which at that part was very deep - and started to swim across, holding the bread in our teeth. Sir Lowry, in an agitated tone that did honour to his kind heart, called out, "Come back, men, for God's sake. You'll be drowned! Come back, and I'll not punish you."

But the General's fears were needless for we soon landed safely on the other side. When we arrived at our camp we found that the roll had been called over several times and that we had been set down 'absent without leave'. We were lucky, escaping with a slight reprimand.

During the whole of our advance from the frontiers of Portugal, until we entered the Pyrenees, on average not more than one biscuit per day was served out to each man. No soldier, weighed down by a heavy knapsack, and from 60-80 rounds of ammunition (such as we riflemen carried at the time), could march 20-30 miles a day on so short as allowance. It was not unusual therefore, after a day's march, to observe groups of our regiment, and indeed of the Division, rooting up the fields with their swords and bayonets in search of potatoes, etc[9].

The reader will probably think that, in the Peninsula, the men of our battalion who were in the habit of foraging after a day's march, were indifferent soldiers, but that was not so because the bravery and daring of these men in the field far exceeded the merits of those comrades who were more quiet in quarters. It was they who were able to undergo the fatigue of the next day.

During the war, our men might be said to have been composed of three classes, the first of which was zealous and grave to absolute devotion in their 'fighting duties', but who considered some little indulgence as a right at other times. The second class barely did their duty when under the eyes of their superior. The third - and I am happy to say these were by far the smallest number - were skulkers and poltroons [cowards], who used weakness from want of rations as an excuse to crawl to the rear. They would not be seen in the ranks again until after a battle had been fought; then, when the commissary again placed them on short allowance, off they would go again. In this manner they swelled the muster-rolls. It was the men in the first of these three groups who placed the Duke on his present pinnacle as one of the great captains of the age.

In their hurried retreat, the French had been obliged to stock themselves in advance with several days' provisions. These were hung very temptingly from their knapsacks - the French did not carry haversacks - in defiance of our hungry jaws. This gave rise to a well known remark in the Light Division: "Damme boys, if the commissary don't show his front we must either find a potato field, or have a killing day!"

We were always in the front, and but for our resourcefulness, which was so dependant on our individual energies, his Grace might have found half his Light Division 'stiff', and the other half tucked under the blankets as Belem Rangers.

On 17 June, the Light Division left Medina de Pomar and began a tedious march through mountainous country covered with woods. They spent the night upon the side of a steep hill. Early the next morning, the 1st battalion moved off preceded by a troop of German hussars and their own pickets. About midday, they reached the village of San Millan.

On 18 June, we passed along the banks of a fine river. Our company, along with half a troop of our German hussars, formed the advance, and on turning a winding of the road, we saw a party of the enemy's cavalry, which formed the tail of their rear-guard. Our Germans, who were commanded by a very smart young fellow, immediately charged them. The French, perceiving the number of our cavalry equal to their own, instantly wheeled about and calmly awaited the attack. A sharp combat took place. It was supported with great resolution on both sides, but terminated in the flight or capture of the enemy. Several prisoners were brought in. All were badly wounded, and scarcely one of our gallant Germans escaped without some sabre-wound. One of the German cavalry, as he came up to us bringing a wounded prisoner and his horse, exclaimed in broken English, "Mine Got! He is mine own broder!" The prisoner was his brother, who was in the French service.

Lord Wellington came up. The officers of both parties had been killed in the charge, and so pleased was he with our cavalry that he promised the sergeant a commission which, I was told, he obtained a few days after. The whole of our battalion, which soon came up, was ordered to push forward.

Simmons: *"It was learned that a division of French infantry was at San Millan."* Wellington directed the 1st and 3rd battalions of the 95th to attack them. Simmons: *"The 1st batt. Rifles was conducted by Colonel Barnard through wooded steep ground beyond the left of the town, the rest of the brigade being moved forward when we became engaged."*

We found the French rear-guard in possession of a little town called San Millan, in front of which they had drawn themselves up, apparently with the intention of defending it. As we continued to advance in extended order, they changed their minds and turned tail. This day I noticed a novel system many of the retreating enemy adopted, which was to fire their muskets over their shoulders without turning round to face us. This was probably due to excessive fatigue.

Simmons: *"We made a sad example of the enemy in a short time, and drove Johnny through Villanueva to Villanaña. Several regiments had formed in column, but were completely cut off. Under cover of night they dispersed, and got away as they could; many were made prisoners. Our 2nd Brigade took all the enemy's baggage. Our loss was trifling when compared with the enemy's. We encamped on the Omecillo, below Villanueva. This was the first day we had fired a shot since breaking up from our winter quarters."*

217

The zest of the riflemen in this, the first affair of the campaign of 1813, was ascribed to the fact that they were, according to Kincaid, *"red hot for an opportunity of retaliating for the Salamanca retreat."*

The next day, the 19th, they passed through Salinas to Pobes, crossed the river Bayas by a wooden bridge, and formed an encampment where they remained for two days.

CHAPTER 20

The Battle of Vitoria
20 June - 4 July 1813

The quick forward movements of Wellington's army cut off King Joseph Bonaparte from the Spanish coast, and the French were forced to abandon all the sea ports except Bilbao and Santander. The armies of King Joseph and Marshal Jourdan retreated to Vitoria.

On 20 June we remained encamped near Puebla [Puebla de Arganzón], a town within ten miles of Vitoria.

They were very close to the French Army. In his diary, rifle lieutenant William Cox wrote: *"I ascended a hill this evening and saw the fires of the enemy distinctly, on the plain in front of Vitoria."*

The total number of Anglo-Portuguese troops Wellington had available was 60,000, with 20,000 Spanish soldiers. Joseph Bonaparte had 70,000 men. At daylight on 21 June, Wellington's forces advanced from their bivouacs on the Bayas river, through the valleys which had been assigned to them. The Light Division was to occupy the centre of Wellington's position.

On the following morning we fell in rather earlier than usual, a general rumour among the ranks auguring that we should have a busy day. We marched along the left of the high road towards Vitoria, leaving Puebla a little to the right. Our battalion, as the advanced guard, preceded the remainder of the Division until we came in sight of the enemy, which was on the other side of the river Zadorra.

Simmons: *"Passed through Subijana de Morillo and other villages. On arriving at some heights, the Division drew up. The enemy could be very distinctly observed in very large force, also drawn up, with the right of his army resting upon the river Zadorra beyond the village of Abechuco, the centre upon some very commanding heights in front of Ariñez, and the left upon Subijana de Alva, having a body of men posted somewhat in advance, on very rugged and high ground named La Puebla. The river took a serpentine course along their position. As soon as General Hill opened the ball by attacking the enemy's right, we moved nearer the river with the 1st and 3rd Battalions. We now had a fine view of the centre on the heights of Najara, which was destined to*

219

be attacked by the Light, 3rd, 4th and 7th Divisions. Three bridges (Tres Puentes) over this river were left undefended by the enemy."

Kincaid: "About 12 o'clock, we were moved rapidly to our left, followed by the rest of the Division, till we came to an abrupt turn of the river, where we found a bridge unoccupied by the enemy, which we immediately crossed, and took possession of what appeared to me to be an old field-work, on the other side."

We commenced a smart brush with their *voltigeurs* [light infantrymen], who slowly retreated and took up a position in the rear of some rocks, from whence their fire swept a bridge in our immediate front. While thus occupied in skirmishing, we heard a loud cheering on our left, where we beheld the 3rd Division charge over a bridge much lower down the stream. Fired by the sight, we instantly dashed over the bridge before us in the face of a galling discharge from the enemy.

Kincaid: *We had not been many seconds there before we observed the bayonets of the 3rd and 7th Divisions glittering above the standing corn, and advancing upon another bridge, which stood about a quarter of a mile further to our left, and where, on their arrival, they were warmly opposed by the enemy's light troops, who lined the bank of the river (which we ourselves were not on), in great force, for the defence of the bridge. As soon as this was observed by our Division, Colonel Barnard advanced with our battalion, and took them in flank with such a furious fire as quickly dislodged them, and thereby opened a passage for these two divisions free of expense, which must otherwise have cost them dearly."*

We then drove them from the rocks, and in our turn had to sustain a heavy fire from several guns mounted upon a hill that commanded our position. The rocks were splintered round us in every direction from this fire, and many of our men were killed or wounded by shot and fragments of stone.

Kincaid says the riflemen advanced so quickly that allied batteries confused them with the enemy, and it was not until they became intermingled with some of the redcoats of the 3rd Division that the cannonade ceased.

We were soon joined by the remainder of our Division, and pushed forward up a hill, from the summit of which we could clearly discern the city of Vitoria.

Simmons: "We moved up the heights to the attack. Johnny was very soon put off them, and took shelter in Ariñez, which place he held very obstinately."

By this time the action had become pretty hot and general with the other divisions, as well as our own. The chief scene of conflict was on an extended plain within a mile of two of the city on the left. Continuing to advance, we arrived at a small village on the main road [Ariñez], from which we were annoyed by a furious fire until, rushing in, we drove them out. In the market-places, we captured a howitzer, the first that was taken.

Verner reports that the first gun captured that day was taken by Lt. John Fitzmaurice and two riflemen of the 1st battalion. *'Observing that the French Artillery, a battery of six guns, was retreating and believing that he could intercept it, Fitzmaurice started with his company, but they, being in heavy marching order, were not able to keep up with him. Five guns had passed before he reached the road, but he caught the leading horse of the sixth and stopped them. The driver drew a pistol and fired at him but the bullet passed through his cap. He called on the two men with him to fire, and one of the horses fell, which completely checked the gun. Then the rest of the company came up, cut the traces, and made the three drivers and four gunners prisoners.'*

It was in our possession but a short time: a whole regiment of the enemy came charging upon us and our force, which consisted of only two companies, had to retreat with precipitation. However, when we turned around, we beheld our favourite 3rd Division coming double quick down the main road to our assistance, with Picton, who was never absent in time of need, at their head. This sight encouraged us and, after retiring for about 100 yards, we were at them again.

While thus engaged, a grape or round-shot struck my pouch with such violence that I was hurled several yards along the ground. From this sudden shock I imagined myself mortally wounded but, on being picked up, I found the only damage I had sustained was the partial destruction of my pouch, which was nearly torn off. I afterwards learned that Hodgson, one of the pardoned deserters at Rodrigo, while running to my assistance, was struck in his mouth by a bullet, which knocked out several of his teeth, and came out at the back of the ear. Severe as this wound was, he recovered[1].

Placing some of the ammunition in my haversack and the remainder in my cap, we were at them again, and recaptured the howitzer in the village, with the assistance of part of the 3rd Division.

Still pursuing them, the chief part of my company kept on the right of the main road.

Simmons: *'To the right the mountains ran at right angles with our front. On their very top you could see the contending parties engaged. From thence, as far as the eye could reach along the line to our left, a continual tiralade going on, the enemy gradually retiring, and the British, Portuguese, and Spaniards moving close upon their heels.'*

The Battle of Vitoria, 21 June 1813
Painted by W Heath. Engraved by T Sutherland. Published by J Jenkins, 4 June 1815. ©British Museum

In all my military life, this sight surpassed any thing I ever saw: the two armies, which had been brought beautifully into action, were hammering at each other, yet with all the coolness of a field-day exercise.

At this moment I noticed a regiment which by its yellow facings was, I think, the 88th, or Connaught Rangers. They were marching in close column of companies to attack a French regiment, which was drawn up in line on the verge of a hill with a small village in its rear. Although at the time under a heavy cannonade from the enemy's artillery, the 88th continued advancing gallantly. Seeing this, we took ground to the left, close to the road, in order to enable them to oppose this line in front. Though hotly engaged at the time, I determined to watch their movements.

Advancing all the time towards their opponents, who seemed to wait very coolly for them, the 88th deployed into line. When they had approached to within 300-400 yards, the French poured in a volley. or should say a running fire from right to left, and then started to reload. The British regiment recovered from that first shock, closed their files on the gap it made, and commenced advancing at double time. When they were 50 yards nearer to the enemy, they halted and in their turn gave a running fire from their whole line. Then, without a moment's pause, they cheered and charged up the hill against them, allowing the French no time to give a second volley. The French were so hard pressed that they came immediately to the right about, and made their way as best they could to the village[2].

We had several Spaniards in our regiment and they were generally brave, but Blanco was one of the most skilful and daring skirmishers we had in the battalion. He was always in front, and had been so in every affair since the advance from Portugal[3]. It was a wonder how he managed to escape the enemy's shot, but his singular activity and intelligence frequently saved him. He had great courage, but it was sullied by a love of cruelty towards the French, whom he detested, and never named but with the most ferocious expressions. I believe his hatred of them was occasioned by the murder of his father and brother, who were peasants, by a French foraging party. On this day he gave many awful proofs of this feeling by mercilessly stabbing and mangling the wounded French he came up to. This massacre was stopped by a veteran of our regiment who, although suffering from a severe wound in the face[4], was so exasperated at the Spaniard's cruelty, that he knocked him down with a blow from the butt of his rifle. It was only by force that we could prevent the Spaniard from stabbing the veteran on the spot.

I now observed the Duke come riding up with some of his staff. Seeing the enemy's confusion, he cried out to one of his aides-de-camp, "Send up a few of Ross's guns; here is work for them". Then he said to us, "That's right, my lads; keep up a good fire," and galloped in our rear to the right[5].

223

In an instant up came Ross's guns and commenced peppering them at a distance of not more than 300 yards, at a place where they seemed blocked together in a mass. We stuck to them like leeches.

During this battle, Kincaid was: *"struck with an unusual appearance of unsteadiness and want of confidence among the French troops. I saw a dense mass of many thousands occupying a good defensible post, who gave way in the greatest confusion before a single line of the 3rd Division, almost without feeling them."*

The French army was carrying with it all the plunder it had acquired during its campaigns in Portugal and Spain, and here at Vitoria, having made no provision for a retreat, wagonloads of it began to clog the road.

Simmons: *"Towards evening, the road became covered with baggage of every description, artillery, caissons, and French carrying away their merchandise and plunder by all sorts of conveyances. We were advancing rapidly. Occasionally a rifleman would shoot a horse yoked to a gun. This stopped the rest behind and blocked up the way. Now and then a few soldiers would fire shots at us from among the baggage."*

When we arrived close to the barriers of Vitoria, we found them blocked up by a great portion of the French waggons, bearing the 'materiel' of their army. We passed the gates. Through the town we were engaged in skirmishing with their rear-guard. Despite the street-firing, many of the inhabitants threw open their windows and appeared at their balconies to welcome us with *vivas*. The ladies, according to the established mode, threw flowers into the streets as we passed along.

In following up the enemy, myself and a few others left the company a little in the rear. I went through the square where I saw a wounded French soldier. With the help of his musket, the poor fellow was endeavouring to follow in the route of the French. When he saw me coming up, he dropped his musket and intimated that he surrendered, but he was also observed by a Spanish vagabond brandishing a club, who intended giving the Frenchmen the *coup de grace*. I knocked the Spaniard down. The Frenchman expressed his gratitude, but I was obliged to leave him and, unless he fell into the hands of our troops who were coming up at the time, probably to the same fate from which I had just rescued him.

A few minutes later, some of the 10th Hussars, and a party of the Life Guards, came dashing through the town, swords in hand, shouting as if they had taken it by storm.

I forced my way through the immense quantity of baggage that blocked up the further end of the town, and through which the cavalry could scarcely pass. There I beheld a French mounted officer, sword in hand, escorting a carriage and four out of the town. A comrade had followed me and we immediately fired. The officer fell and the carriage stopped. We rushed up to the vehicle. It contained two ladies, evidently of high rank, and they seemed much alarmed by the balls whisking around them from both sides. We were desiring them not to be afraid for their safety, as we would not harm them, when an officer of the 10th Hussars came galloping up, flourishing his sword over his head. At first I did no recognise his uniform and cocked my rifle.

"I am an English officer, sir!" he exclaimed.

Hearing this, I stepped to one side of the carriage. I afterward heard that the lady in the carriage was none other than the Queen of Spain, the wife of Joseph Bonaparte, and that from the same carriage the officer of hussars obtained possession of the baton of Joseph himself[6].

In withdrawing, I observed a Spanish muleteer in the French service carrying a small but exceedingly heavy portmanteau towards the town. I compelled him lay it down, which he did, but only after I had given him a few whacks in the ribs with my rifle. On inspection I found the portmanteau to contain several small bags filled with gold and silver in doubloons and dollars[7]. Although I never knew the exact amount, I should think it was not less than £1,000. As I had contributed most towards it capture, I took it as booty, and with my comrades gone in another direction, I had no one to claim a portion of it.

Costello was not the only soldier to fall in with a fortune at Vitoria because, for years, the French had been living off the country, plundering the inhabitants, and levying contributions from them. By this means they had collected valuables and amassed riches, all of which they had carried with them in their retreat towards France from Salamanca. And now, with Vitoria clogged up in the manner described by Costello, they could not get it away, and it fell into the hands of the advancing soldiers, as did the French military chest. Many soldiers secured both gold and silver in large quantities, although the bulk of it was looted by camp followers. Officers tried to keep the men in the ranks, but the soldiers knew that by doing so, the prizes would fall to others.

All who had the opportunity were employed in reaping some personal advantage from our victory, so I determined not to be backward. My chief anxiety now was to secure my prize, but how was it to be accomplished? I could not carry the portmanteau because of its weight, so to bear the valuable load I took one of the many mules that were blocking up the road. A sergeant and two men of the 10th Hussars were passing and, being at a loss how to fasten the portmanteau, I resorted to them for aid. Incautiously, I rewarded them too liberally, and in giving them several handfuls of dollars they got a glimpse of the gold, half of which they demanded. Perceiving the probability of being deprived of the only prize I had made after years of hardship and suffering - and particularly to newcomers for this regiment had newly joined from England - I inwardly resolved not to forfeit it except with my life. Having leant my loaded rifle against a gun carriage, I instantly caught it up and cocked it. Retiring three or four paces, I brought it to my shoulder and swore I would shoot dead the first man to place his hands upon my treasure. My determined air, and the ferocity of my appearance - my face was covered with perspiration and gunpowder - induced them to pause, and finally to desist. With the assistance of the sergeant, who gave his word not to molest me, I completed the strapping of my treasure.

Strange to say, after the battle of Waterloo, in the hospital in Antwerp, this very sergeant, whose name was Lee, and who was the best boxer in his regiment, lay wounded in the bed next to mine.

"Hallo, Rifleman!" he said, when he first perceived me near him, "don't you recollect me!"

At first I did not.

"By God," said he again, "you frightened me more than a bit at Vitoria when guarding your money-bags."

This soon settled the matter, but the poor fellow died after the amputation of his arm.

At this time, almost all our men, to use a phrase much in vogue among us then, were endeavouring to see what they could *make* - in other words *take*. I departed for the camp with the intention of gaining the battalion, but had not gone far when I observed the Duke of Wellington and some of his staff, forcing their way through gun-carriages and waggons into Vitoria. To my great relief he took no notice of myself and my mule, being much too occupied in securing the results of our brilliant victory - the capture of the entire *matériel* of the French army, which had fallen into our hands. I reached the camp in safety.

As evening approached, those riflemen not distracted by the plunder in Vitoria, skirmished with the French beyond the town where they spotted a carriage. Kincaid, who was with them, says that it *'was in the midst of a stubble-field, for some time between us and the French skirmishers, the driver doing all he could to urge the horses along. But our balls began to whistle so plentifully about his ears, that he at last dismounted in despair, and his box was quickly occupied by as many of our fellows as could stick on it, while others were scrambling in at the doors on each side. There were not a few on the roof, handling the baskets there so roughly as to occasion loud complaints from the fowls within. I rode up to the carriage to see that the people inside were not improperly treated. The only one there was an old gouty gentleman who, from the nature of his cargo, must either have robbed his own house, or that of a very good fellow, for the carriage was literally laden with wines and provisions. Never did victors make a more legal, or useful, capture; for it was now six in the evening... We had not tasted anything since 3 o'clock in the morning, so when one of our men knocked the neck off a*

226

bottle, and handed it to me to take a drink, I nodded to the old fellow's health, and drank it off without the slightest scruple of conscience. It was excellent claret... We did not cease the pursuit until dark, and then halted in a field of wheat, about two miles beyond Vitoria. The victory was complete."

Simmons: *"Night at last drew its sable curtain over the scene of slaughter and confusion, and afforded a fine opportunity to many to go in quest of plunder."*

When the Division halted beyond Vitoria, Quartermaster William Surtees was sent back to find the 3rd battalion's baggage and bring it forward:

"I again passed through Vitoria in returning to the Division, but oh, what scenes had I now to witness! The followers of an army are sometimes very numerous, and here they were abundantly so: muleteers, Portuguese and Spanish concubines, with every description of vagabond you can imagine, were by this time all labouring hard in their vocation of breaking open and plundering the carriages and waggons that had been left by the enemy. Among these were hundreds of soldiers, who were now beginning to feel the effects of the wine which they had found in the enemy's baggage. Such a Babel was here to be witnessed as is not easy to conceive.... Had I done as many others did, I might have obtained a great deal both of money and other valuables..., but plundering was never my forte. One officer whom I knew, got, I believe, near £1,000 worth of money, and other valuable property, and innumerable others got considerable sums, more or less... One officer I heard of who, while in the rear where he ought not to have been, found a box full of money, most likely silver, but very heavy. A German dragoon coming up at the same moment laid claim to half of it, and when this officer took hold of it to remove it, the German also laid hold to prevent him. A sort of scuffle ensued, when the German made use of most abusive and mutinous language, with threats, which the officer was obliged to submit to, knowing, as both of them did, how far he had descended from his station, thus putting it in the power of the soldier to treat him as a brother plunderer."

This night we encamped amidst the wreck of the French army. The ground occupied by our regiment was near a small village, a little off the main road that leads to Pamplona[8]. Every man brought into his camp ground whatever he fancied because the unfortunate enemy had been compelled to leave everything behind them, including their women and children. Even if our fellows had been inclined to be honest, their good fortune would not allow them.

As soon as our fires were lighted, the men, who had been under arms from 3 o'clock in the morning until eleven at night, and consequently had not tasted food for the whole of the day, began to fill their hungry maws from the luxuries of the French camp. Roast fowls, hams, mutton etc, were in abundance.

Simmons: *"We had fought over 20 miles of ground. I seated myself by a fire with the officers of the company, and was fortunate enough to get part of a ham and some claret which one of the soldiers had taken from a cart belonging to the enemy. In a little time we had a variety of eatables brought by men of the company. I never ate with a better relish in my life. I lay down by the fire in a French officer's cloak, which one of the men gave me; he had that day shot its wearer."*

At midnight, the wine and brandy went round in horn tots which we generally carried about us. The men mostly lay stretched on the ground, their feet towards the fires, and their elbows resting on their knapsacks. When the grog had roused up their spirits from the effects of the day's fatigue, each one commenced inquiries about absent comrades, for riflemen are always extended in action and seldom know who has fallen until the affray is over.

"Blood 'n 'ounds," said Dan Kelly, bouncing up from his reclining posture; "don't drink all the wine, boys, until we hear something about our absent messmates. Do any of you know where Jack Connor is?"

"He was shot through the body when we took the first gun in the little village near the main road," was the reply.

"Where is Will John?" asked Bob Roberts, with a sudden glance of suspense.

"A ball passed through his head," said another. "I saw poor Will fall."

"Musha, boys! is there any hope of poor Jemmy Copely getting over his wounds?" said Tom Treacy earnestly, lifting his head from his knapsack.

"Poor Copely!" said another. "Both his legs were knocked off by a round shot."

Treacy laid his head on his kit again. He was silent as each man gave a short account of a fallen comrade, but he was eagerly listening. "Why, by Jasus!" he exclaimed. "By Jasus, they have kilt half our mess. But never mind boys, fill a tot, fill a tot. May I be damned but here's luck." He placed the wine to his mouth, but took it away again untasted and laid it on the ground. "Poor Jemmy Copely! poor Jemmy! They have drilled him well with balls before, damn them, now they have finished him. The best comrade I ever had, or ever will have."

The last part of the sentence was uttered in a broken accent and he wiped his eye. He commenced filling a wooden pipe, whose bowl was made from a tailor's thimble, his head stooping all the while as if to hide the large tears that unconsciously rolled over his nose. There was a pause among the group, then Treacy, having recovered himself a little, took up the tot of wine and drank it off. He then jumped up, and in a loud voice, called out to all. "Here me boys! Hear what I am going to say."

A deep silence followed. Treacy knelt on his knapsack, and squeezed his hands together in the attitude of prayer. "May the Lord God grant that those fellows in yonder camp remain where they are until we have the pleasure of thrashing them for the gap they have this day made in our mess."

"Amen! amen!" responded a dozen voices, with an emphasis that would have done credit to a clerk in a country church and, I am certain, with a better inclination for the desired object. And Treacy laid himself at his length once more[9].

After recapitulating their different losses, and the good qualities of their fallen comrades (but taking care not to mention any of their bad ones), every man relaxed into a sleep, from which nothing could arouse them save the sound of the bugles, or the hard cracking of the rifle. These always bring soldiers to their legs again, ready to advance or retreat, the same soldiers who, as the night closed over the column, would lament, or be lamented as one of the fallen or absent messmates.

I was on guard at the time, and having a round sum of money by me, I kept one eye on the direction of the French camp some distance from us, and the other on the money bags. The crackling of the fires soon ceased for want of fuel, and nothing remained but the embers. The whole camp was as still as the grave, with nothing to disturb the soldiers' repose but the casual braying of the donkeys who answered each other from camp to camp, the sound gradually dying away as an echo in the distant woods.

Riflemen seldom pile arms and, as was our usual custom, each man's rifle was loaded and leaning on his arm, close to his breast. It was hugged with the affection a fond lover would use to press to his bosom the girl of his heart, yet I never knew an accident to occur by rifles going off. I quietly walked round the fires to see that none of the men's pouches were near it, but no.

It was a noble sight to see these scathed warriors stretched on the ground. By the clear moon that then shone, I could see that some had had balls through their caps, and that blood was oozing from the furrow of some French bullet. Such trifles were unnoticed by these hardy veterans, who had stood the pelting of many a storm as pitiless as that which they had that day contended with.

The losses to the allies at the battle of Vitoria were 33 officers, 19 sergeants and 688 rank and file killed, and 230 officers, 158 sergeants and 3,782 rank and file wounded. The losses in Costello's battalion were one sergeant and three riflemen killed; four officers were wounded, three seriously. The total number of casualties in the Regiment's three battalions was only 79.

The next morning, the sale of the spoils which fell into our hands took place in the village, near the camp ground where our battalion lay.

In general, the Spaniards were the purchasers, and property which had belonged to the French, such as uniforms, horses, camp-equipage, etc, was sold in abundance at about one-tenth of its value. Mules worth 30-40 dollars brought on average three.

As I had no means of conveyance for the spoil I had obtained, I set about depositing it where I thought it would be safe: £300 I entrusted to our quartermaster[10], and several sums to officers of the battalion, distributing most of the remainder of the silver - about £100 - among the men of my own squad, who undertook to carry it for me. Of the latter, I received very little back. Money was of little use during some of the hardships we afterwards endured, and although I frequently offered a doubloon for a single glass of rum, I was not always able to obtain it.

The next day, the Light Division was ordered in pursuit of the enemy. Simmons: *'The Division fell in and moved by the Pamplona road (the only one left to retreat by) in pursuit of the enemy. The French lost yesterday about 10,000 men killed and wounded, and had 151 pieces of cannon, 415 caissons, the military chest, and the whole of their baggage, taken. Moved through Salvatierra, preceded by the lst German Hussars, 14th Dragoons, and one troop of Horse Artillery.'*

About 12 o'clock we marched in pursuit of the enemy through the town of Salvatierra, many of the men gibing me for my wealth, saying, among other agreeable things, that if I fell they would take care of my knapsack for me. To tell the truth, I was not over anxious to go much to the front, as I now began to look upon my life as of some value.

Simmons: *'We followed the French, and found all the villages abandoned by the inhabitants. The Dragoons came up with the enemy's rear-guard and took fifty stragglers encamped near the village of Alvisera.'*

On 23 June, they followed the French army through Ziordia. So hot was the pursuit that in their hurry to get away, the French did not have time to destroy several bridges, but they tried to retard the progress of Wellington's army by setting fire to villages. Though the weather was bad, the pursuit continued through Extarri-Arantz to Lakuntza, where the Light Division encamped. At dawn the next morning, they were on the move again.

Simmons: *'Cavalry, guns, and the 1st and 3rd battalion Rifles soon came up with the enemy's rear-guard and attacked it. They fought for a while and retired as fast as possible to another position. We as rapidly followed, and again turned the rascals out of it. The road, from the quantities of rain, were very bad indeed, frequently up to the knees. I never in my life saw our Horse Artillery do such wonders in crossing the country. They passed over ditches and through places that no one would credit or think possible; the horses were noble animals and in the finest order. Towards afternoon we got upon the high road from Madrid to Pamplona. The only gun the enemy had brought from Vitoria was now turned against us."*

On our second day's march we came up with the rear guard of the enemy, who made a stand in the road, assisted by the only gun they had carried from Vitoria. The first shot fired from this piece took off at the socket the arm of one of our corporals[11]. We dashed at them and they soon abandoned their gun, which we took, making it the first and last piece of ordnance we captured from them on this retreat.

Simmons' recollection of this incident is both more detailed and more gruesome: *"Johnny, in the hurry to get away, overturned gun, horses and all. The road had been raised fifteen feet over a flat, the side built up like a wall. It was just the worst place for miles that the animals and gun could have been trundled over. Elated with our success, I came up to the spot, but was sadly hurt at a melancholy spectacle. Five French soldiers, who a few moments before were in rude health, now lay with their limbs frightfully lacerated and broken... I pitied them and gave them a little wine from my calabash. They seemed to wish to be shot; one in particular requested it as a boon. The sight was too much. I turned away from it with horror, and if a tear fell, what then!"*

The British column halted in the villages of Santa Barafra, Berrioplano, and Aldaba, and on 25 June, the Light Division closed on Pamplona, moving by a mountain road to Villava where they encamped.

We halted a couple of days in a small village opposite Pamplona [Villava]. As I considered that our fellows had contributed towards my greatness in money matters, I could do no less than treat them to a dinner. Unfortunately, the place afforded no other luxuries than bacon, eggs, and wine, for which the inhabitants took care to charge treble. I paid ten doubloons for three flitches of bacon and three pig skins of wine. This we enjoyed within the walls of a house which had no roof - the French had burnt it off on their retreat. There were some excellent toasts given, such as:

"May we have another brush with them before they get to Paris."

For some time after, we continued in pursuit of one division of the French army, night and day. During this period, the fatigue we underwent was incredible, and we could not have supported without the excellent wine with which that part of the country then abounded, and which we all had plenty of money to purchase.

The fatiguing marches were for the purpose of intercepting a French division of 14,000 men commanded by Clausel, who had been on his way to Vitoria when he heard of King Joseph's defeat. Realising the danger he was in, he had fallen back to Logroño. Early on 26

June, the 3rd, 4th and Light Divisions, led by Wellington, went in pursuit of him, marching south of the city to Olite, then turning east. They crossed the river Aragon at Caseda in the early hours of 30 June. The next morning they learned that Clausel had escaped.

Kincaid: *"It was discovered that Clausel had been walking blindly into the lion's den, when the alcalde of a neigbouring village warned him of his danger, and he was thereby enabled to avoid us, by turning off towards Zaragoza. We heard that Lord Wellington had caused the informer to be hanged. I hope he did, but I don't believe it."*

They continued on to Sangüesa where they remained until 2 July when they marched back to the vicinity of Pamplona, encamping near Monreal.

> After continuing these harassing marches for several days, we at length chased them into France. We next retraced our steps in some degree to Pamplona, in the suburbs of which city we remained a few days.

On 3 July, they moved through Villava to small villages between Villava and Pamplona, from where, over the next two days, working parties were sent to cover the pickets before Pamplona, which was being rigorously blockaded.

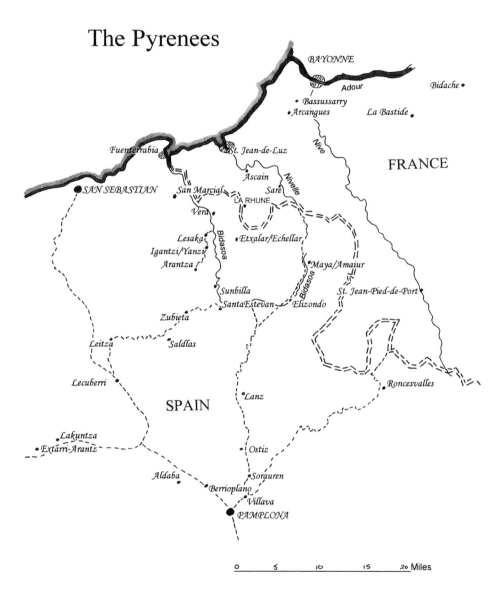

The Pyrenees

BAYONNE

Adour

Bidache •

• Bassussarry

• Arcangues

La Bastide •

Nive

Fuenterrabia

St. Jean-de-Luz

FRANCE

Ascain

Saré

SAN SEBASTIAN

San Marcial

Nivelle

LA RHUNE

Vera

Etxalar/Echellar

Lesaka

Bidasoa

Igantzi/Yanzi

Arantza

Maya/Amaiur

Sunbilla

Bidasoa

St. Jean-Pied-de-Port

SantaEstevan

Elizondo

Zubieta

Leitza

Saldias

Lecuberri

Roncesvalles

• Lanz

SPAIN

Lakuntza

• Extarri-Arantz

Ostiz

Aldaba

Sorauren

• Berrioplano

Villava

PAMPLONA

0   5   10   15   20 Miles

CHAPTER 21

The Pyrenees
5 July - September 1813

The battle of Vitoria had been decisive, and the French army retreated into the Pyrenees on the border between Spain and France. They left behind only their garrisons in Pamplona and San Sebastian, which the British and their allies swiftly set about besieging.

The French forces amalgamated into one army under Marshal Soult, who deployed his men in the Pyrenean mountain fastnesses. Their purpose was no longer to force Wellington's army out of Spain and Portugal, but to prevent it entering France. In July, Wellington began deploying his troops against Soult. On the 5th, the Light Division were relieved from their duty in support of the blockade of Pamplona by the 4th Division, and began their advance into the Pyrenees.

> From thence [the suburbs of Pamplona] we again advanced in the direction of the Pyrenees.

Simmons: *"The Division assembled from different villages at Sorauren, proceeded up a narrow valley to the town of Ostiz, and encamped upon a rivulet."* On the 6th they *"marched up the stream to Lantz, which is situated at the foot of the celebrated Pyrenean Mountains. Encamped in a fine grove of chestnut trees. The hills, which are numerous and richly covered with sturdy old oak and other magnificent trees, with the mountains towering above them in every direction, the tops of which are buried in the clouds, gives a grandeur to the surrounding appearance that can only be felt by those on the spot."*

On the 7th, says Simmons, they *"marched by a most romantic road, and ascended hills, many of them covered with fine trees, oak, beech, and larch, and the ground covered with wild strawberries. The valleys are delightfully irrigated, and abounding with fruits, corn, and oil... Halted for three hours upon the side of a steep hill, and afterwards moved to San Estevan, a charming village, where we fared sumptuously."*

> We and took up our quarters at the pretty little town of San Estevan. Here we halted some days.

Simmons: *"Major-General Skerret took command of our 2nd Brigade, as General Vandeleur was appointed to the cavalry. The Bidasoa rises in the Pyrenees near Elizondo, passing through this valley, and ultimately disembogues itself into the sea at Fuenterrabia, where it divides France from Spain... Remained quiet here until the afternoon of the 14th then moved out of the town and marched and encamped upon the heights above Sunbilla. The Division at daybreak moved down the Bidasoa by a mountain track, sometimes close to the river, at other times winding along the side of the mountain a considerable height from it. On arriving at the bridge of Lesaka, we discovered the enemy's advanced post upon the summit of a mountain. Ordered immediately to move up and dislodge the enemy."*

Our next march was to Lesaka. The enemy had possession of the heights of Santa Barbara, from whence we dislodged them after some hard fighting.

Their advance upon the French position was, says Simmons *"done very leisurely, as the sides were very steep, and it was necessary not to waste our strength and vigour, as we might have occasion for it. On arriving near the top, the French fired occasional shots at us, but ultimately we got to the top, and soon made Johnny scamper down the other side. These heights, Santa Barbara, are named after a convent, the ruins of which still remain. We now had a fine view of the enemy's position on the Spanish side of the ridge of mountains which separate France from Spain. At their base stands the small town of Vera... The enemy were dislodged towards evening from Vera, with the exception of a picket posted near some outhouses. Our picket occupied some houses in the town. The Division encamped upon the heights... We remained in position, going on picket in turn, till the 25th."*

Kincaid described what he could see from the height of Santa Barbara: *"The mountain which the French army occupied was the last ridge of the Pyrenees. Their sentries stood on the face of it, within pistol-shot of the village of Vera, which now became the advanced post of the Division. The Bidasoa takes a sudden turn to the left at Vera, and forms a natural boundary between the two armies from thence to the sea. All to our right was open, and merely marked a continuation of the valley of Vera, which was a sort of neutral ground, in which the French foragers and our own frequently met and helped themselves to forage while any remained, and all in the greatest good humour, without exchanging words or blows."*

Wellington's army was extended across a wide area with the left at San Sebastian and the right near Pamplona. In order to maintain communications, he ordered the Light Division to manoeuvre in the mountains between the two places. On 25 July, they marched through Lesaka and Yanzi [Igantzi] and encamped near the heights of

Sunbilla. Meanwhile, Soult's army began to manoeuvre into the passes of Maya and Roncesvalles to attack Wellington's right near Pamplona.

> We remained upon these mountains for several days, but when the enemy endeavoured to relieve Pamplona, which some of our troops were then besieging, part of our Division was ordered to cross the Bidasoa to frustrate them. This could only be done by a forced march at night. The mountains were in most places rugged and precipitous, without even the semblance of a path, and in order to find our way over, we were obliged to have torches, and to light straw.

This particular march began in the early hours of 27 July. Simmons: *"Marched off in the dark and blundered along the whole night. Arrived at Zubieta after daylight, which was only 2½ leagues, the road being very bad, and amongst rugged mountains."*

> The fatigue incident to that night march was greater than any the men of our battalions had before endured, yet at the end of it you could fire a rifle-ball to where we started from[1]. Accidents were numerous; many of our men had severe falls, and numbers of rifles were broken[2].

When they encamped the next morning (28 July), Simmons *"continually heard a heavy cannonade and peals of musketry, indicating hard fighting upon our right."* The 3rd and 4th Divisions, which had been attacked by Soult's army on the 15th, had fallen back to Sorauren, within ten miles of Pamplona. There, on 28 July, after another engagement, the French were held, and eventually forced to retreat.

> All our hurry was of no avail, as the enemy had been frustrated in their attempt to throw supplies into Pamplona.

Kincaid: *"About midnight we heard the joyful tidings of the enemy's defeat. Our Division proceeded in pursuit at daylight on the following morning."*

At 9am on the 29 July, the Light Division proceeded to Saldlas, on the 30th to Lecunberri, and on 31st to Leitza, where they encamped. Simmons: *"Soult having been worsted in all his attacks upon the British, was now in full retreat, having suffered very considerably in killed and wounded and prisoners."*

The Light Division was now ordered to return the way it had come and *"made a forced march this day by Zubieta, along a mountain track on the left bank of the Bidasoa to the bridge of Yanzi... the greater part of that day under a burning sun, which sadly exhausted the men."*

Again we had the agreeable task of retracing our steps, and with the same hurry we had advanced. By this addition to our fatigue, we lost many men, who were unable to endure it. There was a rivalry between the regiments of our Division as to who should hold out the longest and many, urged by this feeling, continued marching until they fell and expired by the roadside. On the second day, I myself fainted, but after my stock was taken off, I recovered sufficiently to stagger on and finish the march.

That day, the Light Division came up with the French. Kincaid: "*After a forced march, we found ourselves, when near sunset, on the flank of their retiring column on the Bidasoa, near the bridge of Yanzi, and immediately proceeded to business.*"

Descending from the mountains we pursued our march till we came to the bridge that crosses the Bidasoa, where we beheld the French moving along on the other side of the river. Like ourselves, the poor fellows who were retreating seemed dreadfully harassed.

Surtees: "*At length we got two companies posted just over the bridge, in front of which all the rear of the French column had to pass. Poor creatures! They became so alarmed, that they instantly began to cut away and cast off all the loads of baggage, both cavalry and infantry, to make the best of their way. But the mountain on their right was inaccessible and they had all, as it were, to run the gauntlet. Great was the execution done amongst the enemy at this bridge, and many were the schemes they tried to avoid passing it.*"

Part of our battalion commenced firing upon them across the river, and every shot told.

Kincaid: "*Foes as they were, it was impossible not to feel a degree of pity for their situation: pressed by an enemy in the rear, an inaccessible mountain on their right, and a river on their left, lined by an invisible foe, from whom there was no escape, but the desperate one of running the gauntlet. However, 'as every dog has his day' and this was ours, we must stand excused for making the most of it. Each company, as they passed, gave us a volley, but as they had nothing to guide their aim except the smoke from our rifles, we had very few men hit.*"

Happily, and to the honour of the British soldiers, many of our men, knowing what the French suffered from what they had themselves endured, declined firing, and called out to the others to spare them, as it was little better than murder.

We remained encamped here this night, and the next morning marched back to the heights of Santa Barbara.

They returned to Santa Barbara on 2 August. **Simmons:** *"Encamped on our original ground and took up the line of pickets without firing a shot. The enemy remained upon a rocky steep connected with Puerto de Echellar. It was found necessary to dislodge this force from that place. In the afternoon the 1st Brigade was drawn up upon the heights of Santa Barbara, and the 1st and 3rd Battalions were sent up the face of a craggy, almost perpendicular steep."*

As soon as we arrived on the hill, and were anticipating a little rest, the assembly sounded, and we were ordered to drive the enemy from a high mountain which they occupied on our right. This was a heavy task at the time; but to it we went, and in extended order mounted the hill, on the summit of which the enemy were clustered as thick as bees on a hive.

Simmons: *"The enemy opened fire upon us... Several men were knocked over as we gradually approached the top. The enemy made a charge but were soon stopped and, a fog coming on and we still advancing and firing upon them, they gave up the hill without fiercely contending for it."*

After some very hard fighting we carried their position, but not before we had lost many men. One was a sergeant named Kelly, a friend to whom I was much attached. He invited me to take a draught of wine out of his canteen, and was in the act of handing it to me, when he received a shot through the right temple. It came out at the eye. I never before saw a man die so hard. He writhed about, poor fellow, in the greatest agony, without it being in my power to afford him the slightest relief. I was obliged to leave him for a time when some of our men raised a shout that the enemy were flying. On my return I found him quite dead[3].

This was a bad day's work. Another regiment was left in charge of the hill, and we returned to our camp ground by the river-side.

The riflemen again took up a position at Santa Barbara and there they remained quietly until the end of the month, watching the French as they strengthened their position in front with numerous field-works.

August 25th was the Regiment's 'Birthday', and being the anniversary on which the regiment was raised[4], a general jollity was kept up throughout the regiment.

The officers - 73 of them - celebrated with an open air banquet on their camp ground on the banks of the Bidasoa. Kincaid: *"Two trenches, calculated to accommodate 70 gentlemen's legs, were dug in the green sward, the earth between them stood for a table, and behind was our seat, and though the table could not boast of all the delicacies of a civic entertainment, the earth almost quaked with the weight of the feast. And the enemy certainly did, from the noise of it, for so many fellows holding such precarious tenures of their lives, could not meet together in commemoration of such an event, without indulging in an occasional cheer - not a whispering cheer, but one that echoed far and wide into the French lines. As it was a sound that had often pierced them before, and never yet boded them any good, we heard afterwards that they were kept standing at their arms the greater part of the night in consequence."*

Leach: *"Neither vocal nor instrumental music was wanting after the feast, and with the aid of cigars and blackstrap, we enjoyed the most extraordinary 'fête champêtre' I ever witnessed."*

On this occasion I had the pleasure of saving a gallant soldier from the consequences of a pecuniary loss he had sustained, one which might have embittered the remainder of his life. He was a pay sergeant of one of the companies of our battalion, and he got rather tipsy. While in this state, he was robbed of £31 belonging to his company. Having only just been appointed pay sergeant, it was the first money entrusted to his hands, and the circumstance had such a strong effect upon him, that when he woke me up the following morning and acquainted me with his loss, he said he was determined to desert. He said his credit would be for ever destroyed in the regiment, and he could not endure remaining with the battalion afterwards. Having money by me, I was able to make up his losses. I felt much pleasure in arresting the despair that seemed to have taken possession of the mind of this soldier, whom I much esteemed. Some time after, he obtained a commission in the 2nd battalion of our regiment. He was the late Quartermaster Robert Fairfoot[5].

I still had by me a very considerable sum, the remnant of my prize at Vitoria, and as I had no place to keep it but in my knapsack - which I could not always carry about with me - I was naturally apprehensive respecting its safety, and I was consequently obliged to entrust my treasure to the care of a comrade. His name was Bandle, and true to his charge, he never gave me reason to repent my confidence. Many were the stratagems resorted to to persuade him to relinquish his guard. Sometimes he would be suddenly warned for duty by the non-commissioned officers - 'for fun' only they assured me - in the hope that he would leave it behind him, but Bandle was always awake, and on these occasions would take my knapsack on his back and leave his own. He was wakeful as a weasel, and faithful as the dog, for both of which qualities I took good care not to be ungrateful[6].

During August, the Spanish army was blockading Pamplona while Wellington's men blockaded San Sebastian. By 29 August, they were ready to storm San Sebastian.

San Sebastian was now closely invested by the British. Eventually, the breaches being considered practicable, preparations were made for the assault.

Simmons: *"Lord Wellington paid the Light Division a high compliment by allowing a subaltern's party from each battalion, totalling 250 men, to go as a storming party."*
Kincaid: *"The post of honour was claimed by the senior lieutenant (James Percival), in a manner to shut the mouths of all the juniors, yet there were some whose mouths would not be shut. One in particular, Lieutenant H[amilton], had already seen enough of fighting to satisfy the mind of any reasonable man."*

Volunteers were required from our regiment. The duty was so attractive that although two only were to be selected out of each company, myself and five others stepped forward from ours. This brought on a controversy, and lots were drawn according to regulation, which decided in favour of two, named Royston and Ryan[7]. The reader may judge of the value attached to this service, when I tell him that the offer of £20 was made and refused for the exchange[8].

The next day, when the town was to be attacked, our men were all on the fidget to know the result, and every tree and hillock within sight or hearing of the scene was taken possession of. At about 12 o'clock, the breaches were assaulted, and the place carried after a severe contest.

San Sebastian was stormed on 31 August. Percival and Hamilton (who was an Irishman) were both severely wounded, but survived.

The morning San Sebastian was stormed, Soult concentrated a large force at Vera with the intention of relieving the town. Kincaid: *"We turned out before daylight, as usual, and as a thick fog hung on the French position, which prevented our seeing them, we turned in again at the usual time. We had scarcely done so, when the mist rode off on a passing breeze, showing us the opposite hills bristling with their bayonets, and their columns descending rapidly towards us. The bugles instantly sounded to arms, and we formed on our alarm posts."*
Leach: *"The French presented at Vera, opposite to the Light Division, a force estimated at 15,000 men."*
Simmons: *"The enemy soon began to move down the steep hill towards the river, and crossed at a ford below the bridge, having previously driven our pickets from the town. Some French moved forward to take possession of the bridge and were repulsed by two Rifle companies in good style. A stronger force was sent to the bridge, and the two companies occupied some houses and fired upon the enemy from them. A few shot and shell were thrown to cover the advance of the French in passing the river."*

Kincaid: *"We thought at first that the attack was intended for us, but they presently began to pass the river, a little below the village of Vera, and to advance against the Spaniards on our left. They were covered by some mountain guns, from which their first shell fell short, and made such a breach in their own leading column, that we could not resist giving three cheers to their marksman. Leaving a strong covering party to keep our Division in check at the bridge of Vera, their main body followed the Spaniards who, offering little opposition, continued retiring towards San Sebastian."*

Simmons: *"Don Manuel Freyre, with his Spanish Division, fought very spiritedly in the town, and also upon the heights of San Marcial, when the French attempted to crown them. The Spaniards beat the enemy back. Lord Wellington was an eye-witness on this occasion and was highly pleased. Before dark, Marshal Soult was completely beaten in all his attacks, as well as having gained no advantage by his manoeuvres."*

The 1st Brigade of the Light Division (which included 1st battalion 95th), was ordered to pass the bridge of Le Secca, and to move in a parallel direction with the French. Simmons says they *"marched from hill to hill and towards evening crowned the heights above Lesaka and remained there for the night. The day had been exceptionally hot, and our march up the sides of high mountains was trying to the soldiers. Just before dark I was placed with 30 men upon the side of a mountain. The night now set in stormy and rainy, and we had difficulty in keeping our fire from going out... The rain ran down the sides of the mountains in torrents, and the thunder and lightning were very frequent. By the occasional glare which illumined the mountain above me, I saw the enemy in full retreat, no doubt much alarmed for fear of finding the river not fordable."*

Posted at the bridge at Vera was a company of the 2nd battalion 95th, commanded by Captain Daniel Cadoux. Stationed nearby in support was a company of the 3rd battalion under Lieutenant Travers.

Simmons *"Our riflemen still occupied the right bank of the river as far as keeping a double sentry close to it, and the other pickets in loop-holed houses nearby."* At 2am in the morning (1 September), the retreating French, unable to ford the Bidasoa, tried to force their way over this bridge.

Simmons: *"The enemy, finding no possible way of retreating but over the bridge and through Vera, made a desperate attack with a most overwhelming force on the bridge, and carried it. Captain Cadoux brought his company to the bridge and tried to drive the enemy back, or prevent more from passing. They fought most heroically, but he soon fell, after receiving several musket balls in his breast. His lieutenant, Llewellyn, had his jaw shattered. Several men were killed and wounded. They were obliged to retire a little distance, but kept up a fire as long as the enemy continued to file over the bridge."*

Three or four hundred French, unable from the great rains to ford the Bidasoa, charged fiercely upon one of our companies, and another of the 2nd battalion, then posted at the bridge of Vera. After a sanguinary struggle they effected their purpose, and escaped. They were the remnant of the French troops that had forded the river in the morning, and whom our Spanish force distinguished themselves in repulsing[9]. After this we remained quiet for several days in our camp ground.

Kincaid: *"At daylight the next morning we found that the enemy had altogether disappeared from our front."* The Light Division returned to their camp ground above Vera.

CHAPTER 22

La Rhune; Battle of the Nivelle
September - 13 November 1813

The Light Division remained quietly encamped above Vera until 7 October.

For several weeks, we remained encamped, close to the river Bidasoa, with Lesaka in our rear, and Vera in our front. It was about this time that the men of the 52nd who were fortunate enough to have survived the forlorn hope of Rodrigo and Badajoz, were distinguished with a badge of laurel on the right arm, with the letters VS for 'valiant stormer' placed beneath the wreath. This was given by their commanding officer as a testimonial of their gallant conduct. Why the men of our battalion, and those of the 43rd, who had equally distinguished themselves on those occasions, were not similarly honoured, I know not. For my own part, all I ever received in the way of reward for my services as a stormer, was the sum of six dollars after the taking of Badajoz[1].

In the French service, those men who volunteered in the ranks of 'les enfants perdus' were always first in the list for commissions, and were distinguished by a cross of the *Legion of Honour*, which was so respected amongst their countrymen that even their comrades were obliged to salute those who wore it. How must their hearts beat at the possession of such a distinguishing mark, and how different is the case of the British soldier! This 'hope' in his country remains unnoticed, and he quits its service equally 'forlorn' for obscurity, undistinguished other than by his empty sleeves, or his wooden stump, as he limps to Chelsea. Some may argue that an improvement took place at Waterloo. That may be, but on that occasion there were some who performed their first and last military feat and came away unscathed. How 'pleasant' it must be for the old Peninsulars, whose battles fought and won outnumber perhaps the men of their company, to see whole squads of 'Waterloos' strutting about with medals dangling on jackets which had scarcely been on long enough to collect the dust of a donkey's trot.

In this camp also, an order arrived from Horse Guards for the appointment of a colour-sergeant in each company, to be considered as senior, or sergeant-major, with an extra sixpence per day. As no badges (the cross swords) had arrived from England, the deficiency was supplied by our master tailor, who formed an imitation with coloured silks, worked on the arms of the men appointed.

While here we used to amuse ourselves bathing. We were soon to cross the river which divides the French and Spanish territories [the Bidasoa], and it was heart-stirring to see our riflemen unconsciously expose to Spain, the evidence of the dangers they had endured for her liberation, for as they stripped on its banks, and prepared to dash into the clear water, their perforated and wounded exteriors proved what they had seen and suffered. On these occasions, the veterans would generally amuse themselves by remarking and jesting to one another on the peculiar situation of the different bullet holes, and the direction the shot had taken in passing through them.

One day, I nearly lost my life through my own folly. A very handsome little Spanish girl was attached to Dillon, one of our sergeants[2]. Her name was Louisa, and she by some means got to the other side of the river, which was generally occupied by the enemy. She was afraid to go to a bridge lower down lest she should be taken by the French. She cried bitterly and begged the men on our side to get her over. Just here the river was not wide but deep, and having a respect for her, I instantly stripped off all except my trousers, and swam across, intending to bring her to our side. Without a moment's hesitation, I placed pretty Louisa on my back, put her arms round my neck, waded as far as I was able, and then commenced swimming; but as soon as I got into the deep water, she squeezed me so tight round the neck that, although I was a good swimmer, I lost all power. Down I went. Our fellows thought I was playing tricks, but when I rose and bellowed out for assistance, they became alarmed. She struck to me like a leech, and several of the men, seeing me go down a second time, stripped and jumped in to my assistance. The water was 12 feet deep and Kelly, of my own company, dived down, seized her by her long hair, and brought us both to the surface of the water, insensible. Assisted by the rest, he dragged us to land[3].

When I came to myself, I found our head surgeon, Dr. Burke, and some of our fellows, rubbing me back to life. Assisted by the little brandy they poured down our throats, we both recovered. After a little while, I was able to walk to my tent, but not so the pretty Louisa, who was kept wrapped in blankets the whole day. Poor thing. She remained with the regiment while in Spain, and afterwards followed us to England, but what ultimately became of her, I know not.

Here too my old friend, Tom Crawley, got the whole of our regiment out of a precious scrape. Our Division were given linen bags, made exactly to fit across our knapsacks, with three days' biscuit (3lbs) for each bag. The bags were to be kept well tied, and strapped on the top of each man's knapsack. The brigadier expected us to be on short commons while on the Pyrenees and, as this was to be our last resource in case of scarcity, no man was to taste a morsel of biscuit unless given written orders to that effect.

The bags were examined every morning by officers commanding companies. Seeing them strapped snugly on the knapsacks, they considered them to be all right. However, our fellows were never at a loss for subterfuge, and they planned to evade the officers' vigilance by eating all their biscuits except one whole one, which they kept at the top to be seen. In place of the others, they substituted chips. These did very well for some time, but one day, whilst on private parade, Captain Johnston[4] took it into his head to see his company's biscuit shaken out. The first man on the right of his company was the unfortunate Tom Crawley.

"Untie your bag, Crawley," said the Captain.

Tom did as he was ordered, and showed the Captain a very good-looking biscuit a-top.

"Shake the whole out. I want to see if they are getting mouldy."

"Faith, there is no fear of that," said Crawley, looking the Captain hard in the face, then casting a woeful eye on his bag.

But the Captain was not to be baulked. Taking the bag by both ends, he emptied out its contents, which was no more and no less than a few dry chips. Poor Tom, as upright as a dart, stood scratching his head. His countenance would have made a saint laugh.

"What have you done with your biscuit? Have you eaten it, sir?"

Tom, motionless, made no answer.

"Do you know it is against orders?"

"To be sure I do, sir" says Tom; "but, for God's sake, do you take me for a South American jackass, that carries gold and eats straw?"[5]

This answer not only set the Captain, but the whole company, in roars of laughter, and on further inspection, he found that they, and indeed the regiment, had adopted the same plan. Through this our bags were taken away, and we were relieved from carrying chips.

During September and early October, the French opposing the Light Division were busy erecting works for the purpose of defending the pass of Vera. Kincaid: *"The labours of the French on the opposite mountain had, in the first instance, been confined to fortification but, as the season advanced, they seemed to think that the branch of a tree, or a sheet of canvas, was too slender a barrier between them and a frosty night, and their fortified camp became a fortified town of regular brick and mortar. Though we were living under the influence of the same sky, we did not think it necessary to give ourselves the same trouble, but reasoned on their proceedings like philosophers, calculating from the aspect of the times, that there was a probability of a speedy transfer of property."*

By October 1813, command of Skerret's brigade passed to Colonel Colbourne who, early in the month, and accompanied by Harry Smith, reconnoitred the French works. The Duke of Wellington resolved to cross the Bidasoa and the push the enemy back. Kincaid: *"Late on the night of 7 October, Colonel Barnard arrived from headquarters with the intelligence that the next was to be the day of trial. Accordingly, on the morning of the 8th, the 4th Division came up to support us, and we immediately marched down to the foot of the enemy's position, shook off our knapsacks before their faces, and went at them."*

About the beginning of October we had an opportunity of witnessing the gallantry of our 3rd battalion. Although they had not seen our service in the country, on this occasion they showed themselves 'old hands', worthy of their green jackets. They had to dislodge the enemy, then holding possession of a high hill behind Vera, which they did in most excellent style, in the sight of our Division and the 4th.

Kincaid: *"The action commenced by five companies of our 3rd battalion advancing, under Colonel Ross, to dislodge the enemy from a hill which they occupied in front of their entrenchments. There never was a movement more beautifully executed, for they walked quietly and steadily, and swept them regularly off, not firing a shot until the enemy had turned their faces, when they served them out with a most destructive discharge."*

Our battalion was not suffered to remain idle, and we soon joined in pursuit of the enemy, who took refuge in the valleys of France.

Simmons: *"The Light Division had innumerable obstacles to encounter - redoubts and field-works on every eminence presenting themselves to our view - but the steadiness and daring intrepidity of the men eventually surmounted all obstacles, and the French were driven into their own country, of which we now had a fine view."*

On taking possession of their camp-ground we found a whole range of huts, constructed in the most ingenious manner, of turf and stone. One of our men came in for a rather novel prize - a large monkey, which we kept in the regiment for some time. This animal had a strange prejudice - he utterly disliked the sight of a woman.

Kincaid: *"We now found ourselves firmly established within the French territory, with a prospect before us that was truly refreshing, considering that we had not seen the sea for three years, and that our views, for months, had been confined to fogs and the peaks of mountains. On our left, the Bay of Biscay extended as far as the horizon, while several or our ships were seen sporting upon her bosom. Beneath us lay the pretty little town of St. Jean-de-Luz, which looked as if it had just been framed out of the Lilliputian scenery of a toy shop. The town of Bayonne too, was visible in the distance, and the view to the right embraced a beautiful, well-wooded country, thickly studded with town and villages, as far as the eye could reach."*

Simmons: *"One particularly high mountain named La Rhune was still in possession of the enemy, and from the top the French were amusing themselves by firing long shots at the Spaniards all day. In the evening their force was withdrawn and this morning [9 October], La Rhune was occupied by the Light Division.*

La Rhune today

On the morning of the 9th, the day after the preceding skirmish of Vera heights, we took ground considerably to the right, marching along the summit of the Pyrenees until we came to a very high hill, on the top of which stood the remains of an ancient castle. Our men styled the hill the 'father of the Pyrenees', as it was by far the highest mountain we had ever seen. It was called La Rhune by the French, who had possession of it. On our arrival we had the satisfaction of compelling them, after a smart skirmish, to evacuate their lofty tenement. This was difficult because our men had, in most instances, to crawl up the mountain on their hands and knees, in consequence of its steepness. Fortunately for them, the French had a less precipitous side to retreat down, or they would all have been destroyed.

My curiosity led me to explore the old building, in company with one or two comrades. It was originally the ruin of a very strong fortress or castle, in which, I subsequently heard, the Spaniards once kept state prisoners. After searching about for some time, we discovered a narrow pathway. It conducted us to a cellar, or cavern, which to our surprise, we found tenanted by an old gentleman with a venerable beard. He received us very courteously. From his appearance, he seemed to be a hermit, but how he managed to maintain his residence against the dominion of eagles, vultures, and owls, as well as the occasional jar of contending parties, was a wonder he did not condescend to explain. The only gift we could obtain was a little spring water which, after our scramble, was refreshing. The splendid view from our elevated position, however, made ample amends for our work.

Leach: *"Our Division constantly afterwards had a picket of three companies on that mountain, amongst some ruins called the Hermitage of La Rhune."*

Simmons: *"A small mountain, from its similarity and position was called Petite La Rhune, and divided from it by a valley. Our advanced pickets were now posted on one side upon the slopes, and the French on the opposite side within 200 yards of us. From these stupendous mountains we had a most commanding view of a vast extent of highly cultivated French territory, innumerable villages, and the town and port of St. Jean-de-Luz.*

The view was so good that, on 13 October, Simmons, Surtees, Kincaid and Leach witnessed an action at sea just off St. Jean-de-Luz.

Simmons: *"This morning one of our ships was observed to be chasing a brig of war, and got between her and the shore. We observed the batteries near the town trying to aid the escape of the French ship, but without success. As the boats from the English went to board her, the Frenchmen got into theirs and made for the shore. Some English sailors went on board, but soon left her. A short time after she was one mass of fire and soon blew up. A dense smoke arose from the spot, but in a moment there was not a vestige that we could perceive remaining upon the bosom of the ocean. It was a beautiful morning, and some thousands of veteran Englishmen, having a bird's eye view of the whole affair, took a lively interest in the gallant manner our brave tars performed their duty. How delighted the sailors would have been if they had been aware that so many of their countrymen were observing and applauding them from the tops of the Pyrenees!"*

The Light Division were encamped in the same spot for several weeks, during which time the French, who were encamped on Petite la Rhune, again built fortifications. By 30 October, the weather was starting to get very cold, with frequent storms of hail and rain.

Leach: *"A continuation of tremendous gales of wind and rain tormented us for a whole fortnight. They blew down our tents as fast as we pitched them, and almost tore them to pieces, so that we were never dry.... I believe that troops have but rarely been exposed to 24 hours of such weather on so unsheltered a spot... It is enough to say, that day or night, we were never dry. Springs bubbled up from the ground on which our tents stood, and we began to think it was really time to seek winter quarters in more hospitable regions."*

Our battalion at this time was stationed about a mile below La Rhune, and greatly exposed to storms of wind and rain. There was a scarcity of provisions. Few of the country people visited us, so that even those in possession of money found little or no benefit from it. We had reason to believe that the French army, who were encamped about three-quarters of a mile to our front, were more fortunate, as they were plentifully supplied with provisions. Occasionally some of our officers were visited by a supply that was smuggled past the French lines[6].

On 31 October, after being blockaded for four months, Pamplona fell to the allies, and Wellington could now give his mind to a full scale attack on the French in the Pyrenees. To this end, he frequently viewed their position and works at Petite La Rhune. Simmons: *"The enemy's position now had a very formidable appearance upon the summit of the ridge of Petite La Rhune. Where it was at all accessible, strong walls were built, with loop-holes to fire though. The ground was scarped, and at small distances along the front, strong redoubts were placed to strengthen more effectually their line of defence. Four French regiments were encamped upon Petite la Rhune ready to man the works at a moment. The road through the mountains in our rear had been made and put in order by strong parties of soldiers, so that cannon could be brought up with facility at any time.*

A general attack upon the enemy was now daily expected, as Lord Wellington with his staff had been observed inspecting the enemy's position with more than ordinary care for the last two or three mornings. On 9 November every disposition had been made, and the following morning ushered in the battle of the Nivelle.

The attack on Petite la Rhune was allocated to the Light Division. Simmons: *"The whole of the allied army was to co-operate with us and make a simultaneous attack upon the enemy's line of works, redoubts, etc. After dark, the Light Division filed from the encampment behind La Rhune with the least possible noise, formed up into columns, and lay down close behind our advanced picket, which was partly across the deep valley that separated the French from us."*

Colonel Colbourne led the Light Division. With him was Harry Smith: *"When Colbourne and I rode up to our most advanced picket, we found Sergeant Crowther and his men, all sitting with their rifles between their legs, with the sentry a few paces in the front. Without any agitation, they stood up very quietly to reconnoitre us. Colbourne spoke, and commended their vigilance."* Sergeant Crowther was in Costello's company.

This night, the company I belonged to was on picket. Our orders were that, on the first dawn of light, we should attack and drive in the enemy's picket which was opposed to us. We were preparing for the task when, to our surprise, about 100 yards in our rear, we beheld the whole of our Division waiting to support us.

Simmons: *"The French picket was seated around the fire, with no apprehension of what was going to take place. Some heavy cannon sounded the advance, and in a moment every one was in motion up the sides of this tremendous steep."*

As soon as our attack commenced, we heard the alarm given by at least 100 drums and bugles. As the light dawned more clearly, we could see the French columns all in motion. The remainder of our battalion and Division came up, and we were soon hotly engaged, with only a valley partially separating us from the main body of the enemy.

Leach: *"It is impossible to conceive a finer sight than the general advance of our army from the Pyrenean passes against the French position. Almost as far as the eye could reach, was seen one sheet of flame and smoke, accompanied with an incessant fire of light troops, and frequent volleys of musketry, as the lines and columns approached the entrenchments."*

Simmons: *Obstacles of an extraordinary nature were opposed to us, and the enemy kept up a very brisk fire from behind their walls, but... the works were carried in every direction. Other works, more concentrated and filled with men, were now opened to our view and immediately attacked. Many gallant fellows fell to rise no more in this world."*

After we had routed them from their first line, and were getting close to their second, an incident occurred which I, and the greater part of our company, observed. A man of the name of Morely, a shoemaker, fell shot through the head[7]. Nearly the whole time we had been in Spain, he had lived with a Spanish woman, who acted in some degree as one of the sutlers to our regiment. She was tenderly attached to him, and during an action would get as near to her lover as possible, generally on a donkey. On this occasion, some of our wounded men who were passing her, informed her Morely was killed. The poor girl was distracted. Leaving her donkey and stores behind, she rushed down to the spot where he had fallen. We were then in the thick of the fight. With the balls coming thick as hail, our only safety was cover, but she, callous to every danger, threw herself on the blood-stained body of her lover, and gave way to the most appalling ebullition of grief, tearing her hair and wringing her hands. I expected every moment to see the poor woman shot.

The gallantry of Blanco, the Spaniard who was so revengeful at Vitoria, was conspicuous. He had been an intimate friend of Morely, and seeing the danger his countrywoman was exposed to, he rushed boldly from his cover, placed himself in front of her, and continued loading and firing at the enemy, swearing loudly all the time in a way only a Spaniard can do justice to. Such were the fierce grimaces and oaths of Blanco that, notwithstanding the real horror of the scene, it was impossible to resist the impulse to laugh. It was a miracle that he escaped injury.

Meanwhile, the battle was raging. Simmons: *"I saw some French officers standing upon their walls, and trying every means in their power to make their men remain. One young officer was doing prodigies of valour, and would not leave the wall; he was shot, and came tumbling down. The French were driven from all their positions, and our army took up the line of the Nivelle."*

Kincaid: *"Petite la Rhune was more of an outpost than part of their position, the latter being a chain of stupendous mountains in its rear so, while our battalion followed their skirmishers into the valley between, the remainder of our Division were forming for the attack on the main position, awaiting for the co-operation of the other divisions, the thunder of whose artillery, echoing along the valleys, proclaimed that they were engaged, far and wide, on both sides of us."*

At this time, a part of our Division were endeavouring to enter the French lines on our right. The enemy seemed determined to defend their huts, which they had been at considerable trouble to construct, so the action there was close and sanguinary. Part of our battalion took them on the right flank, and they were eventually obliged to yield. We arrived at the huts, which they had arranged in excellent order, and from which they had reluctantly been compelled to retreat. In passing along a row of them, I heard a scuffle going on in one. I entered and beheld a huge French grenadier, with red wings, struggling on the ground with my old acquaintance, Tom Crawley. The Frenchman had been surprised, but he was getting the better of Tom. My appearance determined the matter at once, and the grenadier surrendered.

From what I could make out, in his hasty retreat from the hut, the Frenchman had forgotten some of his needfuls and had returned for them, to be met at the doorway by Tom who, according to his old custom, was preparing to explore the interior. Crawley was immediately attacked by the grenadier with fixed bayonet, and in his attempt to parry off a thrust, had received the blade through his right hand. He bled profusely. We did not kill the Frenchman but left him to the mercy of the caçadores, who were following close behind us.

Tom went to the rear, and I never saw him afterwards. Nor can I say I have heard of him since. Many an anxious inquiry was made, many an old scene was revived and passed current amongst us[8]. Tom Crawley will live in our recollections as long as we can enjoy the good company of a comrade. May this book be extensively read, if it only be to give celebrity to him. May penny publications quote freely from his adventures, in the hope that our veteran sixpenny pensioners, whose small pittance will not permit them to purchase the volume, will have an opportunity of recurring to old scenes.

The enemy, although retreating, did so in an orderly manner, and kept up a tolerably brisk fire. I had no sooner regained the line of skirmishers than I received a severe hit just about the centre of my waist. It nearly knocked me down. For a moment I imagined myself mortally wounded through the body, but on examination I found myself only slightly bruised. A ball had actually stuck in the serpent of my waist belt - the brass clasp or hook that fastens it - from whence it was afterwards taken out with difficulty.

After I had recovered from the shock, I joined in the pursuit of the enemy. Once or twice they attempted to make a stand, but we were close at their heels, so they thought it better to pursue their way at an accelerated pace. They were covered by some battalions of light troops, who displayed considerable coolness.

The French descended the heights, at the foot of which stands the pretty little town of St. Jean-de-Luz, with its white houses. Our battalion, in hot pursuit, was engaged in sharp skirmishing when our gallant Colonel, Sir Andrew Barnard, who had been very conspicuous on a brown, long-tailed horse during the day, received a shot in the breast. I ran up him, as did several other men. We perceived him spit blood, but he would not dismount so one of our buglers supported him on his horse, while another led it to the rear[9].

Immediately after this, my attention was attracted by the 52nd regiment, who charged up the side of a hill on our right, to take a fort. Shots are very strange things. They fly fast, and at this moment, Sergeant Watt of the Rifles received a ball in the head. I was next to him and he laid hold of me with both hands and called out: "Am I dead? Am I dead?"

Poor fellow! He was mortally wounded, and it was with difficulty that I extricated myself from his deadly grasp[10].

The French, after a severe loss, made good their retreat across the river that leads to St. Jean-de-Luz. With our usual luck we took up our camp for the night on the side of a bleak and barren hill.

Kincaid: *"The movements of the two or three days following placed the enemy within their entrenchments at Bayonne, and the headquarters of our battalion in the château d'Arcangues, with the outposts of the Division at the village of Bassussarry and its adjacents... The country was abundant in every comfort, and the chateau was large, well-*

furnished, and unoccupied, except by a bed-ridden grandmother, and young Arcangues - a gay, rattling young fellow, who furnished us with plenty of good wine (by our paying for the same), and made one of our mess. "

After this we got into better quarters on the other side of the river. This was a château called Arcangues.

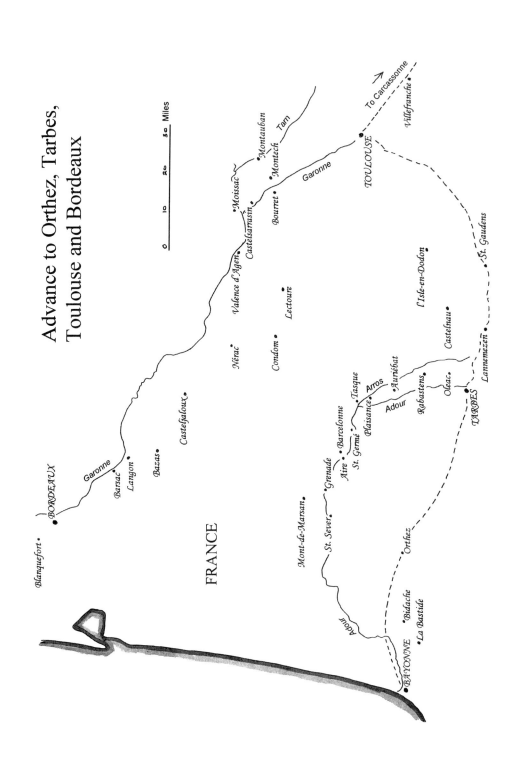

Advance to Orthez, Tarbes, Toulouse and Bordeaux

0 10 20 30 Miles

FRANCE

Blanquefort
BORDEAUX
Garonne
Barsac
Langon
Bazas
Casteljaloux

Mont-de-Marsan
St. Sever
Grenade
Aire
Barcelonne
St. Germé
Tasque
Plaisance
Arros
Aurébat
Rabastens
Oléac
Castelnau
L'Isle-en-Dodon
Lannemezan
TARBES
St. Gaudens

Adour
Orthez
Bidache
La Bastide
BAYONNE

Adour

Nérac
Condom
Lectoure
Valence d'Agen
Castelsarrasin
Moissac
Bourret
Montech
Montauban
Tarn
Garonne
TOULOUSE
Villefranche
To Carcassonne

CHAPTER 23

Actions at Arcangues, the Nive, Tarbes, and Toulouse
14 November 1813 - 13 April 1814

Ejected from Spain, the French were now fighting on their own soil. Wellington, aware of the immense number of casualties the Spanish peasantry inflicted on the French army in retaliation for acts of barbarity and plunder, informed his soldiers that the plundering of French houses would not be tolerated. Simmons: *'The French people do not offer to kill any British soldiers, and we behave to the people the same as if we were in England. The Spaniards were sent back into their own country, as they began plundering, which Lord Wellington would not allow. It is a much better policy to use the inhabitants well. If you did otherwise, the whole country would be in arms, and a soldier durst not go a hundred paces from the battalion without being liable to be murdered by some injured connection.'*

While at Arcangues, the Light Division fortified the château and church, and erected fieldworks.

> We were as usual in the immediate front of the enemy, with our outlying sentinels and theirs little more than thirty yards apart. Such a good feeling reigned among the French and our men, that we frequently went into each other's picket houses. These terms of intimacy the French extended to neither the Spanish nor Portuguese troops, for whom they expressed an unmeasured contempt. This state of things at our outposts was too subversive of discipline to be tolerated by those in command, and it was only done on the sly, upon a reliance of mutual honour. Nevertheless, it exhibits a pleasing picture of the absence of all revenge and prejudice on either side among men of opposing interests. This feeling, however, could not stay the effusion of blood that was still to be shed.

At daylight on 10 December, the French attacked in force and drove in the 2nd Brigade of the Light Division at the château of Castilleur. They then made a heavy attack on the 1st Brigade at the château of Arcangues.

> On 10 December[1], the enemy drove in the pickets, which were chiefly furnished by our battalion, and their columns came briskly

255

forward intent on driving us from our position. Our company had been ordered to line some brushwood on the side of a lane that led from the château and, as they came on, we received them with a fierce and deadly fire. They replied with spirit, and endeavoured to outflank our position. Assisting to repel this attempt, we came in for a shower of shot, and Lieutenant Hopwood and Sergeant Brotherwood, with several more of our party, were killed on the spot[2].

By this time they were getting round us, and perceiving how few our numbers were compared to their own, they started to close. We took to our heels down a field and sprang into the lane. In doing so, I dropped my cap, and there it remained during the day, until I regained possession of it on the retreat of the enemy.

Kincaid: *"We found ourselves engaged along with the pickets, and under a heavy skirmishing fire retired gradually from hedge to hedge, as the superior force of the enemy compelled us to give ground. We finally retired within our home, the château, which was the first part of our position that was meant to be defended in earnest. We had previously thrown up a mud rampart around it, and loop-holed the different outhouses, so that we had nothing now to do but to line the walls and show determined fight. The 43rd occupied the churchyard to our left, which was also partially fortified; and the 3rd Caçadores and our 3rd battalion occupied the space between, behind the hedgerows, while the 4th Division was in readiness to support us from the rear."*

Someone made it known that Lord Wellington and his staff were watching our motions through their glasses from the château. Seeing ourselves under the eye of the Commander-in-Chief, we instantly rallied. Our 3rd battalion were hotly engaged on our left.

Kincaid: *The enemy came up to the opposite ridge in formidable numbers, and began blazing at our windows and loop-holes, and showing some disposition to attempt it by storm; but they thought better of it and withdrew their columns a short distance to the rear, leaving the nearest hedge lined with their skirmishers. An officer of ours, Mr. Hopwood, and one of our sergeants, had been killed in the field opposite, within 20 yards of where the enemy's skirmishers now were. We were very anxious to get possession of their bodies, but had not force enough to effect it. Several French soldiers came through the hedge at different times with the intention, as we thought, of plundering, but our men shot every one who attempted to go near them. Towards evening, a French officer approached, waving a white handkerchief and pointing to some of his men, who were following him with shovels. Seeing that his intention was to bury them, we instantly ceased firing; nor did we renew it again that night."*

The enemy found themselves unable to make any serious impression and, I dare say, were not sorry when night closed upon their baffled columns. We had little respite from the fatigues of the day, as we were busily employed in fortifying the château for the attack anticipated on the morrow. However, the following morning, the enemy retreated within their works, upon which we took possession of our former ground. There we found the bodies of Lt. Hopwood and poor Brotherwood. Both had been stripped, and covered partially with a little loose earth[3].

On 9 December, General Hill and his force had crossed the Nive, and Soult expended much energy in unsuccessfully attacking him. Between the 9th and 13th December there was fighting on various parts of Wellington's line, and although these actions are usually referred to as the Battle of the Nive, Costello and Kincaid refer to them as the battle of Bayonne.

After this, for five or six days following, we had a succession of fights or skirmishes, called the battle of Bayonne, although without eliciting any particular result.

At the outposts, an excellent private feeling was kept up on both sides, although a general order had been promulgated prohibiting all intercourse with the enemy on pain of death. On Christmas night, our company was on picket near a dwelling called Garrett's house. We clubbed half a dollar each, and sent Grindley, our comrade, into the French picket-house to purchase brandy, but when he stayed longer than was usual, we became alarmed and sent two other men in quest of him. From the nearest French sentry, they learned that Grindley was lying drunk in their picket-house. Fearful that the circumstances should come to the knowledge of Lieutenant Gardiner, the officer of our picket, they went to bring him back with them. Grindley was very drunk, and just as they were emerging with him from the French lines, who should ride down to the front post but Sir James Kempt, who commanded our Division at that time. Grindley was instantly ordered to be confined; he was very fortunate to escape with only a slight punishment[4].

The campaign of 1813 came to an end. Leach: *'On the last day of the year, we got together some females, French and Spanish, and danced in the new year at the château of Arcangues, in spite of our proximity to such queer neighbours as the French advanced posts consisted of.'*

About the beginning of January 1814, the enemy were seen advancing, as we understood, to straighten our lines, which were in a half circle. With three or four others, I was ordered to hold possession of a small farmhouse which communicated with some cross roads, and keep up a brisk fire. If the *assemblée* sounded, we were to retreat upon the company, which occupied another, larger house, about 200 yards in our rear. On our right was a high stone wall, and on our left, in parallel, was a hedge, which served as a cover for the French who had possession of it. When we heard the *assemblée*, we were on the alert to retreat, but this was risky as our only passage was by the open field between the stone wall and the hedge. The moment we showed our noses we were saluted with a hailstorm of bullets. This put us all in a rather moody condition, and it was proposed that we retire by independent files. The first to run the gauntlet was a tall, gaunt Irishman. The shower that whizzed about him almost unnerved the rest of us, particularly Johnny Castles, who was at a standstill. Since Castles had figured at Badajoz with a rope round his neck, he had made up his mind to live for ever, on which he had grown fat. Now his corpulence threatened to mark him out.

"Oh, dom your limbs. Ye are the rascals to drink and carouse with as ye did yesterday," he growled in a true Caledonian dialect. He gave an awful grin. "Eh, look at 'em! dom their eyes, they are sure to hit me!" He ducked his head and, with his face half averted and covered by his hands, away he bolted, yelling and screaming all the way. The French peppered away at him in prime style, and the dust rose in every direction from the balls. Being spherical, Johnny puffed and blowed like a whale, but he escaped injury, and rolled over the hedge with a brace of samples through his knapsack and mess-tin[5]. Gilbert[6] and I took advantage of the welcome given to Castles to follow, without allowing them time to reload. As the devil would have it, the pair of us arrived safely. There now remained only one - Jones, a fine, tall, good-looking Welshman. He quickly came after us, but the poor fellow was met half-way by a shot in his hind quarters, passing from side to side. As soon as they saw him fall, the French ceased firing and he managed to scramble forward over the hedge to join us[7]. After all that, the enemy never took the house, and with a reinforcement from the 52nd, we beat them back again.

I often laugh at the recollection of Johnny Castles, though I must say, I funked dreadfully. Like the frogs in the fable, though death to us, it was sport to the French, who had roared with laughter as we bolted by. After this affair, Castles could never be induced to drink, or hold any acquaintance, with the enemy.

On 24 January, the 1st battalion was placed in the Light Division's 2nd Brigade, commanded by Colonel Barnard. The 2nd battalion 95th was moved to the 1st Brigade. St. Jean-de-Luz was now the new supply centre for Wellington's army.

We remained some four or five months at Arcangues then, on 21 February 1814, the army broke up their cantonments, and marched for Toulouse. Our battalion, standing in need of new clothing, did not march with the Division, but were ordered into St. Jean-de-Luz to receive them.

Kincaid: *"The new clothing for the different regiments of the army had been gradually arriving at St. Jean-de-Luz and, as the commissariat transport was required for other purposes, not to mention that a man's new coat always looks better on his own back than it does on a mule's, the different regiments marched there for it in succession. It did not come to our turn until we had taken a stride to the front, as far as La Bastide; our retrograde movement, therefore, obliged us to bid adieu to our Division for some time... Our clothing detained us there two days, and on the third, we proceeded to rejoin our Division."*

According to Leach, they received their clothing on 23 February and were posted back towards the army on the 24th.

> Some time afterwards we rejoined our Division. This was after the battle of Orthez, at which our battalion felt much chagrined in not being present.

Surtees described the battle of Orthez, which took place on 27 February, as a *"decided, but withal unfruitful victory"*. From Orthez, most of Wellington's army advanced along the main road to Tarbes in pursuit of the retreating French, but the Light Division took the left flank, through the towns of St. Sever and Grenade to Barcelonne, where the 1st battalion rejoined the Light Division on 12 March.

On 18 March, says Simmons, *"the Division assembled at Ville St. Germé. Crossed the Arros at Tasque. The Division halted at Plaisance. Three companies of our battalion crossed the river, and took up their quarters in a small village. Close to the house that I, with the company, occupied, an inhabitant was murdered. I heard the shot fired just before I lay down, but had no idea that a human being had been deprived of his existence."*

> On 18 March, at Plaisance, near the town of Tarbes, a French peasant was shot, under circumstances that fixed the crime upon some of the men of our company. The greatest endeavours were made to discover the culprit, and although the company was punished to make them give him up, it was to no avail.

Simmons: *"We tried every means to find out the villain, but to no purpose."* Surtees: *"A subscription was set on foot among the officers of the Division, and 100 guineas were collected and paid to the unfortunate widow who, though grieved for the loss of her husband, was thankful for the money. I strongly suspect my friends, the Portuguese, were the culprits on this occasion."* But they were not:

Three months later, I was told who had perpetrated the deed. That evening, Blanco, accompanied by one or two of our men[8], had gone out in search of wine. They entered the house of a peasant, who resisted the intrusion and struck Blanco, for which the Spaniard shot him on the spot. A very handsome collection was made for the widow and children of the poor peasant, for whose distress a very sincere sympathy was entertained by our battalion.

The morning we left Plaisance we had a long and dreary march over a range of hills, until we came to the village of Tarbes.

They marched from Plaisance to Auriébat, where they halted for a few hours before moving to Aget and vicinity. On the 20th, they marched through Rabastens to Tarbes. Simmons: *'The enemy were posted in very strong positions on a chain of heights, and occupying the town of Tarbes.'*

The battlefield at Tarbes today.
The 95th attacked from the trees nearest the camera

A short distance beyond Tarbes we observed the French in possession of a hill both sides of the road to Toulouse. We were immediately ordered to commence an attack upon them. We went down the road at the 'double'. As we passed them, some of our regiments of cavalry gave us an encouraging huzza.

Simmons: *"Our three battalions of riflemen were ordered to dislodge the enemy, which we went about at once."*

Surtees: *"My battalion (3rd) formed the right, the 2nd battalion the centre, and the 1st the left of our line of skirmishers. We found the hills covered in front with a great number of light troops, which occupied us some time in driving in, and in which service we suffered considerably, for they occupied the hedges and dikes on the high ground, from which it was necessary to dislodge them. We had also a considerably-sized brushwood to pass through before we could get at them."*

They had thrown up strong entrenchments and were, to use a nautical phrase, 'tier above tier'.

Surtees: *"At length, after much smart skirmishing, we gained the height, but found the whole of their heavy infantry drawn up on a steep acclivity, near the windmill, which allowed them to have line behind line, all of which could fire at the same time over each other's heads, like the tiers of guns in a three-decker. We continued, however, to advance upon them, till we got within a hundred paces of this formidable body, the firing from which was the hottest I had ever been in, except perhaps Barossa."*

Only at Badajoz were we more warmly engaged. The enemy were in great numbers, our attacking force few, being only our three battalions of Rifles, which their bullets thinned fast as we struggled up the hill: Although under every disadvantage, we, the victors of so many hard fights, were not to be repelled, and the French were obliged to retreat.

Surtees: *"Before an hour had elapsed, the French were driven completely from every position they held on this very strong hill."* He saw them *"posting away with all expedition to the plain below. Some guns, which had just arrived, gave them an occasional shot, but they did not suffer much as they marched with such rapidity. We immediately followed them down to the plain."*

This day, I stuck a poor Frenchman whom I came up with, and I was very sorry for it because I discovered he was badly wounded. I made honourable amends with a sup from my canteen, which he received with grace.

Surtees believed that the French odds at Tarbes, on the hill of Oleac, was that of *"a whole division, consisting of at least 5,000 or 6,000 men, while not a shot was fired by any but the 16 companies of my regiment, amounting probably to 1,000 or 1,100 men... I believe I shall not be far from the truth, if I state their loss in killed and wounded as equal to the whole strength of our sixteen companies. Our loss on this occasion was very heavy, being about 100 men and 11 officers killed and wounded; the proportion of officers being nearly double what usually takes place."*

Major J Blakiston of the Portuguese Caçadores witnessed this action: *"Our rifles were immediately sent to dislodge the French from the hills on our left, and our battalion was sent to support them. Nothing could exceed the manner in which the 95th set about the business.... Certainly I never saw such skirmishers as the 95th, now the Rifle Brigade. They could do the work much better and with infinitely less loss than any other of our best light troops. They possessed an individual boldness, a mutual understanding, and a quickness of eye, in taking advantage of the ground which, taken altogether, I never saw equalled. They were as much superior to the French voltigeurs, as the latter were to our skirmishers in general. As our regiment was often employed in supporting them, I think I am fairly qualified to speak of their merits."*

The Light Division followed the retreating French to Lannemezen, Castelnau, l'Isle-en-Dodon, Mont Ferrand, and Tournefoile.

Surtees: *"On the 28th or 29th [March], we were moved forward, and after a short march we reached a beautiful plain, with Toulouse appearing most magnificent in the distance. Here we went into cantonments in the different villages and châteaus in the neighbourhood, the greater part of which were completely deserted, and many of them most woefully sacked and plundered, which could have been done only by their own troops."*

We saw but little of the enemy until we came within sight of Toulouse, where they seemed determined on a resolute stand. In the beginning of April, we took up our cantonments on the side of the Garonne, where the aspect of the country was very agreeable. It abounded in wine more superior in quality to that which had been served out as our rations hitherto.

On Marshal Soult's orders, the inhabitants had been obliged to fly on our approach yet, I am happy to say, our men were restrained from most of the excesses, and the destruction of property, that had taken place in Portugal and Spain. This was due to Lord Wellington's excellent order, published throughout the army, explaining to the troops that although we were at war with a usurper and his army, we were not at war with the inoffensive country people, who had been subjected by fear[9].

Not all French property remained untouched. Surtees says that the houses which were occupied were not, as a rule, ransacked by the British soldiers, but that those which had been abandoned, often were. Kincaid: *"We were stationed for several days, in the suburb of St. Ciprien, where we found ourselves exceedingly comfortable. It consisted chiefly of the citizens' country houses... and, as the inhabitants had all fled hurriedly into town, leaving their cellars, generally speaking, well stocked with a tolerable kind of wine, we made ourselves at home."*

By the beginning of April 1814, Wellington's army was gathered on the outskirts of Toulouse. A pontoon bridge was constructed over the Garonne some distance above the town, and on 4 April, the 3rd, 4th and 6th Divisions crossed over it. However, the river became so swollen through heavy rain, the pontoon had to be pulled aside, stranding the three divisions on the other side for several days, which exposed them to a French attack. Fortunately, they remained unmolested, and when the water subsided, the pontoon was re-established. At daybreak on 10 April, the Light Division crossed.

> About 12 o'clock on the night of the 9 April, we were ordered to fall in. Having had scarcely any rest the preceding night, most of our men were buried in profound sleep, when we were suddenly roused by the most expressive words to the ear of a soldier: 'fall in'. This was done in an instant, and we were ordered to advance in double time. We marched to the side of the Garonne, crossed it by means of a pontoon bridge, and took up our station behind the walls of a château about a mile from the town.

They were followed by the remainder of the army. Harry Smith: *"It was evidently the Duke's intention to attack Soult's position this day. Nor were we long on the march before each general officer had his point of rendezvous designated."*

With Wellington's army was what Surtees describes as *"a whole host of Spaniards... These latter gentry, on their entering France, had behaved most wantonly, and had committed numerous atrocities His lordship, as Generalissimo, had ordered them back to their own country again. But they had an anxious desire to participate in the honourable achievement of the allied troops so, upon the promise of good behaviour, he had granted them permission to rejoin the army. They were to have a post of honour assigned them at the ensuring battle... They were here in number, I should think, about 6,000 or 8,000 strong."*

The French defences at Toulouse were formidable, and many buildings had been fortified. The 4th and 6th Divisions were ordered to attack the outer side of a well-defended eminence on the east side of the town; the Spaniards were ordered to attack the same defences from the front. The Light Division were allocated the lower ground, from where they were to support the Spaniards, and could threaten a point on the canal. As planned, the Spanish attacked the redoubt on the hill, but they received such a terrible fire, they turned tail and fled.

> As we proceeded, we heard a heavy firing as if from the left of the town, and soon after beheld a disorganised mass of Spanish soldiers

flying towards us. At first some of our fellows took them for the French, and fired among them, by which some lives were lost. They were a part of the Spanish force which attempted to carry a French fort or redoubt, but the enemy had sent them to the right about faster than they had come.

We continued to approach the town, which was protected by a long series of fortifications that appeared to be full of men. When we halted, sheltered by some trees, near to the walls of some houses, they opened up a running fire from some fieldworks, but with little execution. We were not in this quiescent state long, when the thunder of the conflict was heard going on to our left, the salvoes of artillery, the constant cracking of musketry, the rushing sound of shells, and the occasional wild 'hurra', forming a very pretty concert. The scene was still more electrifying when we found it to be the 6th Division engaged in storming the batteries which the Spaniards had just run from. After a hard tug, they carried them in glorious style. General Picton's Division was also conspicuously engaged on our right, close to the river.

The general attack was crowned with the Duke of Wellington's usual success. The enemy retreated over the bridges of the canal of Languedoc into the town of Toulouse, and we took possession of their outworks.

Surtees: *"Thus terminated the battle of Toulouse, our troops maintaining the ground they had gained, while the enemy retired into the town completely beaten. Soult seemed undetermined how to act, whether to endeavour to hold the town, or leave it by the road towards the south, the only one now open to him. We rested on the field all night, the enemy sending an occasional shot or shell in the direction of our camp... Towards evening we heard that the inhabitants of the city had been most urgent on Soult to withdraw from it, and that he had promised to do so. Indeed, had he not, Lord Wellington might, if he chose, have soon reduced the town to ashes, for the heights we had taken were not 500 yards distant from the city, and completely overlooked it."*

Kincaid: *"The canal became their line of defence, which they maintained the whole of the next day. In the course of the following night, they left the town altogether, and we took possession of it the morning of the 12th."*

Surtees: *"Soult marched out, and was not molested by our troops. He took the road to Villefranche and Carcassonne, up the canal of Languedoc, our cavalry following their track."*

The French army on the second day evacuated Toulouse, as the town was completely commanded by the batteries we had taken. Our battalion was ordered to take possession of part of the suburbs, near the canal.

Kincaid: *The inhabitants of Toulouse hoisted the white flag, and declared for the Bourbons the moment that the French army had left it. In the course of the same day, Colonel Cooke arrived from Paris with the extraordinary news of Napoleon's abdication. Soult had been accused of having been in possession of that fact prior to the battle of Toulouse."*

The Light Division was cantoned in the suburbs of Toulouse.

There was a strict order that no man should be allowed to go into the town, but my curiosity induced me to take 'French leave', and I managed to elude the vigilance of the sentry to see a place I had heard so much of. I found almost all the shops open, and business going on as if nothing had taken place.

Hearing that the theatre was open, I was induced to pay it a visit. It was very crowded. One box was magnificently fitted up, and surmounted by laurel. I wondered for whose occupation it was intended. My curiosity was at once allayed by the arrival of the Duke and his staff, who were received with loud acclamations. 'God save the King' was played, and all but myself appeared to testify the greatest pleasure on the occasion. Although wedged into the centre of a dense crowd in the pit, I feared my insignificance would not conceal me from the glance of the Chief, or some of his Staff. However, my dark dress effectually screened me.

The Peninsular War was over. Leach: *'The general and universal feeling (amongst those, at least, who had been participators in the whole of the war in the Peninsula, from the summer of 1808 to the spring of 1814), was that, for the present, we had had enough of campaigning, and that a little rest and time to refit would be desirable."*

CHAPTER 24

The End of the Peninsular War
14 April - 22 July 1814

The Peninsular War ended with the battle of Toulouse. At the time the situation was far from clear, because Marshal Soult seemed inclined to carry on fighting. Surtees: *"Notwithstanding... Bonaparte's career was at that time finished, Soult still made a show of holding out for him; in consequence of which the army was again put in motion to compel him either to send in his adhesion to the new government, or to resign his command or troops, who had not now a master. He had taken up a position near Villefranche. Accordingly, we marched, I think, on the 15th or 16th."*

A few days after, we had to execute our old manoeuvre of allowing the French no time to rest, and were put in motion after them. On the second day, we halted on the Paris road, and as our men were resting from the fatigue of the morning's march, we heard several loud huzzas in our front. This was followed by the appearance of a carriage and four horses, which contained a French officer who we afterwards understood to be Marshal Soult. The carriage was attended by a detachment of English and French cavalry. The shouting arose from tidings that were joyfully repeated, that peace was proclaimed, and Bonaparte had retired to Elba.

According to Surtees, the advance of Wellington's army alarmed Soult, *"and in consequence he despatched Count Gazan with terms to offer to his lordship, the which, after some alterations, were finally agreed upon, and the army returned once more to Toulouse, where we resumed out former quarters."*

We were immediately ordered to the right-about, and marched back to Toulouse. Before we had proceeded many miles, we were overtaken on the road by great numbers of French soldiers who had been disbanded, or had disbanded themselves, and who were returning to their homes. Like ourselves, they were no doubt tired of the war they had been carrying on so long. Generally, these fine-looking Frenchmen had good feelings towards us, and in many instances shared the fatigue in carrying our men's knapsacks.

Surtees: *"Thus finished the Peninsular War... In 10½ months we had marched from the frontiers of Portugal, and had completely traversed Spain, which we had cleared of its long troublesome and insidious invaders. We had penetrated far into the interior of that country which, three years before, gave law to most of the continental nations, and had worsted in various actions those troops which - except when encountering the British - it had been accustomed almost invariably to conquer."*

Harry Smith said that out of the 1,050 men of his battalion who embarked at Dover before the battle of Talavera, and despite the numbers joining during the course of the war, only 500 remained at the end of it: *"There was scarcely a man who had not been wounded, there was scarcely one whose knowledge of his duty as an outpost soldier was not brought to a state of perfection, and when they were told they must not drink, a drunken man was a rare occurrence indeed, as rare as a sober one when we dared give a little latitude."*

The circumstances of the soldiers' lives changed dramatically. Harry Smith: *"The feeling of no war, no pickets, no alerts, no apprehension of being turned out, was so novel after six years' perpetual war, it is impossible to describe the sensation... We had theatres, balls, fêtes, etc., until the army moved into regular cantonments. There we had plenty of room and quarters - no squabbling about the shade of a tree in bivouac."*

Kincaid: *"The news of the peace at this period certainly sounded strange in our ears... for it was a change that we never had contemplated. We had been born in war, reared in war, and war was our trade; and what soldiers had to do in peace was a problem yet to be solved among us... After remaining a few days at Toulouse, we were sent into quarters in the town of Castelsarrasin, along with our old companions in arms, the 52nd, to await the necessary arrangements for our final removal from France."* The move took place at the end of April.

From Toulouse we marched, in a few days, to Castelsarrasin[1], situated on the right bank of the Garonne, between Toulouse and Bordeaux. Here we came in for delightful quarters, being billeted in the houses. We all had excellent beds. One would have thought these would be most welcome, so it was highly amusing to see our rough, hardy fellows contemptuously spurn this luxury. In the previous five of six years we had been almost constantly exposed. With the earth their rude bed, the sky their canopy, and with generally a stone for a pillow, our men could obtain no sleep on beds of down, and preferred wrapping a blanket round them, and using the hard floor as a place of rest. So much for custom[2].

Harry Smith on Castelsarrasin: *"This place is situated on the Tarn, which divided it from Moissac, where were a body of French troops.*

They seldom came to visit us, and we seldom encroached upon them, for the Napoleonist officers were brutally sulky, and so uncivil that John Bull could not put up with it with impunity."

Costello's experience of the French soldiers was very different.

At Castelsarrasin we were on our usual excellent terms with the French quartered in the neighbourhood. To while away the time we had constant matches with them in running, jumping, and gymnastic exercises.

I became acquainted with a very smart fellow, a French sergeant belonging to the 43rd regiment. A friendship was cemented between us by our both being freemasons[3]. One day, we were sitting in a wine house when the subject of fencing - a science at which the French pride themselves in excelling - was introduced. My friend the sergeant, observed that he was a tolerable hand with the foil. A short lump of a fellow, who proved to be the town's fencing-master, overheard, and challenged him to a trial of skill. This the sergeant immediately accepted and, at the fencing-master's cost, showed himself adept. The sport was carried on with perfect good humour until a fierce dispute arose about a hit, and it was mutually agreed to determine the controversy with points. A pair of foils with sharpened points, kept for this particular service, was immediately produced. The combatants took off their coats and bared their right arms for the duel, as the bystanders calmly commenced betting upon them. But some good-natured soul had privately summoned our guard, who came in and put an end to the affair, greatly to the chagrin of the sergeant, who swore he would have killed the professor on the spot.

That evening, the sergeant, whose name in the lapse of years I have forgotten, invited a corporal, myself, and Gilbert[4], to a dinner given by the non-commissioned officers of his regiment. He went to our Colonel and obtained leave for us to visit him at Montauban where his regiment, the 43rd, was quartered.

On the day appointed, away we started. I shall never forget it. It was a fine morning, and after crossing the Garonne in open boats - the bridge had been destroyed previous to the battle of Toulouse - we entered Montauban. Our uniforms were almost new, and fitted us well. My two comrades had the advantage of being tall, and exceedingly smart-looking men. I was fat as a butt, and as strong as I looked.

In the square of the town, the 43rd and two other regiments, formed a brigade and were drawn up on parade, with two splendid bands playing in front. As we went in search of our friend, we had to pass down the front of two of the French regiments, which we did, saluting their officers soldier-like. The latter returned our salute in the manner for which they are so justly remarked, and made us feel not a little proud of their courtesy.

We moved along the line until we fell in with the sergeant, who started out of the ranks and gave us a hearty welcome. We waited beside him while the band played some favourite airs, then the regiments were dismissed. As soon as they broke ranks, their officers crowded around us, severally shook us by the hand, and gave us sundry smacks on the shoulders, with 'Bravos les Anglais, soyez les bien venus,' etc.

The sergeant immediately escorted us to his quarters. The dining-room was a splendid one, and fitted up beautifully; the tables groaned under every delicacy of the season. We did not forget to do justice to the acknowledged merits of John Bull in all matters of this nature, and much good feeling and conviviality followed, with encomiums and compliments being passed on the English. All went on very well until, with the removal of the cloth, singing was introduced. Several famous songs, so far as we could understand, were introduced, and our sergeant gave us an excellent specimen; Gilbert and myself joined in in our own rough manner. It had been agreed among the French that no song should be sung that reflected upon our country, but a French corporal, under the influence of wine, commenced a *chanson de guerre*, for which, by general consent, and with a very proper feeling, he was kicked down stairs. The guests resumed their seats, and all went on as quietly as before. Here we remained enjoying ourselves till three the next morning, when we were accompanied to the boats at the riverside, escorted by a number of their band playing 'Patrick's Day'.

The foregoing anecdote serves to show the hospitality and kind feelings of the French, who have always claimed our highest respect.

Surtees also visited Montauban because it was the seat of a Protestant college, and was famed in romantic lore, but he was less impressed than Costello with the French soldiers there. *'The people were kind and obliging, and showed us every attention but, unfortunately, a French garrison was quartered in it, the officers of which took every opportunity of quarrelling with ours."*

Leach: *"We spent five or six weeks very pleasantly, and received the greatest kindness and hospitality from the inhabitants. Dances, fêtes champêtres on the banks of the Garonne, horse-races and various gaieties, fill up our time; and great regret was expressed when the order arrived which obliged us to leave our new French acquaintances, and the fair females, some of whom had ruined the peace of mind... of many of our gallant gay Lotharios."*

The order arrived on 31 May, and the Light Division marched from Castelsarrasin the next day.

In a few days, we received an order to proceed to Bordeaux, to embark for England. Delightful were the emotions of pleasure this generally induced in our men, after all their hardships and sufferings.

Their route to Bordeaux was via Bourret, Lectoure and Condom, which they reached on 7 June. At night, they were usually billeted upon the local people in the towns in which they stopped.

Surtees: *"We passed through Condom, another fine town, and Nérac, also a good town, and nearly full of Protestants. We next day halted at Casteljaloux... We next reached the town of Bazas. Here there was to be another parting scene exhibited: the Portuguese were ordered to leave us and proceed towards their own country."* This happened on 11 June.

> We stopped at a village[5], the name of which I forget [Bazas], where we had to part from our allies, the Spanish and Portuguese. Many deep feelings of regret were felt, particularly by the men of our battalion, on parting with the Spaniards who had been incorporated in our ranks for so long, and who were so distinguished for their gallantry. Sixteen had been drafted into our company, but only five survived to bid us farewell. The poor fellows had grown attached to the battalion and expressed much grief on leaving it: Blanco, the sanguinary Blanco, actually shed tears.
>
> Notwithstanding the wretched and ineffective state of the Spanish armies during the campaigns in the Peninsula, I am convinced, and have indeed become more so from subsequent experience[6], that the men have the right stuff to make excellent soldiers, and who could be far superior to the Portuguese.

It was not only the Portuguese and Spanish soldiers who were dispatched back to their own countries from Bazas. Surtees: *"The Spanish and Portuguese women who had followed the men were either to be sent home from hence, or their protectors were to consent to marry them. Some adopted the latter alternative, having had children by them, and some others who had not. The remainder, of course, were compelled to separate."*

> Many men of our regiments, bound by the charms of the señoritas who had followed their fortunes through the war, took this opportunity to desert their country's cause, to take up that of their Dulcineas[7]. Among others were two of my own company. Not content with the 'arms' offered by these 'invincibles', they took rifles and all with them, and we never saw or heard of them after[8].

Leach: *"There was much weeping and wailing on the part of the señoras."*

Simmons: *"The Portuguese in our Division formed into a brigade. Colonel Cerquiero commanded it... All the Portuguese boys and women, and the Spanish ones also, had to leave us and to go home in charge of this brigade, in order to be able to draw rations on the road to their different homes"*

The reference to Portuguese boys is explained by Harry Smith who describes how, during the campaign, the officers of each company formed messes, each of which had goats, looked after on the march and in camp, by a boy. On parting at Bazas, the goats were given to the boys.

Simmons: *'The Portuguese regiments (1st and 3rd Caçadores and 17th Portuguese Regiment of the line), formed in contiguous columns. The 52nd and 1st 95th were drawn up on each side of the market place and at 2 o'clock presented arms and gave three cheers to the regiments as they filed through us, which mark of our attention highly flattered the Portuguese."*

Surtees: *"A friend of mine, who was an officer in the Portuguese service, told me afterwards that the women who marched down to Spain and Portugal at the same time his regiment, formed a column 800 or 900 strong, and that they were regularly told off into companies,... but that they were the most unmanageable set of animals that ever marched across a country. The officers had to draw rations for them all the way; but many of them left the column and went wherever they pleased. Few reached Portugal in the order in which they started."*

From Bazas, the Light Division marched to Langon and Barsac. On 15 June, they went through Bordeaux to the village of Blanquefort, where they spent several weeks awaiting ships to take them either to Britain or America, with which Britain was still at war.

It was a time of reckoning for those of the officers' servants who felt they deserved more than a few goats for their many years' faithful service, and a number now absconded with their masters' mules, baggage and money. Three 95th officers fell victim in this way - the adjutant of the 3rd battalion, William Surtees, and Major Balvaird.

The 1st battalion moved on to Pauillac, where they encamped just prior to embarkation on the *Ville de Paris*. Their destination was England.

We embarked in high spirits at Bordeaux [on 8 July?], for Portsmouth, on board the *Ville de Paris*, commanded by Captain Jones. She was a splendid ship, and astonished us all with the size and regularity of her crew. The sailors, who seldom like a red coat but went hand in hand with us green jackets, were a jolly set of fellows. On 22 July 1814, we anchored at Spithead, and as we went ashore, the sailors, who manned the yards, cheered us.

In our regiment at this time, and on board with us going to England, was a sergeant of the name of S----n. This must be a sufficient explanation, as he is, I understand, now living in London. He was a fine, smart-looking fellow, about 6' tall, who had been with us during the whole of the Peninsular campaign. He was one of those who, after the battle of Corunna, had remained in Spain.

Although he had been married for about ten years, some months after the wedding he had been obliged to leave his wife with friends at Portsmouth in order to rejoin his regiment, then going abroad. He was now on his way home to her. However, by some unaccountable circumstance, incidental to long campaigns, he had never received any tidings of, or from, her and was now very uncertain as to where he should find her; or indeed, if she was still living.

As soon as we landed, he asked me to assist him in his search, and we tramped up and down and around Portsmouth in vain. Having grown almost desperate with disappointment, we stood in the High Street, where he made random inquiries of every person he met. This eventually drew a crowd of women of all ages, but not one could answer his inquiry. He was on the point of giving up altogether, when an old woman on crutches, who was at the rear of the crowd, cast a very keen look at him, and asked him to repeat the name.

"Mary S----n," he shouted.

"Ah!" exclaimed the hag. "If you will just inquire at No. -, near the Post-office, at the back of the street, you will, I think, find the party you require."

Away we hurried, with some five or six women straggling after us. In a few minutes we found ourselves at the door of a small neat-built cottage. After knocking - every moment's wait seemed an hour to my poor friend - the door was opened by a pretty looking little girl about ten years old. She inquired after his errand.

The sergeant looked at the child. "Does Mary S----n live here?" he asked

The little girl looked surprised. "Yes," she said, "that's my name."

"Right," exclaimed the sergeant, and he clasped the astonished little girl in his arms, and dashed into a side room well sprinkled with children.

"Where... where's your mother?"

The words were scarcely uttered, when a shrill shriek was heard from the inner apartment. The mother rushed in, gazed at him, and fell into a fit of hysterics. My poor friend looked perplexed, his features alternating between doubt and fear, with uncertain satisfaction. In an instant, the little one was out of the house and soon leading in a square, well-made, good-looking man, by appearance a carpenter.

The facts - the children, the comfortable, respectable air of the place - were plain to everyone, and the two husbands now stood within range of each other, nostrils dilated in agony, hands clenched, awaiting an expected onset. I never saw two better models of manhood in its prime so wrought up with melancholy and excitement. They dug their eyes into each. The shrieking woman, recovering a little, clung as if for refuge to the carpenter.

My poor comrade, from the rack of suspense, now suddenly drew breath. His daughter held a skipping-rope in her hand which he took and threw lightly over his wife's neck.

"Now, Mr Carpenter" he said in a collected tone, "as it appears that Mary, who *was* my wife, has decided on her choice, suppose we have a bargain on the matter? It's no use our skirmishing about. I have no doubt of your abilities," he went on, pointing to the children who crowded round the parents opposite him, "and as Mary seems to prefer your manner of doing business then, with her consent, suppose you clinch the bargain with a sixpence and take her to you altogether?"

The money was handed out in a moment. It as quickly passed between the sergeant's teeth while he employed both hands to withdraw his sash aside. From his pocket he took a guinea, which he threw into his only daughter's lap, then he left. Closing the door, he hurried into a small public-house across the street.

"Come, landlord, a pot of your sixpenny," he said, throwing down the ill-fated bit of silver, "and take that for your settlement. Ned," he said, turning to me, "call for your liking."

He grasped the vessel as the landlord handed it to him, and swallowed the whole at a draught, like a man who had thirsted for a week, smacking his lips in conclusion of the barter He cast two or three glances up and down his person, then rubbing his hands smartly together, he strutted up the street as if nothing whatever had annoyed him[9].

From Portsmouth, the regiment marched to Dover, where they spent the winter.

CHAPTER 25

Quatre Bras;
Aftermath of the Battle of Waterloo
23 July 1814 - 19 June 1815

Safely returned to England, and quartered in Dover barracks, our men soon forgot the fatigues of the Peninsula campaigns. Being joined by a batch of recruits, and supplied with new clothing, the old soldiers once more panted for fresh exploits; peace became irksome to them. Their souls were strong for war, and they were not long disappointed. At the end of April, we received orders to embark at Dover for Ostend.

Although the Peninsular War had ended with the exile of Napoleon Bonaparte, it was not the end of his desire for power, which he left Elba on 26 February 1815 to try to re-establish. He landed in the Golfe Juan on 1 March. The French rallied to his support, and he reached Paris on 20 March.

The British Government heard of his escape on 10 March, and on the 13th, they and their European allies organised a coalition to counter the threat he posed. Napoleon quickly assembled his army, aiming to strike at the nearest allied forces, which were in Belgium. The allies also began to mobilise, and started to deploy their armies on the frontier between Belgium and France. The 1st battalion 95th, who were under orders to follow part of the 3rd battalion to America, were redirected to Dover where, at 7pm on 25 April 1815, they embarked for Ostend.

Simmons: *"Arrived at Ostend at daylight on the 27th, and disembarked from on board the 'Wensleydale' packet. Embarked again on board Dutch schuyts with six companies of the 1st battalion, consisting of 92 per company. The boats were drawn by horses Arrived at Bruges before dark. Our boats halted for the night in the environs of the town. It being dark, had no opportunity of seeing the place. Sailed at 4am [28 April]. The country flat, but highly cultivated and abounding with everything... The country in every directions intersected with dykes and canals. Arrived at Ghent about 3pm."*

We arrived safe at Ostend, and from thence proceeded by canal, in open boats, through Bruges to Ghent, where we halted a few days.

Northern France
and Belgium

*Walcheren
island*

Ostend • - - - • *Bruges*   *Antwerp* •

• *Ghent*

Calais •   BELGIUM   *BRUSSELS* •

St. Omer •   *Waterloo*
                                        Genappe
                        Soignies •   *Quatre Bras*
FRANCE   • *Ligny*
                                                   • *Namur*
        • *Douai*   • *Valenciennes*   *Charleroi*
Marquion •
Moeuvres • • *Bourlon*
              • *Cambrai*
0 10 20 30Miles   • *Le Cateau*

They left Ghent on 10 May, and at 11am on the 12th arrived in
Brussels, where they were billeted.

> We marched to Brussels, where we remained several weeks, not
> even dreaming an enemy was near us.

Within days of their arrival, Costello's comrade Thomas Maher,
one of the sentries captured by the French at Barba del Puerco in
1810, again found himself confined.

> Maher[1], when the exchange of prisoners took place in 1814,
> returned to England and rejoined us at Dover, so he was with us in
> France at the time of Waterloo. A few nights before the battle [about 16
> May], in a wine-house at Brussels, a quarrel originated between some
> of our men, and the Belgian gendarmes. The guard, who the
> inhabitants were forced to send for, were soon on the spot, but they

were attacked and beaten back by the Belgians, who would have driven them into the guard-house had it not been for Maher. Suddenly turning on the assailants, he levelled his rifle and shot the foremost through the body. On this, all the gendarmes retreated, but not before Maher had received a cut on the side of the neck. He was put into prison for this affair, and although a general court-martial honourably acquitted him, it was not until the battle of Waterloo had been fought. Soon afterwards, our company, to which Maher belonged, presented a requisition to Captain Leach, who then commanded us, and through his intercession Maher obtained a Waterloo medal[2].

While in Brussels, they were joined by John Kincaid, who had travelled independently from Leith in Scotland to Rotterdam, and from thence to Brussels.

Kincaid: *"Brussels was a scene of extraordinary preparation, from the succession of troops who were hourly arriving, and in their formation into brigades and divisions. We had the good fortune to be attached to the brigade of our old and favourite commander, Sir James Kempt, in the 5th Division under Sir Thomas Picton. It was the only Division quartered in Brussels, the others being all towards the French frontier, except the Duke of Brunswick's corps, which lay on the Antwerp road."*

"As the middle of June approached, we began to get a little more 'qui vive', for we were aware that Napoleon was about to make a dash at some particular point; and as he was not the sort of general to give his opponent an idea of the when and the where, the greater part of our army was necessarily disposed along the frontier to meet him at his own place. They were of course too much extended to offer effectual resistance in their advanced position; but as our Division and the Duke of Brunswick's corps were held in reserve at Brussels, in readiness to be thrust at whatever point might be attacked, they were a sufficient additional force to check the enemy for the time required to concentrate the army."

There were now two armies in Belgium, a Prussian army under Blücher, and an Anglo-Dutch-German army under Wellington. Napoleon hoped to fight and defeat them separately, but the two commanders agreed to co-operate with one another.

Kincaid: *"On 14 June it was generally known, among the military circles in Brussels, that Bonaparte was in motion... We were, the whole of the 15th, on the most anxious lookout for news from the front, but no report had been received prior to the hour of dinner."*

At 11 o'clock at night on 15 June, as I was retiring to bed, I heard bugles sounding and drums beating through different parts of the city. I equipped myself as quickly as possible and entered the market-place, where I found the whole of our Division assembling.

Simmons: *"Our Division (the 5th) formed in columns of regiments near the park and waited for orders. We had many vague reports in circulation about the French."*

I then belonged to the 5th Division, under the command of General Sir Thomas Picton. Being orderly non-commissioned officer of the company at the time[3], I received orders to draw three days' rations for the men, but most of this was left behind. Few felt inclined to take part with them, because none but the old soldiers knew its value. Some of the men later cursed their hard fate for not taking away a portion.

They left Brussels at daylight on 16 June. Simmons: *"We marched through the Port de Namur. Numbers of people came to see us leave town."*

The village of Waterloo showing Wellington's HQ. Drawn on the spot by Capt. Jones. Published by C Turner, 20 May 1816. © British Museum.

All things arranged, we passed the gates of Brussels, and descended through the wood of Soignies, that leads to the little village of Waterloo.

It was the 16th, and a beautiful summer morning, with the sun slowly rising above the horizon and peeping through the trees. Our men were as merry as crickets, laughing and joking with each other. At times they pondered what all this fuss could be about, for even the old soldiers could not believe the enemy were near. We halted at the verge of the wood, on the left of the road, behind the village of Waterloo, where we remained for some hours. The recruits lay down to sleep, while the old soldiers commenced cooking[4].

I could not help noticing, while we remained here, the birds in full chorus, straining their little throats as if to arouse the spirits of the men to fresh vigour for the bloody conflict they were about to engage in. Alas, how many of our brave companions, ere that sun set, were no more!

About 9 o'clock, the Duke of Wellington and his staff came riding from Brussels and passed us to the front. Shortly afterwards, orders were given to the Rifles to fall in and form the advanced guard of our Division. We moved on through the village of Waterloo. We had not proceeded far when, for the first time, we heard distant cannon. It was, I believe, the Prussians engaged on our extreme left.

Napoleon and his French army, having crossed the border, had become engaged with the Prussian army at Ligny. Napoleon sent Marshal Ney to capture the crossroads at Quatre Bras, which gave direct access to Brussels, which he needed to take in order to strike at the heart of the allied defences.

Kincaid: *"About 12 o'clock an order arrived for the troops to advance, leaving their baggage behind. Though it sounded warlike, we did not expect to come in contact with the enemy on that day, but as we moved forward, the symptoms of their immediate presence kept gradually increasing: we presently met a cart-load of wounded Belgians and, after passing through Genappe, the distant sound of a solitary gun struck on the listening ear. All doubt on the subject was quickly removed for, on ascending the rising ground, where stands the village of Quatre Bras, we saw a considerable plain in our front, flanked on each side by a wood; and on another acclivity beyond, we could perceive the enemy descending towards us in most imposing numbers."*

"At that time, Quatre Bras consisted of only three or four houses, and as its name betokens, stood at the junction of four roads. The village was occupied by some Belgians under the Prince of Orange, who had an advanced post in a large farmhouse at the foot of the road... When we arrived at Quatre Bras, we found the Duke of Wellington near the Belgian outpost. The enemy's guns were just beginning to play upon the spot where he stood, surrounded by numerous staff."

The 5th Division, and the 1st battalion 95th in particular, were at the head of Wellington's army, and were therefore the first of his troops to come into contact with the enemy.

About 3 o'clock in the afternoon we arrived at four roads. At this time there was a smart firing going on in our front caused, I believe, by some Belgians playing at long shot with the enemy. We halted a few moments, and here I again saw the Duke of Wellington looking through his glass. This was at Quatre Bras, and immediate orders were given by one of the Duke's staff to occupy a clump of trees a little on our left. Our company was ordered to take possession of it[5].

Kincaid: *"The moment we approached, Lord Fitzroy Somerset, separating himself from the Duke, said, 'Barnard, you are wanted instantly. Take your battalion and endeavour to get possession of that village.' - pointing to one on the face of the rising ground, down which the enemy were moving - 'But if you cannot do that, secure that wood on the left, and keep the road open for communication with the Prussians'."*

While performing this task I could see the enemy emerging from a wood about a mile on our right. It was on a hill with a clear plain between us.

These were Ney's troops, sent by Napoleon to take Quatre Bras. Kincaid: *"We instantly moved in the given direction, but ere we had got half-way to the village, we had the mortification of seeing the enemy throw such a force into it that, with our numbers, rendered any attempt to retake it utterly hopeless. As another strong body of them were hastening towards the wood, which was the second object pointed out to us, we immediately brought them to action and secured it. In moving to that point, one of our men went raving mad from excessive heat. The poor fellow cut a few extraordinary capers, and died in the course of a few minutes."*

We had just taken possession of the wood when, for the first time, I beheld a French cuirassier on vidette. He was immediately fired at by our men, and his horse was shot. As it was falling, he disengaged himself from the stirrups, and waved his sword over his head to put us at defiance, but was immediately dropped by another rifle shot. I think the men in our company were the first of the British army who pulled a trigger at this celebrated battle.

I soon perceived the enemy's light troops, in extended order, and in great force, coming down to oppose us. This caused a corresponding movement on our part, and we were ordered to take ground to our left. We passed close to a pond of water, with the main road separating us from the enemy. While executing this the French commenced a very brisk fire on us, until we gained possession of a few houses on a rising ground on the main road, which two companies of our Rifles instantly occupied[6]. The remainder of our Division was now enveloped in one blaze of fire on the plain before mentioned.

Kincaid: *"The plain to our right, which we had just quitted, had become the scene of a sanguinary and unequal contest."* Unequal because at that moment, Picton's Division had no cavalry in support, and they were outnumbered by three to one. *"Our Division, after we left it, deployed into line and, in advancing, met and routed the French infantry. But in following up their advantage, they encountered a furious charge of cavalry, and were obliged to throw themselves into square to receive it. With the exception of one regiment, however, which had two companies cut to pieces, they were not only successful in resisting the attack, but made awful havoc in the ranks of the enemy who, nevertheless, continued their forward career, and went sweeping past them, like a whirlwind, up to the village of Quatre Bras... The forward movement of the enemy's cavalry gave their infantry time to rally and, strongly reinforced with fresh troops, they again advanced to the attack. This was a crisis in which, according to Bonaparte's theory, the victory was theirs by all the rules of war, for they held superior numbers, both before and behind us; but the gallant old Picton, who had been trained in a different school, did not choose to confine himself to rules in those matters, and despising the force in his rear, he advanced, charged, and routed those in his front, which created such a panic among the others, that they galloped back through the intervals in his Division with no other object than their own safety.*

"After this desperate conflict, the firing on both sides lulled almost to a calm for nearly an hour, while each was busy in renewing their order of battle. The Duke of Brunswick had been killed early in the action, endeavouring to rally his young troops, who were unable to withstand the impetuosity of the French. As we had no other cavalry force in the field, the few British infantry regiments present, having to bear the full brunt of the enemy's superior force of both arms, were now considerably reduced in numbers."

We remained very quietly where we were until the French brought up some artillery, and began riddling the house with round shot. Feeling rather thirsty, I asked a young woman in the place for a little water. She was handing it to me, when a ball passed through the building, knocking the dust about our ears. Strange to say, the girl appeared less alarmed than myself.

Fearing that we might be surrounded, we left the building. In doing so, we were fiercely attacked by a number of the French *voltigeurs*, who forced us to extend along a lane from whence we as smartly retaliated. A galling fire was kept up for some time on both sides.

Kincaid: *"While our battalion-reserve occupied the front of the wood, our skirmishers lined the side of the road, which was the Prussian line of communication. The road itself however, was crossed by such a shower of ball, that none but a desperate traveller would have undertaken a journey on it."*

It is remarkable that recruits in action are generally more unfortunate than the old soldiers. Many fine fellows, who had joined us on the eve of our leaving England, were killed here because inexperienced recruits, apparently petrified to the spot by the whizzing balls, unnecessarily expose themselves to the enemy's fire, whereas an old rifleman will seek shelter, if there be any near his post.

Being hard pressed by superior numbers, we were at length joined by a number of Belgians[7]. We received orders to advance, and drove the enemy through the skirts of a wood, passing a field of rye, which obstructed them from our view. As soon as we emerged from the wood, a regiment of French infantry on our right received us with a running fire. I was in the act of taking aim at some of our opposing skirmishers, when a ball struck my trigger finger, tearing it off. It also turned the trigger aside. A second shot passed through the mess-tin on my knapsack. Several of our men were killed by this volley, and Lieutenant Gardiner, a worthy little officer of the company, was severely wounded in the lower part of the leg.

Costello's part in the action was now over, but his comrades, supported by the division of Sir Charles Alten, continued to move forward. Kincaid: *'This reinforcement gave us new life, and as soon as they came near enough to afford support, we commenced the offensive. Driving in the skirmishers opposed to us, we succeeded in gaining a considerable portion of the position originally occupied by the enemy, when darkness obliged us to desist.'*

Of the 600 men in the 1st battalion, 60 were killed or wounded in the action at Quatre Bras, which had lasted several hours.

We wounded men made the best of our way to the rear. On my return to the house at the corner of the lane, I found the pretty Belgian still in possession. She was looking out of the window, quite unconcerned, although a dozen shots had perforated the house. We entreated her to leave, but in vain because she said her father had desired her to take care of the place until he returned from Brussels.

The dusk of the evening soon set in, and myself and numbers of others who were disabled, took up our quarters for the night in another farmhouse lower down, some distance from the main road. This soon became thronged with the wounded of our Division who were brought in. The outhouses became literally crammed, and all the straw and hay, of which there was plenty, that could be procured was strewed everywhere to lay the men on. To sleep was impossible with the anguish of my shattered hand, and the groans of my fellow-sufferers.

The men of Costello's battalion also tried to sleep. Kincaid: *'We laid down by our arms, near the farmhouse in front of Quatre Bras... We had been either marching or fighting for 26 successive hours. An hour before daybreak next morning, a rattling fire of musketry along the whole line of pickets made every one spring to his arms, and we remained looking as fierce as possible until daylight, each side expecting an attack, while the pickets blazed at one another without any ostensible cause."*

It was dawn almost before we knew it, but before then, our advanced sentries began skirmishing along the whole line. Indeed, where we lay, the balls kept patting through the doors and windows. Such as were able to walk soon started for Brussels; but several of the severely wounded were obliged to be left behind for want of conveyances.

We proceeded towards the main road along a pathway, partially protected from the enemy's fire by a hedge. We had not gone far, when one of my companions heard the cries of a child on the other side. Looking over he espied a fine boy, about two or three years of age. He was by the side of his dead mother, who was still bleeding copiously from a wound in the head, probably occasioned by a random shot from the enemy. We carried the motherless, and perhaps orphan child, by turns. At Genappe, we found a number of women of our Division, and one of them recognised the little fellow. I think she said he belonged to a soldier of the First Royals.

Genappe was literally crowded with wounded, and they were conveyed with every possible dispatch to Brussels. Anxious to know the fate of our regiment, I stood on a hedgerow on the skirts of the village as the rain came down in torrents. I descried the Division retreating towards us, and remained until some of the regiments entered the village with many of our wounded, who told me that our regiment, with the cavalry, formed the rear-guard.

At 9am, the Division had received the news of Blücher's defeat at Ligny and of his retreat to Wavre, whereupon Wellington began immediately to withdraw his army towards a position at Waterloo. Kincaid: *"Sir Andrew Barnard was ordered to remain as long as possible with our battalion, to mask the retreat of the others... Between 11 and 12 o'clock, every regiment had got clear off, and we followed, before the enemy had put anything in motion against us. After leaving the village of Quatre Bras, and passing through our cavalry, who were formed on each side of the road, we drew up at the entrance of Genappe. The rain, at that moment, began to descend in torrents."*

From Genappe, Costello continued his journey to Waterloo and Brussels.

I now retraced my steps to Brussels by the same road on which we had advanced. On the way, the cries of cart-loads of wounded was most distressing. Many carts broke down through being overloaded, and through their haste to get forward.

It is curious to observe that, in the rear of an army in battle, confusion and uproar generally exists while all in front is order and regularity. Many people imagine the reverse. What happens is that soldiers' wives, and camp followers of all descriptions, crowd about in great numbers, making enquiries after their husbands and friends, for whom they are usually prepared with liquor and other refreshments. I had no such ties except for my comrades, who were now too busily occupied watching their enemies, and with their own personal considerations, to have either time or opportunity to inquire after mine.

Crowds of carts, horses etc, thickly thronged the roadway, and were greeted on all sides by anxious faces and earnest inquiries. One of the vehicles which hurried along seemed to bear a load of a more enlivening nature than that which characterised the others, for every now and then a burst of laughter hailed it. My sound legs - for my arm only was wounded, and hung suspended in a sling - enabled me to approach the cart, and scrutinise its contents. My surprise almost made me forget my wounds for I beheld the merry features of my old friend, Josh Hetherington, who had received a flesh wound in the leg and was being borne to hospital with his fellow sufferers.

Like myself, Josh had no ties. There was no-one to bring him brandy, but being wide awake and well acquainted with the world, he laid himself at his length inside a cart to await the current of fortune in the bustle of a dark night. He knew one or two of the women who were searching for their husbands. Knowing also their spouses, he replied to their inquiries in as exact an imitation of their voices as one could reasonably give a man credit for. The result was that the bottle was instantly handed into his hiding place, where he took sundry deep gulps. The duped woman walked anxiously by the side of the wheels, wishing to heaven that daylight, or some other light, would enable her to enjoy the sight of her better half. The dénouement of the cheat came with the return of the empty flask, and with it a sincere hope from Josh that her husband would find enough liquor left, and be not wounded at all. The disappointment and rage of the woman gave rise to a burst of merriment, in which the wounded men joined heartily, as the cart continued on its way to Brussels[8].

I arrived at the little village of Waterloo, which many of our men never saw again, as our battalion lost more on 16 June than on the 18th at the battle of Waterloo. Here I stopped for the night.

That evening, his battalion also reached Waterloo. Kincaid: *'It was six in the evening [17th], before we drew into the position of Waterloo. About an hour after, the enemy arrived in front in considerable force, and a cannonade took place in different parts of the line. It ended at dark, and we lay down by our arms.'*

The next morning I proceeded slowly onward for my wound had not, as yet, been dressed. On the way through the woods, I saw droves of Belgians, and English also, with fires lighted, busily cooking, having left their comrades in contest with the enemy. There appeared to be nothing the matter with them.

On the field of Waterloo on the 18 June, at about 10am, the 95th received an order to stand to their arms, and they and their Division took up their position to the left of Wellington's centre. This they held throughout the day's fighting, which began about noon and lasted until 7pm. The contest was severe. Kincaid: *'I had never yet heard of a battle in which everybody was killed, but this seemed likely to be an exception, as all were going by turns... However desperate our affairs were, we had still the satisfaction of seeing that theirs were worse.'*

After resisting waves of attacks, the allied army, reinforced by the Prussians, advanced and drove the French from the field. Napoleon was defeated at Waterloo, but at a terrible cost in dead and wounded on both sides.

Kincaid: *'The field of battle, next morning, presented a frightful scene of carnage. It seemed as if the world had tumbled to pieces, and three-fourths of everything destroyed in the wreck. The ground running parallel to the front where we had stood was so thickly strewed with fallen men and horses, that it was difficult to step clear of their bodies, many of the former still alive, and imploring assistance, which it was not in our power to bestow.'*

Among those wounded at the battle of Waterloo were George Simmons (seriously) and Robert Fairfoot. Tom Plunket, who fought in the 2nd battalion, was also injured. Of Tom, Costello says:

> His usual luck forsook him at Waterloo, where a ball struck the peak of his cap and tore his forehead across, leaving a very ugly scar. I had gone wounded to the rear and there saw him under the hands of the surgeon.

It was probably in Brussels that Costello saw Plunket because that is where he remained wounded for several days after the battle.

> I arrived at Brussels and went to my quarters, which I found so crowded with Belgian officers and men - some quite free from wounds - that I could get no reception. It was about 8 o'clock in the evening of the 18th, and I entered the large square and gazed on the hundreds of wounded men there, stretched out on straw. An alarm was given that the French were entering the city, and in a moment all was in an uproar. The inhabitants ran in all directions, closing their doors. In the square were some Belgian troops and they were in great confusion. Loading my rifle, I joined a party of the 81st regiment who had remained on duty here during the action. But it was a false alarm, occasioned by the appearance of about 1,700 French prisoners, under escort of some of our dragoons. The panic over, I partook of a little bread and wine, and lay down for the night on some straw in the square. The continual arrival of waggons loaded with wounded men caused confusion and uproar. Despite this, I slept soundly.

In the morning [19 June], the scene surpassed all imagination. It baffles description for there were upwards of 40,000 wounded French, Belgians, Prussians and English, intermingled with carts, waggons, and every other vehicle attainable, which continued to arrive heaped with unfortunate sufferers. The wounded were laid on straw, with avenues between them, in every part of the city, with no discrimination between friends and foes. They were nearly destitute of surgical attendance, but the humane and indefatigable exertions of the fair ladies of Brussels, greatly made up for this deficiency. Numbers were busily employed strapping and bandaging wounds; others were serving out tea, coffee, soups, and other soothing nourishment. Many occupied themselves stripping the sufferers of their gory and saturated garments, and dressing them in clean shirts, and other habiliments. Careless of fashionable scruples, the fairest and wealthiest of the ladies of the city ventured to assert their pre-eminence on the occasion. That their companions were in need called forth the sympathies that bind the sexes in mutual dependence.

One lady I noticed particularly. She was attended by a servant bearing on his shoulder a kind of pannier, containing warm and cold refreshments. She was about eighteen, and the peculiarity of the moment made her appear beyond the common order of humanity. As she hurried along, her eyes glancing about for those whom she thought most in need of her assistance, a tall Highlander drew her attention with a deep groan, which arose from the anguish of a severe wound in the thick part of the thigh. In a twinkling she knelt at his side. The soldier looked at her with surprise. Gently. she moved aside his blood-stained kilt, and commenced washing the wounded part. The Scotsman seemed uneasy at her importunity, but with the sweetest voice imaginable, she addressed him in broken English:

"I will not hurt you."

The wounded man, ere he could recover his rough serenity, found his wound bandaged, and at ease, under the operations of his fair attendant. Such acts as these must ever draw forth our admiration.

CHAPTER 26

Army of Occupation in France
19 June 1815 - March 1819

For three days I remained in Brussels, where I had ample means - as in other places, such as Salamanca - for witnessing the cutting off of legs and arms. The French I have ever found to be brave, yet I cannot say they undergo a surgical operation with the cool, unflinching spirit of a British soldier. One incident I witnessed here showed the difference of the two nations. An English soldier belonging, I think, to the 1st Royal Dragoons, was undergoing the amputation of an arm below the elbow. He was evidently an old weather-beaten warfarer for he held the injured limb with his other hand. Throughout the operation he betrayed not the slightest emotion, but chewed most unmercifully on a large plug of tobacco, the proceeds of which, to help out his pain, he occasionally spurted forth. Near to him, a surgeon was probing for a ball in the shoulder of a Frenchman, who was bellowing lustily. This annoyed the Englishman so much that, as soon as his limb had been severed, he took it by the wrist and struck the Frenchman a smart blow across the breech with it.

"Here," he said, "stuff that down your throat, and stop your damned bellowing!"

The accommodation at Brussels was not sufficient for the wounded, so many were conveyed to Antwerp, myself included. The whole of the 81st regiment were employed conveying the men on stretchers to the boat on the canal, which communicated between the two cities. At Antwerp I had my wound attended to, and my shattered finger was taken off at the socket[1].

While here, I observed the singular case of a young fellow - no more than nineteen - who had been one of the drivers to the German Artillery. He had lost both his legs by a round shot, which had passed through the horse's belly and carryied away both limbs. While on the ground in this mangled state, he had received a dreadful gash in one arm from a French cuirassier, and a ball in the other. As a consequence had been obliged to undergo the amputation of both arms, one below the elbow, and the other above. Here the unfortunate youth lay, a branchless trunk, and though numbers died from lesser wounds, up to the moment I left, he survived.

At first, so many of the wounded died that it surprised even the doctors. They discovered that the water with which the patients were in the habit of washing their wounds was brought from a spa and, in some instances, had the effect of poisoning the flesh. As this was a report amongst us wounded men, little reliance can be placed on it[2].

In the course of a few weeks, I was sufficiently recovered to rejoin my regiment, at Clichy camp, near Paris.

After the battle of Waterloo, the soldiers of the French army retired from the field pursued by the Prussians. It had been expected that, in Paris, they would make a stand, but this did not happen. Instead the city declared for Louis XVIII as King of France, whom the allies supported. When the armies of Wellington and Blucher reached the city, the gates were opened and, with the permission of Louis XVIII, they entered. They occupied the city and its environs for the next five months.

The 2nd Regiment in the Bois de Boulogne, 1815. By Lt. Scharf. Engraved by T Sutherland. Published by Jenkins, 1 May 1816. ©British Museum.

Leach: *"The swarms of officers and soldiers - British, Hanoverians, Prussians, Russians, Austrians, Dutch, Belgians, Brunswickers, and others - with whom Paris was inundated, and who choked the avenues of the Palais Royal by day and night, were by no means the least interesting objects at that period. Crowds of English families flocked to Paris before we had long occupied it, and there John Bull might be seen, in all his glory, gaping and staring, in every part of the city, at those continental novelties."*

As usual, Wellington was anxious that his men should not make his and their task more difficult by behaviour which would provoke the local people into taking up arms against them, so the punishments for plunder and robbery were as harsh as ever. However, he did not have the same degree of control over soldiers in the armies of other nations in the alliance. These men, whose countries had been occupied by Napoleon's soldiers, nursed grievances against the French, which they frequently acted upon. As early as 26 June 1815, on the march to Paris, Belgian carabiniers were plundering from the French, so Wellington instructed his Adjutant-General to write to their commander, claiming the right to have the men punished by a Provost Marshal.

There were Provost Marshals in every division in Wellington's army, and they were assisted by sergeants drawn from various regiments. Other soldiers were sometimes seconded to swell their ranks, and when Costello rejoined his Division after 33 days absence, he became one of them, the extra pay he received on 25 August perhaps reflecting these provosting duties.

> Shortly after my arrival, I was ordered on the Provost Guard, which is a kind of military police. We were under the command of Stanway, the Provost Marshal. His instructions were to take all those we found marauding about the gardens and neighbourhood of Paris, and march them down to his guard house for punishment. He was a keen fellow, and would sometimes pounce on as many as 20 in the course of a morning. These were immediately flogged, according to the amount of their offence, or the resistance they made, and then liberated. The depredations became so universal that the inhabitants of Paris complained to the generals of divisions, and we received orders to keep a stricter look out. As we had to take into custody and flog every man we caught in the act of plunder, our guard house was daily filled by soldiers of every uniform. Ours was a true Owenite guard, for we made no objection to sect, country, class, or colour, and served them all alike![3]
>
> The Belgians were especially troublesome. These fellows would go forth in sections and lay waste to everything before them. This was not done out of want because they were well supplied with regular daily rations from Paris. As soon as they saw the guard hemming them in on all sides, they invariably saluted us with brickbats and stones. Sometimes they made a regular attack, but Stanway seldom let any escape him.
>
> One morning, we brought in 16 of them. The punishments were generally inflicted in a little yard which, as usual, the Provost marched them into. From the centre of the ground, the triangles stared the culprits in the face, and they gave a bellow of horror. They fell on their knees, commenced praying, crossed themselves, and showed other symptoms of repentance, but Stanway was inexorable. Our men had

288

the greatest difficulty in unbreeching them, and getting them tied to the halberts. The first to be stripped was a short, stubby, fat, desperate-looking fellow who, by the circumference of his seat of honour, and his struggles for its safety, seemed to bear about it all the honour of his native Belgium. At the first whistle of the cat - even before it reached him - he roared to such a degree, and his fellow culprits sympathised so loudly, and with such a crash of Belgic, that they aroused not only those in the vicinity, but their whole regiment quartered in the village. The Belgians flew to their arms and surrounded the guard house, which was soon in uproar.

Stanway was determined not to relax his duty, and ordered every man of us to load. He placed us in different parts of the building, barricaded the doorways, and prepared for every resistance, continuing the flagellation during the intervals. The assailants became furious, and attempted to scale the walls for a rescue, but were kept off by the guard with fixed bayonets. However, a shower of brickbats, etc, were thrown over the walls, which made us retire into the building.

Our lives were now in jeopardy. Not a man of us dared to stir out, but a signal was given to some English soldiers who were passing. They gave the alarm to the Division then encamped outside the village. Our Rifles, followed by the 52nd, came instantly to our assistance, and the two regiments remained under arms the whole night. The Belgians retired to a field a little distance from them, and kept under arms also. The next morning, they were removed from Clichy and we saw no more of them.

A day or two after this disturbance, I went into Paris to draw rations for the guard. I had to pass the Barrière de Clichy, and before entering the gates, in the street adjoining, I perceived a crowd collected round a doorway. Anxious to know the cause, I mingled with the throng. Pushing to the centre I perceived the dead body of a French gentleman, stretched out on some straw literally saturated in blood. On inquiry, I was informed that he had been slain by a Cossack or Prussian officer some few minutes before. It appeared that the deceased, who was a French count, and the Cossack, had quarrelled the night previous and decided on settling the matter the next morning by a meeting with pistols. The seconds had agreed that the two principals should be placed back to back and, measuring six of his own paces, each should, as the distance was completed, turn round and fire. However, as soon as the Count commenced his first pace, the Cossack turned round and discharged his pistol into the back of his head, stretching his adversary lifeless on the ground.

"I have been shot at enough by your cursed countrymen," he had exclaimed; "now for my turn."

Fearful of the consequences, the assassin and his second had fled instantly by taking horse and riding off to their camp. I was told that the Duke, when the circumstances were related to him, offered a reward for their apprehension, but they were never discovered. The unfortunate Count had been an officer in the French service and, to all appearance, had been a very smart young fellow[4].

In Paris, there were amusements for officers and soldiers alike, including two which were particularly popular in that era: horse-racing and bareknuckle fighting. Surtees: *"We had two English boxers over there also, to amuse the people. They only sparred of course, with gloves on, and I rather think they realised a good deal of money by these exhibitions. Balloons also were sent up from the gardens of Tivoli... In Paris, with plenty of money and an inclination to enter into all the gaieties of the place, no city on earth is so fruitful of the means of pleasure and dissipation... If I was asked which I considered the most sinful city in the world, I would without hesitation say Paris."*

Towards the end of December, arrangements were made for the army to leave Paris, a treaty having been concluded between the Allied powers and France. Harry Smith: *"An army of occupation was designated to remain on the northern boundary of France for three to five years, the larger armies (except their quota of the contingent) being marched back to their respective countries. Of the British Army, four divisions alone were to remain."*

This included the 1st battalion 95th, which marched north to Cambrai. Costello and Leach remained in France, but William Surtees, Harry Smith, and the wounded George Simmons, returned to England.

In the beginning of February 1816, we left Paris, and marched to the environs of Cambrai. Shortly afterwards we were presented with medals sent out by the British government, in commemoration of the celebrated battle. Every man who was in the field on the 16th, 17th and 18th June, was distinguished with this honourable badge. But it caused dissension, particularly among some of the old veterans of the Peninsular campaigns[5]. One, named Wheatley, as brave as any man in the service, was unfortunately in hospital in Brussels during the action, and therefore was not honoured with this mark of bravery so, whenever he met with badges on what he termed 'recruits', he would instantly tear them off and sometimes throw them away. For this too often repeated offence, poor Wheatley was tried by a court-martial, and sentenced to three months' solitary confinement.

He was sent to Valenciennes where lay the 43rd Regiment, who had belonged to our Light Division during the Spanish war. The men of that regiment, who knew Wheatley and the offence he had committed, not only fed him well during his imprisonment, but at the expiration of his confinement sent him back with all the pomp a hero could wish. He was conveyed in a carriage drawn by four horses, his head, as well as those of the postilion and horses, decorated with blue ribands. On seeing this gay equipage enter the village, I was much surprised. I was even more surprised when Wheatley jumped from the carriage amidst the loud acclamations of his old companions.

Poor Wheatley felt neglected on receiving no medal, and from one of the bravest men in the regiment, he became one of the most dissipated. He was discharged shortly afterwards[6].

On 26 May 1816, Costello was promoted to corporal, a rank he held until his discharge from the army.

My company was quartered at Moeuvres, a pretty little village off the main road that leads to Douai. Myself and three privates were billeted on the house of an old fellow named Bernard Loude, who was the richest man in the village, possessing upwards of 300 acres of land. He had his own property, with stables, granary, waggons, and cattle; indeed everything that constitutes a farmer's stock. The house, like all others in that part of the country, was built long, with only a ground floor. On entering it, I observed three pretty girls spinning. The youngest, about 16 years of age, was named Léocadie; the next, who was about 19, was Augustine; and the eldest, who was not above 24 years of age, was called Julie. They were all attractive in appearance[7].

After living there some weeks, I looked upon myself as one of the household and, soldier-like, began toying with the girls. The one who attracted my attention most was Augustine, who was a fine young woman, with light hair and a fair complexion. Her manners were playful yet gentle, and there was an air of innocence in her freedom, which showed that her thoughts were untainted by that knowledge of the world which restrains the levity of youth. Her disposition corresponded with her manners, being frank, generous, and confiding. Her sisters used to say she had a most forgiving temper, yet she had a firm and determined spirit. They loved her with more than the love sisters generally bestow upon each other.

Day after day, I became more intimate with the family, and the fair Augustine, whether serious or jesting, was always my favourite. The courtship of a soldier is somewhat rough: I used to steal a kiss now and then, and my pretty Augustine would check me for doing so, but there was so much goodness in her manner that her reproof tempted a repetition of the offence rather than otherwise. To those who know the inconveniences to which soldiers are subjected in being billeted, it must appear that I was now in clover. Certainly, I never shall forget the happy hours I then enjoyed.

One Saturday, I was ordered on duty to the headquarters of our regiment, at a small village called Bourlon, about two miles from Moeuvres. Before my departure, Léocadie told me Augustine was engaged and soon to be married to a young Frenchman who lived our side of Cambrai. She jokingly added that he could speak a little English because he had been a prisoner in England. It was customary for me to dine with the family every Sunday so, next day, on my return off guard,

I joined the domestic party as usual, and noticed a stranger at table who, by his manner, appeared to be the favoured suitor of Augustine. We had scarcely sat down when, after gazing intently upon me, he suddenly started up and seized me by the hand.

"*Mon brave soldat, est-ce vous?*" he exclaimed, nearly bursting into tears.

I recognised him immediately as the faithful Frenchman whose life I had spared in the streets of Badajoz. Returning to his seat, he described to the party the scenes we had gone through at Badajoz, which sometimes called forth fits of laughter, and sometimes tears. All eyes were fixed on me, Augustine's in particular. She looked more serious than I had ever seen her. She neither shed a tear, nor did she smile, during the whole of her young French lover's narrative, but I could plainly perceive by the heaving of her bosom that she was more deeply affected than the rest. He extolled me to the skies, unaware of the interest he was exciting in favour of an unknown rival. The French are a people fond of glory and sentiment, and a story of *la Gloire et l'Amour* will always excite their admiration.

He then related to me the cruelty of the Portuguese soldiers who conducted him, and the remainder of the garrison of Badajoz, on their march to Lisbon. At Lisbon he was put on board a ship and conveyed to England. After Bonaparte had been conducted to Elba, he, along with a thousand other prisoners, returned to their native homes. He had taken no part in the battle of Waterloo. After dinner I and my old companion parted, having both enjoyed mutual good cheer.

The attention of Augustine after this accidental interview was redoubled, and what I before suspected I now plainly discovered: I had won her heart. From this time, we were more frequently alone; and although her father wished her married to the Frenchman, particularly as he was also a relation and in good circumstances, she had never been seriously attached to him.

The affection that subsisted between us became no secret in the family, and was even rumoured about the village. When it burst out in songs composed by the 'troubadours' of the neighbourhood, her father thought it prudent to get my quarters changed, and applied to the Colonel accordingly.

I was sent to another hamlet, which was in charge of tailors making clothing for the regiment. It was a pretty, neat little village called Sains les Marquion, on the main road to Cambrai. I continued to correspond with Augustine at the house of an old widow who lived at Moeuvres, and we enjoyed many stolen interviews. Her family insisted on diverting her affections from me and, harassed by their remonstrances, she determined on leaving her father's roof. One evening, at dusk, she met me at the widow's, where we betrothed ourselves to each other. The Duke of Wellington had given positive orders that no British soldiers should be allowed to marry French women, so we were clandestinely married by an excommunicated priest[8].

On hearing of her elopement, her father unrelentingly pursued her. He went to Cambrai and applied to the executor to deprive her of her patrimony, but the law prevented him doing so. He then appealed to the military authorities and, to my surprise, about 10 o'clock one morning, four gendarmes entered my quarters in search of her. I was about to give them a very rough reception - some of my comrades, who were quartered with me, proposed giving them a threshing - when the corporal commanding the party warned me I should be held responsible for any ill-usage they might receive. He then produced a written order for her return to her father's house. It was signed by General Sir John Lambert, who commanded our brigade, and was countersigned by Colonel Balvaird[9], who was our head colonel at the time because Sir Andrew Barnard was then the Commandant of Cambrai.

I saw that all remonstrance was in vain, and Augustine was obliged to retrace her steps, which she did with a heavy heart. I accompanied her. Her reception by her father was most unkind. He confined her in a room, its windows darkened and secured by cross bars of iron, the handiwork of the village smith, whose services were called in for the occasion. In this gloomy prison she was not permitted to see her sisters, and her meals were sent at long intervals, and scantily supplied.

A priest was sent for and was paid handsomely to try to wean her affections from me. His prayers, and the bars of iron, were alike in vain, and at the first opportunity, she contrived to escape to me from this durance vile. As soon as she returned, we went together to our colonel, who lived at the château of the village, to request that she might be allowed to remain with me. On entering the room, she threw herself in an impassioned manner on her knees, and begged we might not be separated. The Colonel took her by the hand and raised her from her humiliating posture. He said it was not in his power to grant the request, but he would speak to General Lambert on the matter, which he did, and she was allowed to remain with me.

We now fancied ourselves in a great measure protected, but she was again pursued by her father, who one day very unceremoniously rushed into our cottage, and desired her to return with him. She instantly flew to me for protection, throwing her arms around me, exclaiming,

"Mon Edouard, je ne te quitterai jamais."

Her father, as if seized with a sudden fit of frenzy, laid hold of a hammer that was on the table, and struck himself a blow on the forehead with such force that he fell, and remained insensible on the floor for some time[10]. Poor Augustine's distress cannot be imagined, and it was some time before she recovered. After this, we remained unmolested, and lived happily together.

The battalion was in the environs of Cambrai for three years. Towards the end of June 1818, we broke up our cantonments, and encamped on the glacis of Cambrai. There we remained until the latter end of October, when we received orders to proceed to England. The Colonel, who did not know we were married, sent for me, and informed me Augustine must return to her parents, as she would certainly not be permitted to embark with me to England. We now consulted together as to what step to take. It was agreed I should go to her uncle, who resided in Cambrai, and request him to intercede with her father to allow her to receive part of her patrimony. Although her father could not deprive her of it after his death, she was not entitled to receive it during his lifetime. If he consented to do so, I promised to obtain my discharge from the army, and publicly marry her[11].

Costello fails to inform his readers that, at the time of these events, Augustine was expecting their child. At the end of October 1818, she would have been six months' pregnant at least.

Her uncle, after my interview with him, accompanied me to Moeuvres, a distance of about three or four miles, to discuss the matter with her father; but when I entered house, there was uproar. A tumult of voices from all the family assailed me. One of the brothers cried, "*Délie le chien! Délie le chien!*". A huge wolf-dog was unchained, but instead of attacking me, he came and fawned on me because he knew me from when I had lived in the house.

In the confusion, I expected every moment would be my last as there were no British soldiers nearer than Cambrai. Then Augustine entered. She had heard at her uncle's that I had gone with him to her father's and, apprehensive of the consequences, had followed me. Not attending to any other person present, she entreated me to leave the house, and return to Cambrai with her. I did so.

Early next morning, the regiment being in marching order, I was reluctantly compelled to part from my faithful, almost broken-hearted Augustine. It was agreed she should remain with the family of her uncle until I could communicate with her from England, where we hoped happier days awaited us.

Leach: *"The beginning of the winter of 1818 witnessed the evacuation of France by our troops, which were immediately afterwards scattered all over the world, like dust before the wind. A few regiments went to England, many to Ireland, and still more to the East and West Indies, Canada, the Cape, the Mediterranean; in short, to every creek and corner where we had colonies or garrisons. Thus was dispersed an army, many regiments of which had been together from 1808 to 1818, the whole of which time, with the exception of the few months that Napoleon spent at Elba, was passed in the Peninsula and in France. It was the breaking up of a large family, which was, or ought to have been, bound together by those ties which the various scenes inseparable from the life in which they had been actors, might naturally be expected to create. It was impossible to witness, without feelings of regret, this thorough dispersion of regiments and of individuals so long known to each other and who, in all human probability, would not be reassembled under similar circumstances of interest and excitement."*

Disembarking at Dover, our regiment marched to Shorncliffe Barracks. We had not been long quartered there when an order arrived from Horse Guards for two sergeants and two corporals of each company of the Rifles to be discharged. Men who had been wounded were to be first, and old men next. I was only about 31 years of age, but on account of my wounds, I was invalided by our doctor and immediately departed for Chatham, there to await an order from Chelsea to proceed to London, to pass the Board[12].

Costello's discharge papers record that the Rifle Brigade settled his arrears of pay at Shorncliffe on 16 November 1818. He would have reached Chatham a few days afterwards.

Here, to my astonishment, Augustine presented herself before me. Her appearance almost electrified me. Having arrived at Shorncliffe Barracks and inquired for me, Colonel Leach had kindly paid her passage by coach to Chatham, and had directed her where to find me. Here she gave birth to a child[13]. Shortly afterwards I received orders to appear before the Chelsea Board, and we proceeded to London with others.

On our arrival, our circumstances were very needy. We took a single room in Red Lion Street, Chelsea, and resolved to live as sparingly as possible. I passed the Board, but soon found the pittance of 6d per day allowed me, insufficient to maintain us.

Costello's discharge papers were finalised at Horse Guards on 16 February 1819. Three weeks later, on 2 March, Major-General A F Barnard, who commanded the 1st battalion, wrote to Sir David Dundas, Colonel-in-Chief of the Regiment, on his behalf:

Feeling that my case was not understood, I applied to my Colonel, Sir Andrew Barnard, and explained it to him. He gave me a note, which I now hold in my possession, for Sir David Dundas, then Governor of Chelsea. In my uniform, I set out for Sir David's residence and found him at Chelsea College, walking about the grounds in front of his house. I handed him my paper and stood aside while he perused it.

The letter read: *"I strongly recommend to your notice, and to the attention of the Board of Chelsea, the bearer, Edward Costello, late sergeant in 1st Battalion Rifle Brigade, for an increase of pension for his gallant service, he having been discharged in consequence of wounds received in action."*

He scanned it without turning his head, then tossed aside his pigtail with his forefinger, and coolly handed the note over his shoulder to me, remarking that he dared say the Lords Commissioners of Chelsea had given me what they thought I deserved.

I suppose the old gentleman possessed too much Spartan blood to notice me more than he did. He probably thought my return to England highly inglorious, and unbefitting a soldier, since it had made me a sixpenny burden on the country I had served. To this hour, it remains unaltered[14].

Day after day we struggled with our necessities, and I saw nothing but starvation staring me in the face. What was to be done? With great patience, my faithful Augustine deliberated with me in our misfortune, and we agreed that it would be most desirable for her return to her uncle, and endeavour to move her family and her father to a reconciliation with us both. Her infant, she thought, could not fail to excite commiseration, but how were we to defray the expenses of so long a journey?

Having received several wounds in the service, I was entitled to what is commonly termed 'blood money'. A certificate to that effect, and signed by my commanding officer, and by the adjutant of my regiment, I now had by me to present to the parson of the parish in which I was resident one month after my discharge. The Honourable Dr. Wellesley, brother to the Duke of Wellington, was the rector of Chelsea, and I appealed to him. He referred me to a Mr Woodford, Secretary of the Patriotic Fund, at 80 Cornhill, but this gentleman was even more Spartan than the Lords Commissioners. After two or three stiff struts up and down his office, he stopped suddenly, and staring me very stupidly in the face, said,

"Damn it, sir! did you expect to fight with puddings or Norfolk dumplings? If men go to battle, what else can they expect but wounds! I am now busy, and cannot be troubled with you."

I returned to Chelsea and represented my situation to Mr Wellesley. Through him I succeeded in obtaining a small sum of £5 for the wound at Waterloo, but nothing for those I received in the Peninsula. With this scanty supply we proceeded to Dover, thence to Calais, and from there to St. Omer, where I took leave of my beloved Augustine and her infant. She promised to write to me as soon as she succeeded with her family. If not, it was agreed that as soon as my circumstances improved she should return to me.

"*Ne m'oubliez pas,*" were her last words as she squeezed my hand.

> "I felt a sudden tightness grasp my throat
> As it would strangle me; such as I felt,
> I knew it well, some twenty years ago,
> When my good father shed his blessing on me.
> I hate to weep, and so I came away."

Without a farthing in my pocket - I had given the last sou to

Augustine - I determined to forage my way home as best I could. I set off for Calais, where I arrived in much distress. A brother mason befriended me, and gave me a free passage to Dover. Had it not been for this kind assistance, I know not how I should have crossed the straits.

At Dover nothing could exceed my wretchedness. Having struggled with difficulties in a foreign country, I returned to my own like an outcast, without a friend in the world, or a farthing. The thought maddened me. For a day and a night I walked the streets of Dover, scarcely tasting food. A thousand times I asked myself, what can I do, how shall I act? Begging was out of the question, especially for a soldier. In this state of mind, I was more fitted for a highwayman than a beggar. Can I not rob? I asked myself, but without firearms, how should I proceed?

I walked slowly along the road that leads to Canterbury. In an adjoining field, I espied a number of hop poles, and it occurred to me that with one of these I could knock down the first man who came past. Clearing the hedge at a jump, I pulled one of the poles out of the pile, snapped it off at the butt-end, and retired to my position on the road. Resolutely I glanced about in search of the first passenger. At some distance, I observed two men walking smartly towards me. Squeezing my cudgel firmly in my hand, I awaited their approach. Before I could bring myself to a proper sense of what I was about, one of the men was at my side shaking my hand and saying

"Ned! Is that you, my boy? How are you?"

It was Jem Connor, of my own regiment. I could scarcely answer him. He noticed my confusion but little dreamed the true cause of it. While still holding my hand, he insisted on my returning with him to Dover, and I did so.

The poor fellow had been severely wounded at Waterloo and passed the Board. He had married a woman at Dover and now resides at Chelsea and, I am happy to say, is in good circumstances at his trade as a tailor[15]. But it was providential that the person on whom I thus alighted was a friend, and I have often thought how it prevented me from committing an act which would ever have embittered my future life. Perhaps by similar, sometimes imperceptible, interpositions, many men are saved from the commission of a crime.

My generous comrade, although in needy circumstances himself, insisted on my sleeping at his house that night, and provided most liberally with what I most required. I explained to him my abject situation. He advised me to lay my Chelsea discharge before Colonel Ford, the Commandant at Dover, and solicit from him sufficient means to carry me to London. This was begging and contrary to my nature, and I asked Connor what I was to say, how I should act, for having been a soldier since I was 16 years of age, I was unacquainted with the forms of civil life. He gave me such advice as occurred to him, accompanied me on the road, and showed me the house at which the Colonel resided. It was at the end of the town, near the General

Hospital. With an unwilling hand I rung the bell. The door was immediately opened by a footman.

"Is the Colonel at home?" I said.

"Do you wish to see him?" was the footman's answer as he surveyed my person.

"I do. Tell him that a sergeant of the Rifles wishes to speak to him."

The servant then stepped across the hall and went into the room. The door was ajar. I heard the Colonel ask, "Is he in uniform or in coloured clothes?"

"In coloured clothes," was the answer.

"Tell him to come in."

I entered the room slowly. Believe me, I went with more spirit on the forlorn hope at Badajoz than I went into the presence of this officer. He was standing with his back to the fire-place.

"Well, friend," said he, "what do you want?"

"I want to know sir," I answered in a doubtful tone, "if you will lend me a little money to carry me to London. I will pay you when I get my pension."

The Colonel stooped and stared me full in the face, as if he thought me mad, and with a sententious voice, he exclaimed, "God damn you, sir! who are you, what are you, and what do you want?"

Although the Colonel's uncouth manner almost overwhelmed my sinking heart, my spirit rebounded from the shock and instantaneously brought me about again. I recovered myself and said, in a firm, earnest, yet determined manner: "Sir, I am a man brought to the last pitch of distress, without friends or money. If you will assist me, pray do so, but do not insult my feelings." Then laying my papers on the table, I added, "I am a sergeant of the Rifle Brigade, who has seen service. There, sir, are my papers. Keep them until I refund the money."

Taking my Chelsea discharge, he attentively read over the wounds I had received ["At Almeida through the left thigh and in the right knee, at Badajoz in the right leg, at Waterloo in the right hand, with the loss of the forefingers of the same hand."]. He then looked at me with an altered expression.

"You must have been a gallant fellow, or you would not have got so many scars in the service. Which battalion did you belong to?"

"The First."

He asked me what money I wanted to take me to London. As it was only 75 miles, I said that two shillings would be sufficient: I could walk more than 35 miles a day, and as I had no knapsack to carry, a shilling per day would do for me. Then my feelings overpowered me. He was evidently affected at seeing my emotion for he turned himself round to the fireplace. Facing me again, he said:

"Tut, tut! a brave soldier should not mind a little poverty."

I could not answer him. He rang the bell, and the footman who was in attendance came into the room.

"Tell the cook to get a good dinner ready for a gallant soldier," he said. Putting a chair towards me, in a friendly manner he told me to sit down, and began conversing familiarly. He asked a number of questions concerning the Peninsular War; but we were shortly interrupted by the servant, informing him dinner was ready.

"Go now," said he, "and take some refreshment."

But, alas! my appetite was gone. Before, I could have eaten a donkey, but now I could not break bread. The servants, observing me so discomposed, informed the Colonel. He came to me himself and tapped me on the shoulder.

"Come, come, make a good dinner," he said, then turned to the servant and ordered him to bring a bottle of wine.

After my repast the Colonel returned. He was accompanied by a lady who may have been his wife or daughter, to whom he had probably spoken of me, and who may have felt curious to see the rough soldier who had gone through so memorable a campaign. He slipped some 12 half-crowns into my hand, desiring me on no account to walk, but to take a coach to London. He also gave me back my papers. I thanked him, but asked him to keep them until I could return the money.

"No, no," he replied, "I make you a present of it." Then, in a very kind manner, he said, "Your old Colonel, Colonel Barnard, is made a General and a Knight. He is now Major-General Sir Andrew Barnard; and, if you wish it, I will write to him about you."

"The Colonel is well acquainted with me," I said. I left the house with feelings of gratitude which I could not give utterance to. Although many years have passed, never shall I forget the kindness of Colonel Ford.

On my return to London I wrote to Augustine, but received no answer. I waited with anxiety, and then came the mournful intelligence of her death, most likely owing to her father, as he remained inexorable to the last. Poor Augustine! Peace be to thy memory!

But Augustine was not dead. She was probably still alive when Costello was preparing his narrative for its first appearance in the *United Service Journal* of November 1839.

In the *Rifle Brigade Chronicle* of 1945, G W Cole published details of the research he had undertaken in the archives of the district of Cambrai. He revealed that, on 15 February 1822, less than three years after her final parting from Costello, Augustine Laude, a flax spinner, was married to lime burner Jean Baptiste Wiart. They had three children: Pierre Guislain (15 November 1825), Elisa Josephe (17 March 1828), and Bernard (13 March 1836), surely named after her father. Had there been a shred of legality in whatever marriage ceremony she and Costello went through, she would not have been able to marry Wiart.

There are many unanswered questions about the end of Costello's relationship with Augustine, not the least of which is, what happened to their child? If Costello really did believe that Augustine had died soon after their last parting, then what knowledge had he acquired at the same time about 'her infant'? Wouldn't he have been concerned about his child's welfare? That his concern does not appear to have been great can be explained by the fact that he knew, as we now know, that Augustine was alive, and able to look after their child herself.

In his article, Cole suggested that the Laude family, looking for an opportunity to rid themselves of Costello, may have sent him false tidings of Augustine's fate, but it is just as likely that Costello invented the story of her demise for his own convenience because, by 1822, he had a new partner himself - Charlotte Huntley. As their first child was born in 1822, it is possible that the beginning of their relationship pre-dated Augustine's marriage to Wiart. Having striven to present his relationship with Augustine as having some legitimacy, Costello was in danger of portraying his relationship with Charlotte as bigamous. How convenient then that his first 'wife' should 'die'.

Augustine's mother died on 3 July 1822, Augustine herself on 11 October 1839, and her father on 7 January 1843. Julie also died in 1843, and Léocadie in 1848. In 1935, according to Cole, there were in Moeuvres, a number of residents who still bore the surnames Laude and Wiart.

CHAPTER 27

The Carlist War
1819 - 1838

In Costello's narrative there is nothing whatsoever recorded of events in his life between 1819 and 1835, when he joined the British Legion and went back to Spain to fight. This is what he says about those missing years:

> It will be unnecessary for me to drag the reader through my chequered life, from the time I left the British army until my last campaign in Spain.

However, some information has been gleaned from the records held at St. Catherine's House in the Aldwych, and in the Public Record Office in Chancery Lane. Sometime between 1819 and 1822, Costello married Charlotte Huntley, who was his junior by about seven years, although no record of the marriage can be found. The couple had seven children: Edward (1822), William (1824), Samuel (1827), Charlotte (1830), John (1833), Charles (1835), and Henry (1839).

In 1836, the family was living at 29 Hinden St, Vauxhall Road, Westminster, near to what is now Victoria Station, in the parish of St. George's, Hanover Square. According to the 1851 Census, the first six children were born in Westminster, as was Charlotte, but no record of the children's baptisms can be found in the International Genealogical Index, in the registers of St. George's, Hanover Square, or in the registers of St. Patrick's in Soho and the Westminster Chapel in Horseferry Road, which were the two most likely choices for the family if they had been Catholics.

The only member of the family for which a record of birth has been traced is Henry, who was born after 1837 when the registration of all births, deaths and marriages in Britain became compulsory. His birth certificate gives some indication of how Costello may have earned a living between 1819 and 1835 because he is described as a shoemaker.

In 1835, at the age of 47, Costello decided to become a soldier again by joining the British Auxiliary Legion to fight for the infant Queen Isabella of Spain, daughter of King Ferdinand, in the civil war against the rival claimant for the throne, her uncle Don Carlos.

Britain was not involved in this war, therefore the British Legion was regarded by many as a mercenary force. For this reason, in the preface to the 1841 edition of his book, Costello sought to justify his involvement:

> Some military men fancy a man cannot fight unless he has his country's cause at heart, that being the only thing capable of arousing his martial ardour. I beg most humbly to differ. When a British subject is put into uniform, and placed in the ranks with a firelock in his hand, he requires no stimulant nor patriotic impulse to urge him in attacking the enemy opposed to him. Why should a British subject be ridiculed, or prevented from 'earning an honest livelihood'? Why, if he prefers being knocked on the head in serving a foreign power, should he be termed a mercenary and a murderer, as has been the case with the Legion? Kidnapped by a recruiting-sergeant, or pressed by a press-gang into the British service, John Bull and his brethren of the sister kingdoms make the best of a bad matter by going the whole hog on every occasion, as old soldiers well know, and most, like myself, find in their muskets and bayonets, their only title-deeds. However, from the 'smallness' of the estates they represent, these are but poor guarantees, for when 'cut up' and well 'drilled' by bullets on long and active service, old age steals on, and premature infirmities commence their march.

The 1830s were a time of great want among the working classes, and as the Legion offered a bounty to its recruits, Costello, who had a large family to support, was again tempted.

> In the beginning of July 1835, I enclosed documents from officers of rank in the British army, with a statement of my own service and the rank I had held, to Colonel, now Sir De Lacy Evans, expressing a wish to enter under his command.

General De Lacy Evans was the commander of the British Legion. He accepted Costello, appointed him to the rank of lieutenant and gave him orders to recruit a regiment of riflemen for the 7th Light Infantry, B.A.L. Within two months, Costello had 500 men. Some were Peninsular War veterans, and of those a number were former riflemen. They received an initial bounty of £2 each, and embarked at Portsmouth in September 1835. They disembarked at Portugalete, near Bilbao, in Spain.

> On 19 September, about 7 o'clock on a beautiful summer evening, I again landed on that soil where, 24-25 years ago, I had witnessed so many severe contests. Innumerable changes had filled up the interval between my leaving the Peninsular and my return, so revisiting it would have been very interesting but for the very different scenes I was obliged to witness. They occupied the whole of my sympathies in

comparing a British soldier in 1835, with the same character during his glorious career under Wellington.

Within a short time of his arrival, Costello was promoted to the rank of captain. Almost as quickly, he saw that poor quarters and unnecessarily harsh discipline were to be the lot of his men.

It was evident to me, even this early in the campaign, that General Evans did not display much solicitude or feelings for the comfort of his soldiers, when a representation of their situation to the proper Spanish authorities by General Evans would have made things better for them. The poor men, chiefly raw recruits, unaccustomed to the diet and climate of the country, underwent fatiguing military instructions - a severe daily drill of six hours - but this was merely a foretaste of the treatment they were to endure...

The miserable and comfortless condition of the men was nothing to the disgraceful Provost system which was carried on most rigorously in every regiment of the Legion. At first, it was boasted that the rules of the service were to be purely British, but I found it to be entirely different. Every regiment had its provost, and in some there were two, with a proportion of cats. Any officer, for the slightest dereliction of duty, or as he felt inclined, could order a man to receive from one to four dozen lashes. It mattered not whether the soldier was a recruit or an old campaigner, for there were no less than a dozen of these Chelsea pensioners in the company I commanded.

From Bilbao, the Legion marched to Briviesca.

The inhabitants of this and the neighbouring localities had been much oppressed at different periods, particularly by the French during the Peninsular War. The old patrone of the house in which I was quartered, gave me a long recital of the exactions he had been subject to during that period, by soldiers of different armies, tears rolling over his aged cheeks, which no doubt his extraordinary sufferings had helped to wither. Since my last sojourn amongst them, the Spaniards had made very little progress towards improvement. Foreign invasions, priestcraft, and civil strife, had for so long and so continually absorbed their energies, that they had scarcely recovered, and their beautiful country, rich as it was in natural resources, looked like a desert. It was patched here and there by the hands of a cultivator, who planted in fear and gathered in trembling, under the dreadful probability of having his work uprooted or trodden down by soldiers of either party, who might leave himself and his family stretched lifeless amid the ruin.

At Briviesca, the soldier's training continued, but Costello regarded it as inadequate, especially for his riflemen.

At Briviesca we commenced a regular system of drilling, but instead of being drilled collectively, the Rifles... were confined to marching round in columns of companies, saluting the General, and forming lines, etc. I pointed this out to our Colonel and requested that we be allowed 15-20 rounds of blank cartridge to exercise a little in sham fighting. He acceded. This afterwards proved of great service.

During the short time we remained at Briviesca, the drilling and the provost system were carried on most rigorously and this, together with our long and harassing march from Bilbao, and our living in damp convents, laid the foundation of all the sickness and mortality that befell the unfortunate Legion.

About this time an order came from Madrid for the whole of the men to be paid up to the last day of November 1835. This was the only settlement that captains of companies had with the paymaster until the dissolution of the Legion.

They marched from Briviesca to Vitoria, where Costello had fought in 1813.

I cannot describe how I felt on again beholding this place, so celebrated for the victory we had gloriously achieved here under our immortal Wellington, 25 years before. The very hedges were familiar to me. When we arrived at the village on the main road, where we had taken the first gun, and where I so fortunately escaped death, I could no longer suppress my emotions. I turned away from my company and directed my pony off the road and into the fields. There I gave vent to my feelings. I was one of the time-forgotten numbers who had consecrated the scene, and as I stood there alone, I felt as it were amidst them. I looked about as if the soil would throw out some of my old comrades, but all was one bleak flat, edged in on either side by mountains, which seemed to rear their heads like tombstones over the glorious sleepers at their base. Many years had passed, and many cares had done their best to wither up my heart-strings, but in vain; I was still the 'old soldier'! Although garbed and tilted with the appointments of a captain, my nature had not altered, and I believe that if the offer could have been made, I would have given up epaulettes and all for one short hour's converse with my old brother campaigners.

I took the earliest opportunity to look about the town, so on the morning after our arrival, I passed through the gates on the great road leading to Pamplona to the spot where I had fallen in with the carriage of Joseph Bonaparte. It had been built over by a convent, now converted into a hospital for the Spanish soldiers.

The Legion remained in Vitoria where the corporal punishments were carried on with the same ferocity. Costello wanted to inform General de Lacy Evans of the soldier's plight, but was unable to get near him.

> Never were punishments carried to such an extent, nor authority so unlimited or arrogated as that usurped by the chief part of the officers of the British Auxiliaries.

Although the soldiers were quite well supplied (because they were employed directly by the Spanish Government), many died through want and negligence on the part of the senior officers, whom Costello also blamed for pinching out the men's noble spirit.

The winter of 1835-1836 was a very severe one, and in February 1836, while the Legion was living in crowded conditions in Trevina, a few miles from Vitoria, many fell sick and died. The civilians suffered to, and when the Legion eventually returned to Vitoria itself, it resembled a plague city. In each regiment, about ten soldiers died every day, their bodies carried out of the hospitals in cart loads. Almost as many were lost to desertion for the attractions of joining the army of Don Carlos were many. His soldiers appeared to be better fed, and as each deserter was offered more money than the bounty he had originally been paid by Queen Isabella's side, there were many takers. Junior officers in the Legion were treated unfairly and could be dismissed on a whim, without the benefit of a court martial. Many were the ways those in power found to withhold payment of the sums owed to these officers for their service.

Although soldiers of many nations were employed in support of Isabella's cause, including a French Legion, they worked well together. These foreign troops were well led and, awake to the appalling circumstances the soldiers of the Legion laboured under, would often try to screen them from punishment eg. by dragging a drunken soldier from the street and hiding him so that he would not be discovered by his officers.

In April 1836, the British Legion received orders to leave Vitoria, and proceed towards San Sebastian, where the Carlists were laying siege to the fortress. When they arrived they were issued with fresh uniforms, shoes, and other things they were in need of. Costello was quite proud of his riflemen.

> They were a fine set of fellows. They were ripe, and ready for any duty, and only wanted efficient men at their head.

On 21 April, Costello, with four companies of Rifles was transferred to San Sebastian by an English steamer, and on 5 May they went into action against the Carlists. For Costello it was the first time he had fought since being at Quatre Bras 20 years earlier. Attempting to lead his men against a redoubt, he was wounded when one bullet grazed the skin of his left thigh, and another entered the right knee joint, passing downward through the ham and out at the calf of the leg. Some of his men bore Costello to the rear, where he was placed on a stretcher and carried to his quarters in San Sebastian. The Legion were successful in the action, and forced the Carlists to retire.

Back in his quarters, Costello wrote to his wife at 29 Hinden Street:

My dear Charlotte,

I dare say by the time you receive this letter, the streets of London will be crowded with fellows bellowing out, 'the unfortunate Legion is killed to a man, and poor Costello is no more'. But if you have not purchased the widow's weeds, I request you will not do so as I am not yet half killed. Certainly I have an extra ball through my old trunk, and this I should have escaped had I not exposed myself, perhaps rather unnecessarily, in endeavouring to keep the brave fellows of my company in something like military order.

All were commanders, from the second lieutenant to the major. It appeared to me, in truth, the Legion is not a school for the young soldier to acquire knowledge, nor the old to get credit. How different, indeed, were things carried on in the British Army. There, in the very height of the most desperate conflict, all was cool and collected, and every officer's word could be distinctly heard at the slightest cessation of firing.

The officer who commanded our regiment today is a smart young fellow, and might be of some service in a country fair in Ireland, with a good shillelagh, but to command 400-500 men in action with firearms, against a hardy race of well-disciplined mountaineers, is quite a different thing. I cannot say how many of our regiment were killed as I was reluctantly compelled to leave them, by a ball passing through my right knee, yet I hope I shall not lose my limb. My kindest love to our dear children. Do not think the worst, my dear Carlotte - you shall soon again hear from me.

Affectionately yours,
E Costello.

For several days I felt great apprehension about my leg, which had swollen to almost double its natural size. It had changed to a livid colour and the nails of the toes had fallen off. I was not yet 50, and although in excellent spirits, I doubted my constitution was strong enough to undergo amputation.

Costello did not lose his leg. His experience of gunshots wounds helped him to tend his own wound, and within two months he was able to get around on crutches. At leisure in San Sebastian during his convalescence, he was able to examine the town which some of his fellow riflemen had helped to storm in 1813, and he reflected on the changes foreign invaders had wrought in the character of the Spanish people:

Scarcely a monk was to be found at this time, though the monasteries held their old situation. Even the lovely, dark-eyed nuns had forsaken their cloisters, and seemed to breathe a new life under the more enlightened state. As regards religious enthusiasm, I was astonished at its decrease.

Costello was rewarded for his courage in the fighting at San Sebastian.

A despatch was sent from Madrid, conferring the order of St. Ferdinand on those officers who had most distinguished themselves on 5 May. I was named as one, but the honour was almost lost in the indiscriminate manner in which it was distributed, as numbers procured the distinction without the least claim to either skill or courage, which caused dissatisfaction amongst the really deserving officers.

For their conduct, the men were honoured with pewter medals, in imitation of those of Waterloo. These may be frequently observed appended to the ragged vestments of the unfortunate remnant of the Legion, numbers of whom are to be seen daily, begging in every large town of the kingdom.

The medals were no substitute for the pay which the soldiers were owed by the Spanish government. It was six months in arrears, and while they were quartered in the villages and farmhouses in advance of San Sebastian, some of the men mutinied, refusing to do their duty until they were paid. The money was raised by a general levy upon the inhabitants, but it was then spent by the men on drinking sprees, which caused further uproar.

Many of the unfortunates who abused their hard earnings found themselves woefully deficient the next morning, because the more sober and wide awake among them had picked their pockets while they were insensible. On discovering their deficiency, they in turn took to robbing their comrades, even of their greatcoats, shirts, shoes, and rations. This became so universal that complaints to the officers were futile for scarcely one among them could cast the first stone.

A great number of the men had enlisted for a year only, and held documents to that effect, signed by the officers who had enlisted them. As their time of service was up, whole companies of the 6th and 8th Scotch gave notice to their officers, and the next day piled arms, hanging their accoutrements upon them. The Legion was now in such a state of insubordination, that it was with difficulty that they mustered enough men to march the delinquents to the castle. From there they were shipped on board a steamer to Santander and Santona.

I began to feel tired of an inactive life; and as my wounds were of a nature to disable me for future service, I expressed a wish to the

General then commanding the brigade, that a medical board should examine me.

The General agreed that Costello should spend a month or two at Santander in the hope that he might recover sufficiently to rejoin his regiment.

> I was on the point of leaving, perhaps forever, a Legion from which I had expected so much, but which had come to nothing! Truly, with Hamlet, I might have exclaimed 'Take it for all in all, I ne'er shall look upon its like again.' Nor did I ever wish it, so much was it abused, badly used, and officered even worse.

The distance to Santander was about 100 miles and Costello travelled there in a James Watt steamer. When he arrived, he was ordered to take charge of the convent of Carbon, four miles from Santander. It was the auxiliaries' depot.

> The commandant was generally some field-officer, whose power was almost despotic. He was secure from complaint, as Colonel Arbuthnot seldom, if ever, visited it.

The commandant, Captain Deacon of the 1st Regiment, was on his sick-bed suffering from fever. The officer commanding in his place was the depot's quartermaster, whom Costello described as a land-shark. The men at the convent, most of whom were the mutinous 6th and 8th Scotch transferred from San Sebastian shortly before, were in a poor state, and Costello also discovered that 36 invalids had, on the whim of the quartermaster, been imprisoned in appalling conditions, without meat or wine.

> It would be impossible to portray a faithful picture of the miserable creatures before me. They stood like beings just come out of the grave; their eyes sunk in their heads, and their countenances hardly recognizable from want and filth. Scarcely a dozen of them had even jackets or shirts, and not one had either shoes or stockings; many were covered over with a ragged rug. Their daily allowance had been a pound and a half of black bread, and water.

Costello released them all immediately, and tried to place the quartermaster under arrest, but he escaped to Santander. The man was eventually brought to a court of inquiry, but he was released back to his duties. Suspecting corruption, Costello kept an eye on him.

A large proportion of the men who had given up their arms in San Sebastian were, on the promise of better rations and conditions, persuaded to rejoin their regiments. Having hardly any clothing to travel back to San Sebastian, the convent was ransacked for its old carpets to cover their nakedness. Also used were the old parchment records, left in the convent by the monks.

I shall never forget the sight of these poor fellows slowly emerging from the convent. Numbers alone kept them going, when perhaps, singly, each man would have died rather than have undergone such an exposure.

Those who had refused to rejoin remained at the convent. They were a half-starved and apathetic group, and when Costello discovered that two of them had been wounded by the Spanish guards, he tried to get justice for them. This proved impossible because his senior officer, Colonel Arbuthnot, was employed by the Spanish.

My authority as commandant was a mere mockery, for we were entirely at the disposal of the Spanish guard. It was truly painful, despite the frequency of the scene, to witness the daily return of misery. Midnight, that hour when wretchedness generally forgets itself in sleep, seemed to have lost its influence here, and its silence was broken by the footsteps of these unhappy men. Many passed the time telling over again the oft repeated list of grievances... At times, when the moon shone, the whole building had the appearance of a splendid mausoleum, and the sufferers as they passed from cell to cell, looked unearthly, and put me in mind of the fabled and ghastly inhabitants of the other world. I see them still, the gaunt, misery-stricken countenances of 150 men, with all the changes their tyrants had rung amongst them! Finding my complaints so unavailing, I made up my mind to quite the service. At length, an order arrived, and a medical board having sat accordingly, I was pronounced unfit for further service through my wounds. I packed by traps and hastened to leave the neighbourhood.

Costello left the convent and its men in the care of its new commandant, Captain Oakley, but he tarried long enough to witness Oakley turn the already appalling living conditions of the former soldiers into something even more hellish.

I felt as few ever felt before, and even now, seated in my family circle, though years have intervened, seem to breathe anew the freedom I experienced at my deliverance from this worse than purgatory.

Costello returned home to his family in Hinden Street. He never went soldiering again.

Thus ends my military career which, little as it can boast of leading incidents, may yet prove interesting. I shall be contented if it does little more than wile away a dull hour, or keep alive the recollection of personal enterprise among those of my veteran comrades whom war has permitted to live and peruse it.

CHAPTER 28

Yeoman Warder and Autobiographer
1838 - 1869

On 5 March 1838, a year and a half after his return from Spain, Costello was appointed as a yeoman warder at the Tower of London by the Duke of Wellington, who had become Constable of the Tower in 1826. The Duke had established an appointments system - the previous system having become corrupt - whereaby the posts were granted to gallant and deserving ex-sergeants, with occasional exceptions: Costello was not, and never had been, a sergeant.

Although an extremely privileged position, the duties of warders cannot have been onerous because they were able to take up other employment, and in August 1839, when Costello registered the birth of his son Henry, he described himself not as a Warder of the Tower, but as a shoemaker. Warders often lived in the Tower but, initially, Costello does not appear to have done so, his address in 1839 being at 43 Elliot's Row, St George's Road, Southwark, where Henry was born, and then 3 Poplar Row, New Kent Road, Newington, where he was to be found in residence by the census takers in 1841 and 1851.

In November 1839, a year and a half after his appointment as a warder, the first episode of a serialisation of his memoirs appeared in the *United Service Journal*. The idea for publishing articles about his military experiences seems to have stemmed from his association with an aspiring lawyer called Meller, who was in the British Auxiliary Legion with him. That Meller was closely involved in the early stages of the narrative is indicated by the editor of the *United Service Journal*, who wrote a review of Costello's memoirs when they were published as a book in 1841

"With our knowledge of the facts, we cannot overlook an omission which we should not have expected from the worthy old soldier, towards whom we have proved our sincere interest and, had we been consulted, should not have occurred - namely, the absence of all mention of the autobiographer's obligations to Mr Meller, a gentleman now, we believe, studying for the bar, who served in the Auxiliary Legion with Costello, and put together, from the vivid dictation and notes of the latter, the earlier papers of the narrative. This task, we are bound to say, Mr Meller performed with spirit and fidelity, considering his want of intimate knowledge with the subject; and we conceive that in doing him this

justice, we are but discharging a duty which the hurry of publication alone may have caused the hero of this most striking story to omit."

At no point in any edition of his memoirs, does Costello mention Meller by name, or credit him with writing any of his narrative. On the contrary, in the Preface to the 1841 edition, he says that he rescued his story from the hands of others:

"In the late expedition under Sir De Lacy Evans, the objects of those who undertook to serve the regnant Queen of Spain were as varied as their professions and characters. Many went to fight. Amongst these, my own countrymen rather preponderated. Numbers went also to see the world, as they termed it; and received in its organised bands the ugliest of its knocks. Many went to acquire what they had lost or could not gain in their own country, which if not fame and respectability, they hoped would be something approaching very close to the fashionable idea of one or both. Among these last were a certain few who, searching for the marvellous and the profitable, chanced on various occasions to fall into my company, or else introduced themselves with the object of drawing from me, when in the midst of strong waters and strong impulses, recollections of a life which, however humble the actor, yet for the singular characteristics of the circumstances in which I had been placed, could not fail to interest people. It was therefore, with no little surprise, that on my return to England, I witnessed in the various periodicals of the time, certain extracts from my career which I instantly recognised as mine, and mine only. The fact was, like my immortal countryman poor Oliver Goldsmith, I discovered that a lot had been cast for me, and that my fellow-sufferers, kindly keeping it a secret from all but themselves, had already sacrificed me. Nearly all that was palatable had been devoured by their insatiable jaws, and the most tasty portions had nearly vanished when I ventured to claim 'my own'. At length, I succeeded in putting together this volume, the materials of which might have lost their attractions in their distributed and mangled condition."

It is possible that Costello was here referring not to the earlier chapters of his memoirs published in the *United Service Journal*, but to even earlier articles in that publication, perhaps ghost written by Meller, about his experiences in the British Legion. Articles on the Carlist Wars, written anonymously by protagonists on both sides, began to appear in the *Journal* as early as 1836, eg *'Hospital scenes and sketches of the British Auxiliary Legion of Spain, by a veteran'*. Similar articles continued through 1837 then, in 1838, came the first of a series entitled *Recollections of the Camp in Spain by a Captain of the late British Auxiliary Legion*. The author could be describing Costello when he says that:

"even grey-headed veterans of the British service fancied they were going to transcend their former glories under the immortal Wellington. Alas! how bitterly their experience proved the utter fallacies of such anticipation."

This same writer refers to his companion in the Legion as *"a gentlemanly little fellow"*, who had *"left a 5 years' study under the bar for the vicissitudes of a soldier's life."* Given that Mr Meller went to study at the bar after the Carlist War, it is interesting to speculate on whether these articles might have some something to do with Costello and Meller.

Costello's *Memoirs* continued to appear in serialised form throughout 1840 then, in 1841, they were published in enhanced form as a book, *Adventures of a Soldier*. A second edition was published in 1852, the year Charlotte Costello died. After her death - she was buried in a public grave in Nunhead Cemetery - Costello moved to the Tower of London with some of his children, and they eventually occupied the whole of the Salt Tower, the ground floor being his kitchen and the first floor his living room, with two bedrooms above.

While he was a Warder, Costello had several encounters with former comrades, one of whom was Tom Plunket, whose post-war adventures he relates in some detail. The highlights of Plunket's career with the 95th were between the years 1807-1809, for the regimental records reveal that he took very little part in the Pensinsular War after being hospitalised in August 1811. He fought with the 2nd battalion at the battle of Waterloo where he was wounded by a musket ball which skimmed his forehead, leaving an ugly scar. Plunket's wife was even more scarred.

> Shortly after the battle of Waterloo, Tom wedded a lady remarkable for being deficient in one essential to beauty, ie she had no *face*, or at all events, was so *defaced* it amounted to the same thing. She had gallantly followed the camp through the war, and this slight flaw in her beauty arose from the bursting of an ammunition-waggon at Quatre Bras, near to which she had stood, and by which her countenance was rendered a blue, shapeless, noseless mass. The event was commemorated by the government allowing the heroine a shilling a day pension.
>
> After Waterloo, Tom Plunket was invalided to England, where he passed the board at Chelsea but, disgusted at being awarded the pittance of sixpence a day for his wound and long service, he expressed himself to the Lord Commissioners in a way that induced them to strike him off the list altogether.

Plunket was discharged from the 95th on 10 November 1817 not, as Costello here implies, because of the wound he received at Waterloo but, according to his discharge papers, in consequence of *"being a very bad character and being nearly worn out in the service."*

> The following day he started off for Ireland, where he duly arrived in

rags and wretchedness. To relieve himself, he enlisted again, this time in either the 31st or 32nd Regiment of the line, then quartered somewhere in the north[1].

While wearing a red coat, he had a singular meeting with his former Colonel, then General Sir Sidney Beckwith, which I have often heard him relate. It is customary to have half-yearly inspections of our regiments at home, and shortly after Tom enlisted, when his regiment was formed for inspection on one of these occasions, that duty devolved upon Sir Sidney, who was in command of the district. In walking down the front rank scrutinising the appearance of the men, the General came to Tom, who was distinguished by two medals on his breast[2].

"Do my eyes deceive me?" said Sir Sidney. "Surely you are Tom Plunket, formerly of my own regiment?"

"What's left of me, sir," said Tom, who was seldom deficient in a prompt reply.

"And what has again brought you into the service?" inquired Sir Sidney. "I thought you had passed the board at Chelsea?"

"So I did," said Tom. "But they only allowed me sixpence a day, sir, so I told them to keep it for the young soldiers, as it wasn't enough for the old, who had seen all the tough work out."

"Ha! the old thing, Tom, I perceive," said Sir Sidney, shaking his head. "One of my bravest soldiers," he remarked to the Colonel of the regiment as he proceeded down the ranks.

The same day the General dined at the officers' mess. After dinner, Tom was sent for and Sir Sidney handed him a glass of wine, saying "Here, Plunket. I have sent for you to give us a toast."

"Then, sir, here's to the immortal memory of the poor fellows who fell in the Peninsula," said Tom.

The toast was drunk by all with much solemnity, and Tom was dismissed with a present from Sir Sidney. The following day he was made a corporal. Shortly afterwards, I believe through the medium of Sir Sidney, he went up and passed the pension board at Kilmainham, which granted him a shilling a day[3].

Tom was imbued with roving inclinations, partly owing to his nature and more, perhaps, to his profession, for the ever-changing and chequered course of a soldier's life unsettles a man. At one time, he decided to become a settler in Canada. The government held out an offer to all pensioners, which allowed them so much land, and gave them four years' pay for their pensions[4]. Plunket, ever eager for the handling of cash, accepted the offer. He got two years' pay here, and started off with some 200-300 others to try his fortune, which proved to be a very miserable one. Tom was not a man to rusticate on the other side of the Atlantic amid privations, and before a year had elapsed, he had returned to England with his wife, swearing loudly against forest-land, a swampy soil, and a bad climate. He told his friends that his grant of land was so wild and swampy that looking at it every morning out of the chinks of a wretched log hut he had managed to erect upon his estate, made him quite melancholy. He had, of course, forfeited his own pension forever.

Tom Plunket was less fortunate in 'life's march' than myself, and the last time I saw him was in Burton Crescent[5], most picturesquely clothed, and selling matches. I asked him how he got on, and with one of his usual cheerful smiles he informed me that the match-selling business kept him on his legs.

"I should have thought, Tom, that you had seen enough of *firing*, without endeavouring to live by it now."

"A man must do something these hard times for bread," he replied, and he passed his hand thoughtfully across the furrow in his brow, made by the bullet at Waterloo.

Poor Tom. I felt for him, and was sorry to see him neglected. Others, whose service were many days' march behind his, were taken better care of, but Tom's incorrigible failing[6] was his own stumbling-block. I did not leave him my mere reflection only, but a portion of that coin he so well knew how to get rid of. I wished him success in his new business, and went my way, musing on the strange vicissitudes of a soldier's life: 'Alas! the brave too oft are doomed to bear, the gripes of poverty, the stings of care.'

A few months back, while on duty at the Tower, one of the warders informed me that a most extraordinary lady was anxious to see me. To my astonishment, Mrs Plunket then stood before me. With one hand she held a handkerchief to that part of her face where her nose formerly stood, and with her other hand, she squeezed mine and told me in the most plaintive tone, and with many sobs, of poor Tom's death. She and Plunket usually tramped through different parts of the country, procuring a livelihood by selling needles and tapes. While passing through a street in Colchester, Tom suddenly staggered a few paces, fell down, and expired. The death of Tom, and the sight of Mrs Plunket, whose extraordinary countenance excited disgust as well as pity, spread like wildfire through the town. Several retired officers living in that city, who happened to read my description of him, heard about it, and a handsome collection was set on foot. £20 was collected for the widow, and the lady of a colonel, entirely out of her own pocket, paid for the Tom's funeral, and for a handsome tombstone to perpetuate his memory. Thus ended the career of the gallant but unfortunate Plunket[7].

Costello outlived Plunket by a good many years and died in the Salt Tower on 27 July 1869. He is buried in Nunhead Cemetery in a plot purchased by his son Henry, who lies there in sepulchre with him. In the same grave is Edward's second son, William, William's wife Harriet, and their son William. Charles Costello, Edward's fifth son, is buried in a common grave in the Roman Catholic area of Camberwell Old Cemetery. But was Edward himself a Catholic? We just don't know because the church registry entries which would tell us cannot

Edward Costello's medals and musket balls.

be found, and although some of his many descendants are Catholics, others are not.

In trying to get to grips with this problem, we must bear in mind that Queen's County, in which Costello was born, was one of the areas in Ireland pinpointed by James I for Protestant settlement in the early 17th Century, and the fact that there was a freemasonry lodge in Mountmellick Parish at the end of the 18th Century suggests strong English influences in the area at the time of Costello's birth. Also, the Catholic Church objected strongly to the freemasonry movement, which Costello eventually joined. Furthermore, would Costello's father have been appointed to the government service as a tidewaiter in the customs service if he had been a practising Catholic? The Test Act of 1673 required holders of public office to receive the Anglican sacrament and reject the doctrine of transubstantiation, thereby excluding Catholics. As you can see, before the Catholic Emancipation Act of 1829, being a Catholic in Britain and Ireland was, at the very least, inconvenient.

When he died, Ned Costello left to his children many mementos of his service life. They include his medals, the sword he wore as a Captain in the British Legion, and two of the musket balls which wounded him. The medals are the Military General Service Medal, the Waterloo medal, a Regimental Medal granted to the survivors of the

Edward Costello. This portrait was painted in about 1850.

forlorn hopes at Ciudad Rodrigo and Badajoz, the Spanish Medal for his services in Spain with the British Legion, and the Order of a Knight of San Ferdinand and Isabella II. All of these medals, with the exception of the Order of the Knight of San Ferdinand, which was lost while in the possession of his son, Charles, are now on display in the

Edward Costello in old age, pictured with one of his grandsons.

Royal Green Jackets Museum, having been purchased by Colonel Willoughby Verner in 1915. Willoughby also obtained the two musket balls. One of the balls had taken off Costello's fingers at Quatre Bras. The other, which had been lodged in Costello's left thigh since the action on the Coa in 1810 was, at Costello's request, extracted from his body after death by the Medical Officer of the Tower of London. These musket balls are also on display at the Royal Green Jackets Museum.

Costello regarded himself, first and foremost, as a soldier, and the last of his words to be presented here come from the introduction to the 1841 edition of his *Adventures*, in which he expresses how he felt recalling his military experiences for the book:

> The pleasures I have enjoyed in passing anew over the campaigns of old times, are only to be equalled by the pain felt in the retrospective remembrances of my honoured and never-to-be forgotten brother campaigners, for Spain gave rise to my earliest and noblest friendships and social feelings.
>
> Every man's life is a volume of change, felt and expressed according to his peculiar dispositions and feelings, which are as varied under a military life as they can be under a civil one. Could the unforgettable Tom Crawley but give his own details! Could Long Tom of Lincoln - one of the smartest men of our regiment, now the forlorn bone-picker of Knightsbridge[8] - but pen his own eventful track! And Wilkie, Hetherington and Plunket - the exploits of these and many other humble heroes, who were conquerors in such well-contested fields as Rodrigo, Badajoz, Salamanca and Waterloo, form the principal attractions in these volumes. Their stubborn spirits and perforated bodies formed key-stones for the fame of our immortal Wellington, whose standard might have found a sandy support but for the individual bravery of the soldiers of his invincible divisions. Could they but recount their varied casts of fortune, who would fail to read their histories, or help to rear a cypress to their memories?

NOTES

CHAPTER 1: *Militiaman and Recruit, October 1788 - February 1809*

1. Costello's surname is derived from MacCostello, an anglicised version of Mac Oisdealbhaigh. Queen's County, now Co. Laois, was targeted for Protestant colonisation by James I after 1603 in order to reduce the power of the Catholic landowners. The parish of Mountmellick was founded in 1776, the first Roman Catholic church established there in about 1800, and the first Protestant church in 1828. However, a masonic lodge existed before either of them - from 1786. This may be significant because Costello eventually became a freemason. Established in 1725, Ireland's Grand Lodge is one of the oldest in the world, second only to the English Grand Lodge (1717).

2. An officer in the customs service whose duty it was to board ships on their arrival in port and examine their cargos. In his narrative, Costello mentions only his father. Had his mother died young?

3. Wilson's Dublin Directories of the period do not record the existence of a King William Street in Dublin at that time, but there was a King Street, and a William Street, as there are now.

4. Costello would have been 13 or 14. In Wilson's Directories, there are several Costellos mentioned as traders in Dublin. His uncle may have been his mother's brother. As no records of Costello's birth, or his parent's marriage, have yet been traced, his mother's maiden name is not known.

5. In 1801, General Sir Ralph Abercromby (1734-1801) commanded an expedition to Egypt, where he was fatally wounded.

6. It was a year earlier. The muster and pay lists of the Dublin City Militia have survived and are held at the PRO, Kew. Costello was in the militia with his father. Between 1805 and 1808, two Costellos were present in Captain Frood's company - Edward Snr and Edward Jnr. One enlisted on 1 July 1805, but by 25 August 1805, they are both listed. Ned would have been 16. He was probably his father's eldest and, perhaps, his only, son.

7. Costello was in the militia for 3 years, and was 19 when he joined the 95th in Derry on 27 August 1808 for Unlimited Service. He was the only volunteer for the Rifles, but many of his comrades joined the 83rd and the 66th Regiments. He was described as a shoemaker, 5'6" tall, with brown hair and grey eyes.

8. In his 1967 edition of Costello's memoirs, Anthony Brett-James explains that this was a name given to those in Ireland who were in sympathy with French revolutionaries.

9. John Wilkie is recorded as having joined the 95th at the same time as Costello, ie 27 August 1808.

10. Many autobiographers of the period refer to civilian attire as 'coloured clothes'.

11. A reference to the fable about a donkey which, given the choice of two bales of hay, cannot decide which to eat, and dies of starvation.

12. For centuries Ringsend, in Dublin Harbour, had provided the main embarkation point for the city. However, being situated in marshy ground, it was frequently cut off from the city by treacherous tides, so in 1748 building began on the South Wall to ensure that the connection was permanent. It was four miles long, and had a lighthouse at the end. In 1808, the customary landing place for passengers from the packets was at what was called the Pigeon House, a mile from the end of the wall, where it was 250ft. across, wide enough to accommodate several buildings, including a fort and a custom house.

13. Probably Corporal Zemeran Crooks, a steady fellow, who maintained his rank for many years during the 1st battalion's service in the Peninsula. He was promoted to sergeant on 5 October 1814.

14. Captain Francis Glasse first joined the 95th as a 2nd lieutenant on 14 August 1801, then transferred to the 43rd Regiment as a first lieutenant in July 1802. He transferred back to the 95th as a captain on 18 September 1806, and remained with it until September 1816.

15. In his introduction to the journals of George Simmons, Willoughby Verner describes the Baker rifle which Costello used: *"Weight 9½ lbs, barrel seven-grooved and 30 inches in length, rifling one quarter turn in barrel, bullet spherical, 20 to the pound, charge of powder 84 grains, flint-lock. The ball was placed in the centre of a greased leather patch and rammed home, considerable force being necessary to effect this... A supply of greased patches was carried in a small box with spring brass lid in the side of the butt of the rifle. As regards rapidity of fire, the maximum rate at which perfectly steady shot could be taken was reckoned to be one per minute."*

16. William Green said that, after their return, the men received two guineas each for the loss of their kits

CHAPTER 2: *Hythe, March - May 1809*

1. Peter O'Hare joined the Rifle Corps at its formation on 28 August 1800 from the 69th Foot, where he had been a lieutenant since January 1797. Promoted to captain on 6 August 1803, he was a veteran of the campaign in South America.

2. Thomas Sidney Beckwith had been with the 95th since its formation, transferring from the 71st Regiment on 29 August 1800 as a Brevet Major. He became a Lieutenant-Colonel on 20 January 1803. He was

extremely popular with the men and officers, not just for his leadership and coolness under fire but for his humanity. In his book *25 Years in the Rifle Brigade*, William Surtees, who joined the Rifle Corps two years after Beckwith, relates an extraordinary incident involving Colonel Beckwith's wife and some unruly Irish recruits, which took place between May and October 1805 while the regiment was in Kent:

> *"During our stay at Brabourn Lees, a circumstance occurred which called forth an exhibition of as great a magnanimity on the part of Colonel Beckwith as I almost ever remember to have witnessed. We had received about 200 Irish volunteers, who were wild and ungovernable in the extreme. A party of these, in strolling about one day, had fallen in with Mrs Beckwith, with her maid and child, taking a walk along the Ashford road. Not knowing, I imagine, who the lady and her maid were, they set on and assaulted them in the most violent and outrageous manner, proceeding to such lengths as perhaps delicacy forbids to mention. It was, I believe, discovered who they were. Accordingly, the next day, the Colonel formed the battalion into a square and proceeded to relate the circumstances to the regiment. 'But,' says he, 'although I know who the ruffians are, I will not proceed any farther in the business, because it was <u>my own wife</u> that they attacked, but had it been the wife of the meanest soldier in the regiment, I solemnly declare I would have given you every lash to which a court-martial might have sentenced you.' Such a trait of general forbearance is not often met with; but by this, and similar instances of liberal feeling, he completely gained the heart of every soldier in the battalion, a thing not always attainable by very excellent commanding officers."*

3. The Duke of York was Commander-in-Chief of the British Army.

4. Plunket's discharge papers of 1817 describe him as being 5'6" tall with brown hair, grey eyes and a fair complexion. In the action to try to retake Buenos Aires, he and Fisher, another rifleman, were hoisted onto the roof of a low building to act as sharpshooters. Some years later, when asked by an officer of the 95th how many men he had killed from this position, Plunket replied: *'Twenty, sir,'* then added: *'I shot a gentleman with a flag of truce, sir.'* Not understanding the situation, that is exactly what he had done, and the man had died of his wounds. (*United Service Journal*, 1842.)

5. Lt.-Gen. John Whitelocke (1757-1833) commanded the British forces in South America in 1807. He was blamed for the failure of the expedition and court-martialled.

6. Auguste-Marie-François Colbert (1777-1809).

7. General Sir Edward Paget (1775-1849).

8. This was one of the firing positions which the riflemen were taught to use.

9. In his *Random Shots from a Rifleman*, John Kincaid relates another version of this incident, but he was not a eyewitness either. He places the action at Cacabelos not Astorga, and credits Plunket not Paget with the initiative for shooting the general. In *The History of the Rifle Brigade*,

William Cope expressed doubt that Paget would have bribed a soldier to slay such a chivalrous and brave enemy, but enemy officers *were* a legitimate target for rifleman.

10. This appears to be born out at his discharge in 1817, which is ascribed to him 'being a very bad character and being nearly worn out in the service'. It seems that, by 1817, the memory of Plunket's virtues had been submerged beneath his vices, for his general conduct as a soldier is described as 'bad'.

11. Barclay, Perkins & Co. was a company which brewed beer. Established in 1781, it were based in Southwark.

CHAPTER 3: *To Talavera and Campo Maior, May - September 1809*

1. In the 1841 and 1852 editions of Costello's memoirs, the month of departure is given as March, which is wrong.

2. In Boswell's *Life*, Dr. Johnson expressed his dislike of life on board ship.

3. Robert Craufurd (1764-1812) had served in India, Ireland, and South America, and had commanded the Light Brigade during the Corunna campaign.

4. The men, many of them unaccustomed to the hot climate, were probably suffering from sunstroke. Leach: *"Three men of the latter corps [52nd] died between Santarem and this place [Castelo Branco], from the excessive heat and fatigue."*

5. Four hundred is an exaggeration, but the casualty rate over the next few months was very high. Between 25 June and 24 September, 43 of the 1st battalion had either died, were missing, or had deserted. Between 25 September and 24 December, the number had increased to 110 (13 of them from Costello's company), but by then the men were at Campo Maior in the unhealthy Alentejo region of Spain.

6. Leach described how he slept and what he ate: *"I was, unfortunately, one of those restless beings who, after a night spent in marching, could not sleep in the bivouac during the day. Many a time I have envied the happy fellows who lay down like dogs, under a cork-tree, and slept most soundly, until the rations of tough beef (perhaps killed only a few hours before), boiled into an 'omnium gatherum', with an onion or two, some rice, and a mouldy ship biscuit, were pronounced in a fit state for the table; the said dinner-table being neither more nor less than the turf at the foot of a tree, with a soldier's knapsack by way of camp-chair, which, with a pocket-knife, fork, and spoon, and a tin plate, constituted the whole of our dinner service."*

7. Sir William Napier, *History of the War in the Peninsula and in the South of France from 1807 to 1814*, first published 1827-40. Napier's figure was disputed by Willoughby Verner who points out that Spanish leagues, from which Napier's calculations were probably made, were variable. Many of the men who were on the march have accepted Napier's

estimation of the mileage. Verner, in his *History and Campaigns of the Rifle Brigade*, states that it was 42 English miles from Navalmoral to Talavera, which the men covered in 26 hours, of which nearly 17 were spent marching.

8. At this time, Wellington was still Sir Arthur Wellesley. He was created Viscount Wellington on 4 September 1809 as a consequence of his success at the battle of Talavera. The name Wellington is taken from the family estates in Somerset. He became an earl and then a marquess in 1812, and Duke of Wellington in May 1814.

9. Leach: *"To the best of my belief, not one issue of bread was made to the troops during the fortnight."* Harry Smith: *"Honey was plentiful, but it gave dysentery. My mess - Leach's Company (Leach, Smith, Layton, and Bob Beckwith) - were not as badly off as our neighbours. We had a few dollars, and as I could speak Spanish, I rode into the lines of the Spanish troops, where I could always purchase some loaves of bread at a most exorbitant price. With this, and some horrid starved goats, we lived tolerably for soldiers in hard times".*

CHAPTER 4: *Campo Maior and Elvas, September 1809 - February 1810*

1. The Honorouble Captain James H K Stewart commanded the 1st company. He joined as a 2nd lieutenant on 23 July 1803, was promoted to lieutenant in February 1804, and to captain on 1 August 1805.

2. William Johnston joined as a lieutenant on 20 November 1806. His fellow officers called him Willie, and it is possible that the soldiers called him by the same name. A biography of his service life, probably written by fellow Scot John Kincaid, was published in the *United Service Journal* in 1837.

3. In other line regiments, the floggings were usually administered by the drummers, who directed the movement of troops by the beat of a drum. In the 95th, these movement were conveyed by the notes of a bugle, so it was the buglers who were the floggers. William Green became a bugler in the 3rd company on 25 September 1810: *"It must be understood that we had no drums nor fifes; we had two buglers to each company, and three to the two flank companies, making 22. We always went with the company in action. I liked it very well as my pay was somewhat more."*

4. The records of the 95th are contradictory about Plunket's rank at this time. The muster roll states that he was demoted to private on 15 September, which suggests that he was flogged about that time, but an entry in the previous quarter says that he was *promoted* to sergeant on 17 September. Is it possible that he got back into favour with his officers within two days? Nevertheless, by 25 December he was a private again, and a private he remained. Plunket saw little action in the Peninsula after being hospitalised in June 1811. Kincaid says he was *"a bold, athletic Irishman, and a deadly shot; but the curse of his country was upon him, and I believe he was finally discharged, without receiving such a*

recompense as his merits in the field would otherwise have secured to him."

5.   Rifle lieutenant Harry Smith was also unaffected by the fever. He and the Hon. Capt. James Stewart organised the hunting. They got *"some excellent greyhounds. We were always out coursing or shooting, and were never sick for a day; our more sedentary comrades, many of them, were, distressingly so".* Tom Smith, Harry's brother, also in the 1st battalion, was one of those who succumbed to the fever. He travelled to Ouguela where Harry commanded 40-50 weakly Light Brigade convalescents. Harry's regimental comrades came to Ougela from Campo Maior every day to shoot. On one of these expeditions, they encountered 20 Spanish bandits, which a party of the less disabled convalescents cornered and captured in a small chapel. Six of the bandits were known criminals and were sent to nearby Badajoz, where they were sentenced to the galleys for life.

6.   Costello was in the General Hospital from 25 August 1809 to 16 January 1810, and was convalescent for several weeks after that.

7.   William Lawrence of the 40th Regiment, whose autobiography was first published in 1886, and who was recovering from the fever in one of the convents of the town, also witnessed this: *"Having recovered sufficiently to get about a little, I went on the ramparts. There a fearful spectacle met my gaze: the dead - completely naked - were being brought out of the convents, pitched into carts like so many pieces of wood, carried out of the town, and interred in holes scarcely large enough to admit such a number. This unpleasant office fell chiefly on Portuguese convicts and it surprised me to see how readily they went about their work, carrying one body at a time, the legs over their shoulders, and the head dangling down behind. The grave - the piece of ground appropriated for the burials - was so small that they had to pack their burdens with the greatest nicety."*

8.   William Green: *"Those who died were buried without shells about 11 or 12 o'clock at night, without any burial service, and without firing over them... A young man of the same company as myself, a native of Hinckley, fell ill of the fever, was taken to the dead-house and laid on a plank, with his feet tied together; he was to have been buried the same night. As the sentinel was on his post, he heard a noise in the dead-house. He called the corporal of the guard and the door was opened - the poor fellow had fallen off the plank, and was trying to get the string off his feet. He got well and rejoined the ranks with me. His name was John Moore."*

9.   The Hon. Captain Hercules R Pakenham was with the 40th Regiment before being appointed to the Rifles as a lieutenant on 28 April 1804. He was promoted to captain on 2 August 1805. He too was a veteran of the Corunna campaign. He transferred to the 7th West India Regiment as a Major on 30 August 1810.

10. On 22 February 1810, Private Cornelius Maguire (McGuire), 3rd batt. 27th Regt., and George Chambers, 1st batt. 88th Regt., were arraigned for stopping on the highway and forcibly robbing some Portuguese

inhabitants, notably Antonio Lopiz di Nis, on a march from Tondela to Vizeu on or about 20 February. They were found guilty and sentenced to be 'hanged by the neck until dead'. The sentence was confirmed by Wellington. The execution of Maguire was ordered to be carried out on the afternoon of 2 March in the presence of the troops stationed in Celorico, under the direction of the Assistant Provost of the 4th Division. Chambers was ordered to be executed on 3 March. These two men were used by Wellington as an example to the rest of the army, and he issued general orders expressing his determination to prevent such acts in future.

11. William Lawrence agrees: *"It was near Rodrigo that one of our cavalrymen was flogged for selfishly trading his horse's corn to buy himself grog. His poor horse was miserably thin, but then most of the horses looked like that, probably for the same reason. This was the first man to be caught and he was made an example of. He was tried by court-martial and sentenced to 50 lashes... It is true that horse's forage, particularly in winter, could not always be procured, which was why they had more need of it when it was available. During the Peninsular campaign, the best horses seemed to be those of the German hussars. The hussars had no more chance of gaining forage than our men did, but they were not so fond of drink, which probably accounts for the better condition of their animals."*

12. John Kincaid, who joined the 95th in Portugal later that same year: *"The 1st Regiment of Hussars were associated with our Division through the war, and were deserved favourites. In starting from a swampy couch and bowling along the road long ere dawn of day, it was one of the romances of a soldier's life to hear them chanting their national war songs, some three or four voices leading, and the whole squadron joining in the chorus... They were no less daring in the field than they were surpassingly good at outpost duty. The hussar was at all times identified with his horse; he shared his bed and his board, and their movements were always regulated by the importance of their mission. If we saw a British dragoon at any time approaching at full speed, it excited no great curiosity among us, but whenever we saw one of the 1st Hussars coming on at a gallop, it was high time to gird on our swords and bundle up."*

CHAPTER 5: *Barba del Puerco and Gallegos, 1 March - 9 July 1810*

1. In previous editions, the river is named incorrectly as the Coa.

2. Lt. James Mercer joined on 13 March 1806 as a 2nd lieutenant, and became a first lieutenant on 3 March 1808.

3. There were three Coanes in the 95th between 1804 and 1812 - Alexander, Anthony and James, but by March 1810 only Alexander remained. He had joined as a 2nd lieutenant from the 59th Regt. on 19 November 1807 and was promoted to lieutenant on 4 June 1809. In the 1841 edition, the surname is transcribed as Cohen.

4. In the 1841 and 1852 editions, Thomas Maher's surname is transcribed as Meagher, but regimental records spell it Maher. In Chapter 25, Costello relates this man's experiences during the Waterloo campaign.

5. Kincaid explains this as *"a name given by our soldiers to the point of war which is beat by the French drummers in advancing to the charge. I have, when skirmishing in a wood, and a French regiment coming up to the relief of the opposing skirmishers, often heard the drum long before we saw them, and on those occasions, our riflemen immediately began calling to each other, from behind the different bushes. 'Halloa there! look sharp! for damme me, but here comes old trousers!'"*

6. Simmons' explanation of how Beckwith came so near to being shot in the head is a little different: *"A young Frenchman that was taken, fired into Colonel Beckwith's face. A rifleman was just going to blow his brains out, when the Colonel stopped him, saying, 'Let him alone; I daresay the boy has a mother. Knock the thing out of his hand, that he may do no more mischief with it, give him a kick on the bottom, and send him to the rear'. The next morning, the boy was given a hearty breakfast at the Colonel's house. On being questioned about firing so wantonly, he said he was in such agitation that he was not aware his finger was upon the trigger of his gun. The ball went through the Colonel's cap peak which, being turned up, made it take a slanting direction; it passed through and grazed the top of his head."*

7. George Ballard's (Ballar/Baller) courage did not go unrecognised. On 25 January 1811, he was promoted from a private in Costello's company to a corporal in the 2nd. On 25 March 1812 he was promoted to sergeant, a rank he held for many years.

8. There were two officers of the name of Stewart who were killed on the advance from Santarem in March 1811, Lt. James Stewart and Major John Stewart. Another Stewart, the Honourable James H K, was captain of the 1st battalion's 1st company. The adjutant Costello refers to was Lt. James Stewart who joined as a 2nd lieutenant on 2 June 1804, and became a 1st lieutenant on 6 May 1805. He was killed at Freixedas on 28 March 1811.

9. John Kincaid had a better opinion of the Portuguese soldiers, but agreed with Costello about their fondness for cards: *"Although the two caçadore regiments attached to our Division were, at all times, in the highest order, and conducted themselves gallantly in the field, yet I am of the opinion that, as a nation, they owe their character for bravery almost entirely to the activity and gallantry of the British officers who organised and led them. The veriest cowards in existence must have shown the same front under such discipline... The soldiers, though fainting with fatigue on the line of march, invariably group themselves in card-parties whenever they are allowed a few minutes' halt, and a non-commissioned officer, with half a dozen men on any duty of fatigue, are very generally to be seen as follows, viz. one man as a sentry to watch the approach of the superintending officer, one man at work, and the non-commissioned officer, with the other four, at cards."*

10. George Elder joined the 95th as a 2nd lieutenant on 5 November 1800, was promoted to 1st lieutenant on 24 March 1803, and to captain on 23 May 1805. He became a major on 13 April 1809, being appointed the same day to special service in Portugal. He was promoted to Lt.- Col. on the Portuguese and Spanish staff on 30 May 1811, and died at Madras in 1830 after falling from his horse.

11. In previous editions, mistakenly identified as the 3rd regiment

12. Harry Smith was with one of the most advanced videttes, who was a German of the 1st Hussars. The rifle officers had orders to watch the enemy with their telescopes but the Germans were able to observe a patrol or body of men with the naked eye. The rifle officers on this duty were allowed to take with them only their horses and their telescopes, so Harry Smith, who grew hungry waiting for his servant to arrive with his dinner, was pleased to accept the one provided for him by the ingenious hussar, who kept everything he needed with him. Within ten minutes, Smith was enjoying bacon broiled on the embers of their fire, and a cup of coffee with sugar and biscuit. He could only repay the German in kind when his servant arrived.

13. Simmons said that the Duke was also being kept informed by the guerilla leader Don Julian Sanchez who, with his orderly, dashed through the French outposts to maintain communication with the Governor. It was also reported that the Governor sent a letter to the Duke via an old man.

14. 2 April 1810.

CHAPTER 6: *Battle of the Coa, 10 - 24 July 1810*

1. Harry Smith describes Fort Conception as *"the neatest fortification I ever saw, and the masonry beautifully executed"*.

2. Leach agrees that the force which Craufurd sent to oppose the French patrol was large - seven companies of the 1st batt. 95th, two companies of the 52nd, two pieces of artillery, the 14th Light Dragoons, and part, or all, of the 1st German Hussars.

3. Leach on these same two cavalry actions: *"Their troop of cavalry was soon sabred and made prisoners, but with their infantry it was otherwise. Instantly forming a small square, they retired rapidly and in good order, in the direction of the ford... No troops on earth could have conducted themselves with greater gallantry than the old and often-tried 14th Light Dragoons... Colonel Talbot, whose body I saw a few minutes after he was killed, bore the marks not only of bullets but of bayonets, and it is true that he and many of his brave fellows who actually reached the square, met their death by the bayonets of this invincible little body of Frenchmen, who steadily resisted their charges. Without leaving in our hands any of their brave band, they succeeded in making good their retreat over the plain."*

4. John Garlies McCulloch, a Scot, joined as a 2nd lieutenant on 11 July 1805, and was promoted to first lieutenant on 16 December 1807. His

wounds did not prevent him from escaping from the French and returning to his battalion, but he was wounded again in March 1811, when he lost the use of one arm. He was promoted to captain on 21 October 1812, and to major on 21 December 1815, despite losing the use of his other arm as a consequence of a wound acquired at Waterloo. John Kincaid gives more details of McCullock's colourful career, and his untimely death in London in 1818, in his *Random Shots of a Rifleman*.

5.   Coane survived this action but died in 1812.

6.   Thomas Charity, from Cambridge, joined in April 1805. He was transferred to the 3rd company when the 9th was disbanded. Although only 34 when discharged in 1817, he was described as 'old and weakly'. He had black hair, black eyes and a dark complexion. He was recommended for a pension, and his conduct as a soldier was 'good'.

7.   This was a footnote in the 1852 edition of Costello's book. The musket ball was extracted on 27 July 1869, at Costello's request, after his death, by the Medical Officer at the Tower of London. This ball, and another which took off his trigger finger at Quatre Bras in 1817, are on display at the Royal Green Jackets Museum in Winchester.

8.   There was no Little in the 1st battalion. There was a Robert Liddle in the 8th Company, but he appears to have suffered neither wounds nor capture during this battle. However, John Lidiner, who *was* in Costello's company, was taken prisoner that day, and remained a POW until December 1811 at least.

9.   It is interesting to speculate on the identity of this comrade because William Green, who was neither wounded nor taken prisoner, states that, during this action, he *"carried a poor fellow on my back about half a mile; he had a musket ball through his thigh."*

CHAPTER 7: *Belem and Arruda, 25 July - November 1810*

1.   Harry Smith: *"In collecting transport for the wounded, a sedan chair between two mules was brought, the property of some gentleman in the neighbourhood, and fortunately for me, I was the only person who could ride in it. By laying my leg on the one seat, and sitting on the other, I rode comparatively easy to the poor fellows in the wretched bullock carts, who suffered excruciating agony; poor brother Tom (who was very severely wounded above the knee) among the rest."*

2.   M Pratt joined as a 2nd lieutenant on 18 May 1805, and became a lieutenant on 23 March 1807. Simmons' journal reveals that Pratt died on 1 August, after they had boarded the boats to take them down the Mondego: *"Pratt went ashore to get some milk for our breakfast, as we rested to give the rowers breathing time. I suppose the exertion he used, the day being very hot, had assisted to remove the slough in the wound in his throat, the carotid artery being injured; he died instantly from one gush of blood."* Harry Smith: *"At one house a landlord was most insolent to us, and Lt. Pratt, shot through the neck, got very angry. The carotid artery must*

have been wounded, for it burst out in a torrent of blood, and he was dead in a few seconds, to our horror, for he was a most excellent fellow."

3. Simmons: *"Oil was found the best thing to take them away, as when applied, it killed them, obstructing their breathing."*

4. Harry and Tom Smith were not taken to the hospital but were billeted, in awful agony, in a 'miserable empty house'. Tom's leg was so bad that he was sent home to England. During his convalescence, Harry Smith was billeted with George Simmons, and both of them bathed in the sea to improve their health.

5. On his MGS Medal, Costello has a bar for Busaco yet, on his own admission here, he was not at the battle.

6. Samuel Mitchell joined the Rifles as a lieutenant from the 71st Regiment on 6 August 1802. He was promoted to captain on 9 May 1805, a major on 2 September 1813. He became a Lt.-Col. in the 31st Regiment in 1829, and died at Berhampore in 1833.

7. William McNabb, of the 1st company, was in the General Hospital in December 1810 and remained 'convalescent in Belem' until 24 June 1811, when he was invalided to England. He had joined the 95th in Antrim on 21 July 1800, having served in the Dunbarton fencibles since 1794. His 1800 attestation papers describe him as a merchant from Falkirk, Stirling, and it appears that he was literate. Apparently, McNabb remained in the 1st battalion throughout the Peninsular War, though he may not have fought in it. Given Costello's testimony, it is surprisingly to find his name on the roll call for the Waterloo campaign. What is less surprising is that, afterwards, instead of remaining in France with his battalion, he was sent back to the army depot on the Isle of Wight while his case was 'finally determined'. It was decided that he should be discharged on the grounds that he was old, worn out, and unfit for further service abroad. There appears to have been no obvious blot on his record because, in a letter attached to his papers, Colonel Barnard states that McNabb had always conducted himself well and was deserving of the consideration of the Board (in the matter of a pension). He was discharged on 26 April 1816.

8. In his 1967 edition of Costello's memoirs, Anthony Brett-James explains that General Sir David Dundas (1735-1820) was the author of *Principles of Military Movements, chiefly applicable to Infantry*, published in 1788.

9. There is no evidence that Hetherington was a rifleman. Costello mentions him three times, but on every occasion the situation is one in which men of different regiments were thrown together.

10. A few companies only; the majority were in Cadiz, as was John Wilkie.

11. On 25 October, Simmons records that he found an old woman dead, near the altar of the church at Arruda, and that he and Lt. John Strode did her a final service by placing her in a splendid vault, which they opened with a crowbar. Kincaid also claims a part in this affair: *"The day*

after our arrival, Mr Simmons and myself had the curiosity to look into the church, which was in nowise injured, and was fitted up in a style of magnificence becoming such a town. The body of a poor old woman was there, lying dead before the altar. It seemed as if she had been too infirm to join in the general flight, and had just dragged herself to that spot by a last effort of nature, and expired. We immediately determined that, as hers was the only body we had found in the town, either alive or dead, that she should have more glory in the grave than she appeared to have enjoyed this side of it and, with our united exertions, we succeeded in raising a marble slab, which surmounted a monumental vault, and was beautifully embellished with armorial blazonry. Depositing the body inside, we replaced it again carefully."

In his *Random Shots*, Kincaid describes how, in the thatch of a deserted cottage in Arruda, under his company's post, two soldiers discovered two silver salvers, which the captain of the company ordered to be placed in safekeeping. Such a rich discovery set the soldiers prowling about in the neighbourhood, hoping for similar discoveries. Not long after, the Portuguese owner of the cottage arrived to claim some plate he had concealed at the cottage, but when he was shown the salvers, he said they were not his. Says Kincaid: *"What he wished to remove was concealed under the dunghill, and he accordingly proceeded there and dug out about a cart load of gold and silver articles, which he carried off, while our unsuccessful searchers stood by, cursing their mutual understanding which had suffered such a prize to slip through their fingers. Many an innocent heap of manure was afterwards torn to pieces in consequence of that morning's lesson."*

In the deserted house at Arruda that he shared with fellow officers, Kincaid found a very fine saddle. *"The seat was as soft as a pillow, and covered with crimson silk velvet, beautifully embroidered, and gilt round the edges."* When the battalion left Arruda to pursue Massena, that soft saddle went with it, lodged firmly between Kincaid's bottom and his horse. It was worth far more than the few *vintems* for which Private McGuire was hung for stealing six month's earlier.

12. William Lawrence of the 40th also recalls friendly relations with the French at this time.

CHAPTER 8: *Winter Quarters before Santarem, Nov. 1810 - February 1811*

1. There were three John Murphys in the 3rd company: a labourer from Kilhaven in Co. Wexford, a whitesmith from Balinaslaney in Co. Wexford, and a mason from Cashel in Co. Tipperary.

2. Harry Smith and the Hon. James Stewart spent their leisure hours coursing on the plains of Valle, using Moro, Smith's Spanish hound. The Duke of Wellington also coursed. He had his own dog which he wanted to run against Moro.

3. Some of the Brunswickers tried to desert on 17 January. William Hay, a new recruit to the 52nd Regiment, heard the commotion: *"One night,*

after we had retired to rest, we were called up by the alarm sounding 'to arms', and several shots were fired toward the front. It turned out, however, to be 14 of those unfortunate men making an attempt to desert to the enemy. Some were shot by the picket, and five were taken prisoners. These were tried by court-martial and condemned to be shot." According to general orders, 10 of these deserters were court-martialled at Cartaxo on the 19th. Found guilty, four were shot on the afternoon of 23 January, but the other six, who had been sentenced to 200 lashes each, were pardoned. The first blood William Hay saw shed in the Peninsula was at the execution of the four Brunswickers: *"The Division was drawn up for the purpose, and the sentence carried into execution on four of them; the fifth, a mere child, was pardoned, after having had his eyes bandaged, etc. The whole spectacle I did not forget for some time."* Wellington then directed that the rest of the corps should be sent away from the Light Division.

4. Patrick Fleming was not a sergeant at the time, but a corporal in Costello's company. He was promoted to sergeant, in the same company, on 21 March 1812, only two weeks before the storming of Badajoz, in which he was killed.

CHAPTER 9: *In Pursuit of Massena, February - 13 March 1811*

1. Kincaid: *"The few starved male inhabitants who were stalking amid the wreck of their friends and property, looked like so many skeletons who had been permitted to leave their graves for the purpose of taking vengeance on their oppressors; and the mangled body of every Frenchman who was unfortunate or imprudent enough to stray from his column, showed how religiously they performed their mission."*

2. Simmons: *"The houses were nearly all unroofed, and the people in a starving condition. Two young ladies had been brutally violated in a house that I entered, and were unable to rise from a mattress of straw."*

3. Green: *"The German hussars and the 4th heavy dragoons soon overtook us; the latter carried our knapsacks that we might run and keep up with their horses at full trot, which we did."*

4. John Palmer and Thomas Treacy (Treacey/Tracy/Tracey) were in Costello's company. John Palmer, a labourer from Abingdon in Berkshire, joined the 1st batt. on 26 August 1807, and served with it until 25 October 1814. On 16 July 1816, he joined the 3rd batt. and served until 12 December 1818, when it was disbanded.

    Thomas Treacy, from Roscrea, Co Tipperary, had also been a labourer. He joined the 26th Regiment in May 1805, and then the 95th in March 1807. He served until 23 June 1823. On leaving the army, his conduct was described as 'Irregular. Has served in Germany, Denmark, during the whole of the Peninsular War and at Waterloo, and has been twice wounded'. He was then 44, 5'8½" tall with dark hair, hazel eyes and a fresh complexion, and he was illiterate.

5. Fleming was a corporal at the time.

6. Lt. John Hopwood joined as a 2nd lieutenant on 13 April 1809. He was promoted to 1st lieutenant on 6 February 1811, the same day Simmons transferred out of O'Hare's company and into Beckwith's. He was killed at Arcangues on 10 December 1813.

7. The baggage belonged to Colonel Pierre Soult, brother of Marshal Soult.

8. Kincaid: *"We light folks were employed in the early part of the action clearing the opposing lights from the woods which flanked his position; and in the course of an hour about 30,000 British, as if by magic, were seen advancing on the plain in three lines, with the order and precision of a field day."*

9. One of the prisoners recovered was the rifleman who fell at Pombal, shot through the roof of the mouth. They found him, said Green, *"in an out-house. The French doctor had dressed his wounds very nicely, but being unable to march, they left him. His name was John Ibbertson; he never could speak plain after. He was sent to England with some others who were wounded, and was discharged with a pension."*

10. William Balvaird joined the 95th from the 94th as a captain on 15 August 1805. His 10th company was disbanded in February 1810, but a few months later he took over command of the 5th company from Pakenham. He became a Brevet Major on 22 November 1813, a Major on 21 July 1814, and Brevet Lieutenant-Colonel of the regiment on 21 June 1817, when it was stationed in France after the Waterloo campaign.

11. By March 1811, Humphrey Allen had been in the military services for almost 17 years. A labourer from Rock in Worcestershire, he was in the Royal Marines (1794-1798), and the Ross & Cromarty Fencibles (1799-1802), before joining the 95th in Aberdeen on 18 May 1802 for Unlimited Service, at the age of 29. Present in the Peninsula throughout the war, he was wounded at Corunna, and fought in the Waterloo campaign of 1815. In 1811, he was in the 5th company. He was discharged in February 1818 when he was about 45 years old and, according to his discharge papers, was experiencing epileptic fits. He was 6' tall, with brown hair and hazel eyes. In a footnote to the 1841 edition of his book, Costello recorded a recent sighting of Allen in London: *"Any of my readers passing through Knightsbridge may chance to observe a tall military figure, bent with years, a bag thrown over his shoulders, stooping to pick up bones, etc. This person is no other than the once redoubtable Humphrey Allen, one of the smartest and finest looking men in our Rifles."*

CHAPTER 10: *Casal Nova, Foz de Arouce and Sabugal, 13 March - 7 April 1811*

1. Simmons: *"I ordered some soldiers to remove several chairs and some straw under a staircase, which was then on fire. By this timely removal, the house was saved, and most likely many others."*

2. John Stewart joined the Rifles as a lieutenant from the 79th Regt. in August 1800. He was appointed captain on 11 March 1802, and major on 10 December 1807. At Casal Nova, says Simmons: *"Poor Major Jack Stewart, a dear little fellow, a friend of mine, was shot through the lungs and died in three days."* Leach: *"By his death the regiment was deprived of an officer who thoroughly understood the command of light troops, and was quite at home at outpost duty. He had a quick and accurate eye in taking advantage of ground, was devoted to the particular nature of our service, and his mind soared far above the uninteresting minutiae of barrack-yard drill, the exact distance from button to button on the soldier's jacket, the width of his leather stock, and other matters of the kind."*

3. O'Hare was promoted to major on 11 April 1811. Lt. John Uniacke, who was promoted to captain a few weeks later on 1 May, took over the command of O'Hare's 3rd company.

4. John P Strode joined with John Kincaid on 30 March 1809 from the North York Militia, in which Strode had been a captain and Kincaid a lieutenant. They brought with them sufficient numbers of militiamen to gain commissions in the 95th. Before his militia service, Strode had been with the 7th Fusiliers and with the 96th Regiment. At Casal Nova, he was in the same company as Simmons. Harry Smith: *"Strode, a lieutenant, received his death wound while talking to me."* Before dying at Coimbra. Strode gave his rifle to Simmons, who carried it into action at Foz de Arouce a few days later, when the butt was shattered by a musket ball.

5. These comments about officers carrying rifles was a footnote in the 1841 edition.

6. In November 1811, Patrick Mahone (Mahony/Mahoney/Mayon) of the 8th company, was invalided to England. This is the same Patrick Mahone who joined in Ireland on 10 September 1806, at about the same time as Benjamin Harris. He later fought in the Waterloo campaign.

7. Green was one. He fell sick, and soon after the action at Casal Nova, was conveyed to Coimbra where he remained for about 6 weeks, four of them as a groom to the wounded Lt. Hopwood. He rejoined the battalion shortly before the action at Fuentes de Oñoro.

8. So pleased was Wellington with the conduct of the 95th at Foz de Arouce that he mentioned them in his despatch to Lord Liverpool. In a general order of the same date (16 March 1811), as a sign of his particular approbation, he requested the commanding officers of the 43rd, 52nd and 95th regiments to name a sergeant in each to be recommended for promotion to ensign. The man chosen from the Rifles was Sergeant Simpson, then acting Sergeant-Major, who was appointed an ensign in the 2nd (Queen's) Regiment of Foot.

9. The Humane Society was founded in 1776 for the rescue of drowning persons. I wonder what Costello means when he refers to the 'men of the wooden shoes'?

10. This sight is mentioned by nearly every autobiographer present. It affected them all deeply. Kincaid: *"So disgusted and savage were our soldiers at the sight, that the poor donkeys would have been amply revenged had fate at that moment placed 500 Frenchmen in our hands, for I am confident that every one of them would have undergone the same operation."*

11. Kincaid visited a church on the other side of the river from the village. He found *"the doors standing wide open, the valuable paintings destroyed, the statues thrown down, and mixed with them on the floor lay the bodies of six or seven murdered Portuguese peasants. It was a cruel and a horrible sight, and yet in the midst thereof I was tempted to commit a most sacrilegious act, for round the neck of a prostrate marble female image, I saw a bone necklace of rare and curious workmanship - the only thing that seemed to have been saved from the general wreck - which I very coolly transferred to my pocket, and in due time to my portmanteau."*

12. There was only one Wilkie in the 95th and that was John Wilkie, who joined with Costello. This incident at Mello may have occurred as Costello describes it, but it cannot possibly have been Wilkie who was his companion. On 25 April 1809, Wilkie, probably on account of his lack of previous military training, was transferred out of the 1st battalion, which was about to embark for the Peninsula, and into the newly-formed 3rd battalion. The muster lists, and the account of William Surtees, who was the 3rd battalion's quartermaster, reveal that they remained in Hythe until June 1810 when several companies, which included Wilkie, sailed to Cadiz to a posting on the Isla de Leon. It was not until 21 August 1811, five months after the incident at Mello, that these same companies joined Wellington's army in Portugal. Unfortunately, this is not the only discrepancy I have unearthed in Costello's account of Wilkie's career in the Rifles (see Notes to Chapter 13).

13. Kincaid: *"He imprudently rode into the main street of the village, followed by a few riflemen, before the French had time to withdraw from it, and was shot from a window."* James Stewart had joined the 95th as a 2nd lieutenant on 2 June 1804 and was promoted to lieutenant on 6 May 1805. Leach: *"He was open-hearted, manly, friendly, and independent, a most gallant and zealous officer, and much devoted to his own corps. He neither cringed to, nor worshipped any man, but did his duty manfully, and with impartiality - two qualities inestimable in adjutants. By the soldiers he was idolised, and very justly."* Simmons recalls that the riflemen were so enraged at the manner of Stewart's death that it was only with difficulty that they were prevented from taking revenge upon some French prisoners.

14. Arbuthnot had joined on 20 August 1807, having served in the 77th Regiment and the 6th Garrison Battalion. Two officers of the 1st battalion (Colonel Beckwith and Lt. Haggup), and 12 men were wounded at Sabugal.

CHAPTER 11: *Fuentes de Oñoro, 8 April - 10 May 1811*

1. There were several 1st battalion riflemen called Burke. In 1811, there were two James Burkes, one a labourer from Curlingford, Kilkenny. The Burke referred to by Costello was in the forlorn hope at San Sebastian, a duty which Kincaid tried to prevent him taking (see Notes to Chapter 21). He died in France on 29 June 1815, the action at Quatre Bras being fought on 16 June. The other James Burke joined the battalion on 11 September 1809. He was also in the Waterloo campaign.

2. William Tidey (Tidy) was in Costello's company.

3. In the riflemen's autobiographies, there are several stories (or variations of the same one?) in which a pair German brothers, both hussars but fighting on opposite sides, encounter one another upon the field of battle.

CHAPTER 12: *Almeida and El Bodon, 10 May 1811 - January 1812*

1. According to Verner, the person responsible for this failure may have been the ever unpopular Sir William Erskine, then in charge of the 5th Division, who apparently pocketed Wellington's order to Colonel Bevan to hold the bridge, and then forgot about it.

2. General Rowland Hill (1772-1842).

3. The Great Comet of 1811 was one of the most spectacular on record. The head - the coma - was larger than the sun; its tail was long and straight and stretched a third of the way across the sky. Two months later, lying out in the open on a particularly cold night, Kincaid refers to *"the wonderful comet of 1811, that made such a capital claret, and wishing that he would wag his fiery tail a little nearer to my face, for it was so stiff with hoar-frost that I dared neither to laugh nor cry for fear of breaking it."*

4. Joseph Burke MD, had been appointed assistant surgeon to the 97th Regiment in November 1802, and had joined the 95th as surgeon on 29 June 1809. He remained with the Rifles until 1828, when he went on half pay. He died in Dublin on 16 September 1838.

5. In his *Random Shots* of 1835, Kincaid describes an incident so similar, that it may be the same one. There were many venomous reptiles and scorpions at Reguengo but, says Kincaid, they caused only one casualty in his regiment, and that was *"to a soldier who had somehow swallowed a lizard. He knew not when or how, and the first hint he had of the tenement being so occupied, was in being troubled with internal pains and the spitting of blood, which continued for many months, in spite of all the remedies that were administered. But a powerful emetic eventually caused him to be delivered of as ugly a child of the kind as one would wish to look at, about three inches long. I believe that Dr. Burke, late of the Rifles, has it still preserved."*

6. Harry Smith says that Beckwith went to the rear suffering from violent ague.

7. On 25 July 1811, Thomas Sarsfield joined the 95th as a 2nd lieutenant, and there is every likelihood that he was not only Costello's Tommy Searchfield, but the Tommy Dangerfield referred to by John Kincaid in *Random Shots*. If so, Kincaid was one of the officers who baited him.

   Kincaid's Dangerfield was of middle height, *"rather bull shouldered and walking with bent knees. His face was a fresh good-natured one, but with the usual sinister cast in the eye worn by common Irish country countenances. In short, Tommy was rather a good-looking. and in reality, not a bad fellow, and the only mistake which he seemed to have made was in the choice of his profession... I don't know whether we differed from other regiments in the same respect, but our first and most uncharitable aim was to discover the weak points of every fresh individual, and to attack him through them. If he had redeeming qualities, he of course came out unscathed, but if not he was dealt with most unmercifully. Poor Tommy had none such; he was weak on all sides, and therefore went to the wall."*

   When he joined the 95th, Sarsfield was in a difficult position because, although a gentleman, he was not really an officer; but neither was he a common soldier. This anomaly can be explained by the fact that he was a volunteer, which Kincaid describes as a well connected young man, *"who, being without the necessary influence to obtain a commission at home,"* could get *"a letter of introduction to the commander of the forces in the field, who, if he approves, attaches them to regiments, and while they are treated as gentlemen out of the field, they receive the pay, and do the duty of private soldiers in it... and, if a bullet does not provide for him in the meantime, he eventually succeeds to the commission of some officer who has fallen in action."*

   Sarsfield was promoted to first lieutenant on 21 October 1813. He transferred to the 47th Regiment in April 1815, and died at Grattan's Hill, Cork in January 1840. He was alive when Kincaid's *Random Shots* was published, which may account for his surname being disguised as Dangerfield.

8. The battle of Talavera was fought on 28 July 1809.

9. In early 1810, there were four Kitchens in the 1st battalion - George (8th company), James and William (5th company), and John (3rd company). The only Kitchen to make sergeant was William, although not until 14 October 1812. At the time of these events, he was a corporal, having been promoted on 24 July 1811.

10. Doctor Sangrado of Valladolid, who features in *Gil Blas*.

11. Kincaid: *"About the middle of the night, we received an order to stand to our arms with as little noise as possible, and to commence retiring. The rest of the army had been already withdrawn, unknown to us- an instance of the rapidity and uncertainty of our movements, which proved fatal to the liberty of several amateurs and followers of the army who, seeing an army of 60,000 men lying asleep around their camp-fires at 10 o'clock at night, naturally concluded that they might safely indulge in a bed in the village behind until daylight, without the risk of being caught napping; but long*

ere that time, they found themselves on the high road to Ciudad Rodrigo, in the rude grasp of an enemy."

CHAPTER 13: *Ciudad Rodrigo, 4 - 20 January 1812*

1. Verner says that Colbourne had 10 companies for the task, two from the 43rd, two from each of the battalions of the 52nd, two from the Rifles, and one company from each Caçadore Regiment (650-700 men). However, Colbourne may have detailed only four companies for the actual storming party, which is why most of the autobiographers who were present state that the numbers of stormers was between 300-400.

2. Preventing the Portuguese from assaulting and stripping the prisoners?

3. In the 1841 and 1852 editions, Costello identifies this division as the 3rd, but Simmons, Leach, and Kincaid say it was the 1st.

4. Simmons: *"The weather was keen and it froze sharply. Our poor fellows had to cross the river nearly up to their shoulders, and remain in this wet state until they returned to their quarters."*

5. Capt. Samuel Mitchell, and Lts. William Johnston (?) and John Kincaid.

6. John Uniacke joined as a 2nd lieutenant in July 1804. He was promoted to 1st lieutenant on 9 May 1805 and to captain on 1 May 1811, when he took over the command of the 3rd company from Peter O'Hare.

7. Simmons, who before the assault had fetched the ladders and handed them to the Portuguese, was also there and was *"saved from being blown up with a friend of mine, Lt. Uniacke... When we got into the ditch together he observed, 'This is the way'. In the bustle I said, 'Impossible. Here are the ladders; I shall go up them,' fancying my Portuguese friend had placed them right. Ultimately the ladders served me; poor Uniacke got round the corner just in time to get scorched from head to foot in a frightful manner."*

8. John Wilkie was not killed at the storming of Ciudad Rodrigo because by 19 January he was already dead. He died on 11 December after a long illness. From October he was in the General Hospital, and a large number of 3rd battalion riflemen were either with him in hospital, or convalescent in Belem. Why Costello chose to lie about Wilkie's fate, I cannot say. Perhaps he felt that Wilkie's parents would prefer to hear that their son had died bravely in battle rather than in hospital of disease alongside 30 of his comrades?

9. While they were clearing their foes from the ramparts, the riflemen were not always humane. Kincaid: *"On going a little further, we came opposite to the ravelin... It was still crowded by the enemy, who had now thrown down their arms, and endeavoured to excite our pity by virtue of their being 'Pauvres Italianos'; but our men had somehow imbibed a horrible antipathy to the Italians, and every appeal they made in that name was invariably answered with, 'You're Italian, are you? Then, damn you, here's a shot for you', and the action instantly followed the word."*

10. The firing was indiscriminate and, says Kincaid: *"some heads began to be blown from their shoulders in the general hurricane, when the voice of Sir Thomas Picton, with the power of 20 trumpets, began to proclaim damnation to everybody, while Colonel Barnard, Colonel Cameron, and some other active officers, were carrying it into effect with a strong hand. Seizing the broken barrels of muskets, which were lying about in great abundance, they belaboured most unmercifully about the head, every fellow who attempted either to load or fire, and finally succeeded in reducing them to order. In the midst of the scuffle, however, three of the houses in the square were set on fire, and the confusion was such that nothing could be done to save them."*

11. A common defence in siege situations, a *chevaux de frise* was a large beam studded with long spikes, or swords, and placed in front of, and across, the breaches to impede the enemy's advance.

12. A puncheon is of variable capacity, but usually extremely large, capable of holding 70-120 gallons.

13. Leach: *"Bodies with limbs, and limbs without bodies, were scorched and scattered about in different directions. The houses near the breaches were filled with such of the wounded as were able to crawl away from the ramparts, with a view to find shelter from the severe frost, which numbed their wounds."*

14. Lt. John Cooke of the 43rd, met Uniacke as he was being helped from the breach: *"I ran towards the large breach, and met an officer slowly walking between two soldiers of the rifle corps. I asked who it was, when he faintly replied, 'Uniacke' and walked on. One of his eyes was blown out, and the flesh was torn off his arms and legs."*

CHAPTER 14: *Burials and Executions, 20 January - 17 March 1812*

1. 'Corporal Miles' cannot be identified with any accuracy in the muster lists of the 1st battalion, therefore the date of this court-martial is not known.

2. Harry Smith joined as a 2nd lieutenant on 8 May 1805 and was promoted to lieutenant on 15 August 1805. He served in South America and was on the retreat to Corunna but, disappointingly, his autobiography records almost nothing of his experiences during the two campaigns. In March 1808, he helped to obtain a commission in the 95th for his brother Thomas, who was promoted to first lieutenant on 7 June 1809. Harry Smith became a captain on 28 February 1812 and took over Uniacke's 3rd company, but being on the staff, the command was held by his brother, who never attained the rank of captain. In 1819, Thomas Smith went on half-pay, and in 1824 he became barrack master at Rutland. He retired in 1833, but served as barrack master at Roscrea, Galway, Parsontown, and finally in December 1838, at Chatham.

3. In the notes to the previous chapter, Kincaid discloses the dislike many of the riflemen had for Italians serving in the French army.

4. In the 1841 and 1852 editions, this name is transcribed as Hudson. He was in the 4th company. He rejoined from desertion on 21 February, which was probably the date of the executions.

5. Cummins was not a corporal at the time. The muster lists of the 1st battalion offer no evidence that the riflemen deserted together: Mills deserted on 2 December, McInnes on 5 December, and Hodgson on 10 December.

6. William Green: *"At their execution, 'the Dead March of Saul' was played by the band."*

7. Kincaid regarded the scene with disquiet: *"Shooting appears to me to be a cruel kind of execution, for twenty balls may pierce a man's body without touching a vital spot."*
    Surtees: *"I cannot describe the uncomfortable feelings this spectacle produced in my mind. Nay, not only there, but in my body also, for I felt sick at heart. A sort of loathing ensued; and from the recollection of what I then suffered, I could not easily be persuaded to witness such another scene, if I had the option of staying away. Death in the hundred shapes it assumes on the field of battle seems honourable, and not near so revolting to the feelings, and withal comes suddenly; but to witness the slow and melancholy preparations for an execution such as this, is productive in any heart that can feel, of the most unpleasant sensation imaginable."* One of the deserters was *"a little shoemaker in our Highland company, by name McGuiness [Malcolm McInnes], whom I had known for many years, and who formerly bore an excellent character; but he had most likely been seduced by some of his companions to commit this heinous crime."*

8. In the 1841 edition of Costello' *Adventures*, this man's name is given as Ormond, but in the 1852 edition it was was changed to Arnal. The regimental records confirm that he was Joseph Almond (or Allman).

9. Kincaid says with some admiration that *"when he was paraded for that purpose, he protested against their right to shoot him, until he first received the arrears of pay which were due at the time of his desertion."*

CHAPTER 15: *The Siege of Badajoz, 17 March - 5 April 1812*

1. James Brooks, from Leicestershire, was in Costello's company. He was killed on 21 March. Before joining the 95th, he had been a frameworker and knitter. According to the muster list, Thomas Treacy was not hospitalised as a consequence of this injury.

2. It is not clear whether Green and Gea were sappers or riflemen. William Green was from Lutterworth in Leicestershire, which is not far from Coventry, but he makes no mention of these events and, according to his own account, was wounded in the thigh and hand by a musket ball at the storming of Badajoz, not by a cannon-shot a week or two before.

3. From December 1810 at least, Sergeant Esau Jackson of the 3rd company was at Belem in charge of the stores. He was demoted from

sergeant to private on 25 March 1812. Corporal George Ballard of the 2nd Company, had been promoted from private after the skirmish at Barba del Puerco in March 1810.

CHAPTER 16: *The Storming of Badajoz, 6 - 9 April 1812*

1. Verner notes that the order of dress that night was *"without stocks or packs, and with trousers rolled up to the knee".*

2. William Lawrence was one of the ladder party for the 4th Division. His experiences mirror Costello's.

3. Lawrence: *"At the breach, a French sentry on the wall cried out three times 'Who comes there?' No answer being given, a shower of shot, canister and grape, together with fire-balls, was hurled amongst us... I received two small slug shots in my left knee and a musket shot in my side. Despite my wounds, I stuck to my ladder and got into the entrenchment."*

4. Harry Smith: *"The first shot from us brought down such a hail of fire as I shall never forget, nor ever saw before or since. It was most murderous."*

5. Sgt. Robert Fairfoot saw Green, gave him some rum from his flask, apologised for not being able to carry him out of the reach of shot, then went forward, only to be wounded himself. Green *"The whole of the Division made for the breach. A tremendous fire was going on. I heard the bugle-major sound the advance and double-quick. I rolled on my back (for I had fallen on my side) and repeated the sound... As another division came past me, an officer with a sword drawn stepped up to me and said, 'Desist blowing that bugle, you are drawing all the fire on my men!'"* When the firing slackened, Green was able to the hobble to the rear where two bandsmen with a stretcher carried him to the doctor. His part in the war was at an end. He was invalided to England on 24 July, and eventually discharged.

6. There were several O'Briens in the 1st battalion. Patrick O'Brien was in the 1st company, and Corporal George O'Brien was in the 7th company. It was William Brian who was in Costello's company.

7. Fort St. Christoval.

8. If the plunder consisted of a maximum of 150 dollars and Costello received an equal share of 26 dollars then, apart from himself and O'Brien, there can have been no more than four other British soldiers in the house.

9. Surtees: *"I learnt that no house, church, or convent, was held sacred by the infuriated and now ungovernable soldiery, but that priests or nuns, and common people, all shared alike, and that any who showed the least resistance were instantly sacrificed to their fury."*
    "An English army is perhaps, general speaking, under stricter discipline than any other in the world; but in proportion as they are held tight while they are in hand, if circumstances occur to give them liberty, I know of no army more difficult to restrain when once broke loose. A reason

may perhaps be assigned for it in part. On such occasions as this siege, where they were long and much exposed to fatigue almost insupportable, and to the most trying scenes of difficulty and danger which were generally borne with cheerfulness and alacrity, they perhaps reasoned with themselves and one another in this manner - that as they had borne so much and so patiently to get possession of the place, it was but fair that they should have some indulgence when their work and trials were crowned with success, especially as the armies of other powers make it a rule generally to give an assaulted fortress up to plunder. They had also become quite reckless of life from so long an exposure to death; but an English army cannot plunder like the French. The latter keep themselves more sober, and look more to the solid and substantial benefit to be derived from it, while the former sacrifice everything to drink; and when once in a state of intoxication, with all the bad passions set loose at the same time, I know not what they will hesitate to perpetrate... At this time I think I was fairly tired of life, so disgusting and so sickening were the scenes the few last days had presented."

10. John Castles, a labourer of Old Church, Paisley, in Scotland, had been in the Rifles since it was created in 1800, having joined in Galway at the age of 22 from a Regiment of Fencible Highlanders, in which he had served since 1794.

11. John (Jack) Ketch was appointed public executioner in about 1663. He botched the execution of the Duke of Monmouth, taking seven strikes of his axe to complete the task. So notorious did he become that his name was popularly applied to all English executioners for the next 200 years.

12. Surtees gives an excellent description of the defences at the breach with which Costello and his comrades had to contend: *"In one breach (the large one)... the top of it was fixed with a chevaux-de-frise extending the whole width of the breach, and composed of a strong beam of wood, with sharp-pointed sword-blades fixed in every direction, they being generally about three quarters of a yard long, and so closely set together, that it was impossible either to leap over them or penetrate between them, and the whole so firmly fixed to the works at the top, that it could not be moved. In addition, they had fitted a number of long and thick planks, with spikes about an inch or more in length, and laid them all down the breach, but fixed at the top, so that it was impossible for any one to get up without falling on these.*

"Beyond the chevaux-de-frise several ditches had been cut, into which those must have fallen who surmounted the obstacles on the breach; but I believe none did... In addition to all the above, from the covered way down into the ditch was, I should imagine, at least 30 feet. Our people had descended by ladders and, I doubt not, in the dark, and, in the hurry and confusion of the moment, many were thrown down and killed. In the middle of the large ditch a smaller one had been cut, which was filled with water, and in which, added to the inundation close to the right of the breaches (which had been caused by bringing the river partly into the ditch), numbers were drowned. Small mines had been constructed all along the ditch, which were exploded when it was filled with people, and which produced infinite mischief. On top of the ramparts, the enemy had a

considerable number of shells of the largest size, ready filled and fused; and when our people had filled the ditch below, these were lighted, and thrown over on their heads, each shell being capable of destroying from 12 to 20 men or more. They had beams of wood also laid on the ramparts, with old carriage-wheels, and every sort of missile imaginable, which were poured upon the unfortunate people below.

"*When these things are taken into consideration, added to the incessant and destructive fire from 3,000-4,000 men, all emulous to do their duty, at the short distance of perhaps 20 yards, with the ditch as full as it could possibly stow, you will be able to form some idea of the destruction that must naturally ensue: and awful indeed it was*"

13. William Green was sent to hospital in Elvas, and William Lawrence to Estremoz.

14. Costello did not see O'Hare's body but Simmons, who did, mentions only three balls, all in the chest.

CHAPTER 17: *Advance to Salamanca and Rueda, 10 April - 21 July 1812*

1. Kincaid: "*Among other things carried from Ciudad Rodrigo, one of our men had the misfortune to carry his death in his hands, under the mistaken shape of amusement. He thought that it was a cannon-ball, and took it for the purpose of playing at the game of nine-holes, but it happened to be a live shell. In rolling it along, it went over a bed of burning ashes, and ignited without his observing it. Just as he had got it between his legs, and was in the act of discharging it a second time, it exploded, and nearly blew him to pieces.*"

2. Sgt. James Battersby was one of the 46 riflemen who fought at Talavera in July 1809 as part of the 1st batt. Embodied Detachments. He rejoined his own battalion soon afterwards and went into the 2nd Company. By 11 June 1812, when these events took place, he was a private in the 5th Company, having been demoted only a few weeks previously.

3. Costello is wrong about the name of the grenadier, but right about everything else. Private Dennis Farrell, 61st Regiment, was arraigned at Foncastin on 8 July 1812, for the murder by stabbing, of his wife, Ann Farrell, at the camp near Ciudad Rodrigo on or about 12 June 1812. He was acquitted of murder but found guilty of manslaughter, and was sentenced to 12 months' imprisonment in the guard of his own regiment. Surtees had his own views about the couple's relationship: "*They had often, I fancy, quarrelled, and he had probably used her ill... I subsequently learnt that he was a brave soldier, and that he afterwards fell in the hard-fought battle of the Pyrenees. Poor creature! she was one of the gayest of the females which graced our rural balls near Ituero only a short while previous, and had often danced with old General Vandaleur on those occasions.*"

It is interesting to compare judgements under court-martial law at this time. Two men (McGuire and Chambers), who in 1810 stole money from a Portuguese man, were hanged. Three weeks earlier, three soldiers accused of assaulting and murdering two Portuguese women were acquitted, and in April 1812, a soldier of the 30th Regiment, who was found guilty of attempting sodomy with two fellow soldiers, was given 500 lashes and transported for life as a felon.

4. Battersby was already a private when this incident happened and therefore had no rank to lose. He managed to redeem himself later and on 25 December 1813 was promoted to corporal, but was busted back to private again two months' later on 24 February 1814. The casualty returns for the 1st battalion state that he was killed in action at Waterloo on 18 June 1815.

5. Costello's date is surely wrong because by 4 July they were in Rueda.

6. Costello said previously that the men of the 95th readily volunteered to storm towns, but the carnage at Badajoz may have dampened their enthusiasm for the task because, on this occasion, they had to be selected.

7. Surtees said that the Frenchman was a *"sergeant-major of one of their hussar regiments, and of all the men I ever saw taken, this man evinced the greatest trepidation and alarm. He was absolutely likely to sink to the earth, either from fear of what awaited himself, or from the effects of the contest in which he had been engaged. He had lost his cap in the fray, and seemed like a person deprived of his senses. He must, notwithstanding, have been looked upon by the French as a good soldier, and a valuable non-commissioned officer, for I learned afterwards that they sent in a request that he might be exchanged for one of our sergeants whom they had captured, as it was intended immediately to promote him to the adjutancy of his regiment. Of course, this was immediately complied with."*

8. Barclay, Perkins & Co brewed beer in Southwark.

9. In his *Random Shots*, Kincaid says that at Rueda, a rifleman called Taylor, who was nicknamed 'Sir Arthur' because of his facial resemblance to Wellington, mysteriously disappeared. Later, in one of the dark cellars, another riflemen went to take a drink from a large headless butt of wine, and in it found the body of Taylor, who had fallen in and drowned. There is no reason to doubt this story because the muster lists record that William Taylor, who was in Costello's company, died on 10 July 1812.

10. John Gardiner joined the 95th as a second lieutenant on 9 April 1809 and was promoted to first lieutenant on 30 August 1810. He retired from the army in 1842.

CHAPTER 18: *Battle of Salamanca; Retreat From Burgos,*
22 July - 26 November 1812

1. At Salamanca, the British losses were 28 officers and 360 men killed, and 176 officers and 2,491 men wounded. With 70 men missing, the total was 3,125. The Portuguese lost about 2,000.

2. A soldier used as an example for those learning drill.

3. It is unlikely that Mike Connelly and Josh Hetherington were riflemen.

4. Espoz y Mina was a leading Spanish guerilla leader who operated in the region around Pamplona. In 1810, the Spanish Regency conferred on him the title of Colonel and Commandant General of all the Guerilleros of Navarre. By 1813 he held the rank of general, and commanded about 14,000 men.

5. Kincaid on his stay near Madrid: *"I shall ever look back to that period as the most pleasing event of my military life. The only bar to our perfect felicity was the want of money, as independent of long arrears already due, the military chest continued so very poor that it could not afford to give us more than a fortnight's pay during these three months and, as nobody could, would, or should give cash for bills, we were obliged to sell our silver spoons, watches and everything of value we stood possessed of, to purchase the common necessaries of life."*

6. Kincaid: *"We were now walking nearly knee deep, in a stiff mud, into which no man could thrust his foot with the certainty of having a shoe at the end of it when he pulled it out again. And that we might not be miserable by halves, we had this evening, to regale our chops with the last morsel of biscuit that they were destined to grind during the retreat."*

7. Lord Charles Spencer was appointed to the 95th from the 68th Regiment as a 2nd lieutenant on 8 May 1811. He remained with the regiment until 9 September 1813, when he was transferred to the 52nd Regiment as lieutenant. He retired from the army in 1832.

8. Sergeant Alexander Fotheringham, who been promoted from corporal in October 1810, was in the 8th Company and was indeed killed in action on 17 November 1812.

CHAPTER 19: *Winter Quarters in Alameda; Advance to Vitoria*
26 November 1812 - 20 June 1813

1. Kincaid first saw Don Julian Sanchez a year earlier, near Fuentes de Oñoro: *"He was a middling-sized thick-set fellow, with a Spanish complexion, well whiskered and moustached, with glossy black hair, and dressed in a hussar uniform. The peasantry in that part of the country used to tell rather a romantic story of the cause which induced him to take up arms - namely, that the French had maltreated and afterwards murdered his wife and family before his face, besides firing his house (cause enough in all conscience), for which he amply revenged himself by becoming the most celebrated throat-cutter in that part of the world. His band when he first took the field did not exceed 50 men, but about the period I speak of [ie 1811] his ranks had swelled to about 1,500. They were a contemptible force in the field, but brave, enterprising, and useful in their mountain fastnesses, in cutting off supplies and small detachments. I did not see his troops until some time after, when his heavy dragoons one day crossed our line of march. They afterwards cut a more*

respectable figure; but at that period they looked a regular set of ragamuffins, wearing cocked-hats with broad white lace round the edges, yellow coats with many more than button-holes, red facings, breeches of various colours, and no stockings but a sort of shoe on the foot with a spur attached. Their arms were as various as their colours; some with lances, some with carbines; in short, every one seemed as if he had equipped himself in whatever the fortune of war had thrown in his way."

2. Eight Spaniards were recruited into the 1st battalion between 25 May and 10 June 1812, and a further 50 were enlisted between September and December the same year. Those who stayed were brave, but over 30 deserted, their names forming a long list in the regimental records in December 1812. Three of them - Alonso, Miguel and Montero - were from Costello's company.

3. Alex Cameron had joined the 95th on 6 September 1800 from the 92nd Regt. as a lieutenant. He became a captain on 6 May 1805, and a major on 30 May 1812. He had been in command of the covering part of four companies of riflemen at the storming of Badajoz.

4. There were two Robinsons in the 1st company, both called Thomas. One received a Waterloo medal in 1816.

5. George Stratton. On 25 December 1812, he was in the 1st company, but by 24 March 1813, he was in the 2nd company with Costello. He is recorded as a deserter in the muster list for the period 25 September - 24 December 1813. If this was the occasion to which Costello refers, then it was later than he implies, unless Stratton deserted twice?

6. The army was well prepared for the new campaign, and both Surtees and Cooke record improvements made in equipping the soldiers. Surtees: *"This campaign, each company received four tents, thus allowing about 20 men for each. The officers of each company had one among them, and the field and staff officers in like proportion. These were carried on mules, which before had carried the camp-kettles; but these being exchanged for smaller ones, the men carried them in turns upon their knapsacks. Thus it rarely happened that the tents were not on the ground nearly as soon as the men; but strict orders were given always to encamp out of sight of the enemy, if practicable, that they might not be able to calculate our numbers."*

   Cooke: *"Previously to our advance, the greatcoats belonging to the soldiers were delivered into store, it being considered that the blanket was a sufficient covering for them at night, the more particularly as tents were served out for the use of the whole army... Each man was provided with a reasonable supply of necessaries, including three pairs of shoes, and an extra pair of soles and heels, in his knapsack. The daily allowance of rations for soldiers and officers consisted of 1lb of beef, one of biscuit, and a small allowance of rum or wine. The former was invariably preferred by the old soldiers, although frequently much adulterated by the mischievous capitras [muleteers]."*

7. The Royal Horse Guards. Their name of the Oxford Blues was derived from their first colonel, the Earl of Oxford, and from their blue uniform. Leach described them as gentlemen who *"have been campaigning in London, at Brighton, Hampton Court and Weymouth"*, and that they looked *"as fair and beautiful as lilies, when contrasted with the sunburnt visages and battered appointments of the cavalry regiments which had been many years in the country."*

8. Cooke of the 43rd Regiment also had trouble obtaining bread. After crossing the bridge at Puenteareñas, he had purchased some butter, but as no biscuit had been served out that day he had nothing to put it on. The next day he discovered that the villagers would not sell him any bread, and only obtained a loaf by asking a priest for one.

9 In *Random Shots*, Kincaid describes the routine of the older and more experienced soldiers on arriving at a camp ground: *"Let their feelings of fatigue be great or small, they are no sooner suffered to leave the ranks than every man rushes to secure whatever the neighbourhood affords as likely to contribute to his comfort for the night. Swords, hatchets, and bill-hooks are to be seen hewing and hacking at every tree and bush within reach. Huts are quickly reared, fires are quickly blazing, and while the kettle in boiling, or the pound of beef frying, the tired, but happy souls are found toasting their toes around the cheerful blaze, recounting their various adventures until the fire had done the needful."*

CHAPTER 20: *The Battle of Vitoria, 20 June - 4 July 1813*

1. Miles Hodgson.

2. During 1839 and 1840, in the *United Service Journal*, there was a debate about the use bayonets. The correspondents included John Kincaid and Benjamin Harris. The following, which appeared as a footnote in the 1841 edition of his *Adventures*, was Costello's contribution to that debate. In support of his argument, he used the bayonet charge of the 88th, which he was able to witness because "riflemen in action are at all times extended, and have better opportunities of watching the movements of the two armies than those troops who are compelled to march in compact and closely-wedged masses".

"As of late, much has been said concerning the use of the bayonet in action. I shall here take the liberty, supported by the above, of intruding my own opinions. Both parties, it will be observed were with their firelocks unloaded, the British having fired and charged before the French could reload, and both consequently had no resource left but their bayonets. Now I would ask the no-bayonet gentlemen if the French had seen the British advance with bare muzzles, or with no bayonets, would they have given way with their own bayonets fixed to oppose them? If they did, they ought to be hanged, from the colonel downwards. On the other hand, if the English had attempted to charge with bare muzzles against fixed bayonets, each man from the commanding officer down should be sent to a madhouse. Upon this then I should say, if my opinion be acceptable, that the bayonets had better remain in present use until such time as we can bargain with the French or other enemies to disuse them."

3. Lazaro Blanco had enlisted in the regiment only a year before on 1 June 1812, therefore the only advances he would have been in were those from the army encampments around Ciudad Rodrigo in Spain.

4. Miles Hodgson had a serious wound to his face.

5. Kincaid also saw Wellington. A shell had exploded nearby, frightening Kincaid's horse, which he had trouble controlling. Wellington gave him a reproof, and told him to concentrate on keeping his men together.

6. There is some dispute about the identity of these ladies, and the ownership of the baton. According to Simmons: *"General Gazan's wife was taken, but sent back in her carriage under an escort this morning"* (ie the day after the battle). The baton is thought to have been Marshal Jourdan's. Verner: *"Jourdan's travelling carriage with his Field Marshal's baton was taken by a private of the 87th"* However, Joseph's carriage was captured as well. Simmons: *"King Joseph was so hard pressed that he was compelled to leave his carriage, mount a horse, and gallop off."* Verner: *"King Joseph's travelling carriage, in which every dish and toilet article was of solid silver, was captured by the 14th Light Dragoons of the Light Division."*

7. According to Anthony Brett-James, there were about 16 dollars to one doubloon, which was the equivalent of about £4.

8   Pampluna in the 1841 and 1852 editions

9. Daniel Kelly, Robert Roberts, William John, and two men by the name of John Connor, were in the 2nd Company with Costello. Thomas Treacy was in the 6th Company. Daniel Kelly had been promoted to corporal on 25 March 1812, but was reduced back to the rank of private on 25 February 1813. William John died of his wounds on 12 July. Of someone called 'Jemmy' Copely there is no trace in the 1st battalion muster lists or casualty returns, and although the 2nd company had a sergeant called Richard Copley at this time, he was neither killed nor incapacitated at Vitoria. John Connor, an Irishman and formerly a labourer from Drumlane, Co. Cavan, was reported in the muster lists as being in hospital from the middle of June to the middle of August 1813. By 24 September he was convalescing in Vitoria. However, the casualty returns list the death in France on 13 October 1813 of a man of this name, The other John Connor, originally a tailor from Liverpool, joined the battalion from England between September and December 1812. He was unhurt at Vitoria, but was wounded later at Waterloo. In Chapter 27, Costello recalls meeting a former comrade called Connor in Dover in 1819, and from the description he gives of the man's circumstances, it is surely the Liverpool tailor.

10. The battalion's quartermaster sergeant was Isaac McLeod.

11. Two corporals were recorded as being wounded at about this time. They were David Cloudsley of the 2nd company, who was invalided to England, and George White.

CHAPTER 21: *The Pyrenees, 5 July - September 1813*

1. Kincaid: *"Although we were kept on our legs during the whole of the night, we found, when daylight broke, that the tail of the column had not got a quarter of a mile from the starting-post. On a good broad road it is all very well, but on a narrow bad road, a night march is like a nightmare, harassing a man to no purpose."*

2. Harry Smith had been in the gruelling retreat to Corunna in January 1809, yet he describes this particular march as *"one of the most fatiguing to the soldiers I ever witnessed. On the Pyrenees, as on other mountains, the darkness is indescribable. We were on a narrow mountain path, frequently with room only for one or two men, when a soldier of the Rifle Brigade rolled down a hill as nearly perpendicular as may be. We heard him bumping along, pack, rifle, weight of ammunition, etc., when from the bottom he sang out, 'Hallo there! Tell the Captain there's not a bit of me alive at all; but the devil a bone have I broken; and faith I'm thinking no soldier ever came to his ground at such a rate before. Have a care, boys, you don't follow. The breach at Badajoz was nothing to the bottomless pit I'm now in'."*

3. There were three riflemen called Kelly in the 1st battalion, but there is no record of any of them being killed at this time. Daniel Kelly was a private in Costello's company; John McKelly of the 7th company received a medal for Waterloo; Maurice Kelly of the 5th company, was in the General Hospital for all three musters between 25 June and 24 September 1813, and died on 24 March 1814.

4. The 95th Regiment was formed in January 1800 as an experimental corps of British riflemen, the men being drawn from various other regiments. It was in the attack on Ferrol in northern Spain on 25 August that same year that those soldiers first saw action as rifleman.

5. Robert Fairfoot was for many years in the same company as Costello, and is mentioned in the same approving tones by George Simmons and William Green. At Waterloo, Fairfoot helped the wounded Simmons, who wrote to his parents: *"All the officers know how much Sergeant Fairfoot merits my praise. If I can do him a service, he may always command me; his character as a brave soldier stands with the first in the regiment. You may tell this to his father."* The record of Fairfoot's service, and information about his wife and children, are recorded in the regimental description books at the PRO in Kew, and in a footnote in Simmons' diary, Willoughby Verner notes that in the cathedral in Galway, where Fairfoot died in 1838, there is a tablet *"inscribed by his brother officers to record his good and gallant service as a Rifle Man in the Peninsular, France, and the Netherlands."*

6. Thomas Bandle was, for many years, in the same company as Costello.

7. Samuel Royston and Philip Ryan.

8. Kincaid was the adjutant of the regiment at the time and therefore had the selection of the volunteers. *"The numbers from our battalion were limited to 25, and in selecting the best characters out of those who offered themselves, I rejected an Irishman by the name of Burke who, although he had been on the forlorn-hope both at Ciudad and Badajoz and was a man of desperate bravery, I knew to be one of those wild untameable animals that, the moment the place was carried, would run into every species of excess."* For two days, Burke pestered Kincaid, who only relented when the officer who was to lead the party applied to him on Burke's behalf.

9. Costello puts the French numbers at the bridge at 300-400 but Leach says there were 10,000, the one sounding far too few, the other far too many. Nearly all the autobiographers have something to say about this action because, had the bridge been reinforced earlier, the French could not have crossed and would have been compelled to lay down their arms. There was considerable debate as to who was to blame for Cadoux's death; Harry Smith places it upon the shoulders of General Skerret. Cadoux and his men fought heroically, and the French suffered appalling casualties. Their bodies were thrown into the Bidasoa in the expectation that the current would carry them away downstream, but this did not happen, and the stench of their decomposition became appalling.

CHAPTER 22: *La Rhune; Battle of the Nivelle, September - 13 November 1813*

1. Costello was later awarded a medal for the storming of Badajoz and Ciudad Rodrigo. See photograph on page 316.

2. Michael Dillon of the 1st Company, formerly a carpenter from Limerick, had been a private since joining at Athlone, Co. Weatmeath in September 1810, when he was 18. His discharge papers describe him as being on the forlorn hopes at both Badajoz and San Sebastian. He was not promoted until 1814, when he became a corporal, a rank he held during the Waterloo campaign. Dillon remained in the Rifle Brigade until July 1830, when was discharged at his own request. He was then about 39, 5'8" tall, with dark hair, hazel eyes and a fresh complexion. The Board which sat to consider his request concluded that, as a soldier, he had always conducted himself with the greatest gallantry. He received a pension and was still alive in 1869.

3. Daniel Kelly, who earlier in the year had been a corporal, was a veteran rifleman. Born in Laughrea, Co. Galway, he joined at Dover on 5 August 1806 at the age of 19. He was in Copenhagen and at the battle of Corunna. He fought throughout the Peninsular War, was at Waterloo and served in France afterwards. His conduct was described as very good when he was discharged on 10 August 1826. He was 5'5" tall, had sandy hair, blue eyes and a fair complexion. On leaving the army, his intended place of residence was given as Rathkeale Post Town, Co. Limerick.

4. William Johnston, who was appointed Captain on 22 October 1812.

5. Tom Crawley had been moved from Costello's company to the 1st company on 25 February 1813. He had served in South American expedition of 1806-1807.

6. Harry Smith was one: *"During the occupation of our present position, I found that Basque inhabitants on the Spanish side and those on the French side of the Pyrenees carried on a sort of contraband trade, and that brandy and claret were to be had."* When General Skerret, on whose staff he was at that time serving, complained that he could get no wine or sheep, Smith told him he could get both: *"My smugglers were immediately in requisition. They got me eight sheep and one dozen of claret."*

7. John Morely was in the 2nd company with Costello. In the 1841 and 1852 editions, his name is transcribed as 'Mauley'. He was killed on 10 November 1813.

8. Costello implies that, after Tom Crawley was wounded on 10 November 1813, he never saw him again, or even learned what happened to him, yet there is no evidence that Crawley was hospitalised through his injury, or that he was sent back to England. The muster lists show him in the ranks until September 1814, when he is marked down as on furlough for about five months. He was in the Waterloo campaign, and remained in the 1st company until the beginning of 1818 at least, as did Costello, who continued in the 2nd company.

9. Kincaid, Simmons, and Harry Smith all say that the impact of the shot knocked Barnard from his horse. Simmons: *"Colonel Barnard, towards the end of this day's fighting, received a musket ball in his right breast, which made him tumble from his horse; he fell upon the hilt of his sword and bruised his side very much. I was near him when he fell, and put my hand into his bosom to feel where the ball entered. I found his lungs had been wounded, as blood in quantities and air issued from the wound; some blood was passing from his mouth also. He, in a most collected manner said, 'Do you think I am dying? Did you ever see a man so wounded recover?' I observed 'Your wound is a very bad one, but there have been many instances of men recovering from such wounds, and your pulse does not indicate immediate dissolution.' 'Thank you,' he exclaimed, 'you give me hope. If a man can recover, I know I shall.' He was immediately bled very largely and taken by four men in a blanket to a farmhouse."*
    Harry Smith: *"Poor dear gallant Barnard was knocked off his horse by a musket-ball though his lungs. When Johnny Kincaid, his adjutant, got up to him, he was nearly choked by blood in his mouth. They washed it out for him... He was borne off then to rear and, when examined by Assistant Surgeon Robson, it was found that the ball had not passed through, but was perceptible to the touch."* The ball was extracted. Barnard sent for George Simmons to organise his carriage to Vera, and to remain with him until every dangerous symptom had passed. Simmons had total responsibility for Barnard's treatment, and did not return to his battalion

until 24 December, by which time it was stationed at the château of Arcangues.

10. Robert Watt of the 8th company, who had been promoted from corporal on 18 November 1812 was killed on 10 November 1813.

CHAPTER 23: *Actions at Arcangues, the Nive, Tarbes, and Toulouse 14 November 1813 - 13 April 1814*

1. In previous editions, the date Costello gives is 9 December, but all other sources say it was the 10th.

2. Simmons: *"A ball passed through both their heads, happening to be standing a little behind one another."*

3. Simmons: *"They were both capital soldiers and were put in the same grave."* William Brotherwood is mentioned by several other riflemen: he was a private when Benjamin Harris fought alongside him at the battle of Vimeiro in 1808; Kincaid recalls him as a sergeant teasing the unfortunate Tommy Sarsfield in 1811; and Harry Smith remembers him at the siege of Ciudad Rodrigo in 1812. John Hopwood had been wounded in 1811 (see Chapter 9).

4. Thomas Grindley was in the 7th company. An illiterate labourer from Co. Roscommon in Ireland, he joined in 1805, aged 18. Discharged in 1816, he was described as having several gunshot wounds.

5. John Castles survived the Peninsular War and the Waterloo campaign and was discharged in April 1817, aged 41. He appears to have had no major wounds, and his conduct as a soldier was described as very good. He "conducted himself much to the satisfaction of his officers in every respect, and merits the favourable consideration of the board". His Military General Service Medal is in the collection held at the Royal Green Jackets Museum. He was in Costello's company.

6. Private Thomas Gilbert was in Costello's company. A few months later he was promoted to corporal.

7. Thomas Jones and William Jones were both in Costello's company. William Jones is reported to have been invalided to England a month or two before these events. There is no indication in the muster lists that Thomas Jones suffered any debilitating wound at this time.

8. Blanco was in Costello's company.

9. Wellington's general order, dated 9 July 1813 included the words: *"The officers and soldiers of the army must recollect that their nations are at war with France solely because the Ruler of the French nation will not allow them to be at peace, and is desirous of forcing them to submit to his yoke."*

CHAPTER 24: *The End of the Peninsular War, 14 April - 22 July 1814*

1. Castle Sarrazin in previous editions.

2. The experiences of William Lawrence were similar. On the way to Bordeaux, he and a comrade were billeted in the house of a gentlemen, where they were treated very well. *"Our berth was a fine feather bed, a luxury we had not seen for years. In fact, it was such a luxury that it was too soft for our hard bones."* Neither of the men could sleep in it. *"With a knapsack for a pillow, we wrapped ourselves into a blanket, lay on the floor, and sank into a profound slumber."*

3. There were freemasons in the ranks of the officers and men of Wellington's army. Early in the war, they had met openly in lodges and held processions but, on 5 January 1810, as freemasonry was contrary to the law of Catholic Portugal, Wellington issued a general order banning such displays to avoid offending the host country.

4. By now, Thomas Gilbert was a corporal in Costello's company.

5. In previous editions, Costello stated that it was on the second day's march that the Portuguese and Spanish left them, but that was not the case.

6. In 1835-1836, Costello served with the British Auxiliary Legion in the Spanish Carlist War (see Chapter 27).

7. Dulcinea del Tolosa was the country girl with whom Cervantes' *Don Quixote* fell in love.

8. Those who deserted from the 1st battalion between 25 March and 24 June 1814 were Thomas Joshua, Samuel Royston, Joseph Cummings, William Hinks and Sergeant White. Royston, who had been at the storming of San Sebastian, was in Costello's company, and deserted on 5 June.

9. It has not been possible to identify this sergeant. Costello says he was in his regiment, not necessarily in his battalion - the 1st and 2nd battalions both returned to England aboard the *Ville de Paris*. The surname of Sergeant Daniel Sugden, who was in the 2nd battalion and is mentioned in his recollections by Benjamin Harris, fits, but unfortunately, what is known about Sugden's movements during the Peninsular War does not. The only riflemen left behind at Corunna and Vigo in February 1809 would have been prisoners of the French, or the sick and wounded, some of whom later formed part of the 1st battalion of Embodied Detachments which fought at Talavera. In his *Recollections*, Benjamin Harris relates a regimental story describing a similar domestic scene, except that the rifleman is named as Allen Cummings.

CHAPTER 25: *Quatre Bras; Aftermath of the Battle of Waterloo; 23 July 1814 - 19 June 1815*

1. Meagher in previous editions.

2. The General Court Martial was held on 5 June 1815. Arraigned were privates Thomas Maher and Henry Day of the 95th *"for murder, in*

wilfully and maliciously shooting Andrew Hubert, an inhabitant of the city of Bruxelles, on or about the night of 16 May 1815." They were found not guilty, released from confinement, and returned to duty. However, the general order giving this judgement was not issued until 23 June 1815. Maher was an illiterate labourer from Johnswell, Kilkenny when he joined the 95th in Kent in April 1809 at the age of 20. He was 35 when he was discharged on 30 June 1824, and described as worn out. His general conduct had been 'extremely bad', and he had been wounded twice.

Two days before the fatal shooting in Brussels, Dennis O'Brien, another rifleman of the lst battalion, had deserted. Recaptured, he was court-martialled on 18 December 1816, found guilty and sentenced to serve for life in any corps the army thought fit. He had to forfeit all the benefits and advantages of increases in pay or pension, and was marked on the left side with the letter D, according to the provisions of the Mutiny Act. This mark had to be not less than half an inch long, five inches below the armpit. It was made with either ink or gunpowder, the aim being than it should remain visible and not easily obliterated. The same punishment was meted out to Patrick Stanton of the lst battalion, who deserted from Baralle in France on 12 June 1817 and was court-martialled on 19 August 1817.

3. Costello must have been acting as a corporal because he was not promoted to the rank officially until 26 May 1816.

4. Simmons: *"We marched through Waterloo and halted. I lay down for an hour.*

5. In their publication *The Rifles at Waterloo*, George Caldwell and Robert Cooper give an excellent account of the movements of the lst battalion at Quatre Bras, complete with maps of the area, and photographs of the battleground showing the local farms around which they fought. They also point out that, in the absence of Captain Leach, Lt. John Fitzmaurice commanded Costello's company.

6. Caldwell and Cooper identify these two companies as being those of Leach and Edward Chawner, and the houses as being in the village of Thyle, on the road to Namur.

7. Kincaid: *We were presently reinforced by a small battalion of foreign light troops, with whose assistance we were in hopes to have driven the enemy a little further from it, but they were a raw body of men, who had never before been under fire."* According to Caldwell and Cooper, these men were Hanoverians.

8. Josh Hetherington was not a rifleman, but he may have been in the Light Division during the Peninsular War, and probably belonged to Picton's 5th Division in the Waterloo campaign because it was his regiments which bore the brunt of the fighting at Quatre Bras. However, there is no Josias or Joshua Hetherington in the present Index to Soldiers' Documents held at the PRO, although not all regimental documents have

been processed. If 'Josh' was a nickname, he may be there under another Christian name; he may even be there as an Etherington, but without more clues, identification is not possible.

CHAPTER 26: *Army of Occupation in France, 19 June 1815 - March 1819*

1. While in Antwerp, he found himself in a bed next to the sergeant of the 10th Hussars who had helped him to load his booty onto a mule at the battle of Vitoria (see Chapter 20).

2. Antwerp was close to the island of Walcheren where so many British soldiers caught Walcheren fever (malaria) in the summer of 1809. Thousands died and thousand more, like Benjamin Harris, were never again fit for active service. The British learned from this experience, and on 28 July 1815, a letter from Wellington's Adjutant General confirmed that it was his intention to have all the sick removed from Antwerp in consequence of the approaching unhealthy season. Those not well enough to rejoin their regiments were to go back to England.

3. Robert Owen (1771-1858) was a Welsh-born socialist and philanthropist. His book, *New View of Society*, had been published in 1813. Later, in the 1830s, he was active in the new trade union movement.

4. That such fatal encounters with French officers were not common, must, says Kincaid, *"be ascribed to our ignorance alike of their language and their national method of conveying offence for, in regard to the first, although 'sacré boeuftake' and 'sacré pomme de terre', with which we were constantly saluted, were not applied complimentarily yet, as the connecting offensive links were lost to most of us, these words alone were not looked upon as of a nature requiring 'satisfaction'... With regard to practical insults, a favourite one of theirs, as we afterwards discovered, was to tread as if by accident on the toe of the person to be insulted. Now, as the natural impulse of the Englishman on having his toe trodden on is to make a sort of apology to the person who did it... many thousand insults of the kind passed unnoticed."*

5. No medal had been given to the soldiers who served in the Peninsular War. They had to wait until 1847, when the Military General Service Medal was issued to those still living who had fought between 1794 and 1814. The publication of the memoirs of the likes of Costello and Kincaid, with their barbed references to the absence of such an honour, may have contributed towards the belated decision to award such a medal.

6. On 2 December 1817, Privates John Wheatley and Joseph Binley of the 1st battalion Rifle Brigade (by which the 95th was then known), were arraigned before a court-martial at Cagnicourt, not for vandalising Waterloo medals, but for stealing several fowls belonging to Maximion Haziz of Cagnicourt on or about 23 November 1817. Wheatley was found guilty and sentenced to 3 months' confinement; Binley was acquitted. The officer presiding was Jonathan Leach who was then a Lieutenant-Colonel. John Wheatley's discharge papers record that he was from

Nottingham and joined the 95th for Unlimited Service in April 1805 when he was 18. His service record was good, and it was noted that he was with his regiment in Denmark, throughout the whole of the Peninsular War, and in France. He had been wounded three times. He signed his own name, but not well. He was nearly 6 feet tall. According to the documents, he was not discharged until 31 March 1824.

7. In the *Rifle Brigade Chronicle* of 1945, G W Cole published the results of his searches in the parish records of the district of Cambrai. He found entries for the Loude family (usually transcribed as Laude). Bernard Loude was born in 1758. He married Marie Joseph, and they had five children, three girls and two boys: Julie (1789), Jean Baptiste (1795), Augustine (1796), Léocadie (1798), and François (1803). In 1816, when Costello met them for the first time, the three girls would have been 27, 20 and 18 respectively. Their mother was alive at the time, for she did not die until 1822. In previous editions, Léocadie's name is transcribed as Leucade.

8. On 30 October 1816, a general order was issued stating that *"the chaplains of the army are forbidden to marry any person without the permission in writing of the Field Marshal"*, ie Wellington. It was *not* a specific ban on marriages between British soldiers and French women as Costello implies, but it did make such unions difficult. Of the 99 women who did marry British soldiers in France between 10 November 1816 and 6 October 1818, 40 were French and 35 were English. The origins of the others were given as Scotland, Ireland, Belgium, the Netherlands and Portugal. There was even one from the West Indies. A study of the names of their soldier husbands reveals only one name which might suggest an Irish origin, and that was James McGrath who was in Costello's battalion, therefore Catholicism may have been the more important factor in the decision.

Before the Act of Catholic Emancipation in 1829, marriages were not recognised unless performed by an Anglican churchman. As all army chaplains were Anglicans, this surely created a dilemma for those Irish soldiers who were also Catholics, particularly if they wanted to marry women who were also Catholics (the majority of Spanish, Portuguese and French women). At Cambrai in April 1816, Sgt. William Lawrence (40th) married Clotilde Clairet, a French woman he had met at St. Germain while stationed near Paris. The legality of their union was probably more important to them than Clotilde's likely Catholicism because, without it, Lawrence would not be able to take her to England when the army quit France. The situation with Costello and Augustine was more complicated because of the objections of her family, and although a service by an excommunicated priest may have been a compromise for the couple, it did not make their union legal, as later events clearly prove.

9. Capt. William Balvaird was promoted to Major on 21 July 1814, and to Brevet Lt.-Col. on 21 June 1817.

10. He hit *himself* on the head with a hammer! Regardless of the difficulties Costello was having with the Loudes, of which his officers appear to have been aware, he retained the rank of corporal.

11. There is a contradiction here. For his readers, Costello defends the status of his relationship with Augustine by stating that he is married yet, in almost the same breath, he acknowledges that the union is not legal. Furthermore, if he was prepared to try to obtain his discharge from the army and publicly marry Augustine if she was given her dowry, then why was he not prepared to do so without it?

12. Soldiers who were to be discharged had to be examined by a doctor and then go before a board at Chelsea to be assessed for a pension. The value of the pension often depended on the degree and severity of the wounds the men had suffered, but even in the worst cases, the pension was ungenerous.

13. Costello does not tell us the sex of his baby, let alone its name. No record of the baptism can be found in either the International Genealogical Index, or the registers of the Catholic church in Chatham.

14. In the letter, Costello is referred to as a sergeant, but there is no evidence in official regimental papers that he ever rose above the rank of corporal with the Rifles. His pension was eventually increased in 1865, to one shilling, and then to two shillings

15. In 1813, there were three John Connors in the 1st battalion, all of them in Costello's company. This has given rise to contradictions in the regimental records, but Costello states clearly that the Connor he met in Dover was a tailor who was wounded at Waterloo and discharged as a consequence. This agrees well with the information in the discharge papers for John Connor, a tailor from Liverpool, who had joined the 95th in 1812. He was wounded in the left breast at Waterloo. This rendered him unfit for further service and he was discharged in 1816 at the age of 27.

CHAPTER 28: *Yeoman Warder and Autogiobrapher, 1838-1869*

1. In the Index to soldiers' discharge papers, now available at the PRO Kew, Plunket is mentioned only once, and that is for the Rifle Brigade.

2. One would have been the Waterloo Medal, the other the medal awarded to him by Colonel Beckwith himself (See Chapter 2).

3. The Royal Hospital at Kilmainham, near Dublin, was the equivalent in Ireland of the Royal Hospital, Chelsea. The hospital records are at the PRO Kew, but not all of them are indexed.

4. It would be interesting to find out more about this scheme, how it came about, and how long it lasted because, in the *United Service Journal* of 1838, there is a letter from Upper Canada written by an old military settler. The Kilmainham records revealed that some soldiers who were

receiving pensions between 1819 and 1822, chose to go and live abroad. Their destinations were varied: Lisbon, Oporto, Valenciennes and New South Wales were mentioned, but so was Halifax, Nova Scotia, Newfoundland and - the majority - Quebec.

5. Burton Crescent (now Cartwright Gardens) is just south of St. Pancras Station.

6. Plunket's 'failing' was probably his fondness for alcohol, but Costello's anecdotes also suggest that he had a tendency to speak his mind.

7. The last paragraph was a footnote in the 1852 edition of Costello's book, which suggests that Plunket died in the early 1850s. The officers in Colchester had probably read Costello's descriptions of the man in his 1841 edition. If Plunket died in Colchester as Costello says, and a local woman paid for his tombstone, then there should be an entry for his death in one of the parish registers, and his grave and headstone, should it still exist, will be in one of the local churchyards.

8. Humphrey Allen. See page 99.

BIBLIOGRAPHY

BOOKS

A - Z of REGENCY LONDON. Introduction by Paul Laxton. Harry, Margary, Lympne Castle, Kent, 1985.

ANON — *Memoirs of a Sergeant late of the 43rd Light Infantry, previously to and during the Peninsular War, including the account of his conversion from Popery to the Protestant Religion.* London, 1835.
Facsimile edition published by Ken Trotman, Cambridge 1997.

ATKINSON, J A — *Naval, Military, and Other Costumes of Great Britain,* 1807.

BLAKISTON, J — *Twelve Years' Military Adventure, in three-quarters of the Globe,* 1829.

CALDWELL, G and COOPER, R — *Rifle Green at Waterloo.* Bugle Horn Publications, 1990.

CALDWELL, G and COOPER, R — *Rifles at Waterloo.* Bugle Horn Publications, (49 Cromwell Road, Great Glen, Leicester LE8 0GU), 1995.

COLE, G.W. — *The Romance of a Soldier of Wellington, Sergeant Edward Costello.* Rifle Brigade Chronicle, 1945.

COOKE, J H — *Memoirs of the late War, a Personal Narrative of Captain J H Cooke, 43rd Light Infantry* (Campaigns of 1811-1814). London 1831.

COOKE, J H — *A Narrative of Events in the South of France and America, 1814-1815* (continuation of the above). London 1835.

COPE, WILLIAM — *The History of the Rifle Brigade (The Prince Consort's Own) formerly the 95th.* London, 1877.

COSTELLO, E — *The Adventures of a Soldier, or Memoirs of Edward Costello of the Rifle Brigade, comprising narratives of Wellington's Campaigns in the Peninsula, etc.* Colbourn & Co, London, 1841. Second edition 1852.
Later published in an edited edition as *The Peninsular and Waterloo Campaigns.* Editor, Anthony Brett-James, Longman, 1967.

FERNYHOUGH — *Military Memoirs of Four Brothers (Natives of Staffordshire) engaged in the Service of their Country, as well in the New World and Africa as on the Continent of Europe,* by the survivor (Lt. Robert Fernyhough's journals of service with the Rifle Brigade form most of this volume.) London, 1829.

FITZMAURICE, F M: — *Recollections of a Rifleman's Wife at Home and Abroad,* London, 1851.

FLETCHER, I
and COOK, A.
Fields of Fire: battlefields of the Peninsular War.
Spellmount, 1994.

GODDARD
Military Costumes of Europe, 1812.

GREEN, W
A Brief Outline of the Travels and Adventures of William Green during a period of 10 years in Denmark, Germany and the Peninsular. Coventry, 1857.
Later edited by J and D Teague as *Where Duty Calls Me: the Experiences of William Green in the Napoleonic Wars.* Synjon Books (18 Manor Way, Orpington, Kent BR5 1NW), 1975.

HARRIS, B
Recollections of Rifleman Harris (Old 95th). With anecdotes of his officers and his comrades. Edited by Henry Curling. London, 1848.
Edition of 1929 published by Peter Davies.
Editions of 1970 and 1985, edited by Christopher Hibbert and published by Leo Cooper 1970, and Century Publishing 1985. Reissued 1996.

HARRIS, B
A Dorset Rifleman: Recollections of Benjamin Harris. Edited by Eileen Hathaway. Shinglepicker Publications, 1995. Paperback edition, published with an appendix, 1996.

HAY, W
Reminiscences 1808-1815, under Wellington, by Captain William Hay, 52nd Foot and 12th Light Dragoons. Edited by his daughter, Mrs S C L Wood. Simpkin, Marshall, Hamilton, Kent & Co., London, 1901.
Facsimile edition, Ken Trotman Ltd, Cambridge, 1992.

HAYDON, P
The English Pub: a history. Robert Hale, London 1994.

HAYTHORNTHWAITE. P J *The Napoleonic Source Book.* Arms and Armour Press 1990. Paperback edition 1995.

KINCAID, J
Adventures in the Rifle Brigade, in the Peninsular, France, and the Netherlands, from 1809 to 1815. London, 1830.

KINCAID, J
Random Shots from a Rifleman. London, 1835.

KINCAID, J
Adventures in the Rifle Brigade published in a combined edition with an abridged version of *Random Shots from a Rifleman,* 1909.
Facsimile of combined edition published by Richard Drew Publishing, Glasgow, 1981

LAWRENCE, W
The Autobiography of Sergeant William Lawrence. Edited by G N Bankes. Sampson, Marston & Low, 1886.
Facsimile of 1886 edition published by Ken Trotman, Cambridge, 1987.

LAWRENCE, W
A Dorset Soldier: the Autobiography of Sergeant William Lawrence 1790-1869, edited by Eileen Hathaway. Spellmount, 1993.

LEACH, J	*Rough Sketches of the Life of an Old Soldier during a Service in the West Indies, at the Siege of Copenhagen in 1807, in the Peninsular and the South of France in the Campaigns from 1808 to 1814, with the Light Division; in the Netherlands in 1815; including the Battles of Quatre Bras and Waterloo, &c.* Longman, Rees, Orme, Brown, and Green, Paternoster Row, London, 1831. Facsimile of 1831 edition published by Ken Trotman, Cambridge, 1986.
LEACH, J	*Rambles on the Banks of Styx.* London, 1847.
LONGFORD, E	*Wellington: the Years of the Sword.* Literary Guild, 1969.
MacLYSAGHT, E	*Irish Families: their Names, Arms and Origins.* Allen Figgis & Co. Ltd., Dublin, 1957.
NAPIER, W	*History of the War in the Peninsula and in the south of France 1807-1814.* 5 vols. First published 1827-1840
NORRIS, A H and BREMNER, R W	*The Lines of Torres Vedras: the first three lines and fortifications south of the Tagus.* The British Historical Society of Portugal, 1980.
OMAN, Sir C	*Wellington's Army.* Edward Arnold, 1912.
PAGE, F C G	*Following the Drum: Women in Wellington's Wars.* Andre Deutsch, 1986.
SIMMONS, G	*A British Rifleman. the Journals and Correspondence of Major George Simmons, Rifle Brigade, during the Peninsular War and the Campaign of Waterloo.* Edited by Lt.-Col. Willoughby Verner. London, 1899.
SMITH, Sir HARRY	*The Autobiography of Lieutenant-General Sir Harry Smith, Baronet of Aliwal on the Sutlej, GCB.* Edited by G C Moore Smith. 2 vols. London, 1901.
SMITH, H STOOKS	*An alphabetical List of the Officers of the Rifle Brigade from 1800 to 1850.* Simpkin, Marshall & Co, London, 1851. (This includes a 6-page sketch of the Field Services of the Rifle Brigade from its formation, to the battle of Waterloo, by Lieut-Colonel Leach.)
SMITH, H STOOKS	*An alphabetical List of the Officers of the 43rd Light Infantry from 1800 to 1850.* Simpkin, Marshall & Co, London, 1851.
SURTEES, W	*Twenty-Five Years in the Rifle Brigade,* 1833. Facsimile of 1833 edition published by F Muller Ltd, 1973.
VERNER, W	*History and Campaigns of the Rifle Brigade,* 1800-1813. 2 vols. John Bale & Sons, London, 1912.
VEVE, T W	*The Duke of Wellington and the British Army of Occupation in France 1815-1818.* Greenwood Press, Westport, 1992.

ARCHIVES

Hartley Library, University of Southampton

Letter books for the Adjutant-General's Dept of the army in Germany, the Low
    Countries and France, 25 April 1815 - 28 July 1816.
Letter books for the Military Secretary's Department of the army in France,
    17 May 1818 - 30 Sept 1818.
Other military records for France, Germany, the Low Countries and the
    Waterloo campaign, 1814-1818 (including a list of persons who have
    obtained permission to marry, November 1816 - October 1818).

National Army Museum

Colbourn's *United Service Journal* 1829-1841
General Orders - Peninsular War and Waterloo Campaign

National Library of Ireland

Records for the parishes of Mountmellick, Rosenallis and Marr
Wilson's Dublin Directories 1790-1807

Public Record Office, Chancery Lane

Census of 1841, 1851 and 1861 for Newington

Public Record Office, Kew

Casualty Returns for 95th - WO25/1334, 1335, and 2143
Description Book for 1st batt. Rifle Brigade - WO25/559
Discharge papers for 95th and the Rifle Brigade - WO97
Index to Soldiers' Discharge Documents
Muster and pay lists for 95th - WO12
Muster and pay lists for Dublin Militia - WO13
Muster lists for 1st and 2nd battalions of Embodied Detachments -
    WO12/10692
Records of Customs Service in Dublin - CUST20/33-49
Records for Kilmainham Royal Hospital - WO118 - WO120

Royal Green Jackets Museum, Winchester: Rifle Brigade Chronicle

St. Catherine's House, Aldwych: Regimental Indexes

Westminster Archives: IGI; Records of St George's, Hanover Square

INDEX

Lines of 74, 77, 80, 87
Toulouse 25, 254, 258, 259, 262, 267
  battle of 263-268
Tournefoile 262
Tower of London 123, 311, 313, 318, 328
Trafalgar 73
Travers, Lt. (95th) 241
Treacy, Thomas (95th) 95, 161-162, 228-229, 331, 339, 347
Tres Puentes 220
Trevina 305
troupadours 292
Trowers (14th Light Dragoons) 123
Trueba River 213, 215
Tucker, Col, (29th) 74
Turones/Tourões River 48, 60, 63, 118
Tylden-Pattenson, Lt. (43rd) 208
typhus 43, 44

Uniacke, Capt. John (95th) 102, 143, 147, 148, 151, 152, 330, 337, 338
United Service Journal 299, 311-312, 321, 323, 346, 356
Upper Canada 356-357

Vadilla River 132
Valada 28, 29, 90
Vale da Mula 48, 54, 59, 60
Vale de Espinho 48, 114
Vale de Santarem, see Valle
Vale Verde 48
Valence d'Agen 254
Valencia de Alcantara 28, 39
Valenciennes 275, 290, 357
Valladolid 25, 196
Valle (Vale de Santarem) 28, 80, *81*-87, 90, 207, 330
Venda Nova 28, 90, 93
Vandeleur, Maj.-Gen. 141, 211, 235, 342
Vera 233, 235, 240-246, 351
Victor, Marshal Claude 26, 30, 33
Vigo 25, 352

Vila Cortes 48, 71, 90
Vila Nova 80
Vila Velha 28, 30, *31*, 32, 90, *128*, 131
Vilar Formoso 48, 117
Villa Puerco 48, 61
Villabuena 181, 214
Villacastin 181, 199
Villalta 213, 214
Villamayor 212
Villanaña 213, 217
Villanueva 213, 217
Villar de Ciervo 48, 54
Villarego 131
Villava 231-233
Ville de Paris 271, 352
Villefranche 254, 264, 266
Vimeiro 18, 29
Viseu 46, 58, 90
Vitoria 25, 195, 198, 213, 219, 231, 234. 304, 305
  battle of 220-227, 229, 239, 347
  plunder at 225-227, 230
Vivian, Sir Hussey
voltigeurs 220, 280
volunteers 336

Walcheren 27, 77, 354
Walcheren fever 77, 354
Waterloo, 275, *277*, 278, 282, 283, 296, 298, 326, 353
  battle of 116, 226, 243, 276, 284, 287, 290, 292, 297, 313, 315, 318, 329, 331, 333, 343, 347-350, 354, 356
Waterloo medals 290, 291, 307, 316, 345, 354, 356
Watt, James 308, 351
Watt, Sgt. Robert (95th) 252
Wavre 282
Wellesley, Dr, rector of Chelsea 296
Wellesley, Sir Arthur. See Wellington, Duke of
Wellington, Duke of 18, 26, 29, 30, 33-38, 46, 54, 56, 58, 61, 68, 69, 74, 77, 79, 85, 89, 97,

ERRATA

Table of Contents. Notes are on page 320, Bibliography and Sources on page 359, and Index on page 363.

Page 192. Caption should read 'Marching the French Prisoners into Salamanca, 1812'. Drawn on the spot by Capt. Wilmot, RHA. Published by Clark and Dubourg.

Index. Numbered references after page 320 are one page out, e.g. read 324 for 323.